50
CAPTIVATING LIVES

H.D. Sharma was educated in the universities of Punjab, Delhi and Michigan. He was the recipient of the prestigious Fulbright scholarship twice. He has worked as a librarian and taught library science in universities in India and abroad. He has also authored and edited a number of books.

50 Captivating Lives

H.D. Sharma

RUPA

Published by
Rupa Publications India Pvt. Ltd 2023
7/16, Ansari Road, Daryaganj
New Delhi 110002

Sales centres:
Prayagraj Bengaluru Chennai
Hyderabad Jaipur Kathmandu
Kolkata Mumbai

P-ISBN: 978-93-5702-207-1
E-ISBN: 978-93-5702-210-1

First impression 2023

10 9 8 7 6 5 4 3 2 1

Contents

Introduction

People do not decide to become extraordinary. They decide to accomplish extraordinary things.

—Edmund Hillary

This anthology is more than just a compilation of different biographies. It is a peek into the very story of a country—the world's largest democracy, India. The real identity of a nation lies within the stories of its people, especially of those gleaming jewels who have impacted it for the better and whose influence lingers in the masses for centuries.

India is sea of countless life stories trickling into one another—a lush forest of various lives that have planted the seeds of revolution, dissent and creativity in the souls of millions. If you want to know your country, culture and background well, reading these biographies in this book might just do the trick, as these people were crucial in shaping our nation's identity and progress.

India's past brims with people who fascinate, move and inspire us. B.R. Ambedkar, for instance, started a powerful movement against Dalit exploitation in India, despite having been born in an ordinary middle-class Dalit family with no sociopolitical backing. His extraordinary legacy continues to impact our modern-day educational as well as socio-economic policies, as well as inspires the desire for an egalitarian, caste-free society. We can also remember Subhas Chandra Bose, one of the most prominent leaders of the Indian freedom struggle, in this context. His ideologies were completely contradictory to that of Mahatma Gandhi, who was highly popular among masses during the freedom struggle. Nonetheless, Bose's stance remained firm as a rock, as he stood for

viii ▪ *50 Captivating Lives*

self-governance or *swaraj,* even if it meant using force and violent retaliation against the British.

Let us also not forget about individuals like Henry Louis Vivian Derozio, an Anglo-Indian poet, who had an intense passion for teaching and imparted knowledge among the young people of Bengal in the early nineteenth century. Annie Besant was a British activist and writer, who was a staunch supporter of the demand for swaraj and became one of the most prominent leaders for the Indian independence struggle. This book also provides a detailed account of of Lord Louis Mountbatten, a member of the British Royal Family who was the first governor-general of India. He was sent to India to oversee the plans for the transfer of power from the British crown to the Indians. Going against the oppressive conventions of the Empire they belonged to, these people found an intellectual and spiritual sanctuary in India and did all they could to nourish it. This book commemorates them and their contributions to India.

Thus, etched within collective history and kept alive by personal memory, these figures are not just the heroes of a wonderful past but continue to be the drivers of change in our present-day lives. As Netaji Subhas Chandra Bose has rightly said, 'One individual may die for an idea, but that idea will, after his death, incarnate itself in a thousand lives.' These victors are the ones who set the stage for those who came after them and continue their great legacies. As knowledge bearers, political leaders, artists, thinkers or daring renegades, they towered against the coarse rigidities of their times with the power of ideas, conviction and utmost faith in themselves and their nation.

This book is a tribute to some of the finest of our country, because of whom we are where we are today. You may read it out of pure intrigue or because you want to feel moved. This book, however, doesn't contain any fictional tales, heroic myths or false instances that glorify the influential lives in question. Rather, it aims to tell you the raw truth, embracing all the humanness, paradoxes and complexities of these iconic figures. At the same time, unlike a history book, this collection doesn't just stick to dates and facts, but provides you insight into these people's origins, personal aspirations and goals.

There have been plenty of awe-inspiring thinkers and leaders such as Mahatma Gandhi, Chandra Shekhar Azad, Bhikaiji Rustom Cama, Aurobindo Ghose, Dr B.R. Ambedkar, Indira Gandhi and Rani Lakshmibai who have done extraordinary service to our nation and left their mark, not just on our currency notes, *chowk*, stadiums, metro stations or *marg* but also in our hearts and minds. We quote their words, we write about them, we read their biographies…but what about the unsung heroes who do not appear in our syllabus, history books, Bollywood films or magazines as often as the above-mentioned names do?

This anthology not only explores the well-known, captivating lives of those who shaped and reformed India (you are already aware of most of these powerhouses) but also includes lives, compelling and substantial, that have gotten overshadowed by names that are more dominant and central in popular culture and media. Some of these captivating lives are lesser-explored gold mines, filled with new mysteries and information for you to delve deeper into. This book is a combination of a plethora of short biographies of our most dazzling gems—those who stood up to the British Empire, those who built their own empires of the mind, those who were the frontrunners of the freedom struggle, those who managed this freedom after it was attained and those who desired some change and became that very change.

India has the world's second largest population (and a heritage as ancient as the beginning of human civilization itself), so you already know that picking just a few lives to talk about wasn't easy. However, there are some men and women who have made remarkable differences and exceptional contributions in various fields, in their own unique ways. These 50 captivating figures have influenced our culture, perceptions, societies, bodies of knowledge and morals, despite some of them remaining completely unrecognized till date. This anthology seeks to include their names among the ones that we celebrate conventionally. It is a tribute to the bravehearts that are eminent as well as the ones who, for some reason, still remain on the margins of history books and official records. From someone as prominent as our very own Bapu, the iconic father of the nation, whose opposition of the brutal British Raj gave us the gift of liberation, to someone like Homi Jehangir Bhabha, who isn't too well-known to the masses but made significant contributions to the fields of quantum theory and cosmic radiations—you can find a diverse array of entities in this book. Like different masalas in our most loved delicacies that work together to create a magical flavour, this anthology fuses various illustrious lives—from singers, dancers, writers, mathematicians and scientists, to political leaders, religious figures, medieval rulers and army generals—together.

The people mentioned in this book have shaped the country into what it is today. They fought hard for its freedom from British rule and set independent India on the path of growth and glory, the fruits of which we relish today. These people can be described by a simple word—captivating. This word is not necessarily linked to popularity; it is given to a chosen few to show gratitude and reverence. This anthology commemorates their courage, their will to aid others and their ability to create other influential thinkers and leaders. Let these 50 life narratives captivate you too.

1

Bhimrao Ramji Ambedkar

(1891–1956)

The life of Bhimrao Ramji Ambedkar or B.R. Ambedkar is a saga of struggle against myriad odds. He showed undaunted courage in facing them. He was a reformer who tried to cleanse Hindu society of its ills, especially that of untouchability and the caste system, on the lines of reformers like Raja Ram Mohan Roy, Swami Dayananda Saraswati, Jyotirao Phule and others.

Bhimrao Ambedkar was born on 14 April 1891 in Mhow, a town in the erstwhile princely state of Indore. He was the fourteenth child of his parents Ramji Sakpal and Bhimabai. The family belonged to the 'untouchable' Mahar caste. However, among the 'untouchables', Mahars were considered a martial race and had played an important role in the Maratha army from the time of Shivaji. Many of them had also joined the British army. Ambedkar's grandfather, father and six uncles held the rank of subedar-major in the British army. His father, Ramji, was serving as a teacher in the Army School when Bhimrao was born. He retired from service after a couple of years and took his family to Dapoli, a village in Ratnagiri district of Maharashtra, and then to Satara where he could get a job.

A child's first school is always the family. Bhimrao grew up in a religious atmosphere. His father was a religious man who recited couplets from the Ramayana and the Mahabharata daily like any devout Hindu. Bhimrao's formal education started at Dapoli, but he finished his primary education at Satara. In school, he faced traumatic experiences for being an 'untouchable'. Students and teachers alike shunned him, heaping unspeakable humiliations on the young Bhim. His attitude towards the caste system and the curse of untouchability could be traced to these ugly degrading experiences in his childhood. While studying at Satara, Bhim used 'Ambavadekar' as his surname, which was derived from the name of his family's ancestral village, Ambavade. A teacher, whose name was Ambedkar, changed Bhim's surname to Ambedkar in the school records because he liked the meek but disciplined boy. From Satara, his family moved to Bombay (now Mumbai), where Ramji got a job. Bhimrao was enrolled in Elphinstone High School and he passed his matriculation examination in 1908 from there. He was an average student, but he developed the habit of reading beyond textbooks at a young age. Even before he had passed the matriculation examination, he was married to Ramabai, an eight-year-old girl.

After school, Ambedkar joined Elphistone College and passed the intermediate examination from there. In school, as well as in college, the orthodox upper caste Hindu teachers did not allow Bhim to opt for Sanskrit as an elective subject and he was compelled to take Persian. However, with his own efforts and with the help of some broad-minded Pandits, he acquired a good knowledge of Sanskrit, which enabled him to study and interpret Hindu scriptures. Surprisingly, leaders like Mahatma Gandhi and Jawaharlal Nehru hardly had any knowledge of Sanskrit. Ambedkar was contemplating discontinuing his studies due to financial difficulties when he received a scholarship of ₹25 per month from the Maharaja of Baroda, Sayajirao Gaekwad, which enabled him to graduate in 1912. For further studies, he went to the United States (US) on the Baroda State Scholarship and joined Columbia University, New York, from where he obtained a master's degree in 1915 and a PhD in 1916. While at Columbia University, he wrote three dissertations—*Ancient Indian Commerce, Caste in India* and *National Dividend of India*—which were later published as books. From the US, Ambedkar went to England and joined the London School of Economics and Political Science (LSE) in October 1916 as well as Gray's Inn for legal studies. While he was still studying, the tenure of his scholarship expired and he had to return to India. He was, however, determined to go back to complete his studies. Back in Bombay, he taught at the Sydenham College of Commerce and Economics for two years (1918–20), saved some money, borrowed some more and returned to London to resume his studies. He was awarded an masters in economics in 1921 and a doctorate in economics in 1923. In the same year, he was called to the Bar and qualified as a barrister. On his return to Bombay, he started legal practice but his heart was in doing social work to help the downtrodden. When he had returned to India from England for the first time, he had started a fortnightly Marathi newspaper, *Mooknayak* (Leader of the Dumb), with the help of Shahu Maharaj. Ambedkar had addressed several conferences expressing his views and they had been received well. After completing his education, he was drawn more and more towards social and political activities. His first concern was eradicating untouchability and instilling confidence and dignity among the untouchables. For that purpose, he set up the Bahishkrit Hitkarini Sabha in July 1924. The Sabha gave priority to the education of the depressed classes and opened free schools, libraries and hostels for them. Within five years, the Sabha was running four boarding houses in the Bombay Presidency, where students belonging to the lower castes could live as those from higher castes refused to stay and dine with them.

Ambedkar started a few journals and newspapers to spread his message. A Marathi fortnightly newspaper, *Bahishkrit Bharat*, was started in April 1927. The same year, in September, he founded the Samaj Samata Sangh to preach social equality and started publishing its organ, *Samata,* in March 1929. Yet another journalistic venture of his was *Janata,* a weekly journal, started in November 1930. None of these, however, survived for long as Ambedkar became involved in social, educational and other activities.

In a country like India, where a vast majority of people are illiterate, a person cannot become a leader of the masses through his writings and speeches alone. The leader has to take recourse to some dramatic action in which people can participate in large numbers, as was demonstrated by Bal Gangadhar Tilak and Gandhi. With that purpose in mind, Ambedkar resorted to a form of *satyagraha* (a policy of passive political resistance) to fight for the right of untouchables to drink water from a *chandan talab* (a public sweet water tank) in Mahad, which was inaccessible to the lower castes. Ambedkar and his followers walked up to the tank on 20 March 1927 and drank water from it. The upper caste Hindus were furious and attacked them. But Ambedkar advised his followers to stay calm and not retaliate. The incident resulted in a court case, which the 'untouchables' won, after a long wait, in 1937 from the Bombay High Court. Ambedkar led another satyagraha in March 1930 demanding the right of Hindus of all castes to enter the famous Ram Mandir (Kalaram Temple) in Nashik. From these events, Ambedkar emerged as the leader of the weaker sections of Hindu society. In recognition of this, he was nominated to the Bombay Legislative Assembly, where he served from 1926 to 1934, fighting for the cause of the lower castes. In 1928, he was appointed as a lecturer in the Government Law College, Bombay, and subsequently, became its principal. In 1935, he was made the Perry Professor of Jurisprudence, a highly coveted chair in academics.

Ambedkar was a delegate to the three Round Table Conferences held in London during 1930–32, as a representative for the Scheduled Castes. In these conferences, he pleaded for separate electorates for the Scheduled Castes as there were for Muslims, Sikhs and Christians. During the Second Round Table Conference, Ambedkar came into direct confrontation with Gandhi who claimed that he was the sole representative of the Congress for all castes and communities in India. As the delegates could not arrive at an agreed solution to the problems confronting India, the British government announced their own decision on 17 August 1932, known as the

Communal Award. In it, the Scheduled Castes were given separate electorates. This was unacceptable to Gandhi and most upper caste Hindu leaders like Madan Mohan Malaviya. Gandhi went on an indefinite fast in Yervada Jail, where he had been interned. Later, a pact was signed between Ambedkar and Madan Mohan Malaviya (on behalf of the upper caste Hindus) known as the Poona Pact. Under this pact, separate electorates for Scheduled Castes were rescinded and additional reserved seats in legislatures were provided for them. Thus, division within Hindu society was avoided. This is rightly considered as a great contribution of Gandhi. However, unwittingly, Gandhi and the Congress party had accepted Ambedkar as the leader of the Scheduled Castes.

The years 1934 and 1935 proved to be quite significant in Ambedkar's life. In 1934, he moved to his new house in Bombay which he had designed himself and named 'Rajgruha'. It was large enough to accommodate his vast collection of books. On 27 May 1935, his wife Ramabai died and he performed all the rites prescribed by the Hindu *shastras,* including the shaving of the head, to the chagrin of orthodox upper caste Hindus. By now, Ambedkar was convinced that it was not possible to reform the Hindu society and its hideous customs like untouchability. The only alternative he could think was to leave the Hindu fold and get converted to another religion which would offer the untouchables better social status and equality. He announced this on 13 October 1935, at a public meeting at Yeola in Nashik. He vowed that, 'Though, I was born a Hindu, I solemnly assure you that I will not die as a Hindu.' He exhorted his followers to do likewise. He spent several years studying the social set-up of various religions—Sikhism, Islam and Christianity. To his horror, he found that some kind of discrimination and caste system existed in all these religions. Conversion was therefore postponed.

Ambedkar now wanted to enter politics to represent the depressed classes as well as the poor peasant and the labour force. He founded the Independent Labour Party in October 1936. The party was confined to the Bombay province. It fought elections in February 1937 for the provincial assembly and won 13 out of the 15 seats reserved for the Scheduled Castes (the term used for the depressed classes in the Government of India Act 1935). In 1942, he founded the Scheduled Castes Federation, an all-India party that brought all the Scheduled Castes under its banner. However, it did not do well in the elections for two reasons: one, there are several castes and sub-castes even among the Scheduled Castes and all the castes were not with Ambedkar; two, some powerful leaders of the Scheduled Castes like M.C. Rajah and R.S. Gavai had joined the Congress and opposed whatever Ambedkar did.

Then came the Second World War in September 1939. Ambedkar was nominated as the labour member of the governor general's executive council. As he was cooperating with the government in the war effort, he was made a member of the Defence Advisory Committee. The need for manpower in the defence forces compelled the government to change their policy towards recruitment in the army. Under pressure from the upper castes, the British government had stopped recruiting people from lower castes in the armed forces by the turn of the nineteenth century. Now, they had to change their policy and allow all castes to join the armed forces. Ambedkar exhorted the Scheduled Castes to join the army in large numbers. The British raised a Mahar regiment after half a century. This contribution of Ambedkar has not been accorded its due by his biographers.

In July 1945, Ambedkar founded the People's Education Society. The society opened several schools and colleges, the most important college being the Siddhartha College of Arts, Science and Commerce, Bombay, founded in 1946. Another college opened by the Society was Milind College, Aurangabad, whose foundation stone was laid by Rajendra Prasad, the then president of India, in 1950. This college became the nucleus of the Dr Babasaheb Ambedkar Marathwada University in Maharashtra.

As the Scheduled Castes Federation did badly in the 1946

elections, the British government did not allow Ambedkar to take part in the final negotiations for the transfer of power, i.e., in the Simla Conference of 1945 and The Cabinet Mission of 1946. However, he was elected to the Constituent Assembly from Bengal in July 1947 from Bombay. The Constituent Assembly started functioning from 9 December 1946 even before the transfer of power. Ambedkar was appointed chairman of the Drafting Committee and played a pivotal role in drafting the Constitution. He was also made the first law and justice minister of independent India in the Nehru Cabinet. 'He brought to bear upon his task of drafting a vast array of qualities, erudition, scholarship, imagination, logic and expertise as a legal luminary. He may not be a modern Manu but he was the last word on interpretation.' Immediately after the work of drafting the Constitution was over, Ambedkar started drafting the Hindu Code Bill and worked on it for one year with his usual diligence. As law minister, he introduced the Bill in Parliament in February 1951. Nehru had promised his support for the Bill but when the time came, he dragged his feet and the Bill could not be taken up for discussion and lapsed. This hurt Ambedkar. In disgust, he resigned from the Cabinet. *The Times of India*, Bombay reported his resignation: 'Bereft of the crown of Manu, Dr Ambedkar nonetheless leaves the Government with a considerable record of achievement behind him. The Cabinet is not overburdened with talent, and the departure of this discerning scholar and industrious student of public affairs cannot but dim its limited lustre.'[1]

For quite some time, Ambedkar was not in good health. In 1948, he went to Bombay for treatment and was admitted to a hospital. Soon after, on 15 April 1948, he married a doctor who was working in the same hospital. His wife Sharada Kabir (who later adopted the name Savita) was a Saraswat Brahmin. They led

[1]Keer, Dhananjay, *Dr Ambedkar: Life and Mission*, Popular Prakashan, Bombay, 1962, p. 437.

a happy married life for the remaining eight years of Ambedkar's life. She died on 29 May 2003 in Mumbai at the age of 94.

Despite his achievements, Ambedkar was a frustrated man as he could not do much for the eradication of untouchability. He remembered the declaration he had made in front of thousands of his followers at Yeola way back in 1935, that he will not die a Hindu. He felt that the time to redeem his pledge had come. He had studied Sikhism, Islam and Christianity and had rejected all the religions. In his later years, he took an interest in Buddhism and its philosophy. He had attended a few international conferences on Buddhism at Rangoon, Colombo and Kathmandu and the rational religion had appealed to him. On 14 October 1956, he converted to Buddhism along with his wife and thousands of his followers in Nagpur. On 16 December 1956, Ambedkar died in his sleep in Delhi. His body was brought to Bombay and cremated. He was a Buddhist for only two months. For most of his life, he was a Hindu and a part of Hinduism, the religion whose casteism he strongly condemned.

Ambedkar was a prolific writer. He wrote highly critical and controversial books on caste and Hinduism such as *Caste in India* (1917), *Annihilation of Caste, What the Congress and Gandhi Have Done to the Untouchables* (1945), *Who Were the Shudras?* (1946), *Untouchables: Who Were They? And Why They Became Untouchables?* (1948); *Riddles in Hinduism* (published posthumously in 1987). He also wrote on economic topics in his books *Problem of the Rupee: Its Origin and Its Solution* (1923) and *Evolution of Provincial Finance in British India: A Study in The Provincial Decentralization of Imperial Finance* (1925). On politics, his most outstanding book remains *Thoughts on Pakistan* (1941), and its second edition, *Pakistan or The Partition of India* (1946). He was perhaps the only leader who saw the inevitability of the Partition way back in 1940. Ambedkar analysed the problem in detail and suggested that a partition seemed to be the only solution along with the complete transfer of population, as advocated by Ambedkar, of the two communities. The country was partitioned in 1947 but a complete transfer of population did not take place.

Ambedkar remained a controversial personality during his lifetime and remains so even after his death, not for what he said, but for the way he said it. Still, nobody doubts his greatness. As mentioned by Koenraad Elst, 'Ambedkar was a man of principles, a man with a spine, a true patriot, a realist, a loyal shepherd to his community, a scholar in his own right, a man for whom words had a definite meaning.'[2] The nation's highest award, the Bharat Ratna, was conferred on him in 1990. An impressive statue of Ambedkar greets the visitors at the Parliament House in New Delhi, reminding everyone of his contribution to the Indian Constitution and to the nation.

---

[2]Elst, Koenraad, *Dr Ambedkar: A True Aryan,* Voice of India, New Delhi, 1993, p. 1.

2

Charles Freer Andrews

(1871–1940)

Charles Freer Andrews was one of those British people who identified themselves with India and Indians and worked for their social and political emancipation. While Sister Nivedita had become a Hindu and Annie Besant a Theosophist (the two other British people who worked for the same cause), Andrews remained a devout Christian till the end.

Charles Freer Andrews was born on 12 February 1871 in Newcastle-upon-Tyne. He was the son of a Christian minister belonging to a very orthodox apostolic church. In 1876, his family moved to Birmingham, where Andrews attended King Edward VI School. He was fond of poetry and painting in school. In 1890, he won an open scholarship and joined Pembroke College at Cambridge and obtained the Classical Tripos in first class and the Theology Tripos in 1895. Due to the influence of his Christian friends at Cambridge, he left the orthodox church of his father and got ordained in the Church of England in 1896. Like a true Christian, he started working for the poor. After a year of working in the north of England, he came to London and started doing social work in the East End where the poor lived, under the aegis of the Christian Social Union.

Andrews decided to come to India when he learnt about the death of the missionary Basil Westcott who had come to India to serve the Indian mission. Westcott, in his writings, had spoken highly of India, placing it alongside Greece. Andrews reached India on 20 March 1904 to join the Cambridge Brotherhood and to teach at St Stephen's College, Delhi. Years later, he claimed this date as a second birthday in his life. Here, he met Sushil Kumar Rudra, an Indian Christian, who was the vice principal of St Stephen's College at that time. A fruitful friendship ensued between the two, which continued even after Andrews left the college eight years later. In 1907, George Hibbert-Ware, the principal of the college, was offered bishopric in one of the British colonies and Andrews was offered the post of the principal. He declined and pleaded that Sushil Rudra, who was the vice-principal at the time and his senior at the college by many years, should get it. Till then, no Indian Christian had been appointed principal of the college. Andrew's forceful plea was considered, and with a lot of misgivings, Rudra was appointed principal by the management. Rudra became very popular with the students and the staff and was an admirable host. Many national leaders used to visit him and some even stayed with him. Through Rudra, Andrews came to know leaders like Gopal Krishna Gokhale, Lala Lajpat Rai and Swami Shraddhanand. Gandhi used to stay with Rudra whenever he was in Delhi, after his return from South Africa, till Rudra's death in 1925. It was also through Rudra that Andrews came to understand India and love the country and her people. Years later, Andrews wrote, 'I owe to Sushil Rudra what I owe to no one else in the world; a friendship which has made India from the first not a strange land but a familiar country.' At St Stephen's, Andrews became the most admired teacher. He could teach any subject in the humanities, but he particularly enjoyed teaching English poetry and history. Even during his stay at St Stephen's, Andrews used to visit the *chamar basti* (cobbler's slum) nearby to help the poor cobblers and their families.

In 1912, during his visit to England, Andrews attended a small private gathering where W.B. Yeats, the famous Irish poet, read some of Tagore's poems from the English version of *Gitanjali*. Like others present, Andrews was extremely moved by the poetic vision of Tagore. The same evening, Andrews had an intimate conversation with the poet and a bond was forged between the two which became stronger with the passage of time. Tagore's poems, according to Andrews, contained a message for the West. Tagore, 10 years senior to Andrews, became his *gurudev* (the sublime teacher).

On returning to India, Andrews met Gokhale, who asked him to visit South Africa and help Gandhi finalize the agreement to the harsh remove poll tax being levied on Indian labourers in South Africa. Andrews, along with another British missionary, Reverend W.W. Pearson, reached Durban on 2 January 1914. Gandhi, along with some of his followers, was at the docks to receive them. This was Andrews' first meeting with Gandhi and Andrews quickly and unobtrusively bent down and touched Gandhi's feet, the Indian way of showing respect. They became friends and started informally addressing each other as 'Mohan' and 'Charlie'. Andrews helped Gandhi in putting an honourable end to his satyagraha, working through Lord Gladstone, governor general of South Africa (son of William E. Gladstone, the then prime minister of England). Andrews had known the Gladstone family in England and with their help 'he was able to infiltrate the entire government of South Africa.' Mission completed, he returned to India via London. During this period, he studied Tagore and gave two lectures on Tagore in Cape Town—one in the City Hall and the other in the University of Cape Town in February 1914. Andrews was indeed greatly attracted to Rabindranath Tagore and found his peace and permanent abode in Santiniketan, which he first visited in April 1914. The poet welcomed him with a song that he had composed for Andrews.

Andrews joined Santiniketan in 1915 and it was his home till his last days. In addition to teaching, Andrews helped Santiniketan in various other ways. When the institution was in financial trouble, he went door to door to raise funds for it. He helped in developing Sriniketan, the agricultural wing of Santiniketan, and worked in nearby villages to help the poor farmers. He accompanied Tagore when he visited China and Japan in 1916. The letters that passed between Andrews and Tagore project the deep bond of friendship and love they had for each other. In a letter to Tagore on 23 May 1914, Andrews wrote: 'Your letters have been coming to me morning by morning. They have brought me a vision of a larger, fuller life than I had ever known.' From Paris, Tagore wrote to Andrews on 7 September 1920: 'Your letters always bring the atmosphere of Santiniketan round my mind, with all its colour and sound and movements. Your letters are great gifts to me. I have not the power to repay them in kind.'[1]

Nehru met Andrews for the first time in 1920 when he visited Santiniketan along with Gandhi. Nehru wrote about their meeting saying: 'I remember C.F. Andrews giving me some books which interested and influenced me greatly. They dealt with the economic aspects of imperialism in Africa. About this time or a little later, Andrews wrote a pamphlet advocating independence for India. I think it was called *Independence: the Immediate Need*. This was a brilliant essay and it seemed to me not only to make out an unanswerable case for independence but also to mirror the innermost recesses of our hearts.'[2]

Andrews admired Gandhi and was fascinated and surprised by the respect and reverence the masses held for him. As mentioned earlier, he first met Gandhi in South Africa early in 1915. He also worked with Gandhi to help the indigo workers in the Champaran district of Bihar in 1917. Later, he was with Gandhi during his serious illness in 1918 and 1934, nursing him around the clock. During the Second Round Table Conference in London (1931), he was with Gandhi, explaining his views to English people, bureaucrats and media. He was with Gandhi whenever the latter required 'Charlie's' help. But in spite of the admiration and friendship, he was highly critical of some of Gandhi's policies and idiosyncrasies. He opposed Gandhi for going from village to village to get recruits

---

[1]Jaggi, O.P., *Friends of India*, Munshiram Manoharlal, Delhi, p. 7.
[2]Nehru, Jawaharlal, *An Autobiography*, Oxford University Press, 1980, p. 66.

for the British army during the First World War and criticized him for going against his own principles of non-violence. Andrews, along with Tagore, came down heavily on Gandhi when he made a dramatic bonfire of foreign clothes during the Non-cooperation Movement. 'What advantage there was in burning the noble handiwork of one's fellow men and women?' he asked. 'I almost fear now to wear the *khadaar* you have given me,' he wrote, 'lest I should appear to be judging other people as a Pharisee would, saying I am holier than thou.' Once again, he was critical of Gandhi, along with Tagore and others, for asking students to leave their educational institutions. In the words of Tagore: 'It would be like using the fire from the altar of sacrifice for the purpose of incendiarism.' Andrews felt that the movement should not be run by a rabble-rouser and criticized Gandhi for his greed to enlarge his following with men of doubtful integrity. Andrews also felt dismayed when Gandhi attacked Christian missionaries (being a part of the community himself) and wrote strongly to Gandhi about it.

Few had realized at the time that Andrews' spirit of nationalism was more militant than that of Gandhi. Even during the Non-cooperation Movement, the Congress leaders, including Gandhi, were not sure about what actually they actually meant by 'swaraj.' The maximum they could conceive of was some kind of dominion status. But on 9 January 1921, addressing a large meeting of the Calcutta (now Kolkata) students, Andrews advocated for 'independence, complete and perfect, as against the soul-sapping white-supremacy.' It was left to an Englishman, and a Christian missionary at that, to come out with a clear statement about the objective of the freedom movement. Andrews repeated this sentiment later through hundreds of mediums and in his numerous articles published in India and abroad.[3] It took the Congress another nine years to articulate this agenda, which they finally did during the Lahore session (1929–30).

---

[3]Roy Chaudhury, P.C., *Gandhi and His Contemporaries*, Sterling, New Delhi, 1986, p. 46.

Wherever poor Indians were ill-treated and discriminated against, Andrews rushed to their help, not only in India but also in foreign lands. This mission of his took him to South and East Africa several times. The evil of indenture labour was such that the Indian labourers were transported to various British colonies, where they were treated like bonded labourers. To get them justice, Andrews visited Fiji in 1915 and again in 1917. In 1929, he made a personal investigation about their problems in the West Indies and British Guyana. In India, he fought for the rights of the labour class; in 1918, he intervened in the strike of Madras (now Chennai) cotton factory workers; and in 1919, he helped organize relief work among unemployed tea estate workers stranded at Chandpur (now in Bangladesh). In 1920, he brought to the attention of the government, the plight of forced labour in Rajputana and Simla Bills. In 1921–22, he identified himself with the cause of the striking railway workers at Tundla. In 1925, he was elected president of the worker's union at the Tata factory in Jamshedpur and he got the union recognized and the dispute settled with the company. In 1925 and 1927, he was elected president of the All India Trade Union Congress (AITUC).

He was equally concerned with the plight of the lower caste Hindus and criticized Gandhi for not doing enough for them by frittering away his energy in political work. 'Independence', he wrote, 'can never be won if the millions of untouchables remain still in subjection.' The sympathy with the untouchables made him join the Vaikom Satyagraha in 1925, aimed at getting the road leading to the Vaikom temple opened for the untouchables. He also worked with Ambedkar in formulating the demands for untouchables in 1933.

Andrews was a delightful eccentric. He had no sense of possession and was often seen in clothes which did not fit him well and gave him a sloppy appearance. He often walked barefoot, even to the offices of high officials. Robert Payne has written about Andrews in his book, saying, 'Andrews was one of those quiet men who wear authority like an invisible garment. He had entry into places rarely entered by missionaries. He would sit down over a tea cup with a prime minister, and the next day, without any warning, there would be an official proclamation, or an order in Council, signed by the prime minister and written with the stub of Andrew's pencil.'[4]

From 1935, Andrews divided his time between India and England. He also began to exercise his Christian ministry again. He had never ceased to regard himself as a committed member of his church, notwithstanding his discarding of missionary robes in 1914. Christ remained the centre of his life. Devotion to Him was Andrews' outstanding characteristic as well as the source of his inspiration and strength. During his last months at Santiniketan, he often expressed the hope that, in this place, where the civilizations of the world can share with each other the bases of their strength, there might be established a hall of Christian culture similar to the Cheena Bhavana.

Like most British people in India, the climate did not suit him. Insomnia was another one of his problems. Over the years, he had become very lean, thin and lost much of his vitality. He was operated upon on 31 March 1940, at Dr Riordan's Nursing Home in Calcutta and died of complications on 5 April 1940. In his will, he had written: 'I wish to be buried in the Christian faith, a Christian, near St Paul's Cathedral, Calcutta—if possible, with the blessing of the Metropolitan (archbishop)—as a priest of the Christian Church and minister of the Christian faith which I hold with all my heart.' The Metropolitan did come to bless him before he died. He is buried in the Lower Circular Road Cemetery in Calcutta. Gandhi, in a statement to the press, said: 'He (Andrews) will live through those thousands who have enriched themselves by personal contact or contact with his writings. In my opinion, Charlie Andrews was one of the greatest and best Englishmen.'

---

[4]Payne, Robert, *The Life and Death of Mahatma Gandhi*, Rupa & Co., New Delhi, 1997, p. 267.

3

Abul Kalam Azad

(1888–1958)

Abul Kalam Azad was born in Mecca (now in Saudi Arabia) in 1888, where his father Maulana Khairuddin had migrated to from India. There, Khairuddin had married an Arab lady, Aliya. Their second son was given the name Firoz Bakht, but he was called Muhiyuddin during his childhood and later came to be known as Maulana Abul Kalam Azad. He adopted the name Abul Kalam Azad when he started his journalistic career, just before the First World War. His parents came to Calcutta when he was about two years old. His mother tongue was Arabic as his mother Aliya did not know any other language.

Abul Kalam Azad did not have any formal education, not even in a *madrasa*. Initially, he was taught by his father, who was a scholar of Arabic and Persian. Later, tutors were arranged for the young boy and they taught him various subjects like philosophy, mathematics and logic in Arabic, besides the Islamic scriptures. He completed this informal education by the age of 16, which resulted in his mastery over Arabic and Frisian. It was easy for him to learn Urdu as its script was the same as that of Persian and he became a competent and forceful writer in these languages. His speeches in pure Urdu drew attention and respect among the Urdu-speaking population. However, with his somewhat Persianized Urdu, he could never have a mass following. His claim that he had learned English on his own so he could read books on philosophy and history was not supported by the events of his later life. He was not able to converse in English with the British officials and statesmen and an interpreter always accompanied him. The only book in the English language which stands in his name—*India Wins Freedom*—was dictated by him in Urdu to Humayun Kabir, who translated it into English. Azad never learnt Hindi, even after it became the official language in 1950. Azad even signed the official files in Urdu while serving as the minister of education in Nehru's Cabinet.

Azad had a sharp intellect and was eager to learn. He decided to get out of the rigid orthodoxy of the Muslim theology, as preached by his father and other *ulama* (Muslim scholars). This was the time he changed his name to Abul Kalam 'Azad (freedom)', marking his freedom from orthodoxy. After completing his studies, he began to move in wider circles, which broadened his views. The partition of Bengal by Lord Curzon in 1905 had agitated the Bengalis and a movement had started in Bengal under the leadership of Aurobindo Ghose and others. Azad claims that he had been attracted to revolutionary politics and joined the movement, but there is no record of his joining any revolutionary group in the annals of the freedom movement. In 1908, Azad visited Iraq, Egypt, Syria and Turkey, and as a result, he was attracted to the concept of Pan-Islamism. On his return to India, Maulana Azad started an Urdu weekly newspaper, *Al-Hilal* (The Crescent), from Calcutta in 1912. This was the time when the Balkan Wars started, in which Turkey was involved. His paper carried a strong campaign with Mohammad Ali in favour of Turkey and became the mouthpiece of the anti-British propaganda. In the pages of *Al-Hilal,* Azad highlighted the belief that Abdul Hamid of Turkey was the universal *khalifa* (caliph) of the Muslim world and that the territorial integrity of his empire should be preserved at all costs. He argued that the institution of Caliphate was necessary to secure the organic unity of the Muslim world. The writings of Sir Syed Ahmed asserting that Abdul Hamid was not a khalifa for Indian

Muslims were attacked by him.[1] The anti-British tirade became even harsher when Turkey lost most of the European territory to the Christian nations in 1913. The British government banned the publication of *Al-Hilal* in 1914 and confiscated the security amount. Thereupon, Maulana Azad started another weekly journal, *Al-Balagh* (The Message), in 1914. By that time, the First World War had started and Turkey was fighting against the British on the side of the Central Powers. *Al-Balagh* took off from where *Al-Hilal* had left. The denunciation of British imperialism and the importance of the Khalifa, who was also the sultan of Turkey, continued. *Al-Balagh* met the same fate as that of *Al-Hilal*, the press was confiscated by the government in 1916 and the paper was banned. Maulana Azad was interned and kept at the Ranchi Jail till December 1919. The First World War ended in 1918 with the defeat of the Central Powers, which included Turkey. Under the Treaty of Sèvres, the Ottoman Empire was liquidated. The Pan-Islamic leaders, led by the Ali brothers (Mohammad and Shaukat) and Maulana Azad, started the Khilafat Movement in November 1919 against the treatment of the khalifa by the British. The movement's central demand was that the khalifa should retain the control of places sacred to Islam and be left with sufficient territory to enable him to defend the Islamic faith and holy places. The Khilafat Conference considered the feasibility of non-cooperation with the government to achieve its end. The movement was strengthened when Gandhi joined hands with the Khilafat leaders and started a Non-cooperation Movement, adding Punjab atrocities and swaraj to the agenda for wider support. Gandhi had, thus, reduced the Congress party to the status of an extension of the Khilafat Committee, pushing it in the direction of a conflict with the government. The Khilafat Movement came to an end in 1922, when the khalifa was dethroned due to a revolution

---

[1]Nagarkar, V.V., *Genesis of Pakistan*, Allied, Bombay, 1975, pp. 98–9; Banerjee, A.C., *Two Nations: Philosophy of Muslim Nationalism*, Concept, New Delhi, 1981, p. 209.

led by Mustafa Kemal Pasha, putting Gandhi, Azad and other Khilafat leaders in an embarrassing situation. The Non-cooperation Movement was also suspended by Gandhi in February 1922. When this Pan-Islamic movement fizzled out, the Ali brothers deserted the Congress gradually but Maulana Azad stayed on. As a reward, he was elected to preside over the special session of the Congress in September 1923 in Delhi. As a Congressman, he was imprisoned several times during the agitations done by the Congress party.

During his internship at Ranchi, Azad had started translating the *Quran* from Arabic to Urdu and it was published in 1930 as *Turjuman al-Quran*. It contains a clear view of his religious maturity. It was later translated into English by Dr Syed Abdul Latif and is considered a monumental work of its kind.

In 1928, Azad presided over the All India Muslim Conference. In 1937, he was appointed a member of the Congress Parliamentary Sub-Committee to guide the Provincial Congress Ministries working under the 1935 Act. Maulana Azad came into the limelight when he was elected president of the Congress in 1940. He devoted the best part of his presidential address on 19 March 1940 to the communal question and guaranteed Muslims that their rights and interests would be looked after in any future constitution, leaving it to the minorities to decide the form of safeguards needed by them. He observed that 80 or 90 million Muslims could not be treated as a political minority though they formed only 25 per cent of the population. Moreover, they were more homogeneous and stronger compared to other communities. He further added that any constitution for an All-India Federation would provide full autonomy to the provinces and arm the federal centre with matters such as foreign relations, defence, customs etc. Three days later, the Muslim League passed the famous resolution at Lahore demanding separate areas for the Muslims, which was attended by over a 100,000 Muslims.

Even after his election as Congress president, Maulana Azad did not adhere to all the tenets of Gandhism. He did not spin regularly as was required by the Congress constitution. Azad also did not believe in non-violence. In his opinion, opposing violence with violence was fully in harmony with the natural laws of God. In a letter to Jawaharlal Nehru on 13 July 1942, Gandhi wrote: 'This is my plea about Maulana Saheb. I find that the two of us have drifted apart. I do not understand him, nor does he understand me. We are drifting apart on the Hindu-Muslim question as well as on other questions. I have also a suspicion that Maulana Saheb does not entirely approve of the proposed action (Quit India Movement). Therefore, I suggest that the Maulana should relinquish Presidentship but remain in the Committee. The Committee should elect an interim President and all should proceed unitedly.'[2] Such views deprived Azad of a large Hindu following. During the parliamentary elections, he had to stand from constituencies in North–West Frontier Province (NWFP), Rampur and Gurgaon (now Gurugram), where there was a large presence of Muslim voters. Fortunately for Azad, the Congress leaders, including Gandhi and Azad, were arrested the following month and the question of Azad resigning as president was postponed indefinitely. In fact, he acted as president of the Congress till June 1946. During this period, as the Congress president, he was the spokesman for the party too. He participated in the negotiations during the Cripps Mission (March 1942), Simla Conference (June 1945) and Cabinet Mission (March 1946). His role as the principal negotiator of the Congress, however, came under a cloud. 'It will always remain a matter of speculation whether it was a blessing or the reverse that at this crucial phase of India's history Maulana Abul Kalam Azad happened to be the President of the Congress', wrote V. Shankar.[3] While the Cripps Mission was rejected by the Congress and the Simla (now Shimla) Conference failed on flimsy grounds, the greatest boon offered to the Muslims was by the Cabinet

---

[2]*Collected Works of Mahatma Gandhi*, Vol. 76, Publications Division, p. 293.
[3]Shankar, V., *Sardar Patel Select Correspondence, 1945-1950*, Vol. 1, Navajivan Publishing House, Ahmedabad, 1976, p. 58.

Mission proposals. It stipulated that the Muslim majority areas will be grouped in a way that the whole of Punjab, Bengal and Assam will be included in it; that there will be a very weak centre having jurisdiction to foreign affairs, defence and communications only; and the rest of the subjects will be directly under the provinces, which will have an option to cede after 10 years; that Muslims will have 50 per cent seats in the Legislature (Parliament) and in the Executive (Ministry). Azad could see that Muslims could never get a better bargain and was so excited at that he wrote to the Mission members that he would get the proposals accepted by the Congress, even if Gandhi and others opposed them. Stafford Cripps, a member of the Mission, sent this letter to Gandhi through his emissary, Sudhir Ghosh. Gandhi had just finished reading the letter when Azad walked in. Gandhi asked the Maulana if he had written such a letter. Azad, with a straight face, denied it. Gandhi was stunned. Azad had lost Gandhi's trust. Later, Gandhi in a letter to Nehru on 24 July 1947 wrote that he should drop Azad from his Cabinet.[4] Nehru did not heed the advice as he needed people like Azad and Rafi Ahmed Kidwai as a bulwark against the rising tide of, what he termed as, 'Hindu communalism and revivalist outlook of certain leaders like Purushottam Das Tandon, Rajendra Prasad and others.' Nehru was very unhappy at the victory of this group in getting Hindi, in Devanagari script, recognized as the official language of India in the Constituent Assembly, despite his opposition. The victory of Rajendra Prasad as president of India (1950) and of Purushottam Das Tandon as Congress president (1950) over Nehru's candidates should also be seen in this light. To spite the *Hindi-wallahs*, he had appointed Azad, who did not know Devanagari and did not have in-depth knowledge of Indian culture, as the education and cultural minister. Azad held that position till his death in 1958, although he could not attend office during the last two years of his life, due to ill-health. During

---

[4]*Collected Works of Mahatma Gandhi Vol. 88*, The Publications Division, p. 408.

his tenure as education minister, two education commissions—the University Education Commission (1948) and the Secondary Education Commission (1952)—were appointed. During this period, several other educational and cultural institutions were also created—University Grants Commission, Indian Council of Cultural Relations and the three academies (Sahitya, Sangeet Natak and Lalit Kala). The Delhi Public Library was established in 1950 with the help of the United Nations Educational, Scientific and Cultural Organization (UNESCO). He also took great interest in the Indian Council for Cultural Relations (ICCR). The building in which it is situated is called Azad Bhavan. However, Azad did not take much interest in the development and working of the other institutions, including the academies.

Azad's claim of being a secular Muslim leader must be taken with a pinch of salt because he continued to help the Muslim cause even after independence. He brought many Muslim officers, holding high positions, who had migrated to Pakistan back to India. In his ministry, all the key posts were held by Muslims—Humayun Kabir, K.G. Saidayin, Ashrafaque Hussain, Nurul Hassan. In speech after speech, he advised the Muslims not to migrate to Pakistan as it would weaken the Muslims of India. During the post-Partition days, he exaggerated the death and plight of the Muslims in Delhi, oblivious of the pitiable condition of millions of Hindu and Sikh refugees. Along with Mountbatten, he incited Gandhi to undergo a fast unto death for the release of ₹55 crore to Pakistan, a country at war with India, against the declared policy of the government. Gandhi's fast was camouflaged as being meant for Hindu–Muslim unity, though there were no riots in Delhi at that time. Lord Mountbatten spilled the beans in his memoirs, claiming that the fast was essentially to force the government to release money to Pakistan.[5]

---

[5]Collins, Larry, and Dominique Lapierre (ed.), *Mountbatten and the Partition of India*, Vikas Publishing House, New Delhi, 1983, p. 52.

However, the character of Maulana Azad is revealed to a greater extent in the pages of his memoir *India Wins Freedom*. The first edition of the book was published in 1959 and the complete version, which included the most controversial 30 pages, in 1988. In this memoir, he has reviled people like Gandhi, Rajendra Prasad and even Nehru, his benefactor and faithful friend. But his worst venom was reserved for Sardar Patel, whom he called communal, anti-Muslim and worse. Azad received brickbats for writing such a book from unexpected quarters. Ram Manohar Lohia, while reviewing his book, wrote, 'Maulana's book contains at least one lie on each page and it is wholly unreliable in respect of historical interpretation. The whole story is an uninteresting lie.'[6] Lohia wrote, 'In calling Maulana Azad a better Muslim than Mr Jinnah, I am not concerned with their religiosity. I am only concerned with the extent to which they served the interests of the Muslims in India. Both of them strove outwardly very outspokenly but also perhaps with inward passion, to realize Muslim interests as distinct from the interests of the Indian people as a whole. The Maulana was a better servant of Muslims than was Mr Jinnah'.[7] Ambedkar's views on Maulana Azad were as follows: 'It is extremely doubtful whether the Nationalist *Musalmans* have any real community of sentiment, aim and policy with the Congress which marks them off from the Muslim League. Indeed, many Congressmen are alleged to hold the view that there is no difference between the two and that the Nationalist Muslims inside the Congress are only an outpost of the communal Muslims.'[8] According to Rajmohan Gandhi, 'Pride was Azad's failing. We glimpse it in *India Wins Freedom* in the form of "I-was-wiser-than-the-rest." He refers several times to the errors of Gandhi, Nehru and Patel and not less frequently, to his

[6]Ibid. 16.

[7]Lohia, Rammanohar, *Guilty Men of India's Partition*, Rammanohar Lohia Samata Vidyalaya Nyas Publication Department, Hyderabad, 1970, pp. 12, 16.

[8]Ambedkar, B.R., *Pakistan or The Partition of India*, Thacker & Co., Bombay, 1945, p. 408.

own sounder judgement. "Later events proved how justified my apprehensions were." We encounter such sentences a shade too often.[9] But whatever his own assessment of himself, Azad did not wield much influence in the decision-making process of the Congress. That remained primarily with Gandhi, Nehru and Patel.

Azad did not have much of a family life. His wife Zulaikha Begum gave birth to a baby boy, who died soon after birth. Zulaikha died in 1943 while Azad was interned in Ahmednagar Fort during the Quit India Movement. He did not go to Calcutta for her last rites but wrote a very sentimental letter to one of his friends about her, to unburden his feelings, showing his humane side. During the last years of his life he faced several health issues. Around 1946, he fell down, broke his backbone and could not walk without help. He died at the age of 70 on 22 February 1958. He is buried in the lawns outside Jama Masjid in Delhi.

---

[9]Gandhi, Rajmohan, *Eight Lives: A Study of the Hindu-Muslim Encounter*, Roli Books, New Delhi, 1986, p. 251.

4

Chandra Shekhar Azad

(1906–1931)

Chandra Shekhar Azad was one of the most daring revolutionaries who sacrificed his life for the freedom of the country. He was born on 23 July 1906, in Bhabhra village, now in the Alirajpur district of Madhya Pradesh. His father, Sitaram Tiwari, was a watchman in a state garden and earned a salary of ₹10 a month. His mother, Jagrani Devi, had given birth to three children prior to him, who had not survived. Chandra Shekhar thus got special love and care from his poor parents. As a child, he attended the village school but did not take much interest in studies and used to roam about and play with local boys, using bows and arrows as toys. The village life did not interest him and he left his home without informing his parents. He was 14 at the time. His worried parents were relieved when they received a letter from him telling them that he was in Kashi, studying Sanskrit in a *pathshala* (school). As boarding and lodging was free, he did not have to worry about his daily needs. It is believed that he lived in a room adjacent to the Shri Batuk Bhairava Temple in Kamachha locality of Banaras (now Varanasi) for some years.

In 1920, the Congress party, under the leadership of Gandhi, started the Non-cooperation Movement. The young Chandra Shekhar participated in the movement and took part in picketing. He was arrested and tried before a magistrate. When the magistrate asked his name, he said: 'Azad'. When asked his father's name he said, 'freedom', and on being asked his address, he said, 'prison'. The magistrate was furious and he ordered 15 lashes to be inflicted on Chandra Shekhar's bare body. After every lash, he uttered the words, '*bande mataram*'. He was only 15 when this happened. This incident made Chandra Shekhar something akin to a celebrity in Kashi, and from that time onwards, he came to be known as 'Azad.' Important citizens of Kashi, like Shiv Prasad Gupta, admired the bravery of the boy and he was felicitated at a meeting of the Congress party soon after.

After the failure and suspension of the Non-cooperation Movement, there was a collective feeling of frustration among the people. There was a revival of revolutionary activities, spread over the whole of North India from Bengal to Punjab. A meeting of the revolutionaries was held at Kanpur in October 1924, which was attended by revolutionary leaders from different parts of India. An all-India organization was set up under the name of Hindustan Republican Association, later called Hindustan Socialist Republican Association (HSRA). Chandra Shekhar joined this association. In Uttar Pradesh, it was led by Ram Prasad Bismil. In Punjab, it was guided by Bhagat Singh and his associates. As the association needed money to survive, they planned dacoities. But instead of looting innocent individuals, they decided to loot the government treasury. The most notable exploit was the dacoity on 9 August 1925, on a railway train going from Kakori to Alamnagar, near Lucknow. Ten young men stopped the train, fired to scare the guard and passengers, broke open the iron safe and disappeared with a large amount of money. Chandra Shekhar was one of these young men and had taken a leading part in the dacoity. The government launched a vigorous search for those responsible for this daring act. Indiscriminate arrests were made and the police was able to uncover the whole plot. The leaders were put on trial. Ram Prasad Bismil, Roshan Singh and Ashfaqulla Khan were hanged, while 12 others were sentenced to various terms of imprisonment. Chandra Shekhar had escaped, adopting several guises. The aftermath of the Kakori incident had an adverse effect on the movement of the revolutionaries. R.C. Majumdar, in his book, has written about the revolutionaries, saying, 'Chandra Shekhar Azad, the sole remaining absconder of the Kakori Conspiracy Case took the leading part in re-organizing the revolutionary movement. The name of the Association was changed to Hindustan Socialist Republican Association with a Socialist State in India as its objective.'[1] All this was planned with the help of Bhagat Singh, whom Chandra Shekhar had met in the office of *Pratap* (a Hindi language newspaper founded and edited by Ganesh Shankar Vidyarthi) in Kanpur. Some of the exploits thereafter were performed in collaboration with Bhagat Singh and his colleagues. In 1926, Bhagat Singh along with Chandra Shekhar planned to rescue the prisoners of the Kakori case but the plan fell through. The newly organized association was behind the assassination of John Saunders, assistant commissioner of police, in Lahore on 17 December 1928. They mistook him for John Scott and believed him to be responsible for inflicting *lathi* blows on Lala Lajpat Rai during the Anti-Simon Commission demonstration in Lahore. This was planned by Bhagat Singh, Shivaram Rajguru and Chandra Shekhar, but the shots were only fired by Bhagat Singh. All three left Lahore immediately after the assassination—Chandra Shekhar in the guise of a sadhu.

Like the Kakori Conspiracy earlier, the Lahore Conspiracy Case also adversely affected the activities of the HSRA. Almost all the prominent leaders were either dead or in jail, with the exception of about half a dozen who had managed to evade arrest. In this dark hour, Chandra Shekhar emerged as the leader of the group and organized the association. Their first activity was an attempt to assassinate the viceroy. A few bombs exploded under the viceroy's special train near Delhi in December 1929. The train was damaged but the viceroy escaped unhurt. Next, Chandra Shekhar, with others from HSRA, planned an armed revolution and looted ₹14,000 in an

---

[1]Majumdar, R.C., *History of the Freedom Movement in India*, Firma KLM, Calcutta, 1988, pp. 423–24.

armed robbery from a firm in Delhi on 6 July 1930. In the course of investigation, the police got information about Chandra Shekhar's secret plans. One of his trusted lieutenants was arrested a few days later with a large stock of arms, and the police discovered a bomb factory in Delhi with a stock of chemicals enough to make 6,000 bombs. Chandra Shekhar fled towards Punjab and his presence there resulted in the explosion of a series of bombs which killed and injured a few officials. The police went on a vigorous but fruitless search for him, in the course of which they arrested a number of revolutionaries and discovered several depots of arms and small bomb factories. The government instituted two cases: the Second Lahore Conspiracy Case and the Delhi Conspiracy Case. Chandra Shekhar was the principal accused but he succeeded in staying in hiding. The government offered a reward of ₹10,000 to anyone who could help in capturing Chandra Shekhar, dead or alive.[2] He was constantly on the move, still trying to breathe new life in the association with the help of those who were not yet arrested. But there were not many left and new recruits were hard to come by. He was a worried man. In an effort to elicit the sympathy and guidance of the Congress leaders, Chandra Shekhar met Jawaharlal Nehru in February 1931. Nehru describes the meeting thus:

> I remember a curious incident about this time which gave me an insight into the mind of the terrorist group in India. A stranger came to see me at our house, and I was told that he was Chandra Shekhar Azad. I had never seen him before, but I had heard of him ten years earlier, when he had non-cooperated from school and gone to prison during the Non-cooperation Movement in 1921. A boy of fifteen or so then, he had been flogged in prison for some breech of gaol discipline. Later, he had drifted towards the terrorists, and he became one of their prominent men in north India. All this I had heard vaguely, and I had taken no interest in

---

[2]Ibid. 430.

these rumours. I was surprised, therefore, to see him. He had been induced to visit me because of the general expectation (owing to our release) that some negotiations between the Government and the Congress were likely. He wanted to know if, in case of a settlement, his group of people would have any peace. Would they still be considered and treated as outlaws; hunted out from place to place with a price on their heads, and the prospect of the gallows ever before them? Or was there a possibility of their being allowed to pursue peaceful vocations? He told me that as far as he was concerned, as well as many of his associates, they were convinced now that purely terrorist methods were futile and did no good. He was not, however, prepared to believe that India would gain her freedom wholly by peaceful methods. I tried to explain to Chandra Shekhar what my philosophy of political action was, and tried to convert him to my viewpoint. But I had no answer to his basic question: what was he to do now?[3]

Dejected by Nehru's reply, Chandra Shekhar had no alternative but to continue the struggle with the help of a few remaining revolutionaries. His movements and activities during the last year of his life are not chronicled properly. He must have remained in Uttar Pradesh, visiting places like Kanpur and Banaras. However, we know that he was in Allahabad (now Prayagraj) in February 1931. Most of his revolutionary comrades of the time believe that Azad was betrayed by an associate who turned into a traitor.

On 27 February 1931, Chandra Shekhar's presence in Alfred Park was communicated to the police, who surrounded the area. For quite some time, he held them at bay, firing from his pistol. Two police officials were seriously wounded in the gun battle which lasted for half an hour. Ultimately, his body was riddled with bullets and he died on the spot.[4]

---

[3]Nehru, Jawaharlal, *An Autobiography*, Oxford University Press, 1936, pp. 261–62.
[4]Singh Azad, Prithvi Singh, 'Chandra Shekhar Azad' *Dictionary of National*

Thus ended the life of a great revolutionary. While the country was mourning the death of this martyr, the news of Bhagat Singh, Sukhdev and Rajguru being hanged came from Lahore merely 24 days later. These four men were revolutionary comrades in life and martyrs in death.

Biography, S.P Sen (ed.), Calcutta, 1972.

5

Bahadur Shah II (Zafar)

(1775–1862)

Bahadur Shah II is considered the last Mughal king although he was only de jure king by the courtesy of the East India Company. Bahadur Shah's grandfather Shah Alam II and father Akbar II were pensioners of the East India Company. So was Bahadur Shah, who got ₹1 lakh as his monthly pension. Like it had done for his father, the Company had allowed him to be the titular head of a non-existing 'empire'.

Bahadur Shah, born in 1775, was named Mirza Abu Zafar Siraj-ud-din Muhammad. Little is known about his childhood. There is no certainty even about the place of his birth and where he spent his childhood. However, it is known that he received instruction in Urdu, Persian and Arabic from private teachers and also learnt the military arts of horse riding, swordcraft and shooting with firearms and bows and arrows. We get only faint glimpses of him during his youth. His father, Akbar II, did not want him to inherit the throne, and preferred his younger son Jehangir, who even tried to poison his elder brother twice, perhaps with the connivance of their father. However, the East India Company intervened and declared that they would recognize only the elder brother as heir apparent. Besides being younger, Jehangir was of doubtful character. 'There is no doubt that he (Bahadur Shah) was the best fitted of Akbar's sons to succeed.'

During his youth, Bahadur Shah 'appears throughout the records as a man of culture and upright character.' In 1806, when he was 32, and his father was trying to pass him over in favour of Jehangir, he was described as a 'very respectable character' by Charles Seton, the British Resident for Delhi. As a prince, he lived and dressed simply, was of spare figure and stature and always dressed plainly without ostentation. He retained these habits during his reign as well. In the palace diary of his later years, there are glimpses of him spending whole days reading and writing, studying the *Quran* and composing verses. Bahadur Shah was educated to the life of a mediatized prince and the role fitted him perfectly. Whether he could have developed the qualities of action, we shall never know, for he was denied all opportunities in his early years and the mutiny experience came far too late. But as a philosophic prince he would have adorned any country. Bahadur Shah's interests and tastes were essentially literary and aesthetic.[1]

On ascending the throne in 1837, when he was 62, he assumed the name Abu Zafar Mohammad Sirajuddin Bahadur Shah Ghazi. However, he came to be known as Bahadur Shah Zafar—Zafar being his nom de plume. As he was only a de jure king, he did not have much administrative work to do. But as the king of India, he looked upon the British as his subjects, owing allegiance to him under the terms of the Diwani of Bengal, signed by his grandfather, Shah Alam II, in 1765. The East India Company and the British authorities, however, treated him as their pensioner, to whom they had granted a nominal status of king and whose jurisdiction did not extend beyond the walls of the Red Fort. A regiment of Company guards always camped in the Red Fort. Bahadur Shah accepted this humiliating status stoically. Bahadur Shah was a religious man. He did not suffer from the vice of addiction to drinking but he was a gourmet and loved a variety of food. He married several times and had a number of concubines, slave girls and mistresses. His favourite wife, however, was Zeenat Mahal, whom he married late

---

[1]Spear, Percival, *A History of Delhi Under the Later Mughals*, Low Price Publications, Delhi, 1990, p. 73.

in life and who shared, though unwillingly, the misfortunes of his last years in exile.

But above all, Bahadur Shah was a poet and a literary patron. He tried to write Urdu poetry under the guidance of Zauq and Ghalib—two outstanding poets of the era. Percival Spear has spoken of Bahadur Shah II in his book, saying, 'He composed several volumes of lyrics, some of which attained considerable popularity. Though not quite in the same rank as Ghalib and Zauq, he has his niche in the Urdu literary pantheon and his merit cannot be denied. It is this gift, much more than his crown, which gave him his place in the life of Delhi, and it is this even more than his political misfortunes, which has caused him to be affectionately remembered by the people.'[2] He used to have *mushairas* (poetic gatherings) in his palace which were attended by leading poets and intellectuals of the city. Life in the city was placid and the majority of the citizens, rich and poor, seemed to be content. Bahadur Shah did not interfere in the administration of the city and let the British do the job in his name. It gave the British an aura of legality and Bahadur Shah got unfettered time to indulge in poetic and aesthetic pursuits. He was secure in receiving his pension regularly though it was inadequate to maintain his large establishment. He appealed to the British authorities several times to increase his pension but the appeal was rejected each time.

Then came the Revolt of 1857, when Bahadur Shah was an old, infirm man of 82. A body of mutinous sepoys (Indian soldiers serving under British or other European orders) and officers from Meerut (about 40 miles from Delhi) marched to Delhi and forced their way into the Red Fort on 10 May 1857. The soldiers forced leadership on the reluctant Bahadur Shah and compelled him to sign documents under his seal. The rebels killed 49 Europeans, mostly women and children who were hiding in the Red Fort. They also killed many Christians living in Daryaganj. The rebels

---

[2]Ibid. 74.

also searched every corner of the city for Christians and killed all those they could lay their hands on. Bahadur Shah watched all this helplessly. R.C. Majumdar has talked about this in his book, saying, 'Although the assumption of leadership by Bahadur Shah gave the mutiny of sepoys in Delhi a general character of popular revolt, it was nothing of the kind. Bahadur Shah had no real heart in the business and only yielded to the importunities of the sepoys. He had not the capacity to lead the sepoys and was really led by them.'[3] The reluctance of the king to join the rebels and provide them with fractured leadership was more than compensated by the eagerness of his sons (princes), especially Mirza Mughal, to join the rebels and to provide them with fractured leadership. But the turbulance of the rebels knew no bounds. They paid scant respect to the king and often insulted him. In the city itself, the sepoys indulged in loot and extortion and the people, at large, had no sympathy for the mutineers. The leaderless mob became a curse for the city and the citizens prayed for the return of the Company rule. The mutineers insisted that the king hold a durbar every day and he was paraded by them through the streets of Delhi.

Munshi (native language teacher) Jeewan Lal, (whose diary is one of the most authentic sources of the events of 1857) wrote: 'From house to house the unwilling king was distracted by the cries and petitions—now from the servants of Europeans who had been murdered, now from the shopkeepers whose shops had been plundered, now from the higher classes whose houses had been broken into—all looked to the king for immediate redress. However, seated on a howdah through the streets of Delhi, "he was like a cork on the swelling waves of mutiny'.[4]

It was all over within four months. British enforcements poured into Delhi from Meerut and other nearby areas and the British

---

[3]Majumdar, R.C., *History of the Freedom Movement in India*, Firma KLM, Calcutta, 1988, p. 134.

[4]Llewellyn, Alexander, *The Siege of Delhi*, Macdonald & Jane's, London, 1977, p. 42.

took Delhi by the end of September. Bahadur Shah escaped to the Humayun Tomb but surrendered when the British forces surrounded the tomb and was brought back to the Red Fort. He was tried under the military commission constituted under Act XIV of 1857, contrary to all established norms of national and international laws. The trial started on 27 January 1858 and lasted till 18 September 1858. During his captivity in the Red Fort, he was treated disgracefully—huddled in two small filthy rooms. Bahadur Shah was found guilty and was sentenced to transportation for life. He was not executed like his sons because Lieutenant-General Sir Archdale Wilson had promised Bahadur Shah his life before arresting and taking him into custody.[5]

In October 1858, Bahadur Shah was exiled to Rangoon. The royal assemblage left Delhi on 7 October in the dead of the night. The entourage of the emperor consisted of his beloved wife Zeenat Mahal, their minor son Mirza Jumma Bakht, another wife, four harem women and 16 attendants (both male and female). The royal caravan, travelling in bullock carts and palanquins, took several months to reach Rangoon, where he lived for a little more than three years, pining for his beloved Delhi and writing some memorable plaintive Urdu verses:

Lagta nahin hai ji mera ujde dyar mein, kis ki bani kai alme nepaiedar mein?
Hai kitna badnasib Zafar, dafn ke liye do gaz zameen bhi na mili koi-i-yar mein.

(I am not at ease in this devastated place,
but who has ever been happy in this fleeting world?
How unlucky is Zafar that, for his burial, he could not even get
two yards of land in his beloved's place. (meaning Delhi)]

---

[5]Agarwal, B.R., *Trials of Independence 1858–946,* National Book Trust, New Delhi, 1991, p. 7.

His poetry has kept his memory alive. With the passage of time, a halo of martyrdom and an aura of romantic sympathy has collected around the aged figure. But Bahadur Shah was neither a hero nor a villain. G.D. Khosla has aptly spoken of him saying, 'His role in the uprising of 1857 has been grossly exaggerated by some Indian historians. Bahadur Shah was too weak, too ignorant, too inexperienced in the art of warfare and too resourceless to have taken an effective part as king and leader of a campaign against the British forces. His trial and conviction were clearly a travesty of justice and in the nature of a reprisal.'[6] There was ample proof of his unwillingness to do anything against the British. Still, the Company treated him badly, which led to a fate that he certainly did not deserve.

---

[6]Khosla, G.D., 'Bahadur Shah Zafar' *Dictionary of National Biography*, Vol. 1, S.P Sen (ed.), Institute of Historical Studies, Calcutta, 1972, p. 101.

6

Surendranath Banerjee

(1848–1925)

Surendranath Banerjee was a distinguished teacher, a great orator and one of the foremost leaders of the Indian National Congress for three decades since its inception.

Surendranath was born in Calcutta on 10 November 1848. He was second of the five sons of Durga Charan Banerjee, a reputed medical practitioner. Surendranath's early schooling was done in a *pathshala* and graduated from the University of Calcutta in 1868. The same year, he left for England along with R.C. Dutt and Bihari Lal Gupta to compete for the Indian Civil Service (ICS). He passed the competitive examination in 1869. There was some problem regarding his age but it was resolved in his favour. He qualified in the final examination in 1871 and returned to India. He was posted as the assistant magistrate at Sylhet. His British superior, Mr Sutherland, contrived to show defects in his official work and complained to the higher authorities. An enquiry commission was appointed, the charges were investigated and Surendranath was found guilty of serious dereliction of duty. He was dismissed from service and was sanctioned a pension of ₹50 per month. He went to England to appeal to the India House but did not succeed. Not only was the grievous injustice not undone, but he was also debarred from enrolling at the bar. Surendranath stayed on in England for another year (April 1874 to May 1875), devoting himself to the study of the works of

Western social and political thinkers. In June 1875, he returned
to India as a frustrated man but did not lose heart and started
thinking about another career. As it was proved later, the loss of
the ICS was a huge gain for the country. Surprisingly, in 1882,
seven years after his dismissal, he was made an honorary presidency
magistrate of Calcutta and a justice of the peace.

Soon after his return from England, he accepted the post
of an English professor at the Metropolitan Institution in West
Bengal, at the request of Ishwar Chandra Vidyasagar. In addition,
he also started serving on the staff of the City College, when it was
established in 1879. In 1880, he left the Metropolitan Institution
and joined the Free Church Institution, where he stayed till 1885.
In the meantime, in 1882, he took charge of a school known as
Presidency Institution, which was later upgraded to a college and
renamed Ripon College (now known as Surendranath College) after
Viceroy Lord Ripon, and continued teaching there. As a teacher,
he became very popular among students and inspired them with
a new spirit of political consciousness. He served as a teacher for
37 years from 1875 to 1912, when he was elected to the Imperial
Legislative Council (ILC). While he was working as a teacher, he
had also been taking part in political activities and had managed
to successfully combine a teaching career with a political one.

In 1876, he along with Anandamohan Bose and others, formed
the Indian National Association, a nationalist organization meant to
create a strong body of public opinion about the problems facing
the country. This was achieved to a great extent by the all-India
political tour undertaken by Surendranath, under the auspices of the
Indian National Association, soon after its formation. The apparent
purpose of the tour was to organize a public protest against the
reduction of the age limit of the competitors for the ICS examination
from 21 to 19, but the real purpose 'was the awakening of a spirit
of unity and solidarity among the people of the different parts of
India, through a sense of common grievance'. He visited many
important towns of North India, as far as Lahore. The following

year (1877–78) he covered the Bombay and Madras Presidencies. R.C. Majumdar has written of this tour saying:

> The propaganda tour of Surendranath from one end of the country to another constitutes a definite landmark in the history of India's political progress. It clearly demonstrated that in spite of differences in language, creed and social institutions, the English educated people of this great sub-continent were bound by a common tie of ideals and interests, creating a sense of underlying unity which enabled them to combine for a common political objective. For the first time in living memory, even historical tradition, there emerged the idea of India, over and above the congeries of states and provinces into which it was divided.[1]

Surendranath began to address and educate a much larger audience when he took up the editorship of the newspaper *The Bengalee,* in January 1879, which was started by Girish Chandra Ghosh. Soon, it became a powerful organ of public opinion and a vehicle of mass education. It was subsequently converted into a daily and specially came into prominence during the Ilbert Bill controversy (1880s) when it ably met the diatribes of the Anglo-Indian press. He remained the editor of *The Bengalee* till 1920. While Surendranath was in the midst of the Ilbert Bill controversy, he happened to criticize J.F. Norris, chief justice of the Calcutta High Court, who had insisted in the production of *shaligram shila* (image of Lord Shiva) as witness in a case. Surendranath wrote that it hurt the religious sentiments of the Hindus. He was charged with contempt of court and was imprisoned for two months (May–July 1883). It raised a storm of protest throughout the country, which amply demonstrated his popularity as a national leader. After his release, Surendranath again toured the country. Taking advantage of the

---

[1]Majumdar, R.C., *History of the Freedom Movement in India*, Firma KLM, Calcutta, 1988, p. 328.

newly awakened sense of political unity in India, he organized, under the auspices of the Indian National Association, the first ever All India National Conference in Calcutta on 28 December 1883, which was attended by 100 delegates from different parts of the country. This was followed by the second National Conference in December 1885, a few days before the Indian National Congress (INC) was formed in Bombay. The National Conference, headed by Surendranath, forestalled the INC in all essential aspects. While he could not attend the first inaugural session, after that, he was one of the most respected leaders of the INC till his resignation from its membership in 1918. The National Conference merged with the INC after 1885. Henceforth, Surendranath played a leading part in the INC and presided over its sessions of 1895 (Poona, now Pune) and 1902 (Ahmedabad) sessions.

The partition of Bengal in 1905 led to the emergence of several leaders who tried to mould public opinion against this act of Lord Curzon. Surendranath was perhaps the most prominent among them. 'The strong leadership and personality which he displayed throughout that memorable campaign, particularly at the Barisal Conference, made him the uncrowned king of Bengal.'

Surendranath was a member of the Calcutta Municipal Corporation from 1876 to 1899. He was a member of the Congress deputation which toured England in 1890 to plead for a representative government by reconstitution of legislative councils. He was twice elected by both the Calcutta Municipal Corporation and the Presidency Division to the Bengal Legislative Council, where he was a member for eight years. In 1909, he was the only member from India to attend the Imperial Press Conference. In 1912, he was chosen as a member to the Imperial Legislative Council for the period 1913–16, where he moved several important resolutions.

Surendranath was a moderate like Dadabhai Naoroji, Pherozeshah Mehta, Gopal Krishna Gokhale and others. The Moderates believed in British dispensation, generosity and advocated constitutional methods as a means for achieving a representative form of government. The schism between the Extremists, who believed in agitation, and the Moderates came out in the open at the Surat session in 1907 and weakened the Congress which was controlled by Moderates. The decline in the popularity of the Congress also resulted in the unpopularity of its leaders like Surendranath and others. Thus, he reached the climax of his political career in 1906 and his decline set in. After 1916, the Congress party came under the control of the Extremists. When the Montagu–Chelmsford reforms were announced in 1918, the Congress leadership decided to oppose the reforms. On the other hand, the Moderates, led by Surendranath, wanted to give the reforms a chance as they believed that the proposed reforms were a step towards representative government. When a special session of the Congress was held in Bombay in 1918 to discuss the issue, Surendranath and other Moderates boycotted it. They held a separate conference on 1 November 1918, under the presidentship of Surendranath. It was styled as the All-India Conference of the Moderate Party which became the nucleus for the Indian National Liberal Federation of India, which was formed soon after. Thus, Surendranath walked out of the Congress party which he had nurtured for more than three decades. Consequently, he practically walked out of the history of India's struggle for freedom. Him becoming a minister of local self-government and health in the Bengal cabinet in 1921 and being knighted the same year further tarnished his image as a great national leader. He came down from being the once famous 'Surrender Not Banerjee' to 'Sir Surrender', in the eyes of the masses.

Being a man of principles, Surendranath supported the Montagu–Chelmsford reforms in *The Bengalee* and wrote a series of articles against Gandhi's Non-cooperation Movement. In one of the articles, he wrote, 'Non-cooperation is nowhere as compared to the influence that swadeshism exercised over our homes and our domestic life. There are innumerable villages in Bengal where the *churkha* and *khaddar* are unknown. An industrial movement linked with political controversy may receive a momentary impulse, but in the long run it suffers by such association. An industry must be conducted on business lines. Capital, organization and expert knowledge, these constitute the basic foundations of an industrial enterprise.' He further criticized Gandhi for his manic craze for Hindu–Muslim unity. In the same article he wrote, 'Of course, we admire the supreme solicitude and the earnest efforts of Mr Gandhi to secure Hindu–Muslim unity. But in judging of the communal strife, which we all deplore, let us not, for the sake of historical justice, forget the part the Non-cooperation Movement had in fostering and promoting it.'[2]

However, Surendranath was no more the idol of the masses. His unpopularity was demonstrated by his crushing defeat in the elections for the Bengal Legislative Council by the young Bidhan Chandra Roy of the Swarajist party. The fire that burnt in Surendranath during the Swadeshi Movement had deserted him. He retired from active politics and spent the rest of his years in loneliness, like his contemporary B.C. Pal who had also dared to challenge Gandhi. It was an extremely gracious gesture, however, on the part of Gandhi to visit Surendranath in Calcutta a few months before his death. Gandhi wrote about this visit in *Young India* (14 May 1925) under the title 'The Sage of Barrackpore':

> I was privileged to visit Sir Surendranath Banerjee at his residence at Barrackpore. I had heard that he was ailing and that age had told upon his steel frame. I was anxious, therefore, to pay my respects to him. Though he might not approve of some of my activities, my regard for him as a maker of modern Bengal and a Nester of Indian politics has not suffered any diminution. I remember the time when educated India hung on his lips. Sir Surendranath has a magnificent mansion situated on a river bank among beautiful surroundings. All around there is a great quiet. I expected to see him lying

---

[2]Roy, Chaudhury, P.C., *Gandhi and His Contemporaries*, Sterling, New Delhi, 1972, p. 229.

in bed, weak and care-worn. Instead, I found myself in the presence of a man standing erect from his seat to greet me affectionately and talking to me with the buoyancy of youth.[3]

Gandhi also wrote the obituary for Surendranath on the same lines when he died on 6 August 1925.

The last two years of Surendranath's life were spent writing his autobiography, *A Nation in Making: Being the Reminiscences of Fifty Years of Public Life*. Surendranath concludes his autobiography with a plea for 'cooperation and not non-cooperation, assimilation and not isolation. Any other policy was fraught with peril to our best interests and was suicidal. That is my message to my countrymen, delivered not in haste or impatience, but as the mature result of my deliberations and of my lifelong labours in the service of the motherland.'[4]

That proved to be his swansong.

---

[3] *Collected Works of Mahatma Gandhi*, Vol. 27, Publications Division, New Delhi, pp. 58–59.

[4] Banerjee, Surendranath, *A Nation in Making: Being the Reminiscences of Fifty Years of Public Life*, Oxford University Press, 1925.

7

Annie Besant

(1847–1933)

Annie Besant was born as Annie Wood in London on 1 October 1847. While her mother Emily Morris was Irish, her father William Page Wood was half English and half Irish. Annie was proud of her Irish parentage, always called herself 'an Irishwoman' and had certain pronounced Irish traits in her character. Her father was a doctor but he died when Annie was five years old, leaving his wife, Emily to bring up their two children, Henry and Annie. Emily moved to Harrow and ran a boarding house for Harrow boys. So, in her childhood, Annie had a lot of boys for company and was 'as good a cricketer and climber as any of them'. But soon, one Miss Marryat took responsibility for Annie's education with the permission of her mother. She was taught Latin, French and German, which she perfected during her seven-month stay in Paris and on the Rhine. She read widely and cultivated a love for knowledge which lasted her lifetime. In 1863, Annie completed her education with Marryat and returned to Harrow. Here she devoted her time to archery and croquet, and danced to her heart's content with junior masters, who could talk as well as flirt. Never had a girl a happier home life.[1]

At the age of 20, Annie Wood married Reverend Frank Besant,

---

[1]Stead, W.T., *Annie Besant: A Character Sketch*, Theosophical Publishing House, Madras, 1946, p. 19.

a Cambridge man, who was a clergyman in a small church in a suburb of London. They had two children, son Arthur Digby and daughter Mabel. Mrs Besant found that 'the position of a clergyman's wife was only second to that of a nun.' The couple separated in 1873 and her struggle in life began. She could not get custody of her two children and only got a small annuity. But she was a free person now, not tied down to the dogmas, rituals and myths of orthodox Christianity, which her rational mind discarded. She became an atheist and wrote a tract, *My Path to Atheism*. She was 26 and in search of a job when she met Charles Bradley, a member of parliament (MP) from the Labour Party, who liked her views. He offered her a small weekly salary and a place on the staff of the *National Reformer*, which was the official mouthpiece of the National Secular Society (NSS) of England. She became the co-editor of the journal and thus began a journalist career which lasted till the end of her life. This was in 1874. Along with writing for the *National Reformer*, she indulged in prolific literary activity—writing books and pamphlets in abundance from 1878 to 1886. Some of them are *The Freethinker's Text Book*, *History of the Great French Revolution from the Standpoint of the People*, *Sins of the Church of England* and a popular treatise titled *Light, Heat and Sound*. Besides these, there were innumerable tracts on all sorts of subjects. She also started to work for social reform in many directions, including in the labour unions. During this period, she was busy holding public debates on religion and politics, travelling and lecturing all around the country. She became one of the best orators in England, a fact conceded even by her enemies. From 1885, she became closely associated with the Fabian Society and came in contact with such famous people like Sydney Webb, George Bernard Shaw and Ramsay MacDonald. The same year, she organized a strike of match factory girls and won the fight for them.

The turning point in Besant's life came while she was reviewing Madame Blavatsky's *Secret Doctrine* for *Review of Reviews*. W.T. Stead has written about this saying, 'The moment she read the book, it was as if a long lost synthesis of truth suddenly flashed out in her mind. She asked for an interview with the author, and from that first sight of Madame Blavatsky, Annie Besant's whole life was changed.'[2] She joined the Theosophical Society, which was founded by Blavatsky and Colonel Olcott in 1875 in New York and became the most devoted and brilliant disciple of Blavasky. Blavatsky died in 1891, passing over leadership of the society to Annie Besant, who became the president of the society in 1907, an office she held until her death. Annie Besant represented Theosophy at the Parliament of Religions in 1893 in Chicago, where she met Swami Vivekananda 'in one of the rooms set apart for the use of the delegates, and was highly impressed by the personality and speech delivered by the Swami'. She came straight to India from the US landing here on 16 November 1893, and made it her permanent home. In India, she did not confine her work to the Theosophical Society, the headquarters of which were established at Adyar, near Madras. Soon, she started to work for the social, religious and cultural reforms in her adopted country. She started living like an Indian—wearing a sari instead of a skirt, sitting cross-legged for hours and eating with her hands.

The main thrust of Besant's activities, during this period, was in the educational field. She came to Banaras in 1895 and lived there till 1907. She learnt Sanskrit to understand the Hindu scriptures and soon translated the *Bhagavad Gita* with the help of Dr Bhagwan Das. A branch of the Theosophical Society was opened in Banaras. But her greatest contribution towards the city was the establishment of Central Hindu College in 1898. The principal object of the college was 'to combine moral and religious training in accordance with the Hindu shastras with secular education'. The college started in a rented small building but soon moved to its new campus in Kamacha, gifted by the maharaja of Banaras. The institution became a model for other schools and colleges in the country. The

---

[2]Ibid. 89–90.

Central Hindu College formed the nucleus for the Banaras Hindu University (BHU), which was opened in 1916.

There were several other activities that Besant was involved in for the cause of education, even after she had settled in Adyar near Madras. In 1915, she established the Besant Theosophical College at Madanapalle in the Madras Presidency on the lines of the one started by the nationalists in Calcutta in 1906. In 1917, she started the Society for the Promotion of National Education (SPNE). In 1918, the National University was established by her at Adyar. The chancellor of the University was Rabindranath Tagore and pro-chancellor S. Subramania Iyer. Dr G.S. Arundale was the principal. She also established several schools for boys and girls. In 1917, she started the Women's Indian Association, which later was transformed into the All India Women's Conference. In 1918, she established the Indian Boy Scouts Association in which the boys wore Indian turbans and sang Indian songs but also obeyed the Scout laws. During the 40 years of her active service in India, Besant was, if not the originator, one of the most powerful supporters of all constructive work being done in India.

Besant perhaps will be remembered most for her political work in India. She entered the political arena in 1913. She founded a weekly newspaper, *The Commonweal,* in January 1914. She also purchased a daily paper, *The Madras Standard,* a few months later and changed its name to *New India.* Through these two papers, which soon gained popularity, she conveyed her political views and the aspirations of the Indian people. She declared, 'I am an Indian tom-tom, waking up all sleepers so that they may wake and work for their motherland.' With that aim, she launched Home Rule League at Madras in September 1916. Lokmanya Tilak, who had already formed his own Home Rule League in April of the same year, did not agree to Annie Besant's proposal for a merger of the two Leagues. However, both worked in tandem. Through her Home Rule League, she preached swaraj for India by which she meant 'self-government within the Empire'. The Home Rule Movement made a swift and strong impression on the country. Though her demand was modest enough, her advocacy was militant. Through her speeches and writings, she created an awakening in the country. Swaraj was now in the air. Gandhi, in a speech at the Gujarat Political Conference in November 1917, said:

> The air is thick with cries of swaraj. It is due to Mrs Besant that swaraj is on the lips of hundreds of thousands of men and women. What was unknown to most men and women only two years ago, has by her consummate tact and her indefatigable efforts, become common property for them. There cannot be the slightest doubt that her name will take the first rank in history among those who inspired us with the hope that swaraj was attainable at no distant date.[3]

The government wanted to crush her movement and asked her to abandon the campaign or leave the country. She did not agree to either of the options. In order to stifle her propaganda, the government first forfeited the securities of her two papers and demanded additional deposit. She complied. As a last resort, they interned her on 16 June 1917, along with her two colleagues, B.P. Wadia and G.S. Arundale in Ooty. Protest meetings for her release were held throughout the country and in England. She was released after three months. The imprisonment added to her fame. She was made president of the 1917 Calcutta session of the INC. While concluding her stirring presidential address, she said:

> To see India free, to see her hold her head high among other nations, to see her sons and daughters respected everywhere, to see her worthy of her mighty past, engaged in building a yet mightier future—is not this worth working for, worth suffering for, worth living and worth dying for? Is there any other land which evokes such love for spirituality, such admiration for her

---

[3] *Collected Works of Mahatma Gandhi*, Vol. 14, Publications Division, Government of India, New Delhi, p. 50.

literature, such homage for her valour, as this glorious mother of nations, from whose womb went forth the races that now, in Europe and America, are leading the world? Has any land suffered as our India has suffered—and having suffered, and having survived all changes, unbroken India, who has been verily the crucified among nations, now stands on this her resurrecting morning, the immortal, the glorious, the ever-young, and India shall soon be seen, proud and self-reliant, strong and free, the radiant splendour of Asia, as the light and blessing of the world.

Then came Gandhi on the political horizon of the country. He promised swaraj in one year and started the Non-cooperation Movement, asking lawyers to boycott the courts, students to walk out of schools and colleges, government servants to resign from their jobs and everyone to burn foreign-made clothes. The reason for starting the Non-cooperation Movement was the ill-treatment of the Muslims of Turkey by the British and the atrocities committed by the government in Punjab. The saner elements in the country including Rabindranath Tagore, Bipin Chandra Pal, Madan Mohan Malaviya, Muhammad Ali Jinnah and Annie Besant were horrified. Besant warned the nation that what Gandhi was preaching would lead the nation to lawlessness and anarchy. She went around the country preaching against the Non-cooperation Movement and was hooted down at almost every place where she spoke, including Bombay and Allahabad. With saintly cunning, Gandhi had seen to it that the old lady was insulted. Gandhi could not bring swaraj in one year and the Non-cooperation Movement fizzled out by 1922.

Though Besant became unpopular and lost her position as a leader, she still went on with her work for India. She organized the National Convention with an aim to draft a bill. She succeeded in 1925 when the Commonwealth of India Bill was drafted. She took it to England and got it accepted by the British Labour party and one of its members presented it to Parliament. However, it could not be enacted. Her political career came to an end. She was already in her eightieth year.

The remaining years of her life were spent in Adyar involved in the work of the Theosophical Society. But her health was deteriorating slowly. She passed away on 20 September 1933.

Annie Besant was a prolific writer. It will be impossible to enumerate all the books, pamphlets and tracts written by her. Some of the more important ones are—*My Path to Atheism* (1877); *Annie Besant: An Autobiography* (1893); *Radicalism and Socialism* (1887); *Education as a National Duty* (1903); *The Religious Problem in India* (1909); *Hints on the Study of the Bhagavad Gita* (1906); *Universal Text Book of Religion and Morals*, 3 volumes 1911–15); *Social Problems* (1912); *How India Wrought for Freedom: The Story of the National Congress Told from the Official Records* (1915); *The Ideals of Theosophy* (1912); *Principles of Education* (1918); *Man's Life in The Three Worlds: A Booklet for Beginners* (1923); *On Political Science* (1919); *The Future of Indian Politics* (1922); *World Problems of Today* (1925).

8

Homi Jehangir Bhabha

(1909–1966)

Homi Jehangir Bhabha was a great scientist and an equally great institution builder. He played a decisive role in putting India on the atomic energy map of the world.

Homi Jehangir Bhabha was born in Bombay on 30 October 1909, in a well-to-do Parsi family. His father, Jehangir Hormusji Bhabha, had been educated at Oxford and later qualified as a lawyer. On his return to India, he joined the judicial service in Mysore. But after his marriage to Meherbai Framji Panday (granddaughter of Sir Dinshaw Maneckji Petit), he moved to Bombay, where he was associated with the Tata Industrial House. The Bhabha family became close with the Tata family when Jehangir Hormusji's sister, also named Meherbai, married Sir Dorab Tata, son of Jamshedji Tata. The Tata connection proved very useful to Homi Bhabha later in his life.

Homi started his education at the Cathedral & John Connon School in Bombay, from where he passed the Senior Cambridge examination with honours. Later, he joined Elphinstone College and subsequently, the Royal Institute of Science, Bombay. Homi was not really interested in sports, though he did take part in rowing and played tennis while studying at Cambridge. From the very beginning, he was academically inclined and won several prizes in school as well as in college. He supplemented his formal education by reading a wide variety of books on art, music, literature and science, which were available in the personal collections of his grandfather and father. At an early age, he developed a great interest in science and his parents bought hundreds of books on science to satisfy their son's urge for scientific study. It is said that by the age of 16, Homi Bhabha had studied and understood the special theory of relativity. Homi had not even completed his eighteenth year when his parents decided to send him to England for higher studies. Bhabha joined the Gonville and Caius College of the University of Cambridge in 1927, courtesy of Dorab Tata, who had studied in the same college and had created a trust by donating £25,000 to the college. Homi studied engineering, conceding to the wishes of his father, and obtained a first class in the mechanical science tripos in June 1930. After that, he worked as a research student in theoretical physics—a subject which was more to his liking. After completing the mathematics tripos, Bhabha won the Rouse Ball Travelling Fellowship in 1932, which enabled him to travel to other places and work there. Thus, he was able to work with some of the leading physicists in Europe—Wolfgang Pauli in Zurich and Enrico Fermi in Rome. His own research work had come to the notice of the scientists and he was awarded the Isaac Newton Studentship, which he held for three years. He worked mainly at Cambridge with a short spell in Bohr's Institute, Copenhagen. By 1935, Bhabha had completed the requirements for a PhD degree. In 1937, he was awarded the Exhibition Scholarship which enabled him to continue his research work at Cambridge.

In 1939, Bhabha was in India on a holiday. In the meanwhile, the Second World War broke out and England became a dangerous place to live in. He had to abandon his plans to return to England to continue his research work. By now, he had lived and studied in England for 13 years. Now, Bhabha had to opt for a career in India. He accepted the post of a reader in the department of physics in the Indian Institute of Science, Bangalore, which had been established by Jamshedji Tata way back in 1911 and was a premium science institute in the country. An added attraction for

Bhabha was the presence of C.V. Raman in the institute as the head of the department of physics. Bhabha became a professor in 1944. Homi Bhabha specialized early in quantum theory and cosmic radiation. The Dorab Tata Trust gave him a small grant with which he established the cosmic ray research unit in the department. He published his first scientific paper in October 1933, in which he had described the part played by electrons in the absorption of cosmic rays. His contribution in the field of cosmic ray research was recognized by the world and he was elected Fellow of the Royal Society of Britain in 1941. In 1943, he was awarded the Adams Prize by the Cambridge University for his work on cosmic rays. He was also noted for being the first person to calculate the cross section for electron/positron scattering, which is known as the Bhabha Scattering. He discovered cosmic particles with an enery hundred times greater than any other previously known. He announced his discovery at the International Technical Conference at Stockholm in September 1952.

Bhabha had made ambitious plans in his mind and the Bangalore institute seemed inadequate to him. Bhabha approached the Dorab Tata Trust once again, with plans for an institute fully devoted to nuclear sciences which could play a leading role in offering world class research facilities for Indian scientists. As a result, the Tata Institute of Fundamental Research (TIFR), Bombay, came into being in 1944. Bhabha moved to Bombay, after spending 'six very happy and fruitful years' in Bangalore. After the Second World War, it became clear to Bhabha that the Indian industry and economy would require a tremendous amount of energy, which was not possible to procure from conventional sources of energy. The answer lay in using nuclear power, derived from fuels developed from India's vast resources of uranium and thorium. He devoted his time and energy towards that end. From a research scientist he became an institution builder and almost retired from research in physics. His institution building career had essentially one aim in his mind—to develop atomic energy for peaceful purposes. TIFR was the first step in that direction, but the research done there had to be translated into concrete form. To make that possible, assistance from the Government of India (GOI), in various forms, was necessary. It must go to the credit of Jawaharlal Nehru that he assured full support of his government to Homi Bhabha.

Through Bhabha's efforts, the Indian Atomic Act was passed in 1948 by the Parliament and the Atomic Energy Commission was constituted in the same year, which was essentially a policymaking body. A full-fledged atomic energy programme obviously could not be carried out and overseen on a day-to-day basis by it. For that, a regular department of the government was necessary. The Prime Minister, Jawaharlal Nehru, agreed to Bhabha's proposal and the Department of Atomic Energy (DAE) was created in 1954, with Bhabha as secretary. The department 'would fund, create and operate all the facilities needed for the atomic energy programme'. Bhabha was also the director of TIFR. So far, the atomic energy programme was being executed with the help of TIFR and its scientists. As TIFR was conducting multiphasic research in its laboratories besides atomic research, a new laboratory was created at Trombay, near Bombay, on Bhabha's suggestion. It was called the Atomic Energy Establishment and would be used for the exclusive purpose of atomic research. The name of the laboratory was later changed to Bhabha Atomic Research Centre (BARC), which started functioning in 1954. At the suggestion of Bhabha, the DAE was shifted to Bombay, so that work at the Department, TIFR and BARC could be coordinated expeditiously. In 1954, Bhabha decided that Atomic Energy Establishment, Trombay (AEET) should have a swimming pool reactor to conduct atomic research. The assembly of the systems commenced sometime in 1955 and the reactor itself went into operation in August 1956. Nehru dedicated the reactor to the nation and gave it the name Apsara, which is still functioning. Apsara was a major milestone for the generation of atomic power because the reactor had been designed and built in India. The fuel element alone came from England.[1] It was made clear by the GOI that atomic power would be used for peaceful purposes only.

Bhabha attended the first 'Atoms for Peace' conference in Geneva in 1958, under the auspices of the United Nations, and was elected its president. After the Geneva Conference, an International Atomic Energy Agency was created, with its headquarters at Vienna. Bhabha became a member of its Scientific Advisory Committee and remained so till his death.

Under the expert guidance of Bhabha, two more reactors—CIRUS and ZERLINA—were built. The construction of the country's first atomic power station began at Tarapur in 1963. Unfortunately, Bhabha did not live to see its commissioning, which was done a year after his death. Bhabha also played a pivotal role in conceiving and planning the Indian space programme and helped in setting up the Indian National Committee for Space Research (INCOSPAR), under Dr Vikram Sarabhai. Bhabha was also chairman of the Government Electronics Committee. He also promoted research in radio astronomy and microbiology. The radio telescope at Ootacamund (Ooty) is one of his creations in this direction.

Bhabha died in a plane crash on 24 January 1966 at the age of 57, He died a bachelor. He was a great lover of music, especially of western classical music. He was also drawn to painting, literature, architecture and landscaping. His paintings and drawings are of considerable merit and some of them are preserved in British art galleries. He was a born artist and had acquired refined tastes. The flower beds, the landscaping and the architecture of the TIFR building, all bear witness to the keenness of Homi Bhabha's perception of colour, form and design.[2] However, he will be remembered most as the chief architect of Indian atomic energy establishment, on which the future of our country largely depends.

---

[1]Venkataraman, G., *Bhabha and His Magnificent Obsessions,* Universities Press, Hyderabad, 1994, pp. 150–51.

[2]Kumar, Rajee N., 'Homi Jehangir Bhabha' *Remembering our Leaders,* CBT, New Delhi, 1998, p. 176.

In conclusion, as G. Venkataraman has said in his book: 'Bhabha was a brilliant scientist, imaginative visionary, shrewd planner and organizer, able administrator, sensitive artist, devotee of music and literature, and a passionate lover of trees and gardens. Many are the examples of people who have achieved excellence in one or two areas but seldom one comes across a person so versatile as this.'[3] He was indeed one of the few universal men of our age. C.V. Raman called him 'the Indian Leonardo da Vinci'. He was awarded the Padma Bhushan by the president of India in 1954. Bhabha was awarded honorary doctorates by several universities including Cambridge, London and Perth, besides several Indian universities. Bhabha wrote scores of scientific papers. His publications include *Quantum Theory of Radiation, Elementary Physical Particles* and *Cosmic Radiation.*

---

[3]Venkataraman, G., *Bhabha and His Magnificent Obsessions,* Universities Press, Hyderabad, 1994, p. 200.

9

Bhagwan Das

(1869–1958)

Bhagwan Das was born on 12 January 1869 (he shared the year of his birth with Mohandas Karamchand Gandhi) in Banaras. He belonged to a well-to-do Vaishya family. He was the second of the six children of Madho Das and Chameli Devi. An ancestor of Bhagwan Das, Sah Manohar Das, was the commissariat agent of the East India Company when the battle of Srirangapatna was fought between the British and Tipu Sultan. After the death of Tipu, general loot took place and Manohar Das, taking advantage of it, acquired considerable wealth, left Mysore and settled permanently in Banaras. The family owned valuable property in Bara Bazaar in Calcutta and extensive cultivable land, mostly in the Jaunpur district near Banaras. The family took to banking and usury. The affluence of the family could be judged from the fact that the family had 20 domestic servants during Bhagwan Das' time.

Bhagwan Das' education started at the age of three. His first teacher was a Muslim *maulvi* (a religious instructor) who taught him Urdu and Persian and love for Islam, which he carried throughout his life. At the age of about five, he was admitted to a private school, founded by the famous Hindi poet, Bharatendu Harishchandra near their home, where he learnt Hindi and some English. At the age of seven, he was admitted to the Government Queen's College in Banaras. He was an extremely precocious child. At the age of 12, he passed the matriculation examination and the bachelor of arts examination with a distinction four years later. He had opted for English, sanskrit and philosophy as subjects. In 1886, at the age of 17, he passed the masters examination of the University of Calcutta in mental and moral sciences. He developed great interest in Hindu religion and philosophy, an interest which he maintained throughout his life. He devoted the next four years fully to study these subjects and learnt Sanskrit from Kashi pandits to read the scriptures in the original language. However, at the insistence of his father, he joined government service in 1890 as a *tehsildar* (subordinate revenue officer) and he was promoted to deputy collector and magistrate in 1894. He was posted at various places in Uttar Pradesh. The period of his government service was eventless because his heart was not in it, though he proved to be a man of integrity and was devoid of prejudices. His father died in 1897 and he resigned from government service in 1898.

In the same year (1898), Annie Besant, the president of the Theosophical Society, founded the Central Hindu College 'to rehabilitate all that was great and glorious in the Oriental culture'. She felt that religion was the foundation of all true education as it was the foundation of the family and the state. The existing schools, she felt, were not imparting proper education. Bhagwan Das completely agreed with her views and started working with her in the college as well as in the Theosophical Society, a branch of which was opened in Banaras by Besant. The school proved to be a success; the number of students increased every year and it became a model school for the country. One important contribution of the college was the publication of the *Sanatan Dharma Series* of Hindu religious textbooks. These books give, in a form suitable for students, a graduated outline of the fundamental principles of the Hindu religion. It is quite likely that Besant took the help of Bhagwan Das in planning and writing these textbooks. Bhagwan Das had written the book *Sanatana Dharma: An Advanced Textbook of Hindu Religion and Ethics* in 1904, supplementing the *Sanatana Dharma Series* of textbooks. He, with Annie Besant, published the translation of the *Bhagavad Gita* in 1906, giving original Sanskrit verses and the English translation alongside and a concordance of Sanskrit words at the end. To this day, it remains one of the best translations of the *Bhagavad Gita*. Bhagwan Das served the Hindu College (now Presidency College) as honorary secretary for 15 years (1899–1914). He was also active in the Theosophical Society and played a significant part in the development of the Banaras branch of the society. However, the main interest of his life, by then, had become the study of Hindu scriptures like the Vedas and the *Manusmriti* and their interpretation through his books and articles for the scholar as well as for the layman. A continuous stream of books flowed from his pen year after year and Bhagwan Das became famous as a highly learned man and a *Vedic* scholar.

Through the study of the Hindu scriptures, he came to the conclusion that there was no valid reason to believe and practise untouchability and that all castes should be allowed to enter Hindu temples without any restriction. He also advocated that the *varnas* (four divisions of Hindu society) should be decided by *karma* (actions) and not by birth. Thus armed, he took active part, along with Madan Mohan Malaviya, in the movement against untouchability and restrictive temple entry.

From the mid 1920s onwards, Gandhi had started preaching against untouchability and supporting the temple entry movement. Whenever Gandhi was in doubt about the verdict of the scriptures (as he hardly knew Sanskrit) he used to refer to Bhagwan Das for his opinion. Gandhi used to address him as 'Dear Baboo Bhagwandas' or simply as 'Dear Babooji'. From their correspondence, it is evident that Gandhi had great respect for Bhagwan Das. When the latter started writing to Gandhi's secretary Mahadev, instead of writing directly, Gandhi wrote to Bhagwan Das, 'I know you want to save my time by writing to Mahadev, but it is as well not to do so. It may cause delay and your letters are no strain on me.'[1] When

---

[1] *Collected Works of Mahatma Gandhi*, Vol. 53, Publications Division, Government

Gandhi was undergoing a fast unto death against the verdict of the Communal Award which recommended separate electorates for the Scheduled Castes, Bhagwan Das went to Poona to meet Gandhi in Yervada jail. He remained in Poona for three weeks and met Gandhi in Yervada Jail almost daily. About these meetings Gandhi later wrote about these meetings to Bhagwan Das on 7 January 1933, 'I cannot tell you what a joy it was to have you with me for so many days. It was all so unexpected and therefore a double pleasure.'[2]

Besant collaborated with Madan Mohan Malaviya in the establishment of BHU and merged the Central Hindu College into the proposed university, which started functioning in 1916 in the college campus itself. Das was nominated as one of the five honorary joint secretaries of the management committee of the university. He was also nominated as a member of the University court, senate and other bodies. But soon after, he started criticizing the working of the university and its vice-chancellor, Madan Mohan Malaviya. He wrote articles and open letters expressing his views, which were published in *The Leader* in 1917. The confrontation came to a head in the court meeting of December 1920 and he crossed swords with Annie Besant and Malaviya on various issues. The amendments moved by him lost by heavy margin and consequently he withdrew his membership from the court, the council and other bodies of the university.[3]

It was during 1919–20, at the age of 50, that Bhagwan Das was drawn to politics for the first time. In 1919, he was president of the Uttar Pradesh (UP) Social Conference. In 1920, he presided over the UP Political Conference, and soon became an important member of the INC. He took part in the Non-cooperation Movement launched by Gandhi in August 1920 and was sentenced to a nine-month

of India, 1972, p. 255.
[2]Ibid. 381.
[3]Dar, S.L. and S. Somaskandan, *History of the Banaras Hindu University*, BHU Press, 1966, p. 519.

imprisonment. However, he was released after two months. When
Kashi Vidyapeeth was founded in 1921, Bhagwan Das became its
kulpati (vice-chancellor). He also used to teach philosophy there.
He was nominated as chairman of the Banaras Municipal Board
in 1923 and served in that capacity for about three years. During
his tenure, the municipality functioned efficiently and its debt was
considerably reduced.

In March 1931, serious communal riots took place in Kanpur
after the execution of Bhagat Singh and his two comrades in the
Lahore jail. According to the official estimate, 165 people were
killed and 480 injured. Among the killed was Ganesh Shankar
Vidyarthi, president of the UP Congress. An enquiry committee
was constituted by the Congress to go into the details of the riots,
with Bhagwan Das as chairman. After several months of enquiry
and interviews, the Committee submitted a report. About this
report, well-known historian R.C. Majumdar wrote: 'Bhagwan
Das submitted a report in a bulky volume. It began with a long
historical introduction with sole object to prove that the Muslim
rulers were the most tolerant in respect of other religions. A more
ridiculous parody of history it is difficult to imagine, and yet bore
the signatures of several Hindus who should have known better. It
was a piece of pure political propaganda.'[4] To placate the Muslims,
the Committee had to resort to untruth and the distortion of
history. Fortunately, for the good name of the Congress and of
the authors of the report, it was proscribed by the government.

In 1935, Bhagwan Das was elected unopposed to the Central
Legislative Assembly. His term lasted for two years but he did not
leave any impact on the Assembly proceedings and hardly made
any speeches. His son and biographer, Sri Prakasa writes, 'My father
had no practice of extempore speaking. He was a great writer, but
not a speaker. Whenever he had to say anything, he wrote it out

---

[4]Majumdar, R.C., *History of the Freedom Movement in India*, Firma KLM, Calcutta,
pp. 316–17.

with great care and labour, and read it out in the Assembly. He spent most of his time in the lobbies reading and writing. He never asked any questions. My father delivered very few speeches.'[5] His limitations as a speaker could be the reason for his not taking active part in politics. He was essentially a scholar, a philosopher and a writer. He has written more than 40 books, mostly on religion and philosophy, and almost all of them are in English. Some of these are: *The Science of Emotions* (1900), *Sanatana Dharma: An Advanced Textbook of Hindu Religion and Ethics* (1903), *Science of Peace* (1904), translation of the *Bhagavad Gita* with Annie Besant (1905), *The Science of Social Organization* or *The Laws of Manu in the Light of Theosophy (1910)*, *Religion of Theosophy* (1910), *The Psychology of Conversion* (1917), *The Meaning of Swaraj or Self-government* (1921), *Philosophy of Non-cooperation* (1922), *Krishna: A Study in the Theory of Avataras* (1924), *The Dawn of Another Renaissance* (1931), *The Essential Unity of All Religions* (1932), *The Science of Self* (1938), *Concordance Dictionary of the Yoga Sutra of Patanjali, Bhashya of Vyasa* (1938) and *Mystic Experiences* (1944). Most of these books were published by Theosophical Publishing House, Adyar.

Unfortunately, Das was a difficult writer to understand. It seems too many ideas gushed out of his mind at the same time, confounding the writer and the reader alike. If he had not acquired a style of writing which was difficult to comprehend, he would have been a much more popular philosopher and thinker. He himself confesses, 'I feel keenly and regret exceedingly that Nature has withheld from me the very valuable gift of lucid, bright, attractive and pleasing expression and exposition. Even those kind friends who happen to like my reinterpretations and new versions of the ancient words and thoughts, often take me to task for obscure

---

[5]Prakasa, Sri, *Bharat Ratna Dr Bhagwan Das*, Meenakshi Prakashan, Meerut, 1970, p. 118.

and involved sentences.'[6] However, there is no gainsaying the fact that he was one of the most important thinkers and philosophers produced by this country in the twentieth century. According to S. Radhakrishnan, 'I have been an admiring student of Dr Bhagwan Das' works. His attitude to our ancient works is one to be followed by others: trust tempered with criticism. He had great faith in the central ideas of Indian thought and he was an effective critic of the deviations which took place spoiling the purity and strength of our religion.'

Bhagwan Das was cast in the mould of great *rishis* (sages) and his luxurious beard imparted grace and dignity to his personality, rivalling that of Rabindranath Tagore. Though he was not a good speaker, he must have been a good conversationalist and a charming host as many people used to visit him and enjoy his hospitality. These included Gandhi, Jawaharlal Nehru, Chittaranjan Das, Charles Freer Andrews, Ananda Coomaraswamy and many other Indians and foreigners. However, he was neither a spendthrift nor did his wealth tempt him to be a philanthropist. In spite of his intellectual pursuits, he was very fond of physical exercise and used to do scores of push-ups and sit-ups daily which would have shamed many a wrestler. After seeing Bhagwan Das for the first time, Jawaharlal Nehru remarked, 'He has the straightest back I have ever seen.' And that back remained straight even when he touched his eightieth year.

Bhagwan Das was awarded doctorate degrees honoris causa by the BHU (1929) and Allahabad University (1937). In 1955, he received the Bharat Ratna. In 1959, he died in Banaras. Now, his marble statue greets the visitors at the offices of the Municipal Corporation of Banaras. His son, Sri Prakasa, was the first Indian high commissioner in Pakistan (1947–49) and later served as the governor of Assam, Madras and Bombay.

---

[6]Das, Bhagwan, *Autobiography,* Dr Bhagwan Das Memorial Trust, Delhi, 1961, p. 32.

10

Subramania Bharathi

(1882–1921)

Subramania Bharathi is considered to be the greatest Tamil poet of the twentieth century. He wrote 'Freedom', one of the best patriotic poems in the Tamil language, besides other poetry. His poems created an immense wave of nationalism in Tamil Nadu and inspired people to join the Indian freedom movement.

Subramania ('Subbiah' to his family and friends) was born on 11 December 1882, to Chinnaswami Subramania Iyer and Lakshmi Ammal in Ettayapuram in the Thoothukudi district of Tamil Nadu. Theirs was a middle-class family. His father, a learned Brahmin, was attached to the Ettayapuram *zameen* (land). He was also interested in industry and had installed the first textile mill at Ettayapuram in 1880. Subramania's mother, Lakshmi Ammal, died when he was not even five years old. His father married a second time and his stepmother treated him just like her own son.

Subramania started his primary education at Tirunelveli. He was a precocious child in a limited sense. While he loved and mastered the Tamil language at an early age, he did not like other subjects, especially mathematics. He started composing poetry while still in primary school. He would skip classes and wander about, admiring nature and writing simple, short poems in Tamil. Thus, he became a Tamil scholar very early in life though he did not have much of a formal education. When he was 11 years old, he was invited to the court of the raja of Ettayapuram to recite his poems. The noted poets present at the court were amazed at the quality of the lyrics which he recited. They started calling him 'Bharathi'.

In 1897, Subramania was married to a seven-year-old girl, Chellamma, who later shared the agonies and ecstasies of his life. The following year, his father died and he went to Banaras to live with his aunt, Kuppammal. He passed the entrance examination of the Allahabad University. During his stay at Banaras, he learnt Hindi, Sanskrit and English. His stay there brought a change in his appearance too. He began to sport a thick moustache on the lines of a warrior and an ample turban on his head, tied in a distinct and unorthodox style. Banaras also brought about a change in his outlook and he began to write patriotic poetry and verses about the pathetic condition of India under unsympathetic foreign rule. After four years, he went back to his hometown Ettayapuram but he was disheartened by the caste-ridden and orthodox society. To get away from the suffocating atmosphere, he took up a temporary teaching post as a teacher of Tamil at Sethupathi School in Madurai. He soon left for Madras and took up the job of an assistant editor of a popular Tamil daily, *Swadesamitran*, which was founded by G. Subramania Iyer in 1882. There, he was responsible for translating news appearing in English dailies into Tamil. Besides improving his English, this job gave him a better idea of the political and social developments in the country. He began to write political poems, urging people to wake up from their slumber and to take their destiny in their own hands. He was moving more and more towards writing about the political regeneration of the country. His passion-filled patriotic poems enthralled the people of Tamil Nadu and they started taking an active part in the freedom movement. During those days, he met Sister Nivedita, a disciple of Vivekananda and a great nationalist. She blessed him and exhorted him to devote his poetic talents for the emancipation of the country. As a gesture of gratitude, Subramania dedicated two of his poetry books to her.

In 1907, Bharathi attended the Congress session at Surat. He openly sided with the Extremists led by Bal Gangadhar Tilak, Bipin

Chandra Pal and Lala Lajpat Rai. He believed that the situation called for a revolutionary approach and the policy of appeals and representations would not lead the country to freedom. His poems and writings started becoming more and more volatile and no publisher was prepared to publish his books. Even the editor of *Swadesamitran* stopped publishing his extremist views. Bharati resigned from the paper and started publishing his own weekly, *India*, in 1907. He began publishing his poems and stories, some of them satirical, in *India*.

The Swadeshi Movement in Bengal, and to a lesser extent in other parts of the country, started as a reaction to the partition of Bengal and it was quickly gathering momentum. The government had unleashed repressive measures and hundreds of revolutionaries and freedom fighters had been arrested and imprisoned. Even national leaders like Lajpat Rai, Tilak and Aurobindo Ghose had not been spared. Fearing arrest, Bharathi fled to Pondicherry, a French enclave, in 1908. He spent 10 years in extreme poverty and isolation and was harassed by British spies. His house was ransacked and some valuable manuscripts were stolen. He was forced to discontinue the publication of *India*. But still, he was able to write some brilliant prose and poetry in the beautiful surroundings of Pondicherry. Most of his devotional songs and nature poetry belong to this period. However, tired of the long stretch of an exile's life, he returned to British India. The British administration was prompt in arresting him but released him after a few days free of any conditions. Bharathi first went to his hometown but since he felt out of place in an orthodox society, he went to Madras and joined the editorial staff of the *Swadesamitran* again. After a long time, Bharathi began to live on regular, though meagre, income. But this did not last for long. Bharathi used to visit a temple in Triplicane on a regular basis and offer a coconut to the temple elephant. One day, the elephant was in rut and hit Bharathi with its trunk while he was offering a coconut. Bharathi was badly injured and died after a few days, on 11 September 1921.

Bharathi was a true nationalist and left behind a considerable body of brilliant poetry. His poems could be divided into three categories—patriotic, devotional and miscellaneous poems. Under the first category, come his collection of poems *Swadesa Geetangal* (1909) and *Janma Bhoomi* (1909). Both these books were dedicated to Sister Nivedita, who was a source of inspiration for many Indians. In these poems, Bharathi describes the grandeur of India and her spiritual greatness. He exhorts Indians to work for freedom in true spirit, to abjure political propaganda and to cast away fear and timidness. Some of the poems in this category describe the lives of great men of India and their great deeds as a source of inspiration for the present generation and the generations to come. Some of his poetry and devotional songs are addressed to Lord Krishna and Goddess Shakti and express the ideals of human oneness and universal love as preached by the Vedas. That Bharathi was a deeply religious man is evident from these poems, despite his abhorrence of senseless rituals and customs. Thus, the 'most significant group is formed by his poems on Shakti, Bharati's *ishtadevata* (personal god) the primordial power that makes and unmakes the whole universe'. The Kali worship witnessed in Banaras, his meeting with Sister Nivedita, the powerful poem *Vande Matram* by Bankim Chandra— all influenced his Shakti poems. His poetic approach is personal and approximates the mother-child relationship. Her many aspects are caught within the arc of his poetic creation. Prema Nanadakumar has spoken of Bharathi's work saying, '"*Oozhi-k-Koothu*" is the most audaciously frenzied and most poetically articulate piece in the Bharati canon. It is a description of the Mother's terrible dance of destruction which is at last arrested by the advent of Shiva in his auspicious form, and they unite to recreate the world once again.'[1]

His miscellaneous poems include ones whose subject matter is social reform, scientific and rational thinking and the emancipation

---

[1]Nandakumar, Prema, 'Subramania Bharati' *Dictionary of National Biography*, S.E Sen (ed.), Institute of Historical Studies, Calcutta, 1972.

of women. He also wrote poems for children. This was prompted by his younger daughter Sakuntala and her friends. He sang *The Child's Song* for them and set it to music. Children love to sing *Odi vilaiyadu pappa* even today. Written in very simple Tamil, Bharathi's poems budded with rhyme and rhythm, which even a non-Tamil speaking person could enjoy. His drum-beat song, also popular as a dance piece, proclaims that '*vetri yettu thikkum yetta* (all human beings are equal)'. His other important epic poems are *Kannan Pattu* (1917), *Panchali Sapatham (*1912 and 1924) and *Kuyil Pattu*. The last song composed by Bharathi and sung by him at a public meeting at the beach in Madras, a few weeks before his death, is one of his most popular poems: *Bharatha samudayam* (Long live Bharat Commonwealth), one of his most popular verses.

Bharathi also wrote short stories and an unfinished novel, *Chandrikayin Kathai*. His wisdom tales on the lines of *Panchtantra* and *Hitopadesa* are still popular in Tamil Nadu. Bharati also wrote English poetry and prose, which have been collected in *Agni and Other Poems and Translations* (1937) and *Essays and Other Prose Fragments* (1937).

But today, Bharathi is remembered most for giving a simple and appealing style to Tamil poetry. He showed that the spoken rhythms in Tamil can be easily transferred to the written page. He was one of the first poets of any merit to speak of India as one entity and of her people sharing a common heritage. In poem after poem, he describes the best in each region, the sum of which make India. He exhorts Indians to eschew regionalism to make India great.

Subramania Bharathi has inspired many poets and writers like Bharathidasan (1891–1964) who absorbed his revolutionary zeal and chose the pseudonym to underline his affinity with the great poet. In the memory of Subramania Bharathi stands the Bharati Mandap at Ettayapuram, his native place. There is a statue of Bharathi at the Madras seashore. 'The rhythmic roar of the undying waves seems to recite and repeat his poems.' About Bharathi, C. Rajagopalachari has said, 'The body of national thought that he wove into song was that which preceded Gandhi; it was Vivekananda's and Dadabhai Naoroji's and Tilak's India that forms the material of Bharati's poetry.' Bharathi is known as a national poet and his fame is not confined to Tamil Nadu. He truly lived up to his name—'Bharathi'.

11

Vinoba Bhave

(1895–1982)

Among all the apostles of Gandhi, Vinoba Bhave was the only one who blazed his own trail. After Gandhi's death, most of his followers faded into oblivion, with the exception of Vinoba. He is remembered for the constructive work that he did after Gandhi's death. He was a thinker and a saint, who believed in doing and not preaching.

Vinoba Bhave was born Vinayak Narhari Bhave on 11 September 1895 in Gagode (now in the Kolaba district of Maharashtra) to Narhari Shambhurao Bhave and Rukmini Devi. His father Narhari was a textile technologist and worked in the dyeing department of Buckingham Mills for some time and was credited with producing the first khaki cloth. But later, he shifted to Baroda permanently and served as a senior clerk typist in a government office. Later in life, he developed great interest in music and even wrote books on Indian music. He lived alone in Baroda till 1903, when he brought his family there. For the first eight years of his life, Vinayak was extremely influenced by his grandfather, Shambhurao, and his mother, to whom he was very attached. Vinoba was the eldest of the five children of his parents. One brother and a sister died early, leaving the three brothers— Vinayak, Balkrishna (Baikova) and Shiva—to share the love and affection of their parents and grandfather. All three brothers did not marry and the Bhave family ended with them.

Vinayak started his formal education in a Baroda school and was admitted to Baroda High School later, from where he passed the matriculation examination in 1913. He was not a brilliant student but was good at mathematics and had a knack for learning languages. His English was good and so was his French, which was an optional subject at school. He also knew Marathi, Gujarati and Sanskrit. He then joined Baroda College for his intermediate, for which he had to go to Bombay in 1916. During his train journey, he changed his mind and took a train to Kashi (Banaras) instead. He wanted to learn Sanskrit. It is said that he burned his school certificates so that he would not be able to continue his college education. There were not many certificates to burn anyway. He started studying the Vedas and the Upanishads from some pandits in Kashi, but he did not stay there for long. He had heard about Gandhi and the controversial speech he had delivered at the inaugural ceremony of the BHU, lambasting the princes present on the dais. He wanted to meet Gandhi and reached his Kochrab Ashram in Ahmedabad (Sabarmati Ashram was established later in 1918). Vinayak liked the austere life being led by the ashramites and soon became one of the favourite disciples of Gandhi. The very first day Vinayak met Gandhi, the latter wrote to Vinayak's father Shambhurao (on 7 June 1916), 'Your son Vinoba is with me. Your son has acquired at so tender age such high-spiritedness and asceticism as took me years of patient labour to do.' It is rather surprising how Gandhi could gauge the inner qualities of Vinoba at their very first meeting. The name 'Vinoba' was given to Vinayak after he joined the ashram. At the ashram, Vinoba did all the menial work which was required of all the people there. It is often claimed that even scavenging was being done by the ashramites, including Gandhi. This claim must have a qualified acceptance, as a sweeper had been employed to do the scavenging. In fact, one day, when the sweeper was ill, he had sent his twelve-year-old son to do the scavenging. When the boy could not finish the work, he began to cry. It was at that time that Gandhi decided that the they should do the scavenging work. This was in 1920.[1] Vinoba taught mathematics and Gujarati to the students in the Rashtriya Shala (National School) and also acted as a hotel superintendent. Gandhi used to discuss the intricacies of the Gita and the Upanishads with him and was impressed by the depth of his knowledge and understanding of Hindu scriptures. Gandhi was so impressed by Vinoba that he wrote to him on 18 February 1918, 'Your love and your character fascinate me and so also your self-examination. I am not fit to measure your worth. You seem almost to have met a long felt wish of mine.' It seems that the hard work in the ashram took a toll onVinoba's health. Or there could be some other reasons behind his decision to leave which we will never know. Vinoba left the ashram in February 1917 and went to his ancestral place, Wai. He brushed up on his Sanskrit for six months and studied the Upanishads, Brahmasutra etc., from a learned pandit. For the next few months, he visited several surrounding villages and historical places on foot. Exactly one year later, he returned to the ashram and started doing the daily chores, including teaching, once again.

In April 1921, Vinoba was deputed by Gandhi, at the request of Jamnalal Bajaj, to take charge of the Satyagraha Ashram at Wardha, which was earlier looked after by Ramniklal Modi. Soon, Vinoba extended the activities of the ashram. He founded other ashrams in nearby villages—one at Nalwadi, a Harijan village and another in Pavnar, five miles from Wardha. He also started a Mahila Ashram in Wardha. In 1923, he took part in the flag satyagraha at Nagpur and was imprisoned for three months. He also took part in the Vaikom satyagraha (Kerala) in 1924. He stayed in and around Wardha for 30 years. He ran the ashrams founded by him according to his own beliefs, which were akin to Gandhi but differed in certain important details. There was better discipline and a greater emphasis on 'Harijan' work. Vinoba had several temples and wells opened

---

[1]Tandon, V., *Acharya Vinoba Bhave*, Publications Division, New Delhi, 1992, p. 21.

for Harijans and also founded a tannery for them near Nalwadi in 1935. He had now a team of dedicated workers which enabled him to put into practise what he believed. To better organize the activities in his ashrams, Vinoba founded the Gram Seva Mandal in 1934. He also opened the Maharogi Seva Mandal at Datapur, near Wardha, for service to those with leprosy.

In October 1940, when Gandhi launched the Civil Disobedience Movement, Vinoba Bhave was chosen as the first satyagrahi. He was arrested thrice during this satyagraha and sentenced to various terms of imprisonment each time. When the Quit India Movement was started in August 1942, Vinoba was among the leaders who were arrested. He was kept in Vellore jail and Seoni jail for three years. Back in his ashrams, he started doing constructive work. After Gandhi's death in January 1948, Congress leaders sought out Vinoba for help in transforming the society in independent India. A conference of top political dignitaries and constructive workers was held at the Sevagram Ashram, with Jawaharlal Nehru, Rajendra Prasad, Maulana Azad and others in attendance. It was then that the concept of 'Sarvodaya Samaj' was formulated. The importance of Vinoba Bhave and his work was realized by the government as well as by social workers. After the conference, Nehru invited Vinoba to Delhi to help with the relief and rehabilitation work for the refugees who had been ousted from Pakistan. Nehru wanted to help the Meo Muslims of Gurgaon get back their land which had been occupied by Hindu and Sikh refugees when they (the Meo community) had migrated to Pakistan. Nehru had brought them back to India himself and was now in a dilemma about how to get the land vacated without inviting the ire of the Hindus and Sikhs. The sermons of Vinoba, coupled with the unsympathetic attitude of the Nehru government, succeeded in ousting the Hindu and Sikh refugees, thus fortifying the secular image of Nehru.

To spread the message of Sarvodaya Samaj, Vinoba started the monthly journal, *Sarvodaya,* on 15 August 1949. Vinoba's teachings as well as community work must have come to the notice of people outside India. They had not yet forgotten the devastation caused by war, and were looking for methods which would lead the world to permanent peace. They saw some hope in the teachings of Vinoba. The World Pacifist Conference was held at Sevagram in January 1949, in which delegates from several countries participated. Vinoba inaugurated the conference and Rajendra Prasad presided. In 1950, he began his experiment of Kanchan Mukti (freedom from gold or money economy), which ended in failure for obvious reasons.

Vinoba Bhave is best known for *bhoodan* (a gift of land by the big landlords to the landless). The movement was born accidentally in 1951, when he visited the Telangana area where communists were active. In Pochampalli village, the landless Harijan entreated him to give them land so that they could eke out their livelihood. Vinoba, half in earnest, asked in his prayer meeting if anyone could give them the 80 acres of land that they needed. To everyone's surprise, a young man, Ramchandra Reddy, stood up and said, 'I make a gift of 100 acres of land.' Vinoba realized that it was possible to get land from the big farmers by begging and it could then be distributed to the landless. That was the birth of the Bhoodan Movement. Vinoba and a band of his followers marched from one village to another on foot, persuading landlords to donate their surplus property. They travelled from one corner of the country to the other in a 'sweet-tempered fury', demanding land from landlords. It was a sight to see the 'frail old man with a goat beard striding ahead, lean and sinewy, wearing tennis shoes and carrying a staff.' Vinoba and his movement was covered on the front pages of newspapers across the world. Prime Minister Nehru lauded his efforts in the Parliament. *New York Times* wrote a three-column story on him and his unique movement. *Time* magazine featured this 'man on foot' in its cover story. 'The Bhoodan March' of Vinoba continued for more than 13 years covering a total distance of 36,500 miles. During the *padayatra* (travels on foot) he collected 4.4 million acres of land as free gifts, out of which about 1.3 million acres were distributed among landless farm workers.[2] The number of his followers swelled, which included Jayaprakash Narayan, their differences in the later stages notwithstanding. The Bhoodan Movement led to some other related movements like Gramdan and Sarvodaya. For his exemplary work, Vinoba received the first Magsaysay Award in 1958.

During his *padayatras*, Vinoba Bhave influenced the thinking of many people who met him or heard about him, including the dacoits of Chambal valley. In May 1960, Vinoba, accompanied by Major General Yadunath Singh, toured the dreaded Chambal area which was the safe abode of several dacoits. Word went around among the dacoits and some of them came for his *darshan* and were converted. The first one was the notorious Lachhi, who surrendered at Vinoba's feet. He had read in the newspapers that the 'Baba' (Vinoba) wanted them to repent and surrender. Within a few days, 20 more dacoits, led by the formidable Lokman Dixit (also known as 'Lukka') as well as the Maan Singh gang, surrendered. In a prayer meeting after their surrender, Vinoba said, 'Two thousand and five hundred years ago we witnessed such an incident when Aṅgulimāla was turned into a saint by the touch of Lord Buddha. People say that such happenings are not possible in this *Kali Yuga*, the age of evil. This is nothing but (a) miracle of the Almighty.'[3]

All these years, Vinoba had also been working for the eradication of untouchability and caste restrictions and for the propagation of khadi. But for the last 20 years of his life, he had the feeling that he had done all that an individual could do. Still, he could not resist the temptation of doing something to stop cow slaughter before his death. In February 1982, at the age of 88, he went on a fast and led a satyagraha to secure a total ban on cow slaughter. He did not succeed. On 15 November 1982, he breathed his last in his ashram. Mahadevi Tai, his adopted daughter, lit the funeral pyre.

---

[2]Pandya, Jayant, *Gandhiji and His Disciples*, National Book Trust, Delhi, 1994, p. 52.

[3]Narayan, Shriman, *Vinoba: His Life and Work,*, Popular Prakashan, Bombay 1970, p. 279.

Vinoba Bhave wrote several books and pamphlets, mostly on spiritual and religious topics. His *Gita Pravachan*, translated in English as *Talks on the Gita,* is a collection of his talks which he delivered in Dhula jail in 1932. Others include *Swaraj Shastra* or *Grammar of Politics* (1973) and *Gitai* (a simple rendering of Gita in Marathi verse). His speeches and articles have been collected by his disciples: *Bhoodan* (eight Volumes), selected and edited by Nirmala Deshpande, *Shikshan Vichar* (*Thoughts on Education*) and many others.

Vinoba learnt a lot from Gandhi and even imitated him in some ways but his thinking and constructive work went beyond Gandhian teachings. He clarified this during the Sevagram Constructive Workers Conference in March 1948. He said:

> Gandhiji gave me freely, but I also received from others. Whenever and whatever I got, I made my own. It now forms part of my capital. I do not have separate accounts as to what part of it was derived from Gandhiji and what from others. Of the ideas I read and heard, whatever appealed to me and were imbibed by me, became my own. Hence, I am a man of my own ideas.

Today, nobody talks about Bhoodan or Vinoba Bhave. The Naxalites have taken over once again and have expanded their area of action. The number of landless labourers has increased since Vinoba's death. Land is being grabbed by the powerful and unscrupulous. More and more people are pushed down the enigmatic poverty line. The problem of poverty and landless people is a colossal one. Vinoba tried to do the impossible. He might not have been able to provide a solution, but he showed a way.

12

Jagadish Chandra Bose

(1858–1937)

In the twentieth century, India produced many eminent scientists, but Jagadish Chandra Bose was unique in many ways. His biophysical and plant physiological researches are an attempt at fitting empirical results into the Vedic doctrine of 'unity in diversity'. Thus, he became the only Indian scientist to be admired and eulogized by non-scientists like Swami Vivekananda, Mahatma Gandhi, Rabindranath Tagore, Sister Nivedita and others. Even literary men in Europe such as G.B. Shaw, John Galsworthy and W.B. Yeats, showed great interest in Bose's scientific experiments.

Jagadish Chandra Bose was born on 30 November 1858 in Mymensingh (now in Bangladesh). His father Bhagawan Chandra Bose was in government service, working as a deputy magistrate. In spite of his high government position, Bhagawan Chandra was an admirer of Indian culture and traditions. Thus, it was not surprising that he sent his son to a local school instead of sending him to an English school. 'He should learn his mother tongue before he learnt a foreign language,' argued his father. This early learning of Bengali proved to be an asset for Jagadish later in life, while popularizing science among the masses. At the age of nine, Jagadish joined Hare School in Calcutta and soon after was admitted to St Xavier's College, passing the entrance examination of University of Calcutta in 1875 and enrolling for a BSc in 1879. The following year, he left for England to study medicine but had to switch to natural science because of ill health. He studied at the Christ College in Cambridge. There, he was fortunate to have famous scientists like Lord Rayleigh (a physicist) and Sydney Howard Vines (a British botanist) as his teachers. Rayleigh's inspiring lectures and careful experimentation greatly contributed to the making of the physicist Jagadish Bose. In 1884, he passed the natural science tripos of Cambridge as well as the BSc examination of the University of London.

Jagadish returned to India in 1885 and was appointed as an assistant professor of Physics at Presidency College in Calcutta. He protested against white teachers being paid almost twice as much as Indian teachers. He did not draw his salary for three years and ultimately won his case. The college paid all the arrears to Indian teachers that were being paid to the British ones before. Jagadish wanted to do research work along with teaching but he was saddled with a heavy schedule of class lectures. He was also 'subjected to continuous annoyances and petty difficulties—with the evident earnest desire of those who were about him to end his distinction which was personally galling to them', wrote Sister Nivedita, his friend and admirer. However, a determined Bose overcame all these difficulties and found time to do research work, staying up late into the night. He built a small laboratory for this purpose, designing and fabricating his own tools and instruments in an ingenious way. In this modest laboratory, his research career started around 1894, when his interest in electric waves was roused by the work of German physicist, H.R. Hertz, as explained in *The Work of Hertz and Some of his Successors,* small book by Oliver Lodge. Hertz had shown the existence of electromagnetic waves in free space and found their speed to be the same as that of light. Hertz further showed that such waves had all the usual optical properties i.e., the properties of visible light waves. Hertz died in 1894 and Jagadish started his research work along the same lines. Lodge also started working similarly. Jagadish devised a series of experiments to demonstrate the optical behaviour of electric waves such as reflection, refraction, total reflection, polarization, diffraction and so on. He even managed to polarize the electromagnetic waves in order to further lay bare their identity with light rays. Jagjit Singh, has talked about Jagadish in his book, saying:

> By his contrivance of a wide variety of delightfully simple and yet wonderfully ingenious instruments he proved the underlying unity of electrical and optical beams. As early as 1895, he demonstrated at a public lecture in Calcutta, how electric waves could travel from his radiator in the lecture room to another seventy-five feet away, where his receiver managed to pick up enough energy to ring a bell and fire a pistol. To accomplish this amazingly remarkable feat with his feeble radiator, Bose anticipated the lofty antennae of modern wireless telegraphy.[1]

Today's radio and broadcasting stations are based on the experimentation and theories as propounded by Heinrich Hertz and Jagadish Bose. The results of Jagadish's investigations appeared in leading scientific journals such as *Proceedings of the Royal Society*, *The Electrician* and *The Journal of the Asiatic Society of Bengal*. By the end of 1895, Jagadish ranked high among the successors of Hertz. Further, he concentrated on short radio waves reducing the waves to the millimetre level, unlike Hertz, who dealt with decimetre waves, and Lodge, who studied the centimetre waves. Jagadish was successful in making devices for receiving the polarization of electric waves using simple material such as jute fibre. These receivers were called 'coherers'. He was able to make a perfect coherer, which he could have commercially exploited. His contemporary, Marconi, who worked with other European scientists, exploited his research venture in the same field by designing a long-distance radio signalling device, patented it and made a fortune. But Jagadish had an antipathy towards commercializing science for

---

[1]Singh, Jagjit, *Some Eminent Indian Scientists*, Publications Division, New Delhi, 1991, p. 24.

pecuniary gain. His attitude was called 'unpractical quixotism' by some Westerners. Jagadish wrote a paper based on his research titled 'On the Determination of the Wave-length of Electric Radiation by Diffraction Grating' and sent it to the University of London as a thesis for a DSc. Jagadish was awarded the degree and the University even waived the requirement of his presence at the examination, which was a great honour.

Lord Rayleigh had suggested to Jagadish that he should visit England and meet the scientists there and talk to them about his work. Jagadish reached England in October 1896. With the presentation of a paper on electric waves at the Liverpool meeting of the British Association, Bose made his debut in England as a scientist. He was an immediate success, and brought, in its wake, an invitation to deliver a series of Friday Evening Discourses at the Royal Institution. 'It was during these discourses, with his free exhibition of all his appliances, that Bose revealed his characteristically ascetic trait that astonished many and even disappointed a few.' He never thought of patenting his apparatuses like his improved 'coherer'—an instrument for the reception of radio waves—which had made him justly famous.

Surprisingly, when he was earning laurels as a pioneering physicist, he left this field 'which was still replete with undiscovered nuggets, and ventured into another altogether new one—biophysics or the physics of life'. Jagadish spent less than five years doing research in physics in a ramshackle laboratory fitted with ingenuously made instruments and earned praise from leading physicists of the world. He was really the pioneer in utilizing the Hertzian waves for signalling purposes and laid the foundation of wireless telegraphy. Bose did not care to follow up on his great achievement as his attention was now diverted to an entirely different type of research which evidently, he regarded as of even greater importance. The switchover was accidental. While doing research with the coherer, he found that continuous exposure of metals to electric waves was causing fatigue or lesser sensitivity of the metal. He hypothesized that it was similar to the muscular fatigue of animals. These and many other instances of similitude between the responses of the living and the inert that he discovered encouraged him to take up the study of life. During the remaining years of his life, to prove his point of unity in diversity (between metals, plants and animals), he brought into biophysics the quantitative precision of a physicist. He did so by introducing new experimental methods and inventing many delicate and sensitive instruments for demonstrating the effects of sleep, air, light, food, drugs, irritation etc., in plants, to prove a complete parallelism between the responses of plants and animals and even plants and inanimate materials like metals. This he tried to prove with the help of the crescograph, a supersensitive instrument for recording plant growth by magnifying a small movement as much as ten million-fold. His first demonstration was at the International Congress of Physics in Paris in July 1900. Swami Vivekananda was also present there and congratulated Jagadish after the demonstration and called him the 'heroic son of India'. An even greater compliment came from the French writer and philosopher Romain Rolland, who said: 'You have made us enter into the Kingdom of the universe of silent life, which till yesterday was thought as dead and buried in the night.' Bose visited England and Europe several times on scientific deputation. He lectured at Oxford, Cambridge, London, Aberdeen and Leipzig. During 1923–24, Bose visited Europe for the sixth time. This time, the audience of his lecture at the India Office in London included Ramsay Macdonald, the then prime minister of the United kingdom; Lord Hardinge, former viceroy; and G.B. Shaw. The topic was the 'Phenomenon of the Growth of Plants'. After the lecture, Shaw presented Jagadish with a special edition of his collected works, bearing the inscription: 'From the least to the greatest biologist'. The synthetic philosophical outlook that underlay Jagadish's scientific work had a natural appeal for the sensitive men of literature.

But Jagadish had his detractors, too. Among such critics were Dr Waller and Burdon Sanderson, who had even succeeded in persuading the Royal Society to not publish Jagadish's paper. 'He was blamed for having been carried away by a sort of enchantment exercised by verbal ghosts, like fatigue, sleep, exaltation, irritability, of his own conjuring.' But the urge to satisfy his longing to bring about the unity of animals and inanimate nature sustained Bose in the midst of all the criticism that his biophysical work provoked. And during his lifetime, undaunted by criticism, Bose continued to try to obliterate the boundary lines and establish new points of contact between the domains of the living and the inert. However, his assumption that the phloem tissues in plants are equivalent to nerves in animals was disproved by later investigations.

Jagadish Chandra Bose married Abala Das, daughter of Durga Mohan Das and a cousin of C.R. Das, in 1887. They had only one child, who died in infancy. The couple led a very happy married life. Abala was always by her husband's side whenever he was in difficulty and often accompanied him during his frequent lecture tours to Europe and the US. She was a gracious hostess and acted as a mother to his students, some of whom stayed with them. After Jagadish's retirement from Presidency College in 1915, Abala founded Nari Siksha Samiti, an organization devoted to the education and welfare of women.

Jagadish had many admirers outside the scientific circle as well—the greatest of them being Rabindranath Tagore and Sister Nivedita. He was in constant correspondence with Tagore, who was always anxious to know about the progress of his research and the response to it by scientists as well as non-scientists. In all, 82 letters, written in Bengali, were exchanged between the two. Tagore also immortalized Jagadish through many essays and poems, including the one on mimosa (the *chhui-mui* plant) used by Jagadish in many of his experiments and demonstrations. What really brought them together was the fact that they were both in the quest of an ultimate cosmic unity in the midst of diverse manifestations of nature. 'Another sphere,' wrote Tagore, 'where Jagadish felt affinity towards me was his profound patriotism.'[2] Tagore was three years younger than Bose and outlived him by four years.

Another great friend of Jagadish's was Sister Nivedita, who played an inspiring role in his life. Jagadish's wife, Abala, was equally attached to Nivedita and the latter found solace in their company and was a frequent visitor to the Bose's home. Nivedita died in Bose's summer resort in Darjeeling in 1911. Before her death, Nivedita had urged Jagadish to build a research institute epitomizing the renascent wisdom of India. The Bose Research Institute came into existence in 1917 through the generous donations of people as well as a substantial grant from the government, as a place 'where scholars would ceaselessly pursue the quest for truth'. An inaugural song was composed by Tagore. The famous painter Nandalal's mural decorated the walls of the lecture hall.

During his lifetime, Jagadish was showered with national and international honours. He was knighted in 1917 and was elected Fellow of the Royal Society in 1920. In 1926, he was nominated a member of the League of Nations Committee on Intellectual Cooperation. In 1928, he became corresponding member of the Vienna Academy of Science. He was honorary member of several scientific societies of Europe and the US. He was the general president of the 1927 session of the Indian Science Congress.

He authored a number of books and papers, both in English and Bengali. Some of them are: *Response in the Living and Non-Living* (1902), *Comparative Electro-Physiology: A Physico-physiological Study* (1907), *Researches on Irritability of Plants* (1913), *The Physiology of Photosynthesis* (1924), *The Nervous Mechanism of Plants* (1926), *Collected Physical Papers* (1927), *Motor Mechanism of Plants* (1928) and *Growth and Tropic Movement of Plants* (1929). He also edited several volumes of the *Transactions of the Bose Research Institute*. He also tried to popularize science by writing scientific essays in

---

[2]Mukherji, Visvapriya, *Jagadis Chandra Bose*, Publications Division, New Delhi, 1994, pp. 52–53.

Bengali. He brought out a collection of these essays titled *Abyakta* (*The Unmanifest*), which was written in 1894 and got published in various magazines in 1921.

Jagadish Bose had been suffering from diabetes and high blood pressure for many years, which affected his health. Only his love and enthusiasm for research work sustained him through those years. He died on 23 November 1937.

13

Chaudhry Rahmat Ali

(1897–1950)

Chaudhry Rahmat Ali was born on 16 November 1897, to a Gujjar middle-class family in the Balachaur village, about 30 miles from Jalandhar in East Punjab. It is believed that their ancestors were converted to Islam during the times of Mughal king Aurangzeb. His father Shah Muhammad married twice and Rahmat Ali was the eldest among the three children of his second wife. The other two were his younger brother Mohammad Ali and a sister who died in infancy.

Rahmat Ali's education started in a primary school in Balachaur and continued in Rahon, a small town few miles from his village, which boasted of an Anglo–vernacular middle school. To continue his education further, Rahmat Ali had to go to Jalandhar, the district headquarters and an important city in the area. There, in 1910, he enrolled himself at the Saindas Anglo–Sanskrit High School, which was managed by the Arya Samaj. From there, he passed the matriculation examination in 1912. From Jalandhar he went to Lahore to pursue higher studies and joined the Islamia College, one of the string of colleges founded under the Aligarh Movement. Rahmat Ali graduated from college in 1918, getting a second division with economics, English and Persian as his subjects. It took him six years to graduate, two more than the usual. During these six years, he also tried his hand at journalism and served on the staff of *Paisa Akhbar* and *Kashmir*.

After his graduation, Rahmat Ali continued to live in Lahore, the then capital of Punjab, a seat of learning and political ferment. Most of the Muslim elite of Punjab lived there. Rahmat Ali lived in Lahore till 1930. He wanted to join the Law College but could not do so, perhaps due to a paucity of funds. Instead, he accepted a tutorship in Aitchison College, a public school for the education of the sons of rulers and chiefs of the province. While serving as a tutor, he came in contact with the nawab of Bahawalpur, whose son he taught. Later, he also taught the sons of the Mazari family, who were prominent landlords. He got close to the family and became their legal adviser after attending classes at the Law College (from where he could not earn any degree). The Mazari family paid him well and he lived a life of ease and some affluence. His social contacts widened and the village lad absorbed the culture and etiquette of urban life with ease. Niaz Muhamad Khan, who knew Rahmat Ali during his Lahore days, describes him as, 'well dressed, a joy to listen to, with a discriminating taste in cuisine, with impeccable manners and habits, experienced in the way of the world'.[1] Another friend describes him with the Urdu word *banku*, the nearest English translation of which would be a dandy.

Rahmat Ali had always nurtured a desire of going to England, he even called that his mission in life. The dream materialized in 1930. With all the connections that he had cultivated in Lahore, he did not find any difficulty in getting prominent Punjabi friends to write to men of influence in England about his plans. Armed with the recommendation letters, Rahmat Ali left for England on 31 October 1930. He was already 33 years old. He decided to become a barrister and joined The Honourary Society of the Middle Temple. But for some unexplained reason he could not be called to the Bar until January 1943, taking 13 years, around 10 more than it took most others. It seems that he abandoned the idea of qualifying as a barrister soon after and joined Emmanuel College in

---

[1] Aziz, K.K., *Rahmat Ali: A Biography,* Vanguard, Lahore, 1987, p. 21.

Cambridge in January 1931. He passed the law tripos examination in June 1932. It took him another seven years to get a master's degree in October 1940. His other academic accomplishments at Cambridge remain obscure. However, he came into the limelight after three sittings of the Round Table Conference (1930–32), in which a federal structure of India was discussed and approved by the participants, resulting in the Act of 1935 which served as the Constitution of India until 1947.

Rahmat Ali witnessed this political drama with 'poignant anxiety'. Mohammad Iqbal's presidential address at the Muslim League session of 1930 had thrown up an idea of a separate Muslim region in the north-west of India. This appealed to Rahmat Ali as it diluted the hegemony of 'Indianness'. But that was forgotten and the delegates had unanimously agreed to the federal structure for India. Rahmat Ali claimed that he met the Muslim delegates at the first two sittings of the conference and tried to convince them of their folly of agreeing to an Indian federation which would be perpetually dominated by the Hindus. He said, 'I knew that their action had obliterated the twelve centuries of our history, destroyed the very foundations of our heritage, and crippled all hopes of the fulfilment of our mission.'[2] But he failed to convince them. He went back to Cambridge and published a four-page pamphlet in January 1933, signed by three other students besides him. The pamphlet was titled *Now or Never: Are We to Live or Perish Forever?*. He appealed for 'sympathy and support for our grim and fateful struggle against political crucifixion and complete annihilation'. The homeland of 30 million Muslims was defined in the first sentence as Pakistan, 'by which we mean the five northern units of India, namely: Punjab, NWFP (Afghan), Kashmir, Sindh and Baluchistan'. It was further argued that India was neither a country nor a nation. 'It is in fact, the designation of a state, created for the first time in history, by the British. The heterogeneity of its

---

[2]Ibid. 79.

people was a proven fact. Our religion, culture, history, tradition, economic system, laws of inheritance, succession and marriage are basically and fundamentally different from those of the people living in the rest of India. These differences are not confined to the broad basic principles—far from it. They extend to the minutest details of our lives. We do not inter-dine, we do not inter-marry. Our national customs and calendars, even our diet and dress are different.'[3] Although these ideas did not carry much weight at the time, it must be admitted that all the subsequent arguments in support of Pakistan proceeded from the thesis of Rahmat Ali, and did not cover much new ground. In fact, Jinnah, in his speech in the 1940 session of the Muslim League, while demanding a separate homeland for Muslims, copied extensively, almost word for word, from Rahmat Ali's pamphlet. When the Muslim League came to advocate its own Pakistan plan later, it could not think of any new arguments and repeated Rahmat Ali's points.

That pamphlet was sent to all the delegates of the Round Table Conference and several political leaders, both in England and India. But it attracted little attention and was ignored by the Muslim League and the Muslim Conference. When the representatives of these two organizations appeared before the Joint Select Committee of the Parliament in August 1933, they were asked 'whether there is a scheme for a federation of Provinces under the name Pakistan'. Muhammad Zafarullah Khan replied, 'It was a students' scheme and there is nothing in it.' Another member Yusuf Ali replied, 'We have considered, it is chimerical and impracticable.' The only support which Rahmat Ali's scheme got was from the notorious Sir Michael O'Dwyer, who ruled Punjab during the Jallianwala Bagh massacre in Amritsar (1919). While testifying before the Committee, O'Dwyer argued against the All-India Federation on the lines of Rahmat Ali, saying if the federal government, with a

---

[3]Majumdar, R.C., *History of the Freedom Movement in India*, Firma KLM, Calcutta, 1988, p. 474.

Hindu majority, endeavours to force its will on provinces with a Muslim majority, what is to prevent a breakaway of the Punjab, Sindh, Baluchistan and the NWFP as already foreshadowed and their possibility of forming a Muslim Federation of their own? 'He did not explain the source of the word "foreshadowed" but he appears to have received a copy of Rahmat Ali's pamphlet. Or could he perhaps have helped inspire it.'[4] Obviously, the British hand in the whole affair could not be ruled out.

To give an impetus to his theory, the 'shadowy' Rahmat Ali identified himself as 'founder of the Pakistan National Movement'. This movement, in his own words, was 'a centre of members to work for Pakistan, for the Pak Plan, and for the Pak ideology'. He published another eight-page pamphlet soon after—*What Does the Pakistan National Movement Stand For?*—a virulent attack on 'Indianness', which he described as Hindu imperialism. A minor but significant change was the spelling of the word 'Pakstan' to 'Pakistan'. He continued issuing and distributing pamphlets widely in which he went on extending the boundaries of the Muslim state or the creation of other Muslim states like Bangistan, Usmanistan or Haideristan comprising Bengal plus Assam and Hyderabad respectively. These will be two independent 'nations' forming a triple alliance, he argued. Still later, he proposed setting up seven more states as Muslim pockets, not only in India but also in Ceylon (Sri Lanka). All these pamphlets bore one address—16 Montague Road, Cambridge—and the later pamphlets of various sizes bore the signature of only one man—Rahmat Ali. The increasing number of '*stans*' touched the limits of absurdity, but the impact of his Pakistan movement gathered momentum, and became a reality in the hands of a great strategist like Jinnah in August 1947.

Rahmat Ali eventually decided to see the Shangri-la of his dreams, towards which he had contributed his bit and spent

---

[4]Wolpert, Stanley, *Jinnah of Pakistan*, Oxford University Press, New York, 1984, p. 132.

many years of his adult life. He reached Lahore on 6 April, 1948, met his friends and traced his family, who were now *muhajirs* (refugees) and found them in a pitiable condition. He found the partition of Punjab and Bengal and the loss of Assam unbearable and blamed Jinnah for his 'treachery' and 'betrayal'. To get back the 'lost territories' of Pakistan of his conception, he planned to start a Pakistan National Liberation Movement. He started calling Pakistan as *Pastan* (a defeated country). He declared, 'all our hopes reduced to dust and ashes by the folly and foul play of one man and one man alone—*Quisling-e-Azam-Jinnah*'. This outspokenness cost him dearly. The few old friends who had welcomed him as a 'hero' now deserted him. The government was soon after him. He was declared persona non grata, denied a Pakistani passport and condemned as a danger to the security and tranquillity of the country. The government did not remember, or even let it be known, that he had named the country over which they ruled. They could not forget that he had criticized Jinnah, the 'Quaid-e-Azam' for accepting an incomplete Pakistan. Rahmat Ali was ordered to leave the country. He left on 1 October 1948 for England, and died a lonely and dejected man in Cambridge on 3 February 1951. He is buried in Cambridge City Cemetery at Newmarket Road. His grave is flat earth. The hospital and burial expenses were paid by Welbourne, his tutor during his Emmanuel College days. 'I am glad that I was able to prevent him dying as an unclaimed beggar in poverty and avert the disposal of his body as an unclaimed person,' said Welbourne. During his lifetime, Jinnah did not show any consideration for Rahmat Ali, from whom he had borrowed his ideal, nomenclature, arguments, even his words and phrases. Jinnah owed such a large debt to Rahmat Ali who had played a pivotal role in the creation of Pakistan.[5]

---

[5]Aziz, K.K., *Rahmat Ali: A Biography*, Vanguard, Lahore, 1987, p. 338.

14

Rash Behari Bose

(1880–1945)

Rash Behari Bose was one of those freedom fighters and revolutionaries who spent a major part of their lives in self-exile working for the freedom of the country from distant lands, braving innumerable sufferings and privations. Other such forgotten heroes are Sardar Ajit Singh (uncle of Sardar Bhagat Singh), Madam Cama, Raja Mahendra Pratap and Shyamji Krishna Varma. Among all these freedom fighters, the name of Rash Behari stands out as he was the founder of the Indian Independence League (IIL) and the Indian National Army (INA), which under the leadership of Subhas Chandra Bose, fought the British army and shook the foundations of the British Empire.

Rash Behari was born in 1886 in the Subaldaha village of Burdwan district. His parents, Binod Behari Bose and Bhubhaneswari Devi, formed an average middle-class family. His father was employed in a government press in Simla as as assistant. His mother died when Rash Behari was barely two. Binod Behari remarried soon after, but Rash Behari seemed to have good relations with his stepmother, who often came to his help whenever he was in difficulty. He had his early education at Subaldaha, under the guidance of his grandfather Kali Charan Bose. Later, he joined Dupleix College at Chandannagar, a French enclave. But Rash Behari was not interested in studies and stopped going to school after Class 2. He was more interested in physical activities. As Bengalis were debarred from joining the army, he tried to enlist in the army under a false name but was detected and punished. Seeing the waywardness of his son, his father took him to Shimla and got him a job as a copyholder in the press. There, Rash Behari learnt English as well as typewriting. But he soon left his job in Simla and returned to Chandernagore (Chandannagar). He came in contact with the revolutionaries of the Jugantar Party operating in Chandernagore and decided to devote his life for the emancipation of the country. But soon after, he left Chandernagore and went back to Simla. With the help of his father's acquaintances, he got a clerical job at the Pasteur Institute of India in Kasauli and later at the Forest Research Institute in Dehradun. Despite being a government servant, Rash Behari started taking active part in revolutionary activities. He was in touch with the members of the Anushilan Samiti of Bengal and had formed a small group of devoted revolutionaries under his leadership. The first daring act of this group was the throwing of a bomb on the procession of Viceroy Lord Hardinge on 23 December 1912, on the occasion of his state entry into Delhi riding on an elephant. The bomb was thrown by Basanta Kumar Biswas from the Punjab National Bank building in Chandni Chowk. Lord Hardinge was badly wounded, the man holding his umbrella was killed and another servant was seriously injured. Most of the members of this group were caught after the incident. Avadh Behari, Bal Mukund and Master Amir Chand (who used to give shelter to the revolutionaries) were executed in Delhi jail and Basanta Kumar Biswas was hanged in Ambala jail. Rash Behari escaped because he had mastered the art of disguise to conceal his identity. Undaunted by the setback, Rash Behari continued his revolutionary activities, enlisting the support of several other revolutionaries from Punjab, Bengal and other parts of India. He felt that stray incidents of daredevilry were not of much help in weakening the hold of foreign power on the country. He felt that an attempt should be made to plan a general uprising by the Indian army along the lines of the 1857 uprising. Rash Behari started working towards that end. By that time, he had formed a larger group of revolutionaries under his leadership. The First World War, which started in July 1914, provided them with an opportunity to execute their plan.

According to R.C. Majumdar, 'Rash Behari directed his main attention to propaganda work among the Indian soldiers with a view to inducing them to join in the general rebellion against the British, which was planned to take place simultaneously all over North India.'[1] Rash Behari sent his most trusted lieutenants to work among soldiers in the various cantonments: Allahabad, Ramnagar, Banaras, Ambala, Ferozepur, Jalandhar, Lahore, Meerut and as far as Rawalpindi. According to the plan, sepoys were to revolt on a particular day overpowering or killing the English troops, whose number had been considerably reduced due to the War in Europe and the Middle East. The date of the uprising was fixed as 21 February 1915 throughout North India. But a police informer and spy, Kirpal Singh, who had managed to enrol as a member of the Rash Behari group, conveyed the information to the authorities who took adequate measures to defeat the plan. Many revolutionaries were arrested and executed. So were many soldiers. Rash Behari once again escaped. As the police was after him, he decided to leave India. He applied for a passport under the assumed name of Raja R.N. Thakur and the declared purpose was to make arrangements for Rabindranath Tagore's ensuing visit to Japan. It is believed that Tagore had come to know about the impersonation but kept quiet. The famous Bengali writer, Sarat Chandra Chatterjee is believed to have contributed money for Rash Behari's passage to Japan. Rash Behari left for Japan on 12 May 1915, by the ship, *S.S. Sanuki Maru,* reaching the port of Kobe on 5 June. From there, he travelled to Tokyo. British secret agents in Japan found out that R.N. Thakur was actually Rash Behari Bose who was wanted in India for the attempted murder of Viceroy Lord Hardinge. Once

---

[1]Majumdar, R.C., *History of the Freedom Movement in India*, Firma KLM, Calcutta, 1988, p. 425.

the identity was established, the British planned to apply for his extradition. In 1915, Britain and Japan had very friendly relations and there would not have been any difficulty in getting him back to India as he was declared as the 'most dangerous criminal'. As Rash Behari suspected that the British secret police were after him, he continuously changed his residence to avoid arrest. One Japanese couple, Mr and Mrs Soma, moved by Rash Behari's hardships and deprivations, let him stay in their house for some time, which ended with Rash Behari marrying their daughter, Toshiko, in July 1918. Still their did not end. They continued to change their residence at short intervals. Rash Behari became a naturalized Japanese citizen in July 1923. Consequently, he could not be deported.[2] However, the health of his wife deteriorated due to the hardships that she had to bear. She died in March 1925, at the age of 28, leaving behind a son, Masahide (who was killed fighting the British during the Second World War), and a daughter, Tetsuko.

Rash Behari kept himself busy by playing host to revolutionaries, especially of the Gadar party who came to Japan from Canada and the US. He had established a dormitory called Ajiu-Go (Centre of Asia) for the convenience of visitors. In 1933, he established a hostel called Villa Asians in Tokyo for Asian students, which he managed till 1941. He also formed an Indo–Japanese Friends Society and undertook an extensive tour in Japan explaining the Indian viewpoint. He could speak Japanese fluently. In 1924, he formed the IIL, which played an important role during the War, especially its military wing, Indian National Army or the Azad Hind Fauj.

While in Japan, Rash Behari wrote several books, some of which are—*Panoramic Views of Asian Revolution* (1929), *Wit and Humours of India* (1930), *India Oppressed* (1933), *Stories of Indian People* (1935), *India in Revolution* (1935), *Victories of Young Asia* (1937), *India Crying* (1938), *Tragic History of India* (1942), *Ramayana*

---

[2]Dharamvira, *I Threw the Bomb: The Revolutionary Life of Rash Behari Bose*, Orient Paperbacks, New Delhi, 1979, pp. 11–12.

(1942), *India of Indians* (1943), *The Last Song* (1943) and *Bose Appeals* (1944). He also started and edited a journal *The New Asia* but its entry into India was banned because of its harsh criticism of the British policy. He was also on the staff of *The Asian Review.*

The entry of Japan in the Second World War ignited the revolutionary instinct which was lying dormant all these years in Rash Behari and he organized a conference in Tokyo on 28 March 1942, under the auspices of the IIL with himself in the chair. General Hideki Tojo sent a message to the conference saying that, 'The Japanese government is fully sympathetic towards your efforts and will not hesitate to render all possible help in this respect.' But no formal declaration by the government of Japan was made, which created some consternation in the Indian camp. The conference passed several resolutions including the one requesting the Japanese authorities to declare their full support for the Indian cause and clarify their stand on the issue without delay. The conference also resolved to have an elected Council of Action (COA) and appointed Rash Behari Bose as interim president. These resolutions were to be ratified by a conference of the IIL representatives from all over East Asia to be held at Bangkok. The Bangkok conference was held for a week starting from 15 June 1942, in which delegates from various countries of East Asia participated. It ratified all the resolutions passed by the Tokyo Conference and the COA was invested with powers of control over the IIL in all territories and over the INA. It also invited Subhas Chandra Bose, who was in Germany, to come to East Asia.

Immediately after the Bangkok conference, both the IIL and the INA plunged into action, with Bangkok as headquarters of the COA and Singapore as headquarters of the INA. Over 20,000 Indian prisoners of war had joined the INA, headed by General Mohan Singh.

An unfortunate development occurred when the Japanese replaced the popular Fujiwara Kikan as liaison officer, with Hideo Iwakura, who was not as understanding and sympathetic to the

Indian cause. The fact that the Japanese government was not officially committing to anything undermined the position of Rash Behari as the president of the COA. Doubts were being expressed about his ability to lead the movement. 'His thirty years stay in Japan, his advancing age, frail health and mild manners made some Indians doubt whether he could withstand the strain of an uncompromising stand vis-a-vis the Japanese.' The schism between the COA, the INA and the Japanese widened. Members of the COA, barring its president, resigned. General Singh was peeved at the interference by the Japanese, who were issuing orders of movements to the INA troops without consulting the COA or their commander. He protested and was arrested on 29 December 1942 in Singapore and was released only after the Second World War was over. With the arrest of General Singh, the INA ceased to exist, leaving Rash Behari in a quandary. 'Six months of mounting suspicion, distrust, misgivings, tactlessness and lack of faith in Japanese sincerity culminated in the dissolution of the Council of Action and disbandment of the first INA. Chaos and confusion prevailed for some time.'

Rash Behari then set about the task of rebuilding the IIL as well as the INA. Dr Lakshmaiah joined him on the civil side and Lieutenant Colonel J.K. Bhonsle on the military side. He shifted the IIL headquarters from Bangkok to Singapore in March 1943 and tried to build the two organizations, working day and night to the amazement of his colleagues. Rash Behari knew that it was a matter of time before Subhas Chandra Bose reached East Asia and assumed the leadership of the movement.

Rash Behari called another conference of Indians in Singapore from 27 to 30 April in 1943 and passed the resolution that 'the Indian National Army is the army of the Indian Independence League and all officers and men of the INA as well as all members of the IIL shall owe allegiance to the League.' The constitution of IIL was amended by another resolution investing Rash Behari with almost dictatorial powers.[3] Rash Behari had saved the IIL and the INA from an ignominious end with his foresight and devotion to the national cause. After resurrecting both the organizations to his satisfaction, he left for Tokyo in June 1943.

Subhas Chandra Bose's journey from Germany to East Asia in a submarine is a part of the romantic saga in the annals of the freedom movement. Bose reached Tokyo on 16 May 1943. The Japanese authorities gave assurance of full support to him. Even before Subhas Bose was brought to East Asia, the Japanese were concerned about the presence of the two Boses, who may not work in tandem and create problems. But when General Seizo Arisue of the Intelligence Bureau broached this question, Rash Behari's decision to step down relieved the anxiety of the Japanese. Rash Behari Bose, accompanied by Subhas Chandra Bose, landed at the Sembawang air base in Singapore from Tokyo on the morning of 2 July 1943. Two days later, on 4 July, before an enthusiastic gathering of 5,000 Indians at the Cathay Cinema Hall, Rash Behari handed over the leadership to the 'younger and dynamic hands of Subhas'. Rash Behari voluntarily receded to the background as an adviser and left for Japan, letting Subhas lead the INA.

Rash Behari died in Tokyo on 21 January 1945. The news was announced by a Royal proclamation over the radio and his body was carried to the Zojoji Temple the next morning, on the decorated Imperial bier sent from the Imperial Palace, for last rites. Hours before his death, the Japanese emperor decorated him with the Second Order of the Rising Sun. However, no honour has been bestowed on him by India for his contribution to the nation.

---

[3]Ayer, S.A., *Story of the I.N.A*, National Book Trust, New Delhi, 1997, pp. 34–37.

15

Subhas Chandra Bose

(1897–1945)

Subhas Chandra Bose was the only soldier–statesman that India has produced in the recent past. By alienating thousands of Indian soldiers in the British army from the Crown, he shook the foundations of the British Empire, compelling the British to leave India in a hurry. Thus, his role in the freedom movement is unique and paramount.

He was born on 23 January 1897 in Cuttack, Orissa, ninth of the 14 children of Janakinath Bose and Prabhabati Bose. Janakinath was a lawyer by profession and had earned a name at the Cuttack Bar. He was the elected chairman of the Cuttack Municipality in 1901 and he was later appointed as the government pleader and public prosecutor—a post from which he resigned in 1917 due to differences with the district magistrate. He also served as a member of the Bengal Legislative Council in 1912.

Before he was five, Subhas was sent to the Baptist Mission's Protestant European school in Cuttack where his brothers also studied. He was good at studies, learnt English well but did not take part in school sports. For seven years, he studied in this school and then joined Ravenshaw Collegiate School at the age of 12 and became proficient in Bengali. He passed the matriculation examination in 1913, standing second in the University of Calcutta. While studying in school, he was influenced by the teachings of Vivekananda who taught him that only the service of humanity can bring about one's salvation. This inspired young Subhas to do social work in the nearby villages at the time of calamities like floods and epidemics. For further education, he was sent to Calcutta, where he joined Presidency College and a new chapter in his life began. Since his younger days, Subhas was influenced by sadhus and ascetics. During college vacations in 1914, he, along with a friend, went out in search of a guru, visiting religious places like Haridwar, Rishikesh, Mathura, Vrindavan, Banaras and Gaya, without informing his family. But after a few weeks, they returned to Calcutta, greatly disappointed at not finding a guru who could guide them in life.

Subhas found studies and lectures in the college quite boring and meaningless but he continued attending classes. He passed the intermediate examination in 1915 with credit. For the degree course, he opted for philosophy and it made him interested in studies as philosophy was his favourite subject. Then the famous Oaten episode happened in 1916. Edward Farley Oaten was a young British teacher at the Presidency College, who, it is alleged, used to denigrate Indians and Indian culture while teaching. Once, he manhandled some students who were making noise in the corridors while his class was on. As a reaction to that, some students assaulted Oaten a few days later. As the representative of the class, Subhas Bose was held responsible for this incident of indiscipline. 'Bose, you are the most troublesome man in the college,' the principal shouted at him. 'I suspend you.' Subhas was rusticated and had to discontinue his studies as he could not join any other college affiliated to the University of Calcutta. That proved to be a turning point in his turbulent life. In a paper presented about the incident at a seminar in 1973, Oaten (who was 88 at the time) tells a different version of the incident and denies assaulting any student. He wrote:

> It seems that I led the students to the office, but to do so violently could have been contrary to my nature; I was merely enforcing discipline. Next day, I was assaulted from the rear by a body of students. Subhas Chandra Bose was supposed to

have been connected with the affair, although I never had any proof of this. I suffered no injury except for a few bruises, and I bore the assailants no malice and refused to prosecute. [...] I have been privileged in a long life to see India obtain her freedom in 1947. Netaji contributed towards obtaining that freedom, although not everybody approved of his method. I do not regret the fact that in the beginning of his career my name was linked with his. Both of us, each in his own way, helped to make modern India.[1]

Oaten also wrote a poem on Subhas Bose (1947), the first two lines of which read: 'Did I once suffer, Subhas at your hand; Your patriot heart is still'd! I would forget!' Subhas wrote about the incident in his autobiography:

> I had stood up with courage and composure in a crisis and fulfilled my duty. I had developed self-confidence as well as initiative, which was to stand me in good stead in future. I had a foretaste of leadership—though in very restricted sphere— and of the martyrdom that it involves. In short, I had acquired character and could face the future with equanimity.[2]

After his suspension from college, Subhas went to his home in Cuttack and busied himself in doing social work. He had to discontinue his studies for two years. He went back to Calcutta and with the help of Ashutosh Mukherjee, the vice chancellor of the University of Calcutta, he was able to join the Scottish Church College in third year in July 1917. He now took studies quite seriously and passed his bachelor's in philosophy, procuring a first class. Along with studies, he joined the University Training Corps (India's Territorial Army) and received military training in a camp

---

[1]Bose, Sisir Kumar, *Netaji and India's Freedom: Proceedings of the International Netaji Seminar, 1973*, Netaji Research Bureau, Calcutta, 1975, pp. 28–34.
[2]Bose, Subhas Chandra, *An Indian Pilgrim: An Unfinished Autobiography*, Oxford University Press, 1997, p. 80.

near Fort William, where the students received training like drilling with rifles for four months. This brief military training was very helpful for him while organizing the INA.

At the suggestion of his father and elder brother Sarat (for whom he had great respect and affection), Subhas left for England in September 1919 to appear in the ICS examination. He joined Cambridge University to prepare for the examination but only studied there for eight months. He must have worked hard because his name was fourth on the result list. While undergoing his probationary training, he started having second thoughts about becoming an ICS officer. He wanted to serve the motherland in a different capacity, working towards her freedom and not as a bureaucrat. He wrote to his father and elder brother, explaining the reasons why he wanted to resign from the ICS. He also wrote a letter to C.R. Das, the most important Congress leader in Bengal, on 16 February 1921. Subhas wrote, 'I would like to know what work you may be able to allot to me in this great programme of national service.' In the letter, Subhas also suggested what type of work he would be able to do as well as the ways to reorganize the Congress. On receiving an encouraging reply from C.R. Das, his mind was made up. He resigned from the ICS and left for India.

On reaching Bombay on 16 July 1921, he met Mahatma Gandhi and had discussions with him about his programme of achieving swaraj in one year. The replies which Gandhi gave to his searching questions did not satisfy Subhas. As already decided through correspondence, Subhas met C.R. Das in Calcutta and at once found the political guide he was pining for. At Das's suggestion, Subhas joined the Congress party—he became the principal of the Calcutta National College started by the Congress; he also became the publicity officer of the Bengal Provincial Congress Committee and the captain of the National Volunteer Corps. When the prince of Wales visited India in November 1921, the Congress high command decided to boycott the visit. Subhas Bose was put in charge of the campaign. The government arrested thousands of volunteers including C.R. Das and Subhas in December. This was Subhas' first imprisonment, 10 were yet to follow. C.R. Das and Subhas were imprisoned for six months. Much of their imprisonment period was spent together, bringing the guru and his *shishya* (disciple) even closer. They had plenty of time to discuss the national problems and the strategy which the Congress should adopt. Then came the most disturbing news—Gandhi had withdrawn the Non-cooperation Movement in February 1922. Non-cooperation had failed. An alternative strategy had to be evolved.

C.R. Das proposed, supported by Motilal Nehru, that they should enter the legislatures and wreck the government from within. When the no-changers (the ardent followers of Gandhi) did not agree, C.R. Das resigned from the Congress and formed the Swaraj Party. They fought the 1924 elections under the newly formed party and won a thumping victory in the Central legislature as well as in the states. C.R. Das was elected mayor of Calcutta and Subhas Bose was elected chief executive officer for the Calcutta Municipal Corporation in March 1924 at the age of 27. Both of them worked hard to provide better civic facilities for the people of Calcutta. But Bengal was once again in the grip of terrorism. Swarajists were suspected for abetting terrorism. Subhas was arrested in October 1924 under the Emergency ordinance. For two months, he performed his municipal duties in Alipore jail; then in January 1925, he was moved to Mandalay, the prison in which Lajpat Rai and Bal Gangadhar Tilak had spent their sentences earlier. The rigours of prison life affected his health. The government offered to release him on condition that he should go to Europe without entering India. He contemptuously rejected the offer. 'I am not a shopkeeper, I do not bargain,' he said. He was released unconditionally on 16 May 1927, on grounds of ill-health. He had spent two years in Mandalay jail. By that time, C.R. Das had died in June 1925. It was a cataclysmic loss for Subhas as he had never been on his own before.

But during the two years of contemplation in prison, he had

matured and came to be regarded by the masses as the natural leader of Bengal. He was elected chairman of the Bengal Provincial Congress Committee soon after. His health improved and he actively took part in political developments again. He became the general secretary of the Congress along with Jawaharlal Nehru. When the Motilal Nehru Report on the proposed constitution of India was released, both Bose and Nehru protested against the acceptance of dominion status under the British. They wanted *purna swaraj* (complete independence). Subhas toured the whole country explaining the need for purna swaraj to the masses. 'His eloquence became more practised, his rhetoric more skilful, his stature as a leader greater and more widely accepted.' The Congress fell in line with his thinking, when during the Lahore session in 1929, under the presidentship of Nehru, it was declared that complete independence was the Congress's goal.

Once again, a full-scale Civil Disobedience Movement commenced in 1930 and Subhas was arrested on 23 January, his birthday. When he emerged from prison on 25 September 1930, he was elected the mayor of Calcutta. The following year, he was elected chairman of All India Trade Union Congress (AITUC). As a result of the Gandhi–Irwin Pact, the Civil Disobedience Movement was suspended in March 1931. After Gandhi returned from the Second Round Table Conference on 28 December 1931, Civil Disobedience was resumed on 1 January 1932 and Subhas was once again arrested on the next day, along with other Congress leaders.

But by the end of 1932, he was gravely ill and he was released on 22 February 1933, 'on the condition that he would go to Europe for treatment'. He was suffering from tuberculosis and this time went to Europe. He was admitted to Dr Furth's sanitorium in Vienna. There he met Vithalbhai Patel (elder brother of Sardar Patel). They enjoyed each other's company and discussed political developments in India. They were stunned when Gandhi suspended the Civil Disobedience Movement on 8 May 1933, calling it an act of 'abject surrender'. They issued this famous joint manifesto on 9 May 1933: 'We are clearly of opinion that as a political leader Mahatma Gandhi has failed. The time has therefore come for a radical reorganization of the Congress on a new principle and with a new method. For bringing about this reorganization a change of leadership is necessary.' Vithalbhai died on 22 October 1933 in a sanitorium near Geneva, with Subhas by his side. Vithalbhai shared Subhas's view that it was impossible for India to achieve independence without foreign help. For that, systematic propaganda was necessary. Vithalbhai left a ₹100,000 to organize such propaganda in Europe and England, making Subhas the trustee of the money. However, Subhas did not get the money due to legal wrangling in a Bombay court. Subhas spent the next two years in Europe, visiting several countries, addressing select audiences and meeting important persons including Hitler and explaining India's case to the world.[3]

He returned to India on 8 April 1936 and was immediately arrested but released on 17 March 1937. During Gandhi's visit to Calcutta, Subhas conferred with him and agreed to be president of the 1938 session of the INC. Hugh Toye has spoken of Bose saying,

> Bose, now was a man of more than national stature. Abroad he ranked after Gandhi and Jawaharlal Nehru as an Indian politician. Within India, his personality had proved to many the most attractive of the three. In some places his reputation rivalled that of Gandhi himself, and his nomination as president of the Congress at the early age of forty-one was without doubt an attempt by the Mahatma to consolidate with the orthodox Congress, those considerable left-wing elements in Bengal and elsewhere, which actually preferred Bose's leadership.[4]

---

[3]Mookerjee, Girija K., *Subhas Chandra Bose,* Publications Division, New Delhi, 1975, p. 107.
[4]Toye, Hugh, *The Springing Tiger: A Study of Subhas Chandra Bose,* Jaico Publishing House, 2001, p. 43.

To Gandhi's chagrin, Subhas did not tow Gandhi's line of thinking as the president of the Congress. In his presidential address at Haripura, he did not attack Gandhi but his socialistic thinking was quite evident. He talked of the need for industrial revolution and the need for a national reconstruction programme through the National Planning Committee. Against the advice of Gandhi, Subhas wanted to be the president second time. Gandhi put Bhogaraju Pattabhi Sitaramayya up against him. The election ensued and Bose won by 1580 to 1375 votes. Gandhi felt humiliated and declared that 'it was his own defeat'. When the Congress met at Tripura (1939), Subhas was too ill to participate actively in the proceedings. Following the instance of Gandhi, the entire Congress Working Committee (CWC) resigned, leaving only Subhas and his brother Sarat in the Committee. Subhas as president could have nominated the members of the Working Committee but he did not. He tried a compromise and pleaded with Gandhi, meeting with him personally and through correspondence. But Gandhi was adamant. Bose was left with no choice but to resign, and so he formed a new party, the Forward Bloc, which had to work within the Congress fold.

In September 1939, the Second World War broke out and Subhas wanted the Congress to make the best of this opportunity to start a movement to oust the British. When the Congress wavered, the Forward Bloc, under his leadership, launched a bitter anti-British propaganda campaign without the approval of the Congress high command. He and his brother Sarat Chandra were expelled from the Congress for three years. He was arrested for his anti-government stance in July 1940, along with hundreds of his followers. He was released in November and interned in his house, guarded by police and the Crime Investigation Department (CID). He did not leave his room for 40 days. But one day, in the third week of January 1941, he disappeared in the guise of a Muslim priest and appeared in Germany in April 1941, after making a hazardous journey through Afghanistan and Russia. This is one of most daring and romantic episodes, of not only Indian history but that of the world. His presence in Germany was kept secret but he started broadcasting anti-British propaganda from a secret radio station from Rome and Germany under the name 'Azad Hind Radio'. After nine months, Free India Centres were established at Rome and Paris in 1941 as anti-British centres. Many Indians in Europe started cooperating with Bose in this venture and started calling him *Netaji* (leader) and saluting him with the slogan 'Jai Hind'. Subhas also raised the military unit of Indian Legion of a regimental strength, comprising Indian prisoners of war brought from North African camps for the purpose. But Bose was not sure how to use the Indian legion to oust the British from India. From the beginning, Italians were more sympathetic towards Bose than the Germans. Bose had an interview with Adolf Hitler on 29 May 1942. The views expressed by Hitler were not very encouraging. Hitler said, 'India was endlessly remote from Germany. The real route to India would have to be over Russia's dead body.' Bose was very sceptical about this 'route'.

While Bose was still pondering over what to do in Europe, news came that the Japanese had attacked the US naval base at Pearl Harbor in December 1941 and had run through the British possessions in Southeast Asia. Since that area was much nearer to India than Europe and had many more Indian prisoners of war, the number of Indians living there was also much larger. Moreover, Rash Behari Bose had already been working in Japan and Asia for India's freedom under the banner of IIL. General Mohan Singh and others had also formed the INA, which was later taken over by Rash Behari Bose. A conference was held in Bangkok in June 1942, presided over by Rash Behari, in which delegates from several Asian countries participated. One of the resolutions passed in the conference was to invite Subhas Chandra Bose to East Asia. On receiving the message, Subhas decided to leave Europe. A U-Boat (submarine) was arranged by the Germans for the purpose. Subhas left Germany with Abid Hasan Safrani on 8 February 1942. They arrived in Tokyo on 13 June 1943 and reached Singapore on 2 July 1943. He was received enthusiastically by an immense surging crowd. On 4 July, Rash Behari Bose handed over the leadership of the IIL and its armed wing, INA, to the younger Bose. Subhas went on a whirlwind tour of several countries in the region and was received with warmth and expectation everywhere. Satisfied, he proclaimed Provisional Government of Free India in the Town Hall of Singapore on 21 October 1943 and took the salute of 20,000 INA soldiers recruited from the Indian Prisoners of War. Several departments of the new government were created, headed by trusted followers. INA men were given proper training. A march towards India, along with Japanese forces, commenced. Subhas shifted his headquarters from Singapore to Rangoon (now Yangon) in January 1944, with Burma (now Myanmar) sharing a border with India. Subhas set foot on Andaman and Nicobar Islands, the first free Indian territory which was handed over by the Japanese to the INA. The INA opened campaign on the Arakan Front on 4 February 1944. On 18 March, they crossed over to Indian soil and reached the plains of Imphal and were in the neighbourhood of Kohima but had to retreat. The US air forces helped the British army, which now had superior arms. Worst still, the monsoon had submerged the supply line of INA. Hundreds of INA soldiers died from hunger, disease and wounds. Japanese forces were on the run too. The British had reoccupied country after country, starting with Burma. With the dropping of atom bombs on Hiroshima and Nagasaki, Japan surrendered on 15 August 1945. All was over. But there can be little doubt that the INA—not in its unhappy career on the battlefield but in its thunderous disintegration—hastened the end of the British rule in India, thus the bringing Subhas's life's struggle and sacrifices to fruition.

Subhas, along with Colonel Habib ur Rahman, left Saigon for Tokyo on 17 August 1945. On 22 August, Tokyo Radio announced the death of Subhas Chandra Bose in an air crash over Formosa. Indians have consistently refused to believe that Subhas died in an air crash. Three enquiry commissions appointed by the GOI have not been able to solve the mystery of his death. His ashes are kept at Renkō-ji Temple in Tokyo, but the GOI is reluctant to bring these ashes to India because millions of Indians believe they are not real. Recent research has revealed that Subhas was alive at least till 1946.

While in Europe, Subhas had written to his brother that he had married a German girl, Emilie Schenkl. Subhas had known Emilie since 1934, when she served as his secretary and had helped him in writing his autobiography. Formal records of his marriage do not exist, but Bose's biographer, Hugh Toye, wrote that Emilie had 'secretly' become his wife. In September 1942, she delivered a baby girl, Anita, who later visited India and was received with love and affection. But at that time, this relationship with Emilie had caused Subhas much mental stress because his high moral reputation was at stake—he had vowed to be a celibate till India got her freedom.[5]

Thousands of INA men were taken prisoner by the British after the surrender of Japan. Some were executed in Rangoon and Bangkok; thousands of others were brought to India to be tried 'for waging war against the Crown'. But the whole nation stood up to cheer them as freedom fighters who staggered the British bureaucracy and the army. Many leading lawyers in the Congress offered their services to defend the INA men during their trial in the Red Fort, Nehru among them—the same Nehru who had said in April 1942: 'I shall fight Subhas Bose and his party along with Japan if he comes to India. Such are the compulsions of politics. The fact is that the attitude of the Congress both towards Bose and the INA has been lukewarm throughout. It was not anxious to publicize their exploits. After all, Bose and the INA actually fought for India's freedom while the Congress leaders had merely gone to

---

[5]Ibid. 77.

jail.[6] In spite of the attitude of the Congress, Subhas stands apart from the other martyrs of the freedom struggle. He has become a national hero and legends have been woven around him.

---

[6]Edwards, Michael, *Nehru: A Political Biography*, Vikas Publishing House, 1971, p. 162.

16

Syed Ahmad Barelvi

(1786–1831)

Syed Ahmad Barelvi was the founder of the Wahhabi Movement in India. Wahhabism had started in Arabia by the efforts of Arabian scholar, Muhammad ibn 'Abd al-Wahhab (1703–92). Wahhab aimed at restoring Islam to the exact form it had in the days of the Prophet, rejecting the impurities which had crept among his followers. In India, the source of inspiration for Syed Ahmad Barelvi was Shah Waliullah (1704–62) who wanted to re-establish the Muslim rule in India with the help of Muslim rulers, like the nizam of Hyderabad and Afghan ruler Ahmad Shah Abdali. In 1761, Abdali had invaded India, defeated the Marathas at Panipat, killed and looted at will but soon left for Afghanistan, without strengthening the tottering Mughal Empire, to the chagrin of Walliullah, who died soon after.

Learning from this experience, Syed Ahmad had come to believe that Muslims in India must take upon themselves the amelioration of their condition which was only getting worse after the death of Aurangzeb. A greater part of the country had come under the control of Marathas, Sikhs, Rajputs and Jats. The Mughal ruler was reduced to a destitute, titular head. When Lord Lake entered Delhi in 1803, he was shown a miserable blind old imbecile, sitting under a tattered canopy. It was Shah Alam II 'King of the World', but captive of the Marathas, a wretched travesty of the Emperor of

India.[1] Such was the condition to which the great Mughal Empire had been reduced. With the change of rulers, Muslims had lost all the privileges which were bestowed upon them by the Mughal emperors. Syed Ahmad believed that Muslims must get organized to fight the 'infidel' rulers, to bring back the 'glory of Islam' to India again.

Ahmad was born in Raibareilly (now Raebareli) in Uttar Pradesh in 1786. He studied in a school in Delhi, run by Shah Abdul Aziz, son of Shah Walliullah. His teacher had already issued a *fatwa* (a nonbinding legal opinion) declaring India as a '*dar-ul-harb* (enemy country)' and no more a '*dar-ul-Islam*' as it was ruled by non-Muslims. Abdul Aziz had begun to organize militant centres in north western provinces (present Uttar Pradesh) and Bihar for the purpose of launching *jihad* (a fight against the enemies of Islam). He selected Ahmad as his principal *jihadi*. To learn the art of warfare, Ahmad joined the army of Amir Khan, a Pathan Pindari leader in 1809 in Rajasthan. His military training was cut short in 1817 when the Pathan leader submitted to the British. Ahmad was back in Delhi. Shah Abdul Aziz then declared Ahmad as his successor, handing over his white robe and black turban to him as a ritual of succession. He also deputed two of his own relatives, Shah Abdul Hai and Shah Ismail, to render all possible help and to work under Ahmad's guidance.[2]

Thereafter, Ahmad started in earnest the work of organizing volunteers for jihad and preaching to remove the evils which had crept in the Muslim society. He asked Muslims to shun Hindus and to not adopt their manners in dress and eating; to not join in their festivities like Holi and Diwali; to shun idolatry by not worshipping at *mazars* (Muslim shrines) or venerating *pirs* (Sufi spiritual guides) and not visit any other places unsanctified by Islam

---

[1]Lane-Poole, Stanley, *Aurangzeb and the Decay of the Mughal Empire*, Low Price Publications, Delhi, 1990, p. 206.
[2]Banerjee, A.C., *Two Nations: The Philosophy of Muslim Nationalism*, Concept Publishing Company, New Delhi, 1981, p. 58.

and its Prophet. He was worried that Indian Muslims were losing their identity. For the first time, Islam was defensive in India. In Uttar Pradesh and Bihar, Ahmad started enrolling volunteers for jihad and collecting funds for the purpose. After reaching Calcutta, Ahmad left for Mecca in 1821. At the holy city, he came in contact with the Wahhabis and his ideas about social reform and political struggle got crystallized. He was now convinced that it was only by overthrowing the non-Muslim rule that the reformed faith could be enforced along the lines of Arabia. Thus, the immediate task before the Wahhabis was the conversion of India from a 'dar-ul-harb' into a 'dar-ul-Islam'.

On his return journey, Ahmad landed in Bombay in October 1823 and proceeded to Delhi with the same fanfare as his earlier journey from Delhi to Calcutta. Wherever he went, he continued enrolling volunteers and the number of volunteers continued to grow. His followers started weaving several myths around him and carried on vigorous propaganda among Muslims to prepare themselves for 'jihad'. Even some Muslim rulers, like the nawab of Tonk, became his followers. The sight of such devoted following who had taken an oath of allegiance to him emboldened Ahmad. With 8,000 armed followers, he proceeded via Gwalior, Tonk, the desert of Rajasthan, Sindh, Baluchistan, Kandahar, Ghazni and Kabul, reaching Peshawar in November of the same year. This circuitous route was apparently chosen to avoid passage through Sikh territory. He established his headquarters at Sittana, near Peshawar. He appealed to the Pathan tribes to join him, and many of them did, giving further strength to his jihadi army. The selection of this region to start jihad against the infidel rulers was an astute one. The area was populated almost exclusively by Muslims, who resented the authority of the Sikh rule. It was not accessible to large armies as the barren hills stood as an excellent barrier against outsiders.

Under the Islamic law, the election of a Khalifa was necessary to provide a leader to direct the jihad. There was no difficulty in Ahmad getting elected as Khalifa by his followers. The news of his election and an explanation of this measure were communicated to the Muslims in different parts of India through circular letters. Coins were minted bearing the legend 'Ahmad the Just, the Defender of the Faith, the Glitter of whose Scimitar Scatters Destruction Among the Infidels', and were put in circulation among his followers.[3] The Khilafat was, however, short-lived. Ranjit Singh, who had annexed Peshawar in 1930, became concerned about the hostile activities of Syed Ahmad and sent his army to contain his activities and ambition. A battle ensued at Balakot in May 1931 and Syed Ahmad and his second-in-command, Muhammad Ismail, were killed. Alexander Gardner, who later became a colonel in the Punjab army and was with the crusaders at the time, gave an account of this skirmish in the following words:

> Syed Ahmed and the Maulvi (Abdul Haye), surrounded by his surviving Indian followers, were fighting desperately hand to hand with the equally fanatical Akalis of the Sikh army. They had been taken by surprise and isolated from the main body of the Syed's forces, which fought very badly without their leader. Even as I caught sight of the Syed and Maulvi, they fell pierced by a hundred weapons. Those around them were slain to a man, and the main body dispersed in every direction…I was literally a few hundred yards of the Syed when he fell, but I did not see the angel descend and carry him off to paradise, although many of his followers remembered afterwards that they had seen it distinctly enough.[4]

But this was not the end of Wahhabism. Ahmad's followers continued jihad for another four decades. 'Syed Ahmad had set-up a regular organization. He had appointed a number of "*Khalifas*" or spiritual viceregents, who not only kept alive the movement after

[3]Nagarkar, V.V., *Genesis of Pakistan*, Allied Publishers, New Delhi, 1975, p. 20.
[4]Gardner, Alexander, *Soldier and Traveller: Memoirs of Alexander Gardner*, William Blackwood and Sons, 1898, pp. 171–72.

the death of their leader, but even made it more vigorous within a short time. Taking advantage of the political chaos in Punjab after the death of Ranjit Singh in 1939, the Wahhabis established their authority over a large tract of territory along the left bank of Sindhu (Indus).[5] When Punjab was annexed by Lord Dalhousie in 1849, the problem of Wahhabis was transferred from the Sikhs to the British. Thereafter, the Sittana camp was a source of chronic anxiety for the British for two decades. Up to the late 1860s, several expeditions, involving thousands of regular troops, were made to NWFP to destroy the rebels but without much success. Then, the British government changed their strategy. Instead of fighting the rebels in their stronghold situated in a difficult terrain, they started taking action against the ring leaders, who were sending money to Sittana, in Bihar, present-day Uttar Pradesh and at other places. Thousands of them were imprisoned and the Wahhabi Movement died down in the early 1870s.

The importance of the Wahhabi Movement lies in the fact that it created a permanent schism between Hindus and Muslims and did not allow the composite culture to develop. The seeds of two-nation theory were thus sown. It is rather surprising that the Wahhabis did not take part in the 1857 uprising and remained completely aloof from it though both the revolts were directed against the British. The only explanation could be that the Wahhabis wanted a purely Islamic uprising and did not want to join the one which comprised Hindus. At the same time, it cannot be denied that the Wahhabi jihad against the infidels was much better planned and organized than the outbreak of 1857, which was disjointed, without effective coordination and leadership. The Wahhabis created a highly developed organization to which there is no parallel in the history of the revolutionary movements against the British during the nineteenth century. Some historians argue that it was

[5]Majumdar, R.C., *History of the Freedom Movement in India,* Firma KLM, Calcutta, 1971, p. 247.

the Wahhabis that waged the first war of independence in India and the credit for that goes mainly to Syed Ahmad Barelvi.

It is interesting to note the reaction of Sir Syed Ahmad Khan, who was trying to construct a bridge between Indian Muslims and the British rulers, to this anti-British movement by Muslims. He was afraid that his efforts towards reconciliation would suffer due to the jihad undertaken by the Wahhabis. As in the case of the 1857 uprising (which was considered by the British as a rebellion mainly inspired by the Muslims), Syed Ahmad Khan tried to contain the damage to the Muslim cause by declaring that the Wahhabi Movement was the work of some misguided youth and it was not really based on true Wahhabism. In a letter to *The Pioneer* (14 April 1871), he wrote, 'Wahhabism, as exemplified by certain misguided men in India, is not Wahhabism at all; and those who are really guilty of conspiring against Government are not acting upon the principles of their religious tenets.'[6] Syed Ahmad's views on Wahhabism were expressed in greater detail in articles published in *The Pioneer*, while reviewing W.W. Hunter's *Indian Musalmans* (1871), in which Hunter had concluded that Wahhabism was a rebellion against the British government as Wahhabis considered them as an infidel government. Due to the efforts of Syed Ahmad and others, the hostility generated by the Wahhabi Movement and the 1857 uprising was gradually neutralized. Muslims became the favoured community, especially after the formation of INC.

---

[6]Malik, Hafeez, *Political Profile of Sir Sayyid Ahmad Khan: A Documentary Record*, Adam Publishers and Distributors, Delhi, 1933, p. 310.

17

Bhikaiji Rustom Cama

(1861–1936)

Among the Parsi national leaders, Bhikaiji Rustom Cama was the only one who sided with the revolutionaries. She took active part in propagating their cause, supplied revolutionary literature and arms and acted as a mother figure to them for 35 years while living in self-exile in England and France.

Bhikaiji Cama was born on 24 September 1861 in Bombay in a wealthy Parsi family. She was one of the nine children of Sohrabji Framji Patel and Jaijibai Sorabji Patel. Not much is known about this affluent family of Bombay besides the fact that one daughter of the family was the first woman revolutionary to fight for India's freedom. She was educated at Alexandra Girls' English Institution in Bombay and later learnt to speak several Indian and foreign languages, including French.

She was married on 3 August 1885, to Rustom Cama, a barrister belonging to one of Bombay's prominent Parsi families. He was the son of K.R. Cama, a scholar and an illustrious Orientalist. The same year, the INC was formed in Bombay and a new spirit of political consciousness swept the country and Bhikaiji could not remain unaffected. She was 24 years old and had developed a strong independent mind. She started doing social work during the plague epidemic of 1896 in Bombay, nursing sick patients in hospitals, which was an unusual job for a lady from a respectable affluent family in those times. The treatment received by Indians at the hands of some British officials during the plague epidemic created anti-British feelings in her and she decided to work for the country's freedom. Her husband did not share her views nor was he supportive of her activities. Bhikaiji was a lady of strong character and she did not yield to her husband's protestations. The schism between the two kept on widening, which resulted in a separation in 1901. In 1902, she left for London for medical treatment. As her father had created a trust for his eight daughters, she was not short of funds. Her mother had also given her ample jewellery as her share of the wealth. She lived frugally while in Europe and spent a major part of her money for the nationalist cause. She did not return to India after the surgery which she had to undergo in London. She met Dadabhai Naoroji in London and worked with him for some time for the INC. But soon, she moved away from Dadabhai's moderate politics and was attracted towards more militant and revolutionary ideas. She was so excited to work as a revolutionary for the country that she decided to stay on in England.

In 1905, Shyamji Krishna Varma, a nationalist who was in England for some time, opened the India House, which became the headquarters of the revolutionaries in London, and the abode of famous revolutionaries like Sardar Singh Rana, Veer Savarkar, Har Dayal, Virendranath Chattopadhyaya and others. It was also in 1905 that these revolutionaries formed the Indian Home Rule Society (modelled on the Irish Home Rule League). Shyamji also started *The Indian Sociologist*, an English monthly, which became the mouthpiece of revolutionary propaganda. Bhikaiji regularly wrote for it. She also addressed meetings at Hyde Park in London, explaining the need for freeing India from foreign domination. Though India House was founded by Shyamji, Savarkar had become the undisputed leader of the group and Cama was very much impressed with his dedication as a patriot and by his intellectual brilliance. Savarkar had written a book called *The History of the War of Indian Independence* (1857), and Bhikaiji helped translate it into French, as the book was banned in India. Savarkar was 22 years younger than Bhikaiji and she played the part of a mother figure for Savarkar, trying to help him in all ways possible.

The year 1907 was a memorable one for her and India when in August she, along with S.S. Rana, was invited to attend the International Socialist Congress in Stuttgart (Germany). There were about 100 delegates from several countries of Europe, Asia, Americas and Africa. In a brief but stirring speech, she talked about conditions in India. She began: 'Friends, Comrades and Socialists, I have come here to speak for the dumb millions of *Hindustan*, who are going through terrible tyranny under the English capitalists and the British government.' At the end of the speech, she dramatically unfurled the Indian flag. It was a tricolour with green, yellow and red with 'Bande Mataram' written on the middle band. It also had eight stars representing the eight provinces. It was precursor to the national flag of free India, and was designed jointly by Bhikaiji and Savarkar. This flag became a permanent companion of Bhikaiji; she always carried it in her suitcase and used to unfurl it after her speeches. It is now displayed in the Library Hall of the *Kesari* and the *Mahratta* in Pune.

Soon after the International Socialist Congress, she made a very successful tour of the US. She visited several cities, addressing meetings and small gatherings, explaining the British oppression and the causes of India's poverty. Though not a powerful speaker, her sincerity and passion for India's cause impressed all. Like Annie Besant, Bhikaiji was also proud of India's cultural heritage and always highlighted the glorious past of India. 'People of India have culture,' she would say, 'the poorest peasants had stored in their memories, all the spiritual truths of the *Mahabharata* and the *Ramayana*.' Her visit to the US was a great success and became a media event there. She returned to Europe in October 1908 to meet Bipin Chandra Pal. The texts of her speeches were in great demand. In one of her famous speeches, which were later printed and circulated as a pamphlet titled *Bande Matram*, she said:

Friends let us put aside all hindrances, doubts, and fears. In Mazzini's words, I appeal to you, "let us stop arguing with people who know our arguments by heart and do not heed them." If our people appear degraded, it is an added reason to endeavour at all risks to make them better. A handful of foreigners, a few Englishmen, have declared war on us. Who can wonder if we millions accept challenge and declare war on them? The price of Liberty must be paid. Which nation has got it without paying for it? [...] We want back our own country. No English oak is wanted in India. We have our own noble banyan tree and our beautiful lotus flowers. We do not want to imitate British civilization; we will have our own which is higher and nobler.[1]

Her activities were being watched by the British government and they banned entry of her post and other material sent by her into India. But such restrictions did not deter her from sending revolutionary literature, arms and explosives, which were being sent through Pondicherry, a French enclave. In this, other revolutionaries like Savarkar and Rana were cooperating with her. Bhikaiji and Shyamji were said to have been named in the British Intelligence Department reports to be financing the revolutionary movement in India. They suspected that both of them would be deported to India. Before that could be done, both Bhikaiji and Shyamji moved to Paris in 1909 to thwart the British move to deport them. Bhikaiji lived in Paris for many years. Her residence, which came to be called Paris India House, became a meeting place for the revolutionaries and she did everything in her power to help them. She started a paper, *Bande Mataram,* from Paris in September 1909 with Lala Har Dyal as editor. This monthly paper appeared for nine years without a break. Through this paper, she carried on her attack on British imperialism. *Madan's Talwar,* later known as *The Talvar,* an organ of Indian Independence, was also published

---

[1]Agarwal, Deepa, *Our Leaders*, Children's Book Trust, New Delhi, 1989, p. 56.

by her sometime later, with Virendranath Chattopadhayaya as the editor. This paper joined *Bande Mataram* in its attack on British misrule in India.

In June 1909, Veer Savarkar's brother, Ganesh Damodar Savarkar, was sentenced to transportation for life in the Andamans, on the pretext of writing a provocative poem. In retaliation, A.M.T. Jackson, the collector and district magistrate of Nasik, was assassinated. Veer Savarkar was accused of sending arms to the assassinators and was arrested in London in March 1910 and was ordered to be sent to India. While his ship docked at the French port of Marseilles, Savarkar jumped from the ship and reached ashore. However, he was arrested and sent to India. Bhikaiji did everything in her power to get Savarkar released, spending a good amount of money, but did not succeed. Savarkar, like his brother, was sent to the Andaman cellular jail where he languished for 10 years. Bhikaiji was very upset and used to write to the two brothers while they were in prison. She also used to send money to the Savarkar family regularly.

When the First World War broke out in 1914, Bhikaiji along with Rana, visited those theatres of war where Indian troops were operating, inciting them to lay down arms as it was not their war. When she visited Marseilles on a similar mission, she was interned by the French authorities under British pressure and was kept at Vichy and later at Bordeaux. She was released after three years, when the war was over. Because of her radical views and revolutionary activities, she was repeatedly refused permission to return to India until 1935, when she was 74 and in failing health and severely suffering from facial paralysis. On her return to Bombay, she directly went to Parsi General Hospital, where she died on the 13 August 1936, unsung and unhonoured. Madam Cama certainly deserved better treatment at the hands of her countrymen. She had written her own epitaph: 'He who loses his liberty loses his virtue. Resistance to tyranny is obedience to God.' Her vision of a free India was a republic with Hindi as the common language and Devanagari as the common script. She firmly believed in the idea of 'one nation, one language, one people', though she remained a devout Parsi throughout her life.

Belatedly and reluctantly, she was remembered during her centenary year—1961. A street was named after her in Bombay, and a postage stamp was issued in her honour in 1962, after much haggling. A commercial complex in Delhi has recently been named after her. But not much has been written about her in the annals of the freedom movement of India.

18

William Carey

(1761–1834)

Some Christian missionaries who came to India contributed greatly towards education, journalism, linguistics and allied fields. One such missionary was William Carey.

William was born on 17 August 1761 in Northamptonshire. His father, Edmund Carey, was a school teacher. William was an extremely adventurous boy and loved sports, travel, nature and reading in his spare time. At an early age, he was apprenticed to a shoemaker at Hackleton and soon became a skilful shoemaker himself. As a hobby, he studied languages and became proficient in Greek, Latin and Hebrew, besides some modern European languages. Later in life, learning several Indian and Southeast Asian languages became a passion with him.

He joined the congregation of Baptists in 1783 and he was publicly baptized in the same year. Baptists form a major denomination of Protestants; their faith was founded in the seventeenth century in Holland but soon spread to other countries including England and the US. After his baptism, Carey started taking a greater interest in religion by organizing prayer groups. By 1789, he was put in charge of congregation at Leicester. He was ordained (became a clergyman) in 1791 and helped in forming the Baptist Missionary Society (BMS) at Kettering in 1792. In this society, he came in contact with Dr John Thomas, who had earlier visited India. Carey was greatly influenced by the zeal of this man and decided to come to India for missionary work. The team left for India on a ship on 13 June 1793. Carey was accompanied by his wife, four children and his sister-in-law. They arrived in Calcutta on 13 November 1793. During this five-month journey, Carey had begun studying the Bengali language. Later, he picked up Hindi, Marathi, Sanskrit and Persian—such was his agility in learning languages.

When Carey landed in Calcutta, the officials of East India Company would not allow any missionary work in their territory in the fear of local backlash (this restriction was removed only in 1813). To earn a living and support his family, he had to take up 'secular' jobs. He accepted work as an indigo planter at Madnabati in the Malda district of North Bengal. During their first year in India, his whole family fell ill and his five-year-old son, Peter, died. His wife was very deeply affected by this. He bore these calamities stoically. In 1799, two other missionaries, Joshua Marshman and William Ward, arrived from England and the three of them decided to establish a mission. As it was not possible to start any mission in Calcutta, it being a territory of the East India Company, the trio, along with their families moved to the city of Serampore, a Danish settlement which is about 15 miles upstream from Calcutta, in 1800. Thus, began the famous Serampore Mission started by Carey and his two associates, Marshman and Ward. A 'mission' in Christian parlance refers to 'a body of persons sent by a church to carry on religious work, especially evangelization in foreign lands'.

Carey started translating the Bible in vernacular languages, including the tribal languages. He ended up contributing greatly towards education, healthcare, printing and journalism. While translating the Bible into Indian languages, he had to study grammar, vocabulary and connotation. In the process, he compiled dictionaries and grammars of at least 26 languages. Carey also edited the Ramayana. Carey's knowledge of Indian languages attracted the attention of authorities of the Fort William College in Calcutta, which Lord Wellesley, the the governor-general, founded in 1801 for training officials of the East India Company. Carey was initially appointed professor of Bengali in the College but later Marathi and Sanskrit were also added to his roster. He served this college as professor till 1830 and had to constantly commute between Serampore and Calcutta. While translating the Bible into Indian languages, Carey took the help of several pandits who were working in Fort William College.

Soon after his arrival in Serampore, Carey bought a large house surrounded by an equally large compound near the river. Here, the community which Carey had planned, took shape and as the years rolled by, they undertook an astonishing range of activities. Among his companions, Marshman and his wife, were schoolmasters and William Ward was a printer. Marshman and his wife started a boarding school for Anglo–Indian boys and girls. Soon, they added new schools, where children of local residents could be taught. These were elementary schools and their number increased to 126 by 1818. Subsequently, they felt the need for providing higher education and planned a college 'for the instruction of Asiatic, Christian and other youth in Eastern literature and European sciences'. Their aim was to produce a class of enlightened men, conversant with both the classical literature of India and the best Western learning of the day. From their own resources, they bought land and built the buildings and named it Serampore College. The building was inaugurated in 1818 and classes opened in 1819, with 37 students. Included in the curriculum were Sanskrit, Arabic, Bengali, English, natural sciences and medicine. In the early years, most of the subjects were taught in Bengali. In 1827, the King of Denmark granted the college a charter, empowering it to confer degrees.[1] Serampore College was one of the pioneering colleges in India, teaching modern subjects with theology. In 1910, the arts and science departments were affiliated to the University of Calcutta, leaving the theology

[1]Firth, C.B., *An Introduction to Indian Church History,* Senate of the Serampore College, Serampore, 1976, pp. 153–54.

department to be run by Christian bodies.

The Bible, translated in various languages, was printed in a press (which was the first modern press in North India) and supervised by Carey's companion, Ward. Gradually they got typefaces of many languages designed and cast in their huge foundry—Arabic, Persian, Nagari, Telugu, Punjabi, Marathi, Chinese, Oriya, Burmese, Kanarese (Kannada), Greek, Hebrew and of course, English. The press was housed in a hall, 170 ft long and with scores of people employed. As this was the only press in the area, they undertook printing of secular books and journals from Calcutta and other nearby areas too. It was a self-contained press, having departments for paper and ink making as well as binding. Soon, the Serampore Mission Press became famous and the types produced in this foundry were used throughout the country for years. So were the press-ink and paper. As a result, the press not only became self-supporting but also started earning handsome profits. Many important Bengali, Hindi and English works of the time were printed in this press. During the initial 31 years, the press had printed 212,000 books in 40 different languages.[2] The press helped to spread education and literacy in the country.

The Serampore Mission also contributed towards journalism. In 1818, the trio started two journals, *Samachar Darpan* (a Bengali weekly newspaper, edited by Marshman and his son, which is believed to be the first newspaper printed in any Oriental language) and another English monthly, *The Friends of India*. Both these papers played a valuable part in enlightening the public on social questions and did not contain a lot of religious preaching. The first issue of *The Friends of India* carried an article on sati. The paper continued to bring the horrible custom before the public by reporting actual cases. Some socially conscious officials, many of Carey's former pupils, prohibited the practice in their districts

---

[2]Kesavan, B.S., *History of Printing and Publishing in India*, National Book Trust, New Delhi, 1984, p. 191.

on their own. Even the Governor-General Bentinck was moved and, helped by Hindu social reformers like Raja Ram Mohan Roy, banned sati in the Company territories in 1829 and made it a criminal offence. Along with others, Carey deserves credit for the abolition of this inhuman practice. He is also credited with the abrogation of child sacrifice at Sagar Island in the Ganges. This was done by Lord Wellesley after Carey submitted a report on the practice in the first decade of the nineteenth century. Besides his other activities, Carey was instrumental in founding an asylum for people with leprosy in Calcutta. The care of those suffering from leprosy has been a special field of Christian service and Carey was a pioneering missionary who contributed towards helping those who were shunned by society. Caring for the lepers by Christians goes back to the times of Jesus Christ.

Carey had a lifelong interest in botany and had developed his own botanical garden in Serampore. He was the founder of the Agri–Horticultural Society of Bengal, a purely 'secular' activity. He died on 9 June 1834 in Serampore and was buried in the Serampore College premises. Carey lived in India for 41 years and never visited England during all these years.

19

Bankim Chandra Chattopadhayay

(1838–1894)

Bankim Chandra Chattopadhayay (or Chatterjee) was born on 26 June 1838 in Kanthalpara in Calcutta. His father, Yadav Chandra Chattopadhayay, was in government service and was a deputy collector at the time of Bankim's birth. In fact, it was a family of deputy magistrates and deputy collectors. Bankim's two elder brothers, Shyama and Sanjib, were deputy magistrates. His younger brother, Puma Chandra, also became a deputy collector in due course. Bankim's early education started in 1844 at Midnapore, where his father was posted at the time. His English education began there, under the care of the English headmaster, F. Teed. This good start helped Bankim to master the English language later in life. But his father was transferred from Midnapore and Bankim was sent to Hooghly and he took admission at the New Hooghly College (renamed Hooghly Mohsin College later) in 1849. He was a brilliant student and successfully got through the junior and senior scholarship examinations, in the years 1854 and 1856 respectively. While still a student at the Hooghly College, he participated in and won a cash prize for a poetry competition organized by *Sambad Prabhakar*, a Bengali newspaper founded by Ishwar Chandra Gupta in 1835. In 1856, Bankim joined Presidency College in Calcutta for study law. But in 1858, the University of Calcutta introduced the BA (bachelor of arts) examination. Ten students took the examination in the first batch. Only two passed—Bankim was one of them and he became the first to graduate from the University of Calcutta. His law studies were discontinued as a result, which he completed later in 1869. He studied Sanskrit privately from a pandit as the language was not taught in his college.

Bankim's career as a government servant started immediately after graduation. He was appointed deputy magistrate and deputy collector and was posted at Jessore (now in Bangladesh). He was married at the age of 11 to a five-year-old girl who died while he was serving at Jessore. His second marriage in 1860, to Rajlakshmi Devi, was a long and happy one. They had three daughters.

During his government service that lasted for 33 years, Bankim travelled and worked in 13 districts of the old province of Bengal. Some of these districts are now in Orissa and some in Bangladesh. As an officer, Bankim showed considerable ability and independence. His aristocratic demeanour, strong personality, wide reading and high intellectual attainments left a mark on people everywhere. At the same time, because of his frank and fearless disposition, he often came into conflict with his immediate British superiors like collector Buckland in 1881, Westmacott in 1883 and Baker in 1888. His controversy with the Christian missionary, William Hastie, principal of the General Assemblies Institution (now Scottish Church College), showed his 'undaunted argumentative, combative and debating powers'. By this time, Bankim had written several novels and other works and had become famous. He lost interest in government service and resigned in 1891 at the age of 53, after serving the British government for 33 years. He was awarded the titles of Rai Bahadur (RB) in 1892 and Companion, Order of the Indian Empire (CIE) in 1894.

Bankim's government service did not seem to be a hindrance in his literary exploits as he continued to write and publish books, one after another, and his literary genius flowered as time passed. He started writing in English and his novel, *Rajmohan's Wife*, appeared serially in the *Indian Field*, edited by Kishori Chand Mitra, in 1864. He wrote English with great facility and was a voracious reader of English fiction. He wrote poetry and gradually started writing prose too. He also realized that he could express himself better in his mother tongue, Bengali. This realization was most fortunate for Bengali literature, and his writings mark the dawn of a new era. His first novel in Bengali, *Durgeshnandini,* came out in 1865 and opened up a new vista in Bengali creative literature, though the influence of English romances was clearly discernible in it. His second novel, *Kapalkundla,* published in 1866, describing the tragedy of a girl brought up in the company of a *kapalika* (a person devoted to Lord Shiva) and later married to the way-worn Nabakumar, captured the imagination of the Bengali readers. His third novel, *Mrinalini* (1869), based on the Mihaj-i-Siraj's story of the conquest of Bengal by Muhammad Bakhtiyar Khalji with the help of only 17 horsemen, 'gave the first sign of his patriotism which later developed into militant nationalism'. Novels and other prose works continued in an uninterrupted stream: *Bishabriksha* (1873), *Indira* (1873), *Jugalanguriya* (1874), *Lok Rahasya* (1874), *Chandrasekhar* (1875), *Kamalakanter Daptar* (1875), *Rajani* (1877), *Krishnakanter Will* (1878), *Prabandha Pustak* (1887), *Samya* (1879), *Rajsimha* (1882), *Anandamath* (1882), *Devi Chaudhurani* (1884), *Muchiram Gurer Jibancharit* (1884), *Kamalakanta* (1885), *Radharani* (1886), *Krishna Charitra, Part I* (1886), *Sitaram* (1886), *Bibidha Prabandha, Part I* (1939), *Dharamatattva, Part I* (1988), *Gadya, Padya ba Kabita Pustak* (1891), *Rajsinha* (1893), *Vividha Prabandha, Part II* (1939), *Kabita-Pustak* (1978) and *Devatattva* (published posthumously). As can be seen from the list, Bankim wrote extensively on religious and spiritual themes in the later stages of his life.

Bankim Chandra started a Bengali literary magazine called *Bangadarshan* in 1872 and edited it for four years. Later, in 1877, he handed it over to his brother Sanjib Chandra, who revived it and continued it till March 1883. His novels appeared serially and many of his famous essays on history, sociology, religion, literature and philosophy were first published in this magazine. After the demise of *Bangadarshan*, Bankim sponsored another journal, *Prachar*, in July

1884, with his son-in-law Rakhal Das Banerji in charge. His tracts on Hindu religion like *Dharmatattva-Anushilan, Krishnacharitra* and *Devatattva O Hindu Dharma* were first published in *Prachar*. He also wrote a commentary on the *Bhagavad Gita*, which remained incomplete.

Although in government service, Bankim was a bitter critic of the way the British administration was being carried on, and his caustic and satirical remarks are clearly evident in his writings such as *Bangla Shasaner Kal* and *Muchiram Gurer Jibancharit*. He had deep sympathy for the poor peasants and cursed the Permanent Settlement Act for their poverty in his work *Bangadesher Krishak*.

The greatest contribution of Bankim was to inculcate a sense of nationalism and patriotism among the masses through his novels and essays. He converted patriotism into religion and religion into patriotism. His famous novel *Anandamath* contains the hymn '*Bande*', which became the rallying cry of the patriotic sons of India—thousands of them succumbed to the British police's lathi blows and many mounted the scaffold with 'Bande Mataram' on their lips. The central plot of *Anandamath* revolves around a band of *sanyasis,* called *santanas* or children, who left their hearth and home and dedicated their lives for the cause of the country. The imagery of the Goddess Kali in the novel leaves no doubt that Bankim Chandra's nationalism was Hindu rather than Indian. This is made crystal clear from his other writings which contain passionate outbursts against the subjugation of India by the Muslims. R.C. Majumdar has written about him saying, 'From that day set the sun of our glory—is the refrain of his essays and novels which not unoften contain adverse, and sometimes even irreverent remarks, against the Muslims.'[1]

The hymn 'Bande Mataram' has made Bankim Chandra one of the most remembered writers of any age in India. The All India

―――――――――――――
[1]Majumdar, R.C., *History of the Freedom Movement in India,* Firma KLM, Calcutta, 1988, pp. 302–03.

Radio programme begins in the early morning with the recitation of 'Bande Mataram', which is in easy Sanskrit. It is officially recognized as the national song and has equal status with the national anthem, 'Jana Gana Mana', composed by Rabindranath Tagore. Aurobindo Ghose has spoken of Bankim as follows:

> What is it for which we worship the name of Bankim today, what was his message to us or what the vision which he saw and has helped us to see? He was a great poet, a master of beautiful language and a creator of fair and gracious dream figures in the world of imagination; but it is not as a poet, stylist or novelist that Bengal does honour to him today. It is probable that the literary critic of the future will reckon *Kapalkundala*, *Bishabriksha* (or *The Poison Tree*) and *Krishna Kanta's Will* as Chattopadhyay's artistic masterpieces and speak with qualified praise of *Devi Chaudhurani*, *Ananda Math*, *Krishna Charitra* or *Dharmatattva*. Yet, it is Bankim of these latter works and not the Bankim of the great creative masterpieces, who will rank among the "Makers of Modern India". The earlier Bankim was only a poet and stylist, the later Bankim was a seer and nation builder.[2]

---

[2]Ghose, Aurobindo, *Collected Works,* Sri Aurobindo Ashram Trust, Pondicherry, p. 345.

20

Alexander Cunningham

(1814–1893)

Alexander Cunningham is considered to be the father of Indian archaeology. He made some important and startling discoveries through untiring excavations and the study of coins to fill gaps in the history of India. His successors like John Hubert Marshall and Robert Mortimer Wheeler carried further the work started by him and were able to discover the Indus valley civilization.

Alexander was born on 23 January 1814 in Westminster, London, and was educated at Christ's Hospital and Addiscombe. That was the end of his formal education. He obtained an Indian cadetship at the age of 14, on the recommendation of the famous novelist, Sir Walter Scott. After training, he was appointed as second lieutenant in the engineering division of the Bengal Army, when he came to Calcutta in 1833. There, he came in contact with James Prinsep, an English antiquary, and got interested in the study of Indian numismatics and archaeology. He soon developed proficiency in these subjects and started contributing articles about them in journals. He made time for this hobby even while serving as an engineer in the army.

In the army, he had quite a varied set of assignments. He served as an aide-de-camp (ADC) to Lord Auckland, the governor-general (1836–40). In 1840, he became executive engineer to the nawab of Oudh and was responsible for the construction of a highway from Lucknow to Kanpur. He was on military duty in Central India and was an executive engineer in the Gwalior state from 1844–45. During the first Anglo–Sikh War (1845–46), he was in Punjab on military duty and was responsible for the annexation of the Kullu and the Kangra valley. He was also responsible for demarcation of the boundary between Ladakh and Tibet and also between Bikaner and Bahawalpur states. After the second Anglo–Sikh War (1848–49), he came back to Gwalior as an executive engineer. This was followed by a series of transfers to distant places—Multan (1853), Burma (1856) and the NWFP (1858)—where he served as chief engineer. After he was promoted to the rank of major-general in 1861, he retired from the army. A new and important phase in his life commenced, for which he is remembered and has earned the gratitude of Indians for revealing their past.

However, Alexander did not wait to indulge in his exciting hobby. According to A.L. Basham, 'From his arrival in India in 1831, Cunningham devoted every minute he could spare from his military duties to the study of the material remains of ancient India, until, in 1862, the Indian Government established the post of Archaeological Surveyor, to which he was appointed.'[1] While he was serving as a bodyguard to the governor-general, he found time to come to Banaras, where his preceptor, James Prinsep, had earlier lived for 10 years and had done some excavations, especially of temples turned into mosques. However, Cunningham's area of excavation was Sarnath, about six miles from Banaras. The mystery about the ruins of Sarnath had excited the curiosity of many scholars of Indian history, especially because both Fa-Hien and Hiuen Tsang (Chinese pilgrims) had described a great monastery and a huge *stupa* (pillar) at Sarnath, where the great Buddha delivered his first sermon to his five followers. There had been irregular and half-hearted excavations at this site, but as mentioned by M.A. Sherring,

The most extensive excavations which have been made were affected under the personal superintendence of Major-General

---

[1]Basham, A.L., *The Wonder That Was India*, Rupa Publications, New Delhi, 1981, p. 7.

Cunningham and Major Kittoe, who dug out of the ruins an immense number of statues, bas-reliefs and other curious objects. The former alone, in 1835, found about a hundred statues and bass-reliefs, all of which worth preserving, were sent to the Museum of the Asiatic Society in Calcutta.[2]

Cunningham studied in detail the great stupa, called *Dhamek* (presumably built by Asoka) at Sarnath, even got a 110 ft high scaffold prepared and went up all the way to study the details of the uppermost end of the stupa. He wrote a detailed report of his findings in the *Journal of the Asiatic Society of Bengal* (Vol. XXXII), which remains the most detailed description of it to this day. After Sarnath, he excavated Buddhist mounds at Sanchi in Madhya Pradesh and at other places. He published the reports of these excavations in the *Journal of the Royal Asiatic Society of Great Britain and Ireland* (1850) and later published them in a book, *The Bhilsa Topes: Buddhist Monuments of Central India* (1854). He deciphered the inscriptions on the pillars and railings of the Buddhist ruins and gave their English renderings in the book. During his mission to Ladakh and Tibet in the 1840s, while in military service, he wrote a book on Ladakh which is still useful.

Cunningham made a great deal of contribution in the field of Indian numismatics also and had written several articles on the subject since 1834, in the *Journal of the Asiatic Society*, Calcutta, *Royal Asiatic Society*, London, and in the *Journal of the Numismatic Society*, London. As a result of his study in Indian numismatics, Cunningham declared that coins were in use in India even before the invasion of Alexander (326 BC) and that there was no import of coins from Greece. All these years, this important work in Indian archaeology and numismatics was done by Cunningham as a hobby while he was serving as an engineer in the British army.

In 1846, Cunningham sent a proposal to The Asiatic Society,

---

[2]Sherring, M.A., *Banaras: The Sacred City of the Hindus in Ancient and Modern Times*, Low Price Publications, Delhi, 1990, pp. 235–36.

Calcutta, and later submitted a petition (1860) to Lord Canning, governor-general, for the establishment of a department for a systematic exploration of historical relics spread over a vast area of the country and their proper preservation. Due to his efforts, the Archaeological Survey of India was set up in 1861, with Cunningham as its head (surveyor general). Now he worked full-time, exploring the ruins and analysing and writing in detail about them. For the first time, he visited historical sites in Punjab as well as the river basin in northern India between the rivers, Jamuna and Narmada. The findings of these explorations (1861–65) were published in two volumes, under the title of *The Ancient Geography of India* (London, 1871). In this work, Cunningham had identified all the historical places of India on the basis of Alexander's invasion and the Chinese travellers down to the seventh century AD.

In 1866, Cunningham had to return to England as the Archaeology Department had closed down due to paucity of funds. However, in 1870, the department was revived by Lord Mayo, governor-general, and Cunningham was called back and put in charge of the department. He worked in the department as surveyor general for another 15 years, 1871–85. During this period, he travelled from Taxila in the NWFP to Gour-Pandua in Bengal, in search of historical sites and recorded his findings meticulously. Of course, he was helped by several able assistants. Findings of these visits were published in 24 volumes as the *Archaeological Survey of India Reports*. Of these, Cunningham wrote the first 13 volumes on the basis of his own visits. The remaining 11 volumes were prepared by his assistants under his guidance. In the 13 volumes of his own reports, Cunningham dealt with 500 historical sites and also gives a description of the coins of various periods. An index for all the volumes was prepared by V.A. Smith under the title *General Index to Cunningham's Archaeological Survey Reports* (1887).

It was Cunningham who, during his tours of the Harappa region (1872–73), came across some rare kind of seals, and gave some indication about Harappa in his report of 1875 as being 'a very ancient site and the likely storehouse of rich antiquities'. This must have provided a hint to his eminent successors, John Marshall and Robert Mortimer Wheeler and others, who were able to discover the Indus valley civilization during the 1920s and 1930s.

In 1877, Cunningham collected and compiled all the Ashokan Edicts (inscriptions) and published them, with photographs, in his *Corpus Inscriptionum Indicarum* (Calcutta, 1877). In 1879, he brought out his work *The Stupa of Barhut* (London, 1879). And in 1883, was published his important work, *The Book of Indian Eras* (Calcutta). In 1892, he published his great work *Mahabodhi*; Or the *Great Buddhist Temple under the Bodhi Tree at Buddha-Gaya* (London). It was this work of Cunningham through which the modern world learnt about the glories of Buddha Gaya, Sarnath, Sanchi, Sraasti and Kausambi.[3]

In 1885, Cunningham retired from the Archaeological Survey of India and returned to England. Out of 79 years of his life, Cunningham spent 50 in India, most of the time trying to unravel the hidden secrets of India's past. He donated a large number of historical relics and some old coins he had collected during his stay in India to The National Museum, which included city gate pillars and railings of Barhut and Sanchi. After retirement, he paid a lot of attention to numismatics and carried a large collection of old Indian coins to England. He is considered an eminent authority on numismatics. This collection is now in the British Museum. He was knighted in 1867. He died in South Kensington on 28 November 1893. As G.G. Sengupta has said, 'Though he made no startling discoveries, and though his technique was, by modern standards, crude and primitive, there is no doubt that after Sir William Jones, Indology owes more to General Sir Alexander Cunningham than to any other worker in the field.'[4]

---

[3]Sengupta, G.G., *Indology and its Eminent Savants: Collections of Biographies of Western Indologists,* Pundhi, Calcutta, 1966, p. 80.
[4]Ibid.

21

Chittaranjan Das

(1870–1925)

Chittaranjan Das was born on 5 November 1870 in Calcutta. He was the eldest son and the second child of Bhuban Mohan Das and Nistarini Devi. His father was a solicitor of the Calcutta High Court with a handsome income. Bhuban Mohan Das was a strong supporter of the Brahmo Samaj and edited the monthly *Brahmo Public Opinion* (later changed to *Bengal Public Opinion*) and also authored some books. He was of a very generous disposition and could not help spending money on the poor and the distressed. In the process, he incurred debt which he could not clear and was declared insolvent by the court. His son, Chittaranjan had to clear this debt later in life.

Chittaranjan received his early education in the London Missionary Society's Institution at Bhawanipur and passed the entrance examination in 1885 as a private candidate. He graduated from Presidency College in 1890. He left for England to study law and to sit for the ICS examination in the same year but he missed clearing it by a narrow margin. He had joined The Honourable Society of the Inner Temple at London and was called to the Bar in 1894. After his return to India, he started practicing as a barrister in the Calcutta High Court. However, when he was still trying to establish himself at the Bar, he was pressured by his father's creditors to clear the debt. When he could not redeem the liability, he too was declared insolvent.

In 1897, Chittaranjan married to Basanti Devi at the age of

17 and led a happy married life. The couple had two daughters (Aparna and Kalyani) and a son (Chiraranjan).

Before he was involved in law (and later politics), Chittaranjan's genius revealed itself in poetry and literature. He inherited the literary trait from his father and was also inspired by Bankim Chandra Chattopadhayay. His first literary work was *Malancha* (1895), a poetry collection, followed by *Mala,* another poetry anthology, published in 1902, *Sagar-Sangeet* in 1911, *Antaryami* in 1914 and *Kishor-Kishori* in 1915. Some of these verses were rendered into English by Chittaranjan himself, with the help of Aurobindo Ghose. In 1914, Chittaranjan started a literary journal, *Narayan,* with which were associated a number of eminent literary persons. He kept in constant touch with important literary organizations and people in the country, including Rabindranath Tagore and Bankim Chandra Chattopadhayay. He presided over the Bengal Literary Conference in 1915. He was one of the founders and a member of the editorial board of *Bande Mataram,* an English newspaper started by Bipin Chandra Pal.

Like many other leaders, Chittaranjan took part in the Swadeshi Movement started after the partition of Bengal put into effect by Lord Curzon in 1905. He also became a member of the Anushilan Samiti, a secret society working under the guidance of Sri Aurobindo Ghose, Sister Nivedita, Pramathanath Mitra and Jatindernath Banerjee.

As a lawyer, success came gradually. The turning point in Chittaranjan's legal career came when he was called upon to defend Sri Aurobindo in the famous Alipore bomb case in which Aurobindo was implicated for waging war against the King. This was a historic case during the freedom movement and Chittaranjan encountered all obstacles with courage and established himself as a barrister par excellence. His elocution originated as if from a divine essence, his vast learning, wisdom and foresight were amply vivid in the concluding remarks of his arguments:

> Long after this turmoil, this agitation ceases, long after he is
> dead and gone, he will be looked upon as a poet of patriotism,

as the prophet of nationalism, and the lover of humanity. Long after he is dead and gone, his words will be echoed and re-echoed not only in India but across the distant seas and lands. Therefore, I say that the man in his position is not only standing before the Bar of this court but before the Bar of the High Court of history.[1]

Never had such eloquence been displayed in Indian courts. It has become a classic and has been repeatedly quoted. Das pleaded for eight days, and Aurobindo was acquitted by the Court of Appeal in May 1909. This elevated Das to the rank of a legal luminary and paved the way for a roaring practice. Success followed success and he served as a counsel on many sensational cases, even outside Bengal, including the Dumraon Adoption Case in 1910. Consequently, he built up a large and lucrative practice and started living like a prince. In 1913, he followed the unusual procedure of applying for the annulment of the insolvency order and cleared his father's and his debts. This is only one of the instances of the magnanimity and large-heartedness which he showed during his life. Some of his other conspicuous court cases were those of revolutionaries and freedom fighters—Manicktala bomb case, Decca Conspiracy Case and the Delhi Conspiracy Case. He did not charge any fee in pleading these cases. He would even bear the travelling and other expenses while going to plead for such cases.

His entry in active politics began in 1917, when he presided over the Bengal Provincial Conference held in April of that year in Calcutta. Soon, Das became the leader of the Extremist group of the Congress in Bengal. When the Montagu–Chelmsford Reforms were announced in August 1917, the Moderates hailed the reforms and wanted to give them a trial but the Extremists opposed this. At both the Special Congress session (Bombay, August 1918) and All India Congress Committee (AICC) session (Delhi, December 1918), Chittaranjan took the lead in moving the resolution, denouncing

[1]Agarwala, B.R., *Trials of Independence*, National Book Trust, New Delhi, 1991, p. 69.

the reforms as 'inadequate, unsatisfactory and disappointing', demanding full provincial autonomy instead. In the autumn of 1919, Das went to Punjab as a member of the enquiry committee appointed by the Congress to investigate into the Jallianwala Bagh tragedy and the working of martial law in Punjab. Das stayed in Punjab for three months, bearing all the expenses himself.

When Gandhi announced his historic Non-cooperation Movement at the Special Session of the Congress in Calcutta in September 1920, where Lajpat Rai presided, Chittaranjan led those who opposed Gandhi's proposal. He was supported by Bipin Chandra Pal, Madan Mohan Malaviya and Annie Besant. He was particularly opposed to the boycott of the Councils. Three months later, at the annual session of the Congress held in December 1920 at Nagpur, he 'made up his differences and endorsed Gandhi's standpoint, after his heart-to-heart talk with him'. He also declared at the session that he would give up his practice at the Bar. Returning to Calcutta, he did give up his roaring legal practice and renounced all comforts and luxuries. The whole country was moved at this supreme act of sacrifice and his reward was the title which his admirers gave him—*Deshbandhu* (friend of the country). Chittaranjan's example in giving up legal practice was followed by some other lawyers in the country. He now put his heart and soul in making the Non-cooperation Movement a success. He toured East Bengal to arouse people for non-cooperation. He helped organize district Congress Committees throughout Bengal. In February 1921, he set up the Bengal National College at Calcutta, which was inaugurated by Gandhi. Thousands of miles away from home, a young man was inspired by the sacrifices Chittaranjan made and wanted to work with him, resigning from ICS apprenticeship. He was Subhas Chandra Bose, who wrote to Chittaranjan from Cambridge on 16 February 1921. After introducing himself and his family, Subhas wrote, 'I should like to know what work you may be able to allot to me in this great programme of national service.' Subhas Bose came back to India and started working under his leadership. They formed a formidable team and would have given an alternative leadership to the country had Chittaranjan not prematurely died after four years.

During the Prince of Wales's visit to India in November 1921, which was boycotted by the Congress, Chittaranajan organized volunteer corps to protest against the visit and to court arrest for violating the ban on demonstrations. In the first batch of volunteers, his only son Chiraranjan, was arrested on 4 December 1921, and was sentenced to a six-month imprisonment. This was followed by the arrest of his wife Basanti Devi and sister Urmila on 7 December. Other arrests included those of Subhas Chandra Bose and his own arrest on 10 December. His wife and sister were released soon after but Subhas and Chittaranajan were imprisoned for six months. These arrests were made by the government in a bid to avert the general hartal proposed for 24 December 1921, the day of Prince of Wales's visit. Incidentally, Lord Mountbatten, the last viceroy and governor-general of India, was the ADC of the Prince of Wales on his visit to India. While still in prison, Chittaranajan was elected president of the Ahmedabad session of the Congress to be held in December 1921. The government did not allow him to attend the session. His presidential address was read by Sarojini Naidu, while Hakim Ajmal Khan presided over the session.

Gandhi formally started the Non-cooperation Movement on 1 August 1920 and suspended it on 24 February 1922, without consulting anyone. After the Ahmedabad Congress session, Gandhi announced mass civil disobedience or Satyagraha in Bardoli, a *taluk* (administrative district) in Gujarat. But before it could be started, Gandhi withdrew it, again without consulting anyone. Chittaranjan Das was upset. So were many Congress leaders. Subhas Bose, who was in the same jail with Chittaranjan Das describes how his mentor was upset with Gandhi's sudden decision and was beside himself with sorrow and anger at the way Mahatma was repeatedly bungling.[2]

---

[2]Bose, Subhas Chandra, *The Indian Struggle, 1920–1942*, Oxford University Press, New Delhi, 1997, p. 82.

On being released from jail in August 1922, Chittaranjan was unanimously elected president of the Gaya session of the INC (December 1922), where he sought to change the strategy of the Non-cooperation Movement and pleaded for 'council entry' as a tactical measure. It was evident to everyone that the programme of boycotting the Councils, courts and educational institutions had failed. All these bodies continued to run as before. Gandhi could not win freedom for the country in one year. Still, when Chittaranjan Das moved a resolution for council entry in the Congress session, it was defeated by the followers of Gandhi, now called 'no-changers'. Das resigned from the INC in disgust and formed the Swaraj Party with Motilal Nehru in 1923. He went around the country, starting with Bengal, propagating the reason for entering the councils to thwart the government from within. More and more people were turning towards the Swaraj Party as an alternative to the INC, which had miserably failed. Ultimately, seeing the writing on the wall, Gandhi yielded and in a special session of the INC at Delhi in September 1923, the Swaraj Party was declared as the 'parliamentary wing' of the Congress.

During the November 1923 Elections, the Swaraj Party swept the elections in Bengal and in some other provinces, as well as in the Central Legislative Council. By mutual agreement, it was decided that Motilal Nehru would lead the Swarajists in the Central Assembly and Chittaranjan Das in the Bengal Legislative Council. The obstructive tactics of the Swaraj Party were a source of great embarrassment for the government and the Viceroy had to use his powers to get things done. In the field of journalism too, the Swarajists made much progress. Das launched a daily newspaper, *Forward*, in October 1923. Subhas was asked to look after the affairs of the paper. As Subhas has written in his book, 'Within a short time *Forward* came to hold a leading position among the nationalist journals in the country. Its articles were forceful, its news service varied and up-to-date and the paper developed a special skill in the art of discovering and exposing official secrets.'[3]

In 1924, Chittaranjan was elected the first mayor of Calcutta with Subhas Bose as the executive officer of the Calcutta Municipal Corporation. He was elected mayor for the second time in April 1925. The last AICC session attended by him was the Belgaum session in December 1924, which Gandhi presided over. There was complete reconciliation between the Swarajists, led by Chittaranjan Das and Motilal Nehru and Gandhi. Later, Chittaranjan presided over the Bengal Provincial Conference held at Faridpur on 2 May 1925.

Chittaranjan Das donated his palatial house at Bhawanipur to the nation and it was turned into a charitable hospital for women, known as the Chittaranjan Seva Sadan.

Since the early months of 1925, Chittaranjan Das suffered from a poor state of health and he suddenly died on 16 June 1925 while trying to recuperate at Darjeeling. His body was brought to Kolkata for his last rites, which were attended by hundreds of thousands of wailing Indians, including Gandhi. The whole country plunged into grief. Subhas Chandra Bose has written about this, saying:

> Though his active political career consisted of barely five years, his rise had been phenomenal. With a reckless abandon of a Vaishnava devotee, he had plunged into the political movement with heart and soul and he had given not only himself but his all in the fight for Swaraj. When he died, whatever worldly possessions he still had, were left to the nation. He was clear headed, his political instinct was sound and unerring and unlike the Mahatma, he was fully conscious of the role he was to play in Indian politics.[4]

Subhas Chandra Bose had lost his mentor. In future, Bose would have to fight his political battles single-handedly against powerful foes.

---

[3]Ibid. 97.
[4]Ibid.122–23.

22

Maharshi Dayanand Saraswati

(1824–1883)

Among all the reformers of the nineteenth century, Dayanand was unique in the sense that he was not influenced by western education and philosophy; in fact, he did not even know English. In spite of that, he has left a more lasting impact on Indian society than any other reformer. The Arya Samaj, founded by him, is still active, not only in India but also in other countries where Indians have settled in considerable numbers like South Africa, Mauritius, Fiji, Trinidad and England. The educational wing of the Arya Samaj, in the form of Dayanand Anglo Vedic (DAV) schools and colleges, is the largest educational network in the country. In addition to these modern institutions, there are also *gurukuls*, established on the ancient pattern of education, for both boys and girls. Such was the impact of the gurukuls that when Gandhi returned from South Africa in 1915, he sent his sons and about 100 other children, who were with him in the Phoenix Ashram in Durban, to Gurukul Kangri in Haridwar for some time. These institutions have kept the name and message of Dayanand alive.

Dayanand's autobiography *Aryamantavya* does not throw light on his place of birth nor about his family. But his biographers Pandit Lekh Ram and Devendranath Mukhopadhyay, who went to Gujarat to find out the truth about his birth and family, have revealed that Dayanand was born in the town of Tankara in Kathiawar (now in Morbi), in 1824. He was given the name 'Mulshankar' or

'Mulji' by his family, who were Brahmins. His father was a small landholder-cum-moneylender and commanded respect in the area. Mulji's family was orthodox Shaivites. Dayanand spent the first 20 years of his life in the village and got the education which such an environment could offer. He committed to memory *Yajurveda* and parts of other Vedas as well as *Rudradhyaya*, the scripture for Vaishnavas.[1] He learnt the Devanagari script at the age of five and was also taught Sanskrit. His father also taught him the rituals which a Shaivite family had to perform. Two events had a great impact on his life. The first being the death of his younger sister from cholera and that of his beloved uncle soon after; the second was a *Shivratri* night, when the young Mulji saw a mouse climbing on the Shivlinga and devouring the offerings, while other members of the family were asleep. These two events were the turning points in the life of the young Mulji. He began to ponder the meaning of life and death and the true form of God as he was now convinced that the symbols of God, as represented in idols of various shapes and forms, could not be the true God. When his parents came to know about his state of mind, they decided that Mulji should get married. Before that could happen, Mulji left his home and family to never return. He was initiated into *sanyas* (renunciation) by Swami Parmananda Saraswati Maharaj, who changed Mulji's name to Dayanand Saraswati. He learned yoga from Jawalanand Puri and Sivanand Giri at Dudeshwar, near Ahmedabad. He traversed all of north-west India for many years in search of a guru and yogi who could clear his doubts and teach him true religion but could find none, till he met Swami Virjanand at Mathura. Here, his real education in Sanskrit and the Vedas started in 1860. He was already 36 years old. He stayed for three years in Virjananda's ashram. His guru found in Dayanand, an extraordinary personality, eager to do something for the Hindu society. At his guru's command, Dayanand took a solemn vow to devote his life to spreading the

---

[1]Sarda, Har Bilas, *Life of Dayanand Saraswati*, Vedic Yantralaya, Ajmer, 1946, p. 4.

Vedic message and for removing superstitions and ignorance from the Hindu society.

He started preaching about the true religion of the Vedas and condemning idol-worship, meaningless rituals and the evils inherent in the caste system. His slogan was 'back to the Vedas', the sacred books of the Hindus which should be read by all Hindus irrespective of the caste to which they belonged. For several years, he confined his efforts to lectures and the practise of *shastrartha* (intellectual debates) with orthodox Hindus to spread his message. He preached at the Kumbh Mela in 1867 at Haridwar and was met with stiff resistance from the orthodox Hindus. His famous shastrartha in Banaras (1869) with 300 traditional pandits did not bring any fruitful result.

His visit to Calcutta in 1872–73 was a turning point in his reforming mission. He had gone to Calcutta at the invitation of the Adi Brahmo Samaj and stayed at the house belonging to the Tagore family. There, he met several leaders of the Adi Brahmo Samaj, including Keshab Chandra Sen, Hem Chandra Sarkar and others. He studied the working of the Brahmo Samaj and learnt many lessons, being receptive to new ideas. Consequently, a major shift in his methods of preaching came about. Instead of preaching in Sanskrit, which only a few could understand, he decided to preach in Hindi to reach a wider audience. He also changed his dress from a loincloth to a long gown, dhoti and a turban, all in ochre—the colour worn by the Indian sadhus. He also learnt that by merely giving lectures and holding debates, he would not be able to achieve much. To reach a wider audience and to give some kind of permanency to his endeavours, he needed an organization on the lines of the Brahmo Samaj. He realized he would also have to write his views to convey his message to people living in different parts of the country and even outside. So, he learnt Hindi and gave his first lecture in Hindi in 1874, a year after his return from Calcutta.

The urge to start an organization fructified when the first Arya

Samaj was established in Rajkot in January 1875. But it did not survive for long. The second Arya Samaj in April of the same year was founded in Bombay, with 100 founding members, and proved to be an important landmark in the history of the Arya Samaj Movement. A committee was formed to supervise the activities and rules (28 in number) were framed for the initiation and guidance of its members.

But for Dayanand, real success came when he visited Punjab in March 1877. He went to Lahore at the invitation of the Brahmo Samajis who had established some branches in Punjab earlier. But soon differences in ideology cropped up and the Brahmo Samaj people disassociated themselves from Dayanand. However, his lectures attracted quite a few influential people, who were impressed by the personality and teachings of 'the Swami'. There was hardly any debate there as Punjab did not have Brahmin orthodoxy. Hindus there had been facing foreign onslaughts for centuries and were ready to try social transformation and wanted to get organized for their emancipation. The first Arya Samaj in Punjab was established in June 1877 in Lahore. From the very start, it was better organized than the one in Bombay. They elected a committee to run the affairs, reduced the number of principles from 28 to 10 (which are still followed by the Arya Samaj everywhere) and formulated by-laws. Arya Samajs sprang up in all major cities of Punjab, except in the princely states, where Dayanand did not preach.

It was in Punjab, while the Swami was preaching, that a new concept emerged, that of *shuddhi* (purification). Christian missionaries and Muslim *mullahs* (clergy) were very active at that time in Punjab, converting Hindus to their religions. Through shuddhi, a person who was converted to another religion could be 'purified' and brought back to the fold of Hinduism. Arya Samaj in Punjab had taken the work of shuddhi in earnest, facing the ire of both Muslims and Christians, especially the former. Many Aryas were martyred while doing shuddhi work including leaders like Lekhram (biographer of Swami Dayanand) and later Shraddhanand.

The Shuddhi Movement has been criticized by a group of historians, forgetting that it was an ancient custom approved by scriptures like *Vratyastoma* and *Devala Smriti*.[2] One of the most famous cases of shuddhi was that of Harilal Gandhi, the eldest son of Mahatma Gandhi. Harilal had become a Muslim to avoid paying back the money borrowed by him from some Muslim moneylenders and also to spite his father, whom he held responsible for his troubles. He was converted to Islam in Jama Masjid, Bombay on 14 May 1936, in front of a cheering crowd of Muslims. This created a stir in the country and was a great embarrassment for the elder Gandhi and Kasturba. It was the Arya Samaj that came to their rescue and Aryas, showing great daring, brought back Harilal to the Hindu fold through shuddhi after six months.[3]

Another development which contributed to Swami's success in Punjab was the publication of *Veda Bhashya* in fascicles, starting in 1878. The response was overwhelming and the subscription for the book ran into hundreds. While in Punjab, Swami had written a small book earlier, *Aryoddeshyaratnamala* (1877), containing a 100 definitions and descriptions of key terms of Hindu religion and philosophy, meant to help people in understanding his discourses and writings. 'Swami spent only sixteen months in the Punjab and was never to pay a return visit, yet, when he left the land of five rivers, a new force had clearly been set in motion in Punjab society, a force that had decisive influence in the history of the province for many years to come.'[4] Lahore had become the unofficial headquarters of the Arya Samaj and gave a lead to Arya Samajs around the world. Lahore, becoming part of Pakistan after the Partition in 1947, proved to be a great setback for the Arya Samaj,

---

[2]Jordens, J.T.F., *Dayanand Saraswati: His Life and Ideas*, Oxford University Press, 1997, p. 170.
[3]Kulkarni, Sumitra Gandhi. *Mahatma Gandhi: Mere Pitamah* (Hindi), Diamond Pocket Books, New Delhi, 1997, pp. 217–17.
[4]Jordens, J.T.F., *Dayanand Saraswati: His Life and Ideas*, Oxford University Press, 1997, p. 160.

from which it has not been able to recover fully, even to this day.

By the time Dayanand left Punjab, he had become famous and his following had increased considerably. Soon, the number of Arya Samajs multiplied and when Swami died, there were 79 Arya Samajs functioning mostly in Punjab and Uttar Pradesh. Today, the number runs into thousands. The Swami spent the last five years and three months of his remaining life in hectic activity, visiting Uttar Pradesh and lastly Rajputana, where he died on 30 October 1883. According to his biographer J.T.F. Jordens, the cause of Swami's death was acute dysentery, double pneumonia and mismanagement of his treatment by his followers, who had brought him from Jodhpur to Ajmer while he was seriously ill.[5] However, the Arya Samaj people believe that Dayanand was poisoned by his enemies, especially suspecting a favourite concubine of the maharaja of Jodhpur.

Dayanand has left a considerable number of books and pamphlets, which he wrote laboriously. His magnum opus, of course, is *Satyarth Prakash*. The first edition of this seminal work was published in 1875 in Hindi, when Dayanand was not quite proficient in the language and thus he was not satisfied with the end result. A second and final edition of *Satyarth Prakash* was published in 1882–83, a part of it after his death. Some of his other important works are—*Sanskar Vidhi*, first edition 1877, second edition after his death in 1884; *Rigvedadibhashyabhumika* published in fascicles from 1877 onwards; *Rigveda Bhashya* and *Yajurueda Bhasha Bhashya*, published in fascicles from 1877 to 1880. His autobiography was written in Hindi by the Swami and subsequently its English translation was published in *The Theophist*, a monthly of the Theosophical Society in 1879–80, at the time when the Swami had a brief association with the society and its founder, Blavatsky.

Besides preaching Vedic lore, Dayanand preached against idolatry, meaningless rituals and the caste system. He was one of the first reformers to advocate swadeshi and swaraj. For the

---

[5]Ibid. 242.

integrity of the country, he favoured Hindi as the national language and set an example himself. Though he did not know English, he encouraged Indians to learn English to understand the modern scientific advancement of the West. The name Dayanand Anglo–Vedic, given to educational institutions run by Arya Samaj, implies just that.

Arya Samaj attracted many luminaries during Dayanand's lifetime and even after his death. Some of them took an active part not only as social reformers but also as freedom fighters like Mahavind Govind Ranade, Lajpat Rai, Bhai Parmanand, Shyamji Krishna Varma, Swami Shraddhanand and many others.

Jawaharlal Nehru sums up the contribution of Arya Samaj thus:

> The Arya Samaj was a reaction to the influence of Islam and Christianity; more especially the former. It introduced proselytization into Hinduism and thus tended to come into conflict with other proselytizing religions. The Arya Samaj, which had been a close approach to Islam, tended to become defender of everything Hindu, against what it considered as the encroachments of other faiths. At one time, it was considered by the government as a politically revolutionary movement, but the large numbers of government servants in it made it thoroughly respectable. It has done very good work in the spread of education both among boys and girls, in improving the condition of women and in raising the status and standards of the depressed classes.[6]

[6]Nehru, Jawaharlal, *Discovery of India,* Jawaharlal Nehru Memorial Fund, New Delhi, 1946, pp. 335–36.

23

Henry Louis Vivian Derozio

(1809–1831)

Henry Louis Vivian Derozio was one of the earliest Indo–English poets. Besides being a poet of rare quality, he was an educationist, a journalist and a reformer, which made him a controversial figure in the educated circles of Calcutta in early nineteenth century. Henry Derozio was born on 18 April 1809 and was of Eurasian parentage (his father Francis Derozio being an Indian of Portuguese descent and his mother, Sophia Johnson, British). As a Christian, he was baptized in the same cathedral where William Makepeace Thackeray, the famous British novelist, was baptized three years later. The house on the Lower Circular Road, where Henry was born, was the property of the Derozio family. It is no longer there but the cemetry on Park Street, where he was buried, still remains.

At the age of six, Henry was admitted in the David Drummond Dharmatala Academy. As the name suggests, it was run by David Drummond, 'a man of great force of character as well as something of a metaphysician and poet'. In the academy, Drummond helped young Henry to sharpen his splendid power of intellect and imagination. During the period of eight years at the Academy, Henry developed a taste for literature and philosophy and read the works of British and European thinkers widely. He did extremely well at school, wrote verses for several events and received prizes for his achievements. He left the Academy in 1822, at the age of 14. He joined the mercantile firm of James Scott & Co., in which his father was the chief accountant. The work at the commercial establishment was not to Derozio's liking, it was 'a mere drudgery', and after enduring it for two years, he left it and went to Bhagalpur (in present Bihar) to stay with Arthur Johnson, his uncle (the husband of his mother's sister), who was looking after an indigo plantation at the nearby Tarapur. Derozio spent almost three years there, lending a helping hand to Johnson and at the same time enjoying the country scenery—the luscious paddy fields, the ripping river, and the company of rustic people around him. These serene surroundings kindled young Derozio's imagination and he began to write verses describing what he saw and imagined. Derozio started sending his poems to Dr John Grant, editor of the Indian *Gazette*, for publication under the assumed name of 'Juvenis'. Grant liked his poems and encouraged him to continue writing. When Derozio came back to Calcutta in 1826, Grant persuaded him to get his poems published in a book. Thus, came out the first volume of Derozio's poems which was appreciated in literary circles. This was when Derozio was still in his teens. Grant also offered Derozio the post of an assistant editor at *Indian Gazette*. Later, he edited the *Calcutta Gazette* for some time. He also contributed poems to the *Calcutta Magazine, Indian Magazine, the Bengal Annual* and the *Kaleidoscope*, which widened his readership. In 1827, the second volume of his poems, which included one of his most famous poems, 'The Fakir of Jungheera', was published. This raised him to fame as a poet of considerable merit, with interest being shown in his writing by literary circles in London too.

On his arrival in Calcutta in 1826, Derozio was also appointed assistant teacher of English literature and history in the Hindu College. Soon he was acclaimed by H.H. Wilson, Visitor of the College, as one of the best teachers of the institution 'who possessed the rare power of weaving interest around any subject that he taught'. Apart from the subject content, the distinctive feature of Derozio's teaching was to awaken in his pupil's mind a love for truth and a spirit of enquiry. Being a free thinker himself, he encouraged his students to do likewise. He had a genuine love and sympathy for his students which he expressed in his poem titled 'Sonnet to the Pupils of the Hindu College':

Expanding like the petals of young flowers
I watch the gentle opening of your minds.

By his method of teaching, Derozio helped his students to develop a spirit of enquiry and rationality and encouraged them to express their views and opinions without any inhibition or restraint. After college hours, the students used to meet Derozio either in the college premises or in his house at Lower Circular Road. These informal meetings took a formal shape in the Academic Association. Initially, the Association meetings were held in Derozio's house, and were later shifted to the garden house of Sri Krishna Singh. During the weekly meetings, discussions were held on varied subjects like freewill, fate, faith, cultivating virtue, patriotism, God and idolatry. Some meetings were attended by a few of the leading intellectuals of the city.

Assisted by Derozio, his students started a weekly, *Parthenon*. The first issue contained criticism of some of the actions of the government as well as highlighted the depraved and perverse practices of Hinduism. The authorities of Hindu College took a serious view of the kind of articles published and the paper had to stop publication. Apart from such unorthodox expressions, the students also indulged in activities which horrified their parents, like eating beef and pork and drinking alcohol. The parents started blaming the kind of instruction which was given in the college. They collectively complained to the college authorities and even threatened to withdraw their wards from the college. The management believed that the very existence of the college was at stake. They blamed the teachings of Derozio for the waywardness of their wards. The authorities soon took steps to remove Derozio from the service of the college. Derozio was charged with atheism and immorality, which he allegedly taught to the students. It was decided that 'Derozio being the root cause of all the evils and cause of public alarm should be removed from the College'. In his reply, Derozio vindicated his stand and repudiated all the allegations. After doing that, he resigned from the college in April 1831.

After quitting Hindu College, Derozio started *East Indian*, an evening daily on 1 June 1831. He was the editor as well as the proprietor of the paper. He turned it into an organ of the Anglo–Indian community, projecting their travails and disabilities and suggesting remedies. It was rather strange that a free thinker and a rationalist should be reduced to a communal crusader. However, his life was cut short and he died of cholera on 26 December 1831 in Calcutta. While he taught rational thinking and virtues of truth and duty, all borrowed from Western philosophers and thinkers, he had not delved into Indian philosophical and religious works like the *Bhagavad Gita* and the *Upanishads*, as his contemporary reformer Ram Mohan Roy had done. As a result, Ram Mohan had a much greater impact on society with wider ramifications. Derozio was never accepted as a role model for social reformers who followed him. But nobody could doubt his patriotism. In one of his poems, *To India—My Native Land*, he wrote:

> *My country! in thy day of glory past A beautious halo*
> *circled round thy brow,*
> *And worshipped as a deity thou wast,*
> *Where is that glory, where that reverence now?*

Derozio was one of the early Indo–English poets who left a mark on the literary horizon. He wielded a powerful pen; his imagery and power of description were of a high quality. There is a music in his words and a rare depth of feeling. However, he lacked the originality of style and he tried to copy Byron and Thomas Moore. But it was perhaps, inevitable. Those were different days and to cut a new line for a youthful writer would probably have been a catastrophe. Despite his limitations, he has an honoured place among the early Indo–English poets.[1]

As mentioned in the book edited by Nirmal Sinha:

> Derozio is remembered most for the influence he exerted on his students and followers, popularly known as "Derozians" or "Young Bengal". They were the harbingers of radical thought which contributed to the Bengal Renaissance of the nineteenth century. In that context, he was coadjutor of Rammohan Roy. Some of the Derozians who became famous and carried on the message of Derozio were Krishna Mohan Banerjee, Ram Gopal Ghosh, Peary Chand, Rashik Krishna Mallick, Dekshinaranjan Mukherjee.[2]

[1]Sinha, R.P.N., *The Birth and Development of Indo-English Verse*, Dev Publishing House, New Delhi, 1971, p. 147.
[2]Sinha, Nirmal (ed.), *Freedom Movement in Bengal, 1818-1914: Who's Who*, Academic Publishers, Calcutta, 1991, pp. 92–93.

24

Morarji Desai

(1896–1995)

Morarji was born on the intercalary day of 29 February 1896, in a Brahmin family in the Surat district of Gujarat. He was one of the six children of Ranchhodji Nagarji Desai and Vajiaben Desai. His father was a teacher in a village school. The early childhood of Morarji, however, was spent at his maternal grandfather's place Bhadeli. He received his primary education in this village and was sent to Bulsar for secondary education. When he was a boy of 15, his father died by suicide after jumping into a well, just three days before Morarji's arranged marriage to an eleven-year-old, Gajraben. However, Morarji went through with the marriage on the appointed day and became the head of the family, which included, besides the child bride, his grandmother, mother, three brothers and two sisters.[1] On passing his matriculation examination in 1912, he won a scholarship which enabled him to join Wilson College in Bombay, where he studied from 1913 to 1917. After graduation, he joined Bombay Provincial Civil Service in 1918 and spent the next 12 years in service there, working mostly as a revenue officer or a magistrate.

In 1930, Morarji resigned from government service and joined the INC. Gandhi had started the Civil Disobedience Movement

---

[1]Mehta, Ved, *A Family Affair: India Under Three Prime Ministers,* Sangam Books, Madras, 1982, p. 7.

in the same year. Morarji took part in it and was imprisoned. But all the satyagrahis were set free after the Gandhi–Irwin Pact in March 1931. Morarji became a member of the local Gujarat Pradesh Congress Committee and came to the notice of Sardar Patel, who was the president of the committee. He was appointed its secretary. During the next four years, Morarji was imprisoned thrice for participating in the anti-government movement led by the Congress party. In 1931, he was nominated as a member of the AICC.

In 1937, the Congress party fought elections for the provincial Assemblies. Desai was elected from his home district and was appointed minister for revenue and forests in the Congress ministry, headed by Chief Minister Balasaheb Gangadhar Kher. In 1939, all the Congress ministries resigned against the British government's decision to involve India in the Second World War without consent. After relinquishing office, Morarji participated in the individual satyagraha and was imprisoned. During the Quit India Movement, he was detained for three years. After the Second World War, elections for provincial assemblies were held in 1946 and Morarji was elected to the Bombay Legislative Assembly and became home and revenue minister (1946–52) again in Kher's ministry. During these six years, Morarji earned the reputation of working of a puritan and a zealot, who would put even Mrs Grundy to shame. The most important of such puritanic measures was the introduction of total prohibition, which led to bootlegging and ultimately gave birth to criminals. Like some of his other measures, this measure also proved to be unsuccessful. Because of the unpopularity of his puritanical crusade, he lost the election to the Provincial Assembly in 1952. But Kher retired and made Morarji his successor, as he was the senior most member of his cabinet. Morarji later got himself elected in a byelection and served as the chief minister of Bombay state from 1952–56. As chief minister, he is remembered for ruthlessly putting down the agitation for the Samyukta Maharashtra Samiti, in which about 80 persons, mostly students, were killed in police firing. In the words of the *Illustrated Weekly*, Desai became 'the most hated person' in the province. Apart from this notoriety, which he earned partly because of the vacillating policy of the Nehru government with regard to the reorganization of provinces on linguistic basis, Desai proved himself a good administrator and a no-nonsense man. He was instrumental in introducing far-reaching reforms in the land revenue administration and also in police and jail reorganization. He thought of both, the peasant and tenant and enacted progressive legislation for them, much before any Indian province did anything in this direction. His experience as a government official during the British Raj helped him in administering the Bombay province, which came to be known for its efficiency, progress and integrity.

In November 1956, Morarji joined Nehru's Union Cabinet, as minister for commerce and industry. He was elected to the Lok Sabha in the 1962 elections and thus continued as finance minister, a portfolio he held from 1958 to 1963. In 1958, at the age of 62, he went out of the country for the first time, visiting Europe, the US and Canada. As finance minister, he led the Indian delegation to the annual meetings of the board of governors of the International Monetary Fund (IMF) and the International Bank for Reconstruction and Development in New Delhi in 1958 and in Washington DC in 1959, 1960 and 1961. He also attended the Commonwealth Prime Minister's Conference in London in 1960 and 1961. He was quite successful as a finance minister. 'Defence through development, creation of a climate of confidence and initiative, export promotion and austerity in government administration, public corporations and companies in the private sector and in the personal lives of the privileged segments of the society, formed the main theme of his economic and fiscal policies.' But as finance minister he is remembered most for promulgating the Gold Control Order as an ordinance in 1962, which prohibited the production of any gold jewellery purer than 14 carat, thus antagonizing many people. In his book, Morarji has spoken of this saying, 'The main purpose of gold control was to prevent the smuggling of gold worth crores of rupees into India from outside. As long as the attraction of gold was not lessened and the demand for gold was not reduced, it would be difficult to control the smuggling of gold. It was, therefore, necessary to take steps to lessen the attraction of gold in the public mind.'[2]

In 1963, he was forced out of the Nehru Cabinet under the Kamaraj Plan which had called on the senior leaders of the Congress to resign from ministerial posts and to work for strengthening the party. Many believe, Morarji included, that the Kamaraj Plan was essentially devised to oust Morarji from the Cabinet.

After Nehru's death in May 1964, the question of who would be his successor arose. By this time, Kamaraj, Morarji's bête noire, had become the INC president, who saw to it that Morarji did not become the prime minister. He put up the name of Lal Bahadur Shastri and managed to get him elected 'unanimously' as the prime minister. When Lal Bahadur died suddenly in 1966, Desai wasted no time in making a second bid for the prime ministership. Though Desai was the most prominent Congress leader, he had antagonized many members in the party. His advocacy of Hindi as the national language turned the entire South block against him. Kamaraj rallied all his forces and proposed the name of Indira Gandhi as a candidate for prime ministership. This time Morarji did not quit and a contest became inevitable. The Congress parliamentary party met on 19 January 1966 to decide the issue. Indira Gandhi polled 355 votes against Morarji's 189. Indira Gandhi initially did not include Morarji in her cabinet. In the 1967 Lok Sabha elections, Morarji was elected from Surat constituency and Indira Gandhi became the prime minister again, without any opposition. She wanted Morarji to join her cabinet because the Congress had suffered reverses in the 1967 elections and she thought that including Morarji in her cabinet would strengthen the party. After some haggling, it was decided that Morarji would be the finance minister and also would be designated

---

[2]Desai, Morarji, *The Story of My Life*, Macmillan India, 1974, p. 190.

deputy prime minister. 'His performance both in Parliament and in councils of the Party was so skilful and the force of his will and personality so evident that he almost came to exert decisive influence in the making of policy'. That made Indira Gandhi somewhat jittery as she did not want to be upstaged and was looking to undermine his position. Controversy cropped up in 1969 on the issue of the nationalization of banks and on the selection of a candidate for presidentship of the Congress. The old guard, including Morarji, opposed Indira Gandhi on these and on some other issues. She gambled and split the Congress party into two. Her wing of the Congress came later to be known as Congress (I) and the other faction as Congress (O). Morarji opted for the latter, and was asked by the prime minister to resign from the posts held by him. From 1969 to the advent of Emergency in 1975, Morarji sat with the insignificant opposition in the Parliament, as the leader of Congress (O). Indira used the Emergency to remain in power after the verdict of the Allahabad High Court against the validity of her election of 1971. Morarji Desai was arrested along with thousands of others whom she considered her adversaries. He remained in prison for 19 months. The Emergency rules were relaxed in January 1977, in preparation for parliamentary elections to be held in March 1977. Various political parties formed a coalition under the name Janata Party, with Morarji heading the Congress (O) faction. The other parties which joined hands to oppose Indira Gandhi's Congress were Bharatiya Lok Dal, Jana Sangh, the Socialists and a splinter group of Congress, led by Jagjivan Ram. Congress (I) was routed and the Janata Party formed the government with Morarji as the prime minister. He was 81 at the time but still active. One of the first acts of his government was to repeal laws imposing internal Emergency. It also initiated an economic strategy based on labour-intensive private industry and voluntary groups in rural areas. But the policy did not shift radically and there was a rising tide of strikes, communal violence and general frustration in the country. Morarji was riding a chariot of 20 horses, each pulling in a different direction. There were ego clashes and factional disputes. The Janata government collapsed in July 1979, making way for Indira Gandhi to come to power again. Morarji's public career came to an end. He led a retired life for another 16 years and died in Bombay on 10 April 1995.

After the 1930s, Morarji led the life of a true Gandhian—wearing khadi, spinning regularly, being a strict vegetarian and teetotaller. He even tried to copy Gandhi's technique of undergoing a fast to win over his opponents. But surprisingly, he was never one of those close to Gandhi. In the most comprehensive and official eight volume biography of Gandhi, written by Dinanath Gopal Tendulkar, titled *Mahatma: Life of Mohandas Karamchand Gandhi*, Morarji Desai's name does not appear even once. Desai's outspokenness could be one of the reasons behind this omission.

Morarji Desai was a tall, handsome man. A man of fixed habits and equally fixed ideas, he did not change with the times. However, he was an extremely good administrator and a man of courage. He was also a man of integrity, though it came under question during his prime ministership when charges of corruption were levelled against his son Kantilal Desai, who was his private secretary. He wrote his autobiography, *The Story of My Life,* in three volumes, which is prosaic and tiresome, and in which he devotes a full chapter to defending Kanti and his relations with him. In the preface of the book, he says: He felt that he had to write the book, 'because it was my duty to write about my experiences so that the reader might get some guidance from them when he is confused.'[3] Modesty was certainly not one of his virtues.

---

[3]Desai, Morarji, *The Story of My Life*, Macmillan India, 1974.

25

Romesh Chunder Dutt

(1848–1909)

The Dutts were a respectable literary family of Calcutta. Toru Dutt, who had become famous as a poet in young age, was a cousin of Romesh Chunder. In fact, a collection of poems by members of the Dutt clan was published as *Dutt Family Album* in 1870. It was natural for Romesh to inherit this literary taste and aspirations. A few members of the family embraced Christianity in 1862, led by Govind Chandra Dutt, Toru's father, which was criticized by other family members.

Romesh Chunder was born on 13 August 1848. His father, Isan Chunder Dutt, was a deputy collector in the revenue department of the government. His early education was in district schools, wherever his father got posted. Unfortunately, his father died by drowning in 1861. His mother had died two years earlier. The four brothers and two sisters came under the guardianship of their uncle, Shashi Chunder Datt. Romesh was enrolled in Hare School, from where he passed the Entrance Examination in 1864. The same year he was married to Matangini (Mohini) Bose, daughter of Nabagopal Bose of Calcutta, at the age of 16. However, the marriage does not seem to have affected his studies. He joined Presidency College and passed the First Arts Examination in 1866 and obtained a scholarship. In March 1868, he left for England to compete for the ICS. He passed and stood third in the order of merit. During this period, he also undertook legal studies and was called to the

Bar. He returned to India in 1871 and his career in the ICS began.

From 1871 to 1897, he served the ICS in various capacities in districts of Bengal and Orissa, beginning as probationer assistant magistrate of Alipore and rising to the position of divisional commissioner of Burdwan and officiating commissioner of Orissa (1895). Realizing that he had no scope of further promotion as permanent commissioner, he took premature retirement in 1897, at a relatively early age of 49. His work as a civil servant earned him praise from official quarters as well as from the public. He was one of the early administrators who showed that Indians could administer as well as any British officer.

As a free man, Romesh started a very fruitful and exciting career as a public person and as a writer. Before retirement, he took leave preparatory to retirement and visited several countries in Europe for months. Soon after, he was appointed a lecturer in Indian history at the University College, London, where he stayed till 1904. Those seven years in England were his most productive period as a writer. In 1898, he came out with the English translation of the Ramayana and that of Mahabharata next year, which helped the West appreciate and understand the great Indian epics better. Max Muller wrote the introduction to the Ramayana, while Mahabharata was dedicated to him. In 1899, another book of his titled, *England and India: A Record of Progress During A Hundred Years, 1785–1885* appeared. Next came *Famines in India*, which included his five open letters to Lord Curzon. His classical work and perhaps the most important one, *The Economic History of India Under Early British Rule*, was published in two volumes in 1902 and 1904 respectively. Apart from other aspects of Indian economic history, he highlighted the causes of famines in India and their remedy. He graphically traced the decline of Indian industries during the early British rule and the deliberate policy of harming and discouraging Indian industries so that India might not offer competition to British products. He also highlighted the drain on the Indian economy in the form of 'home charges'. Another great Indian, Dadabhai Naoroji, was also writing on the same subject at the time. His well-known book *Poverty and Un-British Rule India,* was published in 1901. They were contemporaries, and as nationalists, were concerned with the pathetic situation into which the British rule, with its colonial economic policies, was pushing the Indian masses.

However, Romesh Dutt's *Economic History* is more detailed and he wrote with the background of his administrative experience in the ICS. But, in spite of his criticism of the British administration, Romesh was a 'loyal' Indian and did not believe that the British rule was wrong by itself. It must be remembered that during the second half of the nineteenth century, British rule was accepted as a necessity. Even the INC used to pass a resolution of 'loyalty' in every session from its inception in 1885. Romesh believed that the British connection was basically good and that the future of India lay in advancing within the framework of the British Empire. Because of his 'moderate' attitude towards the British, he was invited to preside over the 1899 session of the Congress at Lucknow. In his address, he concentrated on the economic problems faced by the Indians and did not touch the political aspirations of the people. The idea of swadeshi was still another six years away, when Lord Curzon partitioned Bengal.

Even before his retirement, while serving in the ICS, he had written books on various topics. His first book was *Peasantry of Bengal* (1875), in which he pleaded the cause of the peasants against the government and landlords. In 1889–90, he had published *A History of Civilization in Ancient India*, in which he tried to present the aspects of Indian culture, which until then were known only to scholars and Orientalists, to inquisitive students of Indian culture. In 1894, he had published *Lays of Ancient India: Selections from Indian Poetry Rendered in English* in verse form. This was the translation of some of the best-known passages from the Upanishads, from the edicts of Ashoka and from the short epic, *Bhairavi*.

In the field of social reform, except for his two Bengali novels and *Satnaj*, Dutt made no active contribution, unlike Ranade, who was also a government servant like Romesh Dutt, though in the judicial service. Romesh Dutt made substantial contribution to Bengali literature, which was passing through a phase of revolutionary innovation at that stage, both in form and content. Romesh Chunder Dutt's first homage to Bengali literature was a book, *Literature of Bengal* (1877), written in English. This was perhaps the first scientific attempt to write a history of Bengali literature, from the twelfth century down to his time. He tried to join the galaxy of Bengali fiction writers, led by Bankim Chandra Chattopadhayay. He wrote four historical and two social novels, all of which were well-received by the reading public. *Banga Bijeta* (*The Conquerer of Bengal*) and *Madhabi Kankan* (*Bracelet of Flowers*) depicted the conquest of Bengal by Akbar. The other two historical novels were *Maharashtra Jiban Prabhat* and *Rajput Jiban Sandhya*. All four were published in 1879—an amazing output by any standard, especially by a high official in government service. His two other novels, *Samaj* (1885) and *Sangsar* (1886), were written with social purposes in mind—the first one advocating widow remarriage and the second one, intercaste marriage. Another contribution of Romesh Dutt to Bengali was his translation of the *Rig Veda* (1885).

He left London in 1904, came to India and joined as the revenue minister of Baroda, a state which was ruled by a very progressive and enlightened Maharaja Sayaji Rao Gaekwad who gave him a free hand to handle the reforms in the state, in August of the same year. Romesh Dutt did his job diligently and earned everyone's praise. In an article published in *India*, Sir William Wedderburn praised his work on several fronts: for lessening the burden of revenue on the royals by rationalizing the revenue structure; for giving great fillip to education in the state, by spending 6.5 per cent of the state revenue on education as compared to one per cent in British India. He also revived panchayat system in the state.[1]

---

[1] *Collected Works of Mahatma Gandhi*, Vol. 4, Publications Division, Government of India, pp. 456–7.

His departure from London saw the end of his career as a writer. After 1904, he did not write any books though he continued to deliver speeches and write articles in papers and journals.

In 1903, during the annual session of the Congress, an exhibition of Indian products was held for the first time as an adjunct to the Congress session. Romesh Dutt was requested to preside over the Industrial Conference. In his presidential address, he made a masterly analysis, in simple language, of the current economic and industrial situation in the country and the role which swadeshi could play in helping Indian industries, both small and large scale, to develop.

He was appointed as a member of the Royal Commission on decentralization which visited India in 1907, and had to leave Baroda service. The commission was set up to formulate ways and means to involve an increasing number of Indians in the administration. He was the only Indian member of the commission and signed its report with dissent notes on several points.

Romesh Dutt spent another year in London from April 1908 to March 1909, where he 'freely placed his counsel and criticism at the disposal of John Morley, Secretary of State for India, on the impending scheme of constitutional reforms'.

In June 1909, Dutt returned again to Baroda service as Diwan. However, this time he could not do much as his health started deteriorating. He died on 30 November 1909 in Baroda.

Romesh Dutt was one of the early Indians, who showed that Indians could administer as well as any British or European official. He might not have been a pioneer, but his interests were spread over many areas and his contribution in many of these was significant. Rabindra Chandra Dutt has spoken of him saying:

> If a comparative assessment has to be made, however, his work in the economic field would probably stand out as his most outstanding contribution to the future of the country. His contribution to Bengali literature and his researches in ancient Indian history were substantial, but his two volumes

of Economic History and his Famines India undoubtedly influenced more than any of his other works the future course of the National Movement in the country.[2]

---

[2]Dutt, Rabindra Chandra, *Romesh Chunder Dutt,* Publications Division, New Delhi, 1981, p. 171.

26

Indira Gandhi

(1917–1984)

Indira Priyadarshini Nehru was born on the 19 November 1917 in Allahabad. She was the only child of Jawaharlal Nehru and Kamala Nehru. A son was born to Kamala in 1924, but he unfortunately died after a few days, leaving Indira without any sibling. Indira later described her childhood as 'lonely' and 'insecure'. Soon after Indira's birth, her mother became sick. Later, the sickness was diagnosed as tuberculosis and the family was engrossed with her treatment for the rest of her life. At the same time, Indira's grandfather, Motilal Nehru, and her father, Jawaharlal, joined the Congress party and were greatly involved in the freedom movement led by Mahatma Gandhi. Both of them were often in and out of prison. As a result, Indira's formal education was peripatetic and unsystematic. When she was six years old, she was enrolled in St Cecilia's in Allahabad. However, she did not stay there long because of Jawaharlal's protestations as he was against the Anglo–Indian education that was prevalent in India. In March 1926, Indira accompanied her parents to Europe, where Kamala had to undergo treatment for tuberculosis. Indira was admitted to L'Ecole Nouvelle in Bex, Switzerland, where she picked up French and learnt to speak fluently. Later, she studied at the International School of Geneva. In December 1927, the family returned to India as Kamala's health had improved, as a result of which Indira's education in Europe was interrupted. In 1931, she was admitted to Pupil's Own School at Poona run by a devoted couple, Coonverbai J. Vakil and her husband Jehangir Jivaji Vakil, an Oxford-educated and confirmed socialist. It was a school with a difference and it gave full scope to students to develop individual thinking at their own pace. At the age of 16, Indira passed the matriculation examination of the Bombay University (now University of Mumbai). Soon after, she was admitted to Santiniketan as a student of Shiksha Bhawan and came under the benign influence of Rabindranath Tagore. But in April 1935, Indira had to leave Santiniketan as her mother's health had worsened and she had to accompany her to Europe. Dr Madan Atal, a cousin of Kamala, accompanied them. Jawaharlal was in Almora jail at the time and could not go but he was released on 4 September 1935 and was able to join his wife and daughter at Badenweiler, Germany, where Kamala was admitted in a sanatorium. In January 1936, Kamala was shifted to a sanatorium near Lausanne in Switzerland. Indira was admitted to her old school at Bex nearby but had come to Lausanne to be with her mother during her last days. Feroze, who had been a family friend, also joined them, uninvited. Kamala died on 28 February 1936, with Indira, Jawaharlal, Dr Madan Atal and Feroze Gandhi at her bedside. After studying at Bex for some time, Indira left for London and got herself enrolled at Badminton School in Bristol to appear for the matriculation examination of the University of London. Feroze Gandhi was also in London at that time, as a student at the London School of Economics. Indira met Feroze often and they used to go sightseeing or go to the theatre. A recent biography offering insight into Indira and Feroze's relationship during their stay in London has caused quite a controversy. Indira was in London for one year. After finishing her studies at Bristol, Indira went to Oxford and joined Somerville College on the recommendation of Professor Harold Laski, a friend of Nehru. At Oxford, she fell ill and had to go to Switzerland for treatment of pleurisy. When she recovered, she went back to Oxford but had to leave for India soon after as war clouds gathered over Europe. She sailed in a steamer via Cape of Good Hope with Feroze

Gandhi. After a long and tortuous journey, they reached Bombay in June 1941. Soon after, Indira announced that she wanted to marry Feroze. Kamala had been very much against Indira marrying Feroze. Before her death, Kamala had told Nehru that 'she was worried about Indira's relationship with Feroze because she was sure he was unstable'.[1] She did not think Feroze would enter any profession and be in a position to support Indira. It is not certain if Kamala knew that Feroze came from a doubtful parentage. After an initial reluctance, the Nehru family agreed and Indira and Feroze got married on 26 March 1942 in Allahabad. It was then that she changed her name to Indira Gandhi. The couple went to Bombay to attend the historic Congress session on 9 August 1942, where the Quit India resolution was passed. After some time, both of them were arrested. Indira was sent to Naini jail and was given 'A Class' in prison. On 13 May 1943, nine months after her arrest, Indira was released. Three months later, Feroze was also released from Faizabad jail. They set up home in Allahabad, in a small house on Fort Road. Their son Rajiv Gandhi was born on 20 August 1944. Their second son, Sanjay, was born on 14 December 1946, in New Delhi, where Nehru was heading the interim government at the time. Feroze was appointed managing editor of *National Herald*, an English daily founded by Jawaharlal Nehru, in Lucknow. He moved to Lucknow while Indira lived with her father in New Delhi, in the prime minister's official residence. She not only looked after her father but accompanied him on foreign tours, taking on the responsibilities of a hostess. She also started taking active interest in Congress affairs and was nominated a member of the CWC (1955) and of the Central Parliamentary Board (1958). In 1959, she was elected president of the INC, and held this office till January 1960. Obviously, she was being groomed by Nehru as his successor.

---

[1]Frank, Katherine, *Indira: The Life of Indira Nehru Gandhi*, Harper Collins, London, 2001.

Indira's domestic life during the years of Nehru's prime ministership was not a happy one. Feroze did not relish being referred to as 'Nehru's son-in-law', the phrase that was acquiring the overtones of a taunt. He found the whole business of protocol galling, because it relegated him to a humble position at social functions.[2] In due course, he was elected a Member of Parliament. Resigning his post of managing editor of the *National Herald*, he moved from Lucknow to Delhi, where he was allotted a house as a member of the Parliament. But Indira did not stay with him. She continued to stay with her father with her two sons in Teen Murti Bhavan, as his official hostess. There were rumours that the relations between Feroze and Indira had reached a breaking point. Indira denied the rumours unconvincingly. According to Ansar Harvani, 'When Indira assumed office as Congress president (1959), they were hardly on talking terms. He often used to write letters to her addressing sarcastically as "Comrade Congress president" and ending with "Yours fraternally".'[3] Feroze led a lonely and reckless life though he had emerged as a very successful parliamentarian, even embarrassing Nehru in the Parliament and exposing some serious corruption cases. But due to the strain of public life and an unhappy married life leading to indulgences, Feroze's health deteriorated and he died on 8 September 1960.

He was only 47.

The war with China in 1962 affected the prestige of Nehru as well as his health. He died in May 1964. Though he had groomed Indira for the prime ministership through the CWC and Congress presidentship, and tried to compensate her lack of formal education by writing over 200 odd letters, mainly on history (which did not interest her), the time was not ripe for her to head the government. She was only 47 when Nehru died. Lal Bahadur Shastri

---

[2]Pande, B.N., *Indira Gandhi*, Publications Division, New Delhi, 1989, p. 107.

[3]Harvani, Ansar, *Gandhi to Gandhi; Private Faces of Public Figures*, Gyan Publishing House, New Delhi, 1966, p. 211–12.

was elected 'unanimously' as prime minister, K. Kamaraj played a leading role in this decision. Indira was inducted by Shastri in his cabinet as information and broadcasting minister. In August, 1964, she was elected unopposed to the Rajya Sabha. The sudden demise of Shastri in January 1966 necessitated the selection of a prime minister once again. The weighty Congress leadership, known as 'the Syndicate', backed her candidacy as the successor to Shastri, reportedly because they considered her a pliable *goongi gudiya* (a dumb doll). As Morarji Desai was also an aspirant, an election ensued. Indira won by 355 to Morarji's 169 votes. She was sworn in as prime minister on 24 January 1966. She received a challenging inheritance. The country had to face two wars in four years and an insurgency in the Northeast. On the economic front, successive monsoon failures had affected food grain production, resulting in scarcity. She was handicapped by her own administrative inexperience and awkwardness in the Parliament. Her decision to devalue the rupee in 1966 by a whopping 57.7 per cent, without adequate preparation at home and financial assistance from abroad, had disastrous consequences. The prestige of the Congress was on the wane. When the election to Parliament was held in 1967, the party won only 283 seats of the 520 seats of the Lok Sabha and lost power in eight states. Many Congress stalwarts including Kamaraj and several ministers were defeated. However, she herself won from the Raebareli constituency and was sworn in as prime minister for the second time in March 1967 without opposition. As an act of prudence and as a gesture of goodwill, she invited Morarji Desai to become deputy prime minister holding the finance portfolio. She herself took over the external affairs portfolio in September and made an extensive tour of East European countries and Russia in October 1967 and of South America and Caribbean countries in 1968. She addressed the UN General Assembly on 14 October 1968. She was trying to emerge on the international scene as the prime minister of the largest democracy in the world.

In India, she also toured extensively, first as Congress president and later as prime minister and became quite popular among the masses, earning the sobriquet 'Mother India'. She directly appealed to the people to look to her for their emancipation from poverty and hunger over the heads of the party bosses. Her penchant for populism deepened as her dislike grew for the pressures put on her by the party bosses. The Syndicate had been weakened as many of the leaders had been humbled in the 1967 election. After the death of President Zakir Hussain in May 1969, she came in direct confrontation with the Syndicate over the choice of the new president. V.V. Giri won with the support of Indira Gandhi, defeating the Syndicate candidate Neelam Sanjiva Reddy and the Congress party split into two. The majority of members of Parliament joined the Indira camp and the rump called themselves 'Congress Old (O)'. Morarji had opted for Congress (O) and resigned, to the delight of Indira Gandhi. The former 'meek and shy' young lady had transformed into a great political strategist.

Indira Gandhi had won the battle against the Syndicate but she did not have a majority in the Parliament, which irked her and she felt that she was vulnerable. By now, she had learnt the art of being popular with the masses. To everyone's surprise, she put on the garb of a socialist, though as late as 1962 she had told an interviewer: 'I really don't have a political philosophy. I can't say I believe in any "ism".' She was 45 then and had never evinced interest in socialism, never talked of it, until the expediency of office forced her to.[4] She initiated several populist (leftist) measures like the nationalization of 14 major banks (July 1969), abolition of privy purses of the princes (November 1969) which Sardar Patel had certified at the time of Independence. Such measures had transformed her personal fight into an ideological one. Her 10-point programme aimed at a 'socialist pattern of society'. She thus acquired an image of a leader who felt deeply for the poor.

---

[4]Gopal, Ram, *Indian Freedom: Rhetorics & Reality*, Vimal Prakashan, Ghaziabad, 1988, p. 114.

Armed with such an image, she decided to hold the election in February 1971 instead of 1972, which would have been the normal course. The battle at the hustings was fought under the slogans *'Indira Hatao* (remove Indira)' by the opposition against *'Garibi Hatao'* (remove poverty)' by her party. Throughout January and February, Indira Gandhi campaigned even more strenuously and relentlessly than she had done in 1967. She won a landslide victory; her Congress winning 325 seats, a two-third majority in the Lok Sabha. It was her personal victory. She was sworn in as prime minister for the third time in March 1971 and 'she became the most powerful Indian Prime Minister since independence'. While Nehru first gained power and then office Indira Gandhi first gained office, then power. Her socialist agenda now encompassed several other spheres. She constituted a commission to regulate future expansion of industry and trade, abolished the old managing agency system and nationalized general insurance.

The year 1971 was one which threw up immense problems for Indira's government and ultimately brought unrivalled glory to Indira Gandhi. Trouble had been brewing in East Pakistan (now Bangladesh) from the very birth of Pakistan because of the cultural differences between the Eastern and Western wings. Early in 1971, elections were held in Pakistan and Mujibur Rehman's Awami League won with an overwhelming majority in the state assembly and a majority in the national assembly. But he was not allowed to head the government and was arrested. The army let loose a reign of terror in East Pakistan. 10 million refugees from there entered India, which affected the country, politically and economically. For India, it was no more a domestic matter of Pakistan. Indira Gandhi's government signed a Treaty of Peace, Cooperation and Friendship with the Soviet Union in August 1971. This treaty strengthened India's position vis-a-vis China and to some extent the US. India started training and helping the Bengali guerrilla force, named *'Mukti Bahini* (freedom force)'. Pakistan retaliated by bombing Indian airfields. There is a view that Pakistan offered a lifetime opportunity to India to dismember Pakistan. On 4 December, India declared war on Pakistan and the Indian Army, supported by the Air Force, entered East Pakistan and Pakistan army surrendered on 16 December. Bangladesh was born. Indira had become Goddess Durga for the masses, to the chagrin of her enemies. Her popularity was confirmed in the March 1972 State Assembly elections, in which the Congress captured 70 per cent of the seats contested. The president conferred the Bharat Ratna on her on 26 January 1972. On 2 July 1972, the Simla Agreement was signed by Indira Gandhi and the Pakistan president, Zulfiqar Ali Bhutto. India agreed to return the conquered territories and to release 91,000 Pakistani Prisoners of War. Her prestige and popularity were further enhanced when India conducted a nuclear explosion for peaceful purposes on 18 May 1974. By now, she had established complete dominance over the party, parliament and the country. When the Supreme Court invalidated the nationalization of banks and abolition of privy purses of the princes, she tampered with the independence of the judiciary, making it subordinate to the Parliament. She started depending on the advice of her younger son Sanjay, a school dropout. He was issued a licence to produce a small car and got allotted a huge plot of land near Delhi for the factory, bypassing all bureaucratic norms. Gradually, he became as powerful as Indira Gandhi herself and was surrounded by a score of young sycophants. The mother–son duo was now destroying the very pillars of democratic government. In 1973, she appointed A.N. Ray as the chief justice of India, superseding three judges that were senior to him. A new slogan was concocted, that the country required a 'committed judiciary' and 'committed bureaucracy'. It was argued that these were essential for the progress of the country and for implementing the 'progressive' policies of the government. Actually, it was to snuff out any opposition and to get away with illegal and corrupt dealings. Nationalization of banks and general insurance had enlarged the scope of corruption by Indira Gandhi and Sanjay Gandhi. The Nagarwala case, a bizarre scandal involving

₹60 lakh in 1972, was only the tip of the iceberg. The government treasury was no longer safe.

In 1975, came a bombshell. Justice Jagmohanlal Sinha of the Allahabad High Court set aside Indira Gandhi's election to Lok Sabha on grounds of corruption and debarred her from contesting polls for six years. While she consulted her lawyers to appeal to the Supreme Court, she encouraged her son Sanjay and his associates to organize mass rallies by hired hoodlums in her favour. To add to her woes, her party lost elections in Gujarat. She was also confronted by Jayaprakash Narayan's mass rallies, which were swelling in number by the day. The possibility of Congress losing the support of the people rankled in her mind. Moreover, the decision of the Supreme Court regarding her appeal did not help her either—a stay order against depriving her right to vote was all she got. She did not want to lose power and took the drastic step of proclaiming internal emergency and made President Fakhruddin Ali Ahmed sign the proclamation on 26 June 1975 in the dead of the night. All the opposition leaders, including Jayaprakash and Morarji, were arrested, censorship of the worst type was enforced and courts were closed. Indians did not get newspapers on that day. According to Amnesty International, during the first year of Emergency, more than 1 lakh people were arrested and detained without trial. Some were tortured and a few defiant ones were even killed. The Constitution was tampered with. Presidential orders were issued, suspending Articles 14, 21 and 22 of the Constitution. Sanjay Gandhi became the de facto ruler of the country, an extra-constitutional authority. He aggressively tried to implement his 'Five-point Programme' which included forced sterilization and slum clearance, along with his mother's 20-point programme. The rule of law was being replaced by the rule of Sanjay Gandhi. Everything was being done to save their rule. Election to Lok Sabha was postponed, which was due in 1976. However, there were some advantages of Emergency for the common man: trains were running on time, offices were working punctually and efficiently, there was less crime on the streets. Emergency, at least outwardly, seemed to be a success. But on the whole, there was fear and disgust among the people.

On 18 January 1977, Indira Gandhi took a U-turn and announced that the general elections were to be held in March of the following year. Most of the detainees were released and press censorship was relaxed. The opposition parties joined hands and formed the Janata Party. The results of the election stunned Indira and Sanjay. Both of them lost. The Congress (I) could win only 153 as against 299 by Janata including Jagjivan Ram's Congress for Democracy. The Janata Party formed a government, headed by Morarji Desai. The Janata Party had come to power on a negative vote—a protest vote against the Emergency. It had neither a history nor an organization; neither an ideology nor a programme of its own. The Janata conglomerate had several inner contradictions and the leaders did not work as a team. Their clumsy efforts to punish Indira Gandhi for Emergency excesses, especially arresting her twice, proved counterproductive. It did not come as a surprise to the nation when the Janata government fell in July 1979. Fresh election was held for the Lok Sabha and Indira Gandhi became the prime minister again, for the fourth time, on 14 January 1980. Her party won 351 seats in a house of 542, trouncing all other parties. She herself had won the Raebareli seat with a record margin. Sanjay Gandhi won from neighbouring Amethi. Using undemocratic methods, she dismissed nine Janata state governments, imposing President's Rule. Fresh elections were held. Indira's party won all but one of them. Sanjay once again came to his own element along with his coterie, most of whom were now members of Parliament. However, Sanjay died in an air crash on 23 June 1980 in Delhi. Indira was heartbroken but regained her balance and started working again almost immediately. There were some people who felt that Sanjay's death was the best thing that could happen to India.

The concentration of power, almost dictatorial, at the centre had resulted in the neglect of the states. The Congress lost in Andhra, Tamil Nadu and Karnataka. There was trouble in Assam, Kashmir and above all in Punjab, where the Akali Dal was challenging the supremacy of the Congress and had wrested power in the 1977 election. To meet their challenge, Sanjay Gandhi when alive, with a nod from his mother, had cultivated a demagogue named Jarnail Singh Bhindranwale. He was a fundamentalist at heart and soon gained a large following, which was armed by the Pakistan secret service. As his strength grew, Bhindranwale began to demand a separate, autonomous Sikh state, Khalistan. He moved into the Golden Temple, made the Akal Takht his headquarters and converted it into a fortress. His military adviser, a retired major general Shabeg Singh, who had trained the Mukti Bahini in Bangladesh, gave regular training in arms to the followers of Bhindranwale. They had become terrorists and had spread all over Punjab, killing people at will, mostly Hindus. Even the police were afraid of them. Indira Gandhi watched the tragic drama for some time with patience, but then decided to strike. On 6 June 1984, the army entered Harmandir Sahib (Golden Temple). It was called 'Operation Blue Star'. There was fierce fighting between the Indian Army and the well-entrenched Bhindranwale and his armed followers. Tanks and artillery had to be used. The Akal Takht, where Bhindranwale was hiding with his men, was heavily damaged and had to be rebuilt later. More than 300 army men had died in the confrontation. That was the end of Bhindranwale along with many of his followers who had become a terror in Punjab.

Indira Gandhi now feared her assassination, and even gave out instructions for her funeral. Her security was beefed up. But she refused to be protected by the army. She was assassinated by two of her own Sikh security guards, on the morning of 31 October 1984, in her own residence at 1, Safdarjung Road.

Indira Gandhi did not aspire to be a world leader like her father did, but she was active in the Non-Alignment Movement, founded at the initiative of Nehru at Belgrade in 1961. She attended the fourth Non-Aligned Conference at Algiers in 1973 and chaired the seventh Non-Aligned Conference held at New Delhi in March

1983. Indira Gandhi was not an intellectual like Jawaharlal Nehru and did not write much. Her speeches and reminiscences have been published in several volumes by the Publications Division of the GOI. Some other volumes have also been published by the Indira Gandhi Memorial Trust.

Indira's character was summed up by her father, Jawaharlal Nehru in a letter to his sister, Vijaya Lakshmi Pandit, in 1934, which is in the nature of a complaint. He wrote: 'She (Indira) scarcely writes to her parents; she ignores us completely. Her behaviour is extraordinarily self-centred, remarkably selfish.' In another letter, he complained that 'she is remarkably casual and indifferent to others. Indu revolves around herself, self-centred, she hardly thinks of others'.[5] In the light of her behaviour as prime minister, it seemed as if Indira never lost her sense of solitariness in a hostile world, always sought security in ways that made her intolerant of criticism and identified herself so completely with India that she made little distinction between her person, family and government. There was always authoritarianism lurking behind her cultivated charisma.

---

[5]Frank, Katherine, *Indira: The Life of Indira Nehru Gandhi*, Harper Collins, London, 2001, p. 84.

27

Mohandas Karamchand Gandhi

(1869–1948)

Mohandas Karamchand Gandhi was born on 2 October 1869 in Porbandar (also known as Sudamapuri) in Gujarat. His father Karamchand was the Diwan (prime minister) of Porbandar. His grandfather, Uttamchand, had also been the Diwan of Porbandar and later of Junagadh. Earlier, his ancestors had been grocers, a common occupation of the *Vaish* (Bania) community to which Mohandas belonged. Mohan's mother, Putlibai Karamchand Gandhi, was an extremely religious lady who devoted much of her time in worship, trips to the temples and fasting. The family belonged to *Vaishnava* sect which has a lot in common with Jainism. Gandhi was greatly influenced by the preachings of this sect and his belief in non-violence and the efficacy of fasting in later life could be traced to this early influence. It may be noted that Jainism venerates extreme forms of asceticism, like slow starvation and many spiritual Jain leaders have died in this way. But Gandhi used fasts as a moral force as well as a coercive tactic to achieve his ends.

When he was seven years old, Gandhi's family moved to Rajkot, another state in Kathiawar, where his father, Karamchand, had become a Diwan. There, Mohandas joined a primary school and later a high school. He was a mediocre student and was very shy and timid. He hardly took part in sports or gymnastics but was fond of walking, a hobby which he adhered to till the last days of his life. While still in high school, he was married, at the age of 13 to Kasturba, daughter of a merchant of Porbandar, who was of the same age or a year older than him. A baby was born to the couple within a year of marriage, who died after a few days. But later, four sons were born to the couple—Harilal (1888), Manilal (1892), Ramdas (1897) and the youngest, Devdas (1900). In 1906, at the age of 37, Gandhi claimed that he became a *brahmachari* (a celibate).

While he was still struggling with studies in school, his father died in 1885. Gandhi has devoted a full chapter in his autobiography, *The Story of My Experiments with Truth*, to describe the death of his father in poignant detail. After passing the matriculation examination in 1887, he joined Samaldas College in Bhavnagar, where the shy and introvert found studies difficult and the atmosphere in the college uncongenial. Someone suggested to him that it was much easier to get a barrister's degree in England than getting a law degree in India. Mohandas jumped at the idea and with the support of his family, sailed for England on 4 September 1888. He had already become a father by then. His eldest son Harilal was born in June 1888. Kasturba and the baby boy thus became the responsibility of Mohandas' mother, Putlibai and other members of the joint family. Mohandas spent almost three years in England and was called to the Bar in June 1891. A few days later, he left for India. During these three years, he had tried to live like an Englishman and bought expensive clothes and a silk hat. He learnt ballroom dancing, keeping to himself the fact that he was a married man. He had managed to remain a vegetarian and had even joined the London Vegetarian Society. He was 5 ft 5 inch tall, with an unimpressive personality but there was something in his character and bearing which attracted people to him. During all these years, Mohandas never wrote to his wife Kasturba as she was illiterate.

On his return to India, Gandhi decided to set up his legal practice in Bombay but he did not succeed. Frustrated, he returned to Rajkot and tried his luck there, without much success. While he was wrestling with the problem of his career as a lawyer, help came from an unexpected quarter—an offer came from the firm Dada Abdulla & Co. with headquarters at Durban, South Africa, to advise the firm in a law suit. Mohandas wanted to leave India, where he had not succeeded and was happy to accept the offer. Since his return to India, his wife had given birth to another son, Manilal (1892). Robert Payne has written about this saying, 'Mohandas felt no pangs at the thought of leaving his young sons, and because he had been spending less and less time with his wife, he was not distressed by the thought of abandoning her either.'[1] Gandhi sailed for South Africa in April 1893. On reaching Durban, Gandhi started studying the case and also started looking after the correspondence of the company. He was also helping the lawyers who were already fighting the case. After studying the case in detail, he advised the litigants to settle the matter through arbitration, which to his delight, was accepted by the parties. This exercise had taken one year. The task done, he was ready to go back to India. During this period, he had observed the pitiable condition of Indians in Transvaal and Natal and had some humiliating experiences himself. When he learnt that the situation for Indians was going to be worse through a proposed legislation to disenfranchise all the Indians in the Crown colony of Natal, he decided to stay on and fight for the rights of the Indians. Most of the Indians there were illiterate. They had come there as indentured labourers to work in sugar plantations and mines. Gradually, some of them had become businessmen, most of whom were Muslims like Dada Abdulla. But all of them remained almost illiterate and ignorant of their rights. The Indians were called *coolies* (indentured labour), whatever their profession. Gandhi started with writing petitions to the Natal government, making speeches and demanding interviews with government officials. To provide Indians with an

---

[1]Payne, Robert, *Life and Death of Mahatma Gandhi*, Rupa Publications, 1997, p. 86.

organization, he founded the Natal Indian Congress in 1894. He enrolled himself as an advocate in the Supreme Court of Natal. His legal practice flourished and gradually, he was able to employ a large staff in his office. He rented a big house in Beach Grove, where the elite of Durban lived. His efforts to fight for the rights of Indians were only partially successful.

The Bill for disenfranchisement of Indians was passed, though it was finally agreed that Indians already on the voters list would not be excluded. The £25 tax on Indians (a kind of *jizya* of the Mughal Vintage), was reduced to £3. In June 1896, Gandhi decided to visit India to bring his family to South Africa. During his six-month stay in India, he met several Indian leaders like Pherozeshah Mehta, Bal Gangadhar Tilak and Gopal Krishna Gokhale and was impressed most by the gentle and soft-spoken Gokhale. During his visit to India, he realized that while he was among intellectual inferiors in South Africa; in India, he would be among intellectual giants. He sailed back for South Africa with his wife, two sons and a nephew in December. In his absence, his clerks had been working for him in his office and his legal practice had not suffered. By now, he had become a prosperous barrister. 'His tone became more authoritative and more unyielding.' Besides being a successful barrister, he had become a political representative of the Indians, through his social work. The iron of ambition had entered him. He had set up his home in that big, beautiful house facing the sea in Durban, with his wife, children and quite a few 'friends' who worked for him. The Natal government was determined to restrict the number of Indians and were implementing laws towards that end. Gandhi continued the fight against injustice but it was an unequal struggle, which he rarely won and often lost. But when the Second Boer War broke out in October 1899, he offered his services to the Natal government at once because he felt a great sense of loyalty to the Empire. To help the British army, he formed the Natal Indian Ambulance Corps. For their services, Gandhi and 37 other Indian volunteers were awarded the War Medal after the war was won. When Queen Victoria died in 1901, Gandhi led a procession of Indian mourners through the streets of Durban. But, to his chagrin, all his effort to show his loyalty to the Empire proved counterproductive and after the war, the discrimination and harassment of Indians continued. He felt frustrated. 'On my relief from war-duty, I felt that my work was no longer in South Africa but in India,' he wrote in his autobiography. He left for India with his wife and children, telling his friends in Natal that he would return if they needed him. The family reached India in December 1901. Leaving his family at Rajkot, he hurried to Calcutta to attend the Congress session. Gokhale took him under his wings and got Gandhi's resolution on South African Indians passed in the Subject Committee.

Gandhi reached Rajkot and tried to practice law once again but without confidence and consequently without success. 'The memory of past failures oppressed him. The man who spoke so boldly in Durban, was tongue-tied in his own country.' Once again South Africa came to his rescue—a telegram from Durban summoned him back. He sailed for South Africa in the middle of November 1902, along with his family. He had been in India for about a year then. On his return to South Africa, he found that after Britain's victory in the Second Boer War, the condition of Indians was becoming worse. Consequently, the challenge there was the worst he had faced so far, especially in Transvaal. He, therefore, decided to stay in Johannesburg and enrolled as an advocate of the supreme court of Transvaal. In the meanwhile, Gandhi wanted to live a different kind of life—a community life where everyone would work with their own hands and earn their living. In this, he was influenced by the Trappist monastery near Durban, which he had visited earlier and books like *Unto This Last* by John Ruskin and *The Kingdom of God is Within You* by Leo Tolstoy. He bought a 100-acre farm in 1904, 14 miles from Durban, and established the famous Phoenix settlement. His family and several other persons started living at the Phoenix Farm. Such acts and experiments marked him apart from ordinary men. Even some British men like Henry Polak and Albert West joined him. Now, Gandhi had to commute between Phoenix Farm and Johannesburg, where he was practicing as a barrister. Despite the deteriorating condition of Indians under British rule, he once again wanted the Indians to show their loyalty to the British Empire during the Zulu uprising (1906). He exhorted the Indians not to be afraid of war. 'Wars were relatively harmless. They (Indians) would prove their patriotism by killing Zulus (the local inhabitants),' he argued. This was a strange and perverse argument, which ran counter to his religious beliefs.As Robert Payne has said, 'To the generation accustomed to remembering Gandhi as an apostle of peace, these arguments may startle them. It is strange that not only Gandhi approved of war during Zulu uprising but whenever war broke out, he was in the forefront, calling upon Indians to volunteer.'[2] The Zulu uprising was suppressed brutally by the British in a few months. Gandhi had no remorse in giving a token help to the British in this unequal conflict.

The situation in Transvaal continued to get worse. To plead the Indian case to the government in London, the Indians decided to send a delegation to England. They financed it through contributions. The two-member delegation comprised Gandhi and H.O. Ally. They sailed for England in October 1906, travelling first class and stayed at Hotel Cecil, one of the more expensive hotels in London. A similar delegation was sent in 1909, comprising Gandhi and Sheth Haji Habib. Again, they had travelled first class and stayed at Cecil Hotel. The two delegations did not achieve anything. But the indomitable Gandhi continued to fight the Black Acts of Transvaal and Natal governments and exhorted the Indians to violate the unjust laws non-violently. This he called satyagraha, in which even some whites participated. He spread his ideas through the newspaper *Indian Opinion*, which was published in English, Gujarati, Tamil and Hindi, from his Phoenix Farm from 1904

---

[2]Ibid. 121–22.

onwards. Thus, he had prepared himself and the Indians well for the forthcoming battle. They agitated against the £3 tax on Indians; against compulsory registration and giving fingerprints, and against annulment of all marriages not solemnized according to Christian rites. The fight through satyagraha continued for several years. Gandhi and hundreds of Indians were arrested for violating the law, time and again. In 1910, Gandhi had established another settlement named Tolstoy Farm near Johannesburg to accommodate and feed the satyagrahis. In 1912, Gokhale visited South Africa to argue the case for the Indians. General Smuts agreed to dilute some of the harsh measures but went back on his promise, after Gokhale left. Ultimately, a provisional agreement was arrived at between General Smuts and Gandhi in which some minor demands of Indians were conceded, but the government did not change the policy of apartheid and Indians there continued to suffer discrimination. In July 1914, Gandhi sailed for India via England, where he spent several months for the treatment of pleurisy which he had developed. Mark Thomson has mentioned that, 'Though the limited gains Gandhi realised for the Indian community in South Africa were later nullified by the racialist policies of successive white governments, his *Satyagraha* Movement did reveal the effectiveness of organised non-violent resistance against the more powerful opponent.'[3] In fact, the experiences in South Africa left a permanent imprint on Gandhi's thinking and we find him referring to these experiences time and again during his innumerable discourses in India. According to Jawaharlal Nehru, 'Gandhiji underwent a tremendous conversion during his early days in South Africa, and this shook him up greatly and altered his whole outlook on life. Since then, he has had a fixed basis for all his ideas, and his mind is hardly an open mind.'[4]

---

[3]Thomson, Mark, *Gandhi and His Ashrams,* Popular Prakashan, Bombay, 1993, p. 38.
[4]Nehru, Jawaharlal, *An Autobiography*, John Lane, London, 1936, p. 516.

In South Africa, Gandhi also had some very unpleasant experiences. One such experience happened in February 1908. In that year, he had led an agitation against the Black Act which required every Indian to get himself registered after giving 10 fingerprints. He and some other satyagrahis were imprisoned for refusing to give fingerprints. But soon after, he without consulting any of his colleagues, agreed to register after giving fingerprints 'voluntarily'. He was released. This infuriated some of his followers. When he came out of prison, some Pathans questioned him, 'It was you who told us that fingerprints were required only from criminals. How does that fit in with your present attitude?' The Pathan also bluntly told Gandhi, 'We have heard that you have betrayed the community and sold it to General Smuts for £15,000. We will never give fingerprints nor will let others do so.' When Gandhi went to the Registration Office to give fingerprints, a group of Pathans confronted him and a burly Pathan, Mir Alam, hit him with a heavy stick. Others gave him more blows and kicks. He fell unconscious. A Christian missionary, Joseph Doke, who was passing by, took pity on him, brought him home and nursed him back to health.[5] Gandhi appealed to the government to not take any action against those who had assaulted him. Doke was so impressed by Gandhi and his philosophy of life (which was similar to that of Jesus Christ) that he wrote a biography of Gandhi, the first one among hundreds that were to follow. The incident shows two sides of Gandhi—his inconsistency and whimsical attitude to the problems at hand, and his winning ways through gentleness and what came to be called 'charisma', sowing the seeds of greatness in the man. Gandhi was so excited upon seeing his biography in print that he bought all the copies of the book and distributed them to his friends, acquaintances and to people in power, free of cost. The blow inflicted by Mir Alam seemed to have changed the attitude of Gandhi towards

[5]Tendulkar, D.G., *Mahatma*, Publications Division, New Delhi, 1960, p. 90–91.

Muslims, resulting in the appeasement of Muslims during the remaining years of his life. He wrote a letter (21 June 1909) to a Muslim friend, Habib Mohan, which was in reply to a letter in which Mohan had asked Gandhi's opinion about the demands of the Muslim delegation presented to Lord Minto (1906) and the latter conceding to all the demands. Gandhi wrote, 'My personal view is that, since numerically Hindus are in a great majority, and are, as they themselves believe, better placed educationally, they should cheerfully concede to their Muslim brethren the utmost they can. As a *satyagrahi,* I am emphatically of the view that the Hindus should give to the Muslims whatever they ask for, and willingly accept whatever sacrifice this may involve.'[6] It is evident that the policy of Muslim appeasement was enunciated by Gandhi while still in South Africa. In this, he was neither influenced by Tilak nor Gokhale. He was his own guru.

Gandhi also had some other enemies in South Africa, besides Pathans. In a letter to Chhaganlal Gandhi (11 March 1914) from Cape Town, he wrote, 'Medh (Surendra) writes to say that they are plotting again in Johannesburg to take my life. That would indeed be welcome and a fit end of my work. In case I die suddenly, by the reason this of any other, I want to set down here certain ideas which I have thought out.'[7] The remainder of the letter is somewhat like a testament, giving details of how different members of his extended family were to be provided for. It is not clear who was after Gandhi's life.

Gandhi reached Bombay on 9 January 1915. He had already sent his apostles to India, before leaving South Africa. They arranged a hero's welcome for their mentor as Gandhi was not yet known to the Indian masses. As advised by Gokhale, Gandhi toured India for one year, 'keeping his eyes open and mouth shut', but he

---

[6] *Collected Works of Mahatma Gandhi,* Vol. 9, Publications Division, Government of India, p. 265.
[7] Ibid. 380.

could hardly follow the latter part of Gokhale's advice. He made several speeches during the year. He had become a compulsive speechmaker or rather sermonizer; his weekly 'silence day' later in life, notwithstanding.

After the stipulated year of wandering, he settled down at Ahmedabad, where he founded the Kochrab Ashram on 25 May 1915. It was inititally started at the at the suburb in a bungalow but the bungalow soon proved to be too small for the projected ashram. He then bought 1,130 acres of land on the bank of the Sabarmati River and moved the ashram there. He appealed for funds and donations came pouring. Gujaratis are a rich community and have a tendency towards philanthropy. Gandhi had no dearth of money for his ashram. He named it 'Satyagraha Ashram'. This was the third ashram he had founded. The number of ashramites grew from 30 to about 200, as Gandhi's fame spread. Each member of the ashram had to take some vows—of truth, *ahimsa* (non-violence), celibacy, non-stealing, non-possession and control of palate. But the vows were often broken, especially that of celibacy by both male and female ashramites, some of whom were married couples. In spite of the vows, Gandhi attracted social workers, scholars, minor politicians, students and cranks. Later, his secretary Mahadev Desai remarked that 'the Ashram to me looks like a mad house'. This was a cynical exaggeration. The ashram had developed into a small village with its own farm, dairy and tannery. It also had a school and a small workshop. On 12 February 1926, the Satyagraha Ashram was registered in the name of Mohandas Karamchand Gandhi and Maganlal Gandhi, his cousin, and the value of the property was assessed at ₹275,000. For 15 years (1915–1930), this ashram served as the Gandhi's headquarters.

Soon the time came for Gandhi to launch his political career in India, for which he had done preparatory work in South Africa and later in India. He had studied the psychology of the Indian masses, which helped him to create a mass following. He knew that Hindus were a people who adored sacrifice and identified leaders with what they gave up and less by what they had. He changed his dress to give him a look of a poor Indian farmer. If politics is to be compared with marketing, Gandhi was a marketing genius. He used his appearance to communicate. The communicative power of costume transcended the limitations of language in a multilingual and illiterate India. His apostles, based in his ashram at Ahmedabad, augmented his efforts and strategy by spreading myths about him and soon he earned the reverent title of the 'Mahatma'. The illiterate, superstitious masses now looked to him for miracles. Small miracles did follow. The first one was in Champaran, Bihar in 1917, where he went to look into the problems of peasants working in indigo plantations owned by white planters. Through his efforts, the condition of farmers was ameliorated to some extent and the Mahatma earned the gratitude of thousands of poor farmers. The next satyagraha was for solving the dispute between workers and mill owners at Ahmedabad, which was solved partially through arbitration (1918). Immediately afterwards, he launched a satyagraha at the Kheda district in Gujarat, where farmers were heavily taxed, even when their crops had failed. After four months of 'no-tax campaign', the government agreed to suspend the assessment of tax for the poor farmers. Gandhi was emerging as a miracle man.[8]

However, during the First World War (1914–1918), while freedom fighters like Rash Behari Bose were trying to inspire the Indian soldiers to stage a revolt against the British, Gandhi acted as a recruiting agent for the British army, and earned a medal for his services. Then came the Jallianwala Bagh Tragedy (13 April 1919) at Amritsar, in which hundreds of innocent and unarmed Indians were shot dead and wounded. The ghastly and inhuman act of the British shook the nation and Gandhi was quick to sense the mood of the masses and intellectuals alike. He started an anti-British movement. In the meanwhile, the Muslims in India were angry with the British for the treatment meted out to Turkey and

---

[8]Ibid. 380.

the Khalifa, who was the head of the Muslim *umma* (faithful). They had formed a Khilafat Conference, which decided to start non-cooperation with the British government. The movement was led by the Ali brothers (Mohammad and the burly, Shaukat) and Maulana Abul Kalam Azad. They invited Hindus to join in their anti-government and Pan-Islamic movement. Gandhi not only joined the Khilafat Conference but started acting as their guide and friend. B.R. Ambedkar has spoken of this, saying,

> Thus, the truth is that the non-cooperation had its origin in the Khilafat agitation and not in the Congress movement for Swaraj; that it was started by the Khilafatists to help Turkey and adopted by the Congress only to help the Khilafatists; that Swaraj was not its primary object, but its primary object was Khilafat and that Swaraj was added as a secondary object to induce the Hindus to join it.[9]

According to Annie Besant: 'As the Khilafat was not sufficiently attractive to Hindus, the Punjab atrocities and the deficiencies of Reforms Act were added to the list of provocative causes.'[10] In his autobiography, Gandhi wrote, 'The adoption of non-cooperation for the sake of the Khilafat was itself a great practical attempt made by the Congress to bring about Hindu-Muslim unity.' Many Indian leaders like Madan Mohan Malaviya, Annie Besant, Bipin Chandra Pal, Chittaranjan Das and others tried to dissuade Gandhi from fighting for a cause which did not concern India at all. But Gandhi ignored their protests and convinced himself that he was fighting for a sacred cause. He could not see that the Khilafat Movement was 'oddly unreal, for the Muslims in India had not previously felt any great bond with the khalifa nor was there any concerted movement in any of the Muslim countries for the

---

[9]Ambedkar, B.R., *Pakistan or the Partition of India.* Bombay, Thacker and Company, 1946, p. 148.
[10]Besant, Annie, *Future of Indian Politics*, Theosophical Publishing House, Madras, 1922, p. 250.

restoration of the authority of the khalifa. It was an essentially an Indian Muslim movement and drew its strength from imaginary grievances'. Gandhi gambled dangerously and unwisely. But he felt that he was in a strong position now, Muslim support adding to his strength. He formally inaugurated the Non-cooperation Movement on 1 August 1920 (the very day Tilak died) by returning three medals the government had awarded him for his services to the Empire. Gandhi then reached Calcutta, on 4 September, to attend the special session of the Congress, accompanied by an army of enthusiastic Khilafatists. There, he moved his resolution on non-violent non-cooperation, which stipulated every Indian to surrender all the titles and honours conferred by the government; lawyers to boycott the courts; teachers and students to walk out from government aided schools and colleges; and all government employees to leave their offices, culminating in a no-tax campaign. The idea was to bring the government machinery to a grinding halt. Gandhi did not explain how lawyers and government employees would live and support their families if they left their jobs. There was strong opposition to the proposal, coming from leaders like Chittaranjan Das, Annie Besant, Bipin Chandra Pal. However, Gandhi and the Khilafatists had got a crowd assembled at the venue of the Congress as delegates. Train load of 'delegates', hired by Bombay's merchant Prince Mian Mohammad Haji Jan Mohammad Chotani, arrived and packed the panel, to vote for the resolution of Gandhi. All Muslims, except Jinnah, voted for, and almost all leading Hindus, except Motilal, voted against the resolution. When put to vote, the verdict was 1855 votes for and 873 against the resolution. The Calcutta Congress gave Gandhi his first major victory. Emboldened by this, he reached Nagpur for the regular session of the Congress in December 1920, where the resolution on non-violent non-cooperation passed at Calcutta had to be ratified. By this time, leaders like Chittaranjan Das and Lajpat Rai were won over by Gandhi to his side. Like the Congress session at Calcutta, the Nagpur session was also dominated by the Muslim presence. According to a leading Muslim League leader, Chaudhry Khaliquzzaman, 'The Congress session in Nagpur was almost a Muslim session of the Congress for I believe that the number of Muslims was so large as to give it a Muslim colour.'[11] The only strong voice against the resolution was that of Jinnah. When he stood up to oppose the resolution and addressed Gandhi as 'Mr' he was shouted down. 'Say Mahatma,' the unruly crowd demanded and didn't let him proceed. Jinnah walked away, never to return to the Congress. Many believe that it was the turning point in the history of the Congress, and that of India. Gandhi's resolution was passed with overwhelming majority of votes once again.

Immediately after the Nagpur session of the Congress, Gandhi declared that he would now get swaraj (self-rule) within one year through non-violent non-cooperation and he went around the country accompanied by the Ali brothers propagating his proposed miracle. But while the Muslim leaders were making violent speeches, inciting the religious fervour of the Muslims, Gandhi was speaking on an entirely different level of non-violence and non-cooperation. As nothing startling was happening, Muslims were getting impatient and they unleashed their fury in Malabar, spearheaded by the Moplahs. Murder, rape, pillage and forcible conversion of Hindus followed. Annie Besant wrote in anguish, in her weekly *New India*: 'It would be well if Mr Gandhi could be taken into Malabar to see with his own eyes the ghastly horrors which have been the result of his preachings and his loved Ali brothers, Mohammed and Shaukat. The slaughter in Malabar cries out his responsibility.' But Gandhi not only remained unmoved by the plight of thousands of Hindus but also tried to defend the Moplahs by saying that, 'the brave, God-fearing Moplahs are fighting for what they consider as religion, and in the manner which they consider as religious'. The Congress, under his guidance, suppressed all reports about the atrocities and started blaming the authorities for suppressing the riots and started

---

[11]Khaliquzzaman, C., *Pathway to Pakistan*, Longmans, Lahore, 1961, p. 57.

a relief fund for the Moplahs. The Congress government in free India even went a step further by classifying Moplah rioters as freedom fighters and made them eligible for pension.

The year 1921 ended without swaraj. By this time, leading Congressmen like Chittaranjan Das, Subhas Chandra Bose, Lajpat Rai had been imprisoned. To the dismay of Gandhi, the massive boycott which he had expected did not take place: a large number of students continued to study (even universities like BHU and Aligarh University were not closed); there were long queues in front of government recruiting offices; lawyers did not stop attending courts except a few like Chittaranjan Das, Motilal Nehru and Rajagopalachari, who had amassed wealth and were secure. Fearing dismal failure of the Non-cooperation Movement, Gandhi, without consulting any one, suspended the movement on 24 February 1922, giving the Chauri Chaura incident, in which some policemen were burnt alive as reason for suspension. The nation was stunned. Lajpat Rai wrote a 17-page letter from prison addressed to Congressmen, in which he blamed himself and other Congress leaders for 'surrendering our better judgement to his (Gandhi's) decision'. Along with this, mass 'civil disobedience' as planned by Gandhi in the Bardoli *taluka* (administrative district) in Gujarat was also abandoned, for which hectic preparations had been made earlier.

Congress leaders like Chittaranjan Das, Motilal Nehru and Lajpat Rai lost faith in the infallibility of Gandhi and his methods and formed the Swaraj Party; contested in the forthcoming elections and entered the Councils. The declining popularity of Gandhi emboldened the government to arrest him on 10 March 1922. He was sentenced to six years imprisonment but was released after two years due to his illness. He went to his ashram, spending his time spinning and learning Urdu. He asked his followers to do 'constructive work'. But his hold on the masses did not completely vanish. His charisma remained. The reason was that Gandhi had carried out his propaganda among the masses rather than at the

Congress sessions. His activity was not confined to the podium but was conducted among the people in the streets of rural and urban India. He was a great and astute organizer. When he took over the Congress party in 1920, he turned it into a mass movement. Earlier it was a sort of discussion club of the elite, who passed resolutions during the annual sessions. Now the Congress had committees comprising committed members from the taluka, district, state and culminating into the AICC and, its executive smaller wing, the CWC. He also ensured that Congressmen should demonstrate allegiance to him, and him alone. The spinning wheel was the first item on Gandhi's economic agenda and it served as a barometer to judge the loyalty of the Congress workers to him. He had politicized it by making regular spinning incumbent on every Congressman; failing which his membership would cease. The other criterion was non-violence, absolute non-violence. This was to put a check on the glory earned by revolutionaries for their daring deeds. Muslims were, however, exempt from these two norms. The hold on the Congress machinery was evident when he was elected to preside over the Congress session at Belgaum in 1924.

The failure of the Non-cooperation Movement provoked the Muslims to indulge in large-scale rioting, though the Khilafat question was solved by the Turks themselves by ousting the Kaliph from Turkey. The most serious riots took place in Kohat, West Punjab and Gulburga in the Nizam's territory, both in 1924. The communal riots continued in subsequent years, proving the dangers of dubious methods adopted by Gandhi to bring unity among Hindus and Muslims. Gandhi went on a 21-day fast after the Kohat tragedy, in which almost the whole Hindu and Sikh population of the town was shifted to Rawalpindi. The fast did not bring any change in the communal situation and the riots continued at different places. Frustrated, he lived quietly in the Sabarmati Ashram after that. Though he continued to make speeches, he didn't have anything new to say. People were tired of hearing his familiar sermons on charkha and untouchability. However, he watched the political developments in the country and waited patiently for the comeback. By 1928, top leaders of the Congress were dead—Bal Gangadhar Tilak (1920), Chittaranjan Das (1925) and Lajpat Rai (1928). Motilal Nehru was sick and was worried about the future of his son, Jawaharlal. Gandhi placated the Nehrus by offering the presidentship of the Congress to Jawaharlal in 1929. Once again, Gandhi had no rival. He occupied centre stage. Then he burst on the political scene of India like a tornado. On 1 January 1930, the Congress declared 'purna swaraj' as its political objective and authorized the Working Committee to launch a Civil Disobedience Movement. Gandhi, the great strategist and publicist, started the movement in a most dramatic manner. He was to break the Salt Laws. On 12 March 1930, Gandhi, followed by 78 members of his Sabarmati Ashram, started a march heading towards Dandi, a small village on the sea coast of Gujarat. The party took 24 days to reach Dandi, passing through scores of villages. It was a well thought out publicity gimmick. The march became world news. On 6 April, after reaching Dandi, Gandhi picked up a little lump of salt left by the waves. The whole of India was electrified. Salt laws were being violated at thousands of places in the country. The Civil Disobedience Movement had begun. Gandhi was arrested on 4 May. Always ready to compromise, he wrote a letter from prison to the viceroy, seeking an interview which was granted. This resulted in the famous Gandhi–Irwin Pact, the details of which were announced on 5 March 1931. The Congress agreed to suspend Civil Disobedience. The government agreed to release all prisoners, restore the forfeited lands and allow villagers living near the coast to collect salt for personal use (which they had been doing for centuries anyway). But the government monopoly on salt remained. The Salt Laws were not changed. Gandhi also agreed to attend the Second Round Table Conference in London (for the first one, the Congress did not send its representative), to be held later in 1931. He elected himself as the sole representative of the Congress. The Conference was a complete failure and the parties did not reach a consensus.

It was left to the Prime Minister Ramsay MacDonald to give his verdict. On his return, Gandhi renewed Civil Disobedience and was arrested, along with thousands of Congress workers. While he was still in Yervada jail, the Communal Award was announced by the government in August 1932, which allowed separate electorates for the depressed classes (Scheduled Castes). Gandhi foresaw the bifurcation of the Hindu society and went on a fast unto death to get it annulled. The fast was broken when a pact (now known as the Poona Pact) was signed between B.R. Ambedkar (representing the Scheduled Castes) and Madan Mohan Malaviya, on behalf of the upper caste Hindus. Separate electorates were withdrawn, but a larger number of seats were allotted to Scheduled Castes in the assemblies. This was one of the greatest achievements of Gandhi, saving the Hindu society from a great catastrophe.

While starting on the Dandi March, Gandhi had abandoned the Sabarmati Ashram and sometime later established another ashram called Sevagram, near Wardha. He severed his formal connection with the Congress in September 1934 but remained the undisputed leader of the Congress, taking important decisions till almost the very end. In March 1940, the Muslim League passed what has come to be known as the 'Pakistan Resolution'. Gandhi was the first Congress leader to support the Muslim league contention of an 'autonomous and sovereign Muslim nation'. Under the title 'A Baffling Situation', Gandhi wrote in *Harijan* (6 April 1940): 'Muslims will be entitled to dictate their own terms. Unless the rest of India wishes to engage in internal fratricide, the others will have to submit to Muslim dictation if Muslims will resort to it.'[12] This view, he reiterated again and again in subsequent years.

On 9 August 1942, the Quit India resolution was passed by the CWC, drafted like many others resolutions, by Gandhi. But the government swiftly acted and arrested him and other Congress

---

[12] *Collected Works of Mahatma Gandhi*, Vol. 71, Publications Division, Government of India, p. 388.

leaders during the night of either 9 or 10 August. Gandhi, with 23 of his colleagues, including Kasturba, was kept in the Aga Khan Palace, Poona, where Kasturba Gandhi and Mahadev Desai, died during internment. He was released on 6 May 1944, as usual, on health grounds. Then happened one of the most humiliating incidents in his life. He went to Bombay to meet Jinnah, offering him the Rajaji Formula which contained the 'essence' of Pakistan. For 18 days, 9 to 27 September 1944, Gandhi trudged to Jinnah's palatial house on Malabar Hill. The two met daily, discussed and then exchanged letters summarizing their discussions. Gandhi addressed Jinnah as 'Dear Quaid-e-Azam' and Jinnah addressed his adversary as 'Mr Gandhi' in the letters. How things had changed! In 1920, at Nagpur, Jinnah addressed Gandhi as 'Mr Gandhi' and he was heckled and humiliated. But in 1944, not a single Gandhite came forward to protest. On the last day, Jinnah dismissed Gandhi by writing, 'No responsible organization can entertain any proposal from any individual, however great he may be, unless it is backed up with the authority of a recognized organization, and comes from its fully accredited representative.' Gandhi never again boasted that he was not even a four anna member of the Congress. Gandhi had been warned for undertaking this misadventure by leaders like Mukund Ramrao Jayakar. After the failure of the talks, K.M. Munshi wrote to Gandhi, 'Your formula is now in Mr Jinnah's hands and he will use the formula as a bargaining counter with the British government and also as the starting point in future negotiations with Indian leaders.' About the Gandhi–Jinnah meeting, Lord Wavell wrote in his journal: 'Anything so barren as their exchange of letters is a deplorable exposure of Indian leadership. This surely must blast Gandhi's reputation as a leader. Jinnah had an easy task; he merely had to keep on telling Gandhi he was talking nonsense, which was true and he did so rather rudely.'[13] Indeed,

---

[13]Payne, Robert, *Life and Death of Mahatma Gandhi*, Rupa Publications, 1997, p. 512.

this mistake of Gandhi had weakened his position and that of the Congress, and had brought Pakistan several steps nearer. In July 1946, when his biographer, Louis Fischer, asked Gandhi what he had learned from his 18 days with Jinnah, he replied. 'I learned that he (Jinnah) was a maniac. I could not make any headway with Jinnah because he is a maniac.' It took Gandhi three decades to understand Jinnah, while Mountbatten reached the same conclusion in his first meeting with Jinnah in March 1947. Gandhi returned to his Wardha Ashram, a dejected man. He became ill, suffering from 'bad cold, a bronchitic cough and pain in the chest'. Soon he had his fourth nervous breakdown. As mentioned in *Wavell: the Viceroy's Journal*, 'He felt so spiritually isolated from his flock and from all India, that there were many who wondered whether he would ever resume his political life.'[14]

As the withdrawal of the British approached and the top leaders saw power coming in their hands, differences between Gandhi and his colleagues began to crop up and during the talks with the Cabinet Mission (March–June 1946), they became serious. Pyarelal, Gandhi's secretary, wrote: 'In that hour of decision they had no use of Bapu. The Cabinet Mission invited the members of the Working Committee to meet them. Bapu, not being a member, was not sent for and did not go. On their return, nobody told Bapu a word about what had happened in the meeting.' In a note to G.D. Birla in 1946, Gandhi wrote, 'My voice carries no weight in the Working Committee. Today I feel like *Trishanku*. Is it really time for me to retire to the Himalayas?' He felt that he was not wanted in Delhi and left for Noakhali in November 1946, and later, went to Bihar, where serious communal riots had broken out. He came to Delhi at the end of March 1947 at the invitation, not of his colleagues, but of the new viceroy, Mountbatten. The new viceroy had a one-line brief: 'Hand over India to the Indians'. It

---

[14]Moon, Penderel (ed.), *Wavell: the Viceroy's Journal*, Oxford University Press, London, 1973, p. 91.

had become dangerous for the British to hold on to India. As the Muslim League was adamant to have Pakistan and was resorting to large scale rioting and killings, for which the Congress, wedded to non-violence, had to answer for, the British decided to partition the country.

Gandhi attended the meeting of the AICC, in which the resolution about accepting the partition of the country was to be discussed and passed. He had already made known his views about the partition of the country. The burden of his speeches and writings during 1940–47 was—partition of the country on religious basis is an untruth; the only solution to deal with this untruth is to yield to it; if we do not yield, there will be bloodshed and destruction (a civil war); there was no other, violent or non-violent method, to solve this problem. In his speech in the AICC (14 June 1947), he forcefully advocated the partition of the country and silenced the opposition led by Purushottam Das Tandon, J.B. Kripalani and others. The resolution accepting partition was passed by an overwhelming majority. It is a travesty of truth to claim that Gandhi was opposed to Partition till the very end. Facts do not support that claim. India was partitioned and became independent on 15 August 1947. Two independent dominions were created— India (Bharat) and Pakistan. Gandhi stayed on in Delhi, residing in the Birla House.

That winter of Gandhi's life was a winter of despair. His charisma ceased to work. The masses who used to come for his *darshan* (meeting with a holy figure), more often came now to abuse him. His unsympathetic attitude towards the unfortunate millions of Hindus and Sikh refugees (who believed that Gandhi was mainly responsible for their misery) antagonized them. Several of his prayer meetings were disturbed by angry refugees. Nearly 95 per cent of his mail was full of abuse in those post-Partition days. For millions of Indians, he had become a dangerous man. The worst had yet to come. Late in 1947, a war between India and Pakistan broke out over Kashmir. Gandhi went on a fast, forcing the GOI India to release ₹50 crore to Pakistan, which were held up by the Indian government 'until the Kashmir affair was settled'. This upset many people. He was assassinated on 30 January 1948, while he was coming out to address a prayer meeting in the Birla House garden. His funeral procession was organized as a military operation by the British commander-in-chief. His body went on its last journey in an army vehicle.

The aftermath of the assassination was horrible, but the details were suppressed by the government. Chitpavan Brahmins (to which caste, Nathuram Godse, his assassin, belonged) were the target of the fury of the followers of Gandhi. Nobody knows how many innocent people were killed, their houses burnt down, their property looted in Poona, Bombay, Nagpur, Satara, Belgaum and Kolhapur. One of the rare studies of the post-assassination violence was made by Maureen Patterson who ruefully reported that she was not given access to relevant police files even decades after the incident. She estimated that the death toll may run into hundreds.[15]

After Gandhi's death, a vast hagiography appeared. Miracles were assigned to him; things he had never done and words he had never spoken were credited to him. He became a government institution, with his portrait on the walls of Indian embassies abroad and government offices and courts inside India. Across the Raj Ghat in Delhi, where Gandhi was cremated, stands a museum and library to perpetuate the memory of the great man. His few possessions are carefully exhibited there, including the Australian woollen shawl that he was wearing at the time of his death.

'There is something in Mahatma Gandhi which appeals to the mass of Indian people. Born in another country, he might have been a complete misfit. What, for instance, would he have done in country like Russia or Germany or Italy. His doctrine of non-violence would have led him to the cross or to the mental

---

[15]Elst, Koenraad, *Gandhi and Godse: A Review and A Critique*, Voice of India, New Delhi, 2001, pp. 12–13.

hospital', wrote Subhas Chandra Bose.[16] In an unguarded moment on 10 June 1947, Gandhi said about himself in a prayer meeting,

> In India, public opinion is not as vigilant as in England. Had it been so, a worthless fellow like me should not have presumed to become a *mahatma*. And even after I became a *mahatma,* everything that I did would not have been put-up with. As it is, in India everyone who is called a *mahatma* ceases to be answerable to the public, whatever—right or wrong—he might do.[17]

Gokhale, while living with Gandhi in South Africa, had remarked that 'there is arrogance even in Gandhi's humility'.

The real tragedy of Gandhi was his family life. He did not care to bring up his four sons like a loving and caring father. As head of the family, Gandhi was a bully. His wife and children feared him. None of his sons could be called educated in the real sense. The most tragic life was led by his eldest son, Harilal, who became an alcoholic and a pervert and spent last two decades of his life abusing his father whom he believed was responsible for his plight. By his behaviour, Gandhi almost alienated the feelings of his wife, Kasturba. No one ever saw her laughing or even smiling. Her spirit was crushed by an autocratic and eccentric husband. But Gandhi had no idea that he was tormenting his wife and sons. 'Ba often wondered why her husband acted like God because he was but a mortal like herself. She remembered how he had groaned and moaned when his first molar was extracted.' Her being illiterate was a boon for Gandhi. Many secrets and truths about his life were cremated with her in 1944.

In spite of his concern about his health and about preaching others how to keep oneself healthy, Gandhi was not a healthy man.

---

[16]Bose, Subhas Chandra, *The Indian Struggle, 1920-1942,* Oxford University Press, 1997, pp. 327–28.

[17]*Collected Works of Mahatma Gandhi*, Vol. 88, Publications Division, Government of India, p. 124.

He also suffered four nervous breakdowns, the worst collapse being in 1937. According to Judith Brown,

> Gandhi's collapses were rarely due solely to overwork. The undoubted physical and mental strain to which he constantly exposed himself was often overlaid with emotional tension or distress which led to a "physical collapse". Although the aging Mahatma seemed to the public a tranquil spirit, he was often moody, and experienced a turbulent anger with himself, his family and his close colleagues.[18]

Those who believe that Gandhi lived the life of a poor Indian farmer will be surprised to learn the kind of diet he used to take. In a letter to Satish Chandra Dasgupta (20 June 1933) Gandhi wrote: 'I am taking nearly four lbs of milk and plenty of oranges, pomegranate, juice and grapes. That is my staple food.' In his early life, Gandhi was fanatically opposed to taking milk. In a letter to Chhaganlal (11 March 1914), Gandhi wrote, 'The idea of it (milk) is pure flesh, and not in keeping with the way of non-violence, will never leave my mind. I do not think that I shall ever be able to consume milk, etc. while I inhabit this body.' Gandhi's whole life is full of such contradictions. He could work as recruiting agent for the British army during the First World War and keep intact his faith in the creed of ahimsa. He has spoken of this himself, saying,

> Foolish consistency is the hobgoblin of little minds. My aim is not to be consistent with the previous statements on a given question, but to be consistent with the truth as it may present itself to me at a given moment. The result has been that I have grown from truth to truth. My words and deeds are dictated by prevailing conditions. There has been a gradual evolution in my environment and I react to it as a satyagrahi. What I am concerned with is my readiness to obey the call of Truth,

---

[18]Brown, Judith, *Gandhi: Prisoner of Hope*, Oxford University Press, 1990, p. 284.

my God, from moment to moment, and, therefore, when anybody finds any inconsistency between any two writings of mine, if he has still faith in my sanity, he would do well to choose the later of the two on the same subjects.[19]

Gandhi was not only a compulsive speaker and preacher but also a compulsive writer. He believed in the power of the written word. He did not write many books, but three of them stand out. The first is a small booklet, titled *Hind Swaraj* (1909), which contains criticism of modern civilization and machinery, but comes across as outdated and Utopian over time. *Satyagraha in South Africa* (1928) describes his experiences in South Africa. His bestselling work has been *The Story of My Experiments with Truth,* which was initially written in Gujarati but later translated by him in English (1927). It ends with the Nagpur session of the Congress (1920) but has been the major source of information for his biographers, especially British and American. It has been translated into almost every Indian language and many foreign languages as well. 'Inevitably it omits much that is important and the accounts of the later years are sketchy and disorderly. He occupies the centre of the stage, and has not gift for bringing any other character to life.' However, the autobiography does provide a peep into the fascinating character of Gandhi.

He has edited or has been associated with at least five journals. Most of his journalistic writings are either in Gujarati or in English. In South Africa, he took charge of *Indian Opinion,* a weekly in Gujarati and English in 1903. In India, he was responsible for bringing out *Navajivan* (Gujarati). *Young India* (English) a weekly started by the Home Rule Party of Bombay was taken over by Gandhi in 1919 (ceased publication in 1932). *Harijan* (English), *Harijan Bandhu* (Gujarati) and *Harijan Sevak* (Hindi), started in 1933. Most of his letters, speeches, addresses and miscellanies

---

[19] *Collected Works of Mahatma Gandhi,* Vol. 55, Publications Division, Government of India, p. 61.

appeared in these journals, which have been published and meticulously edited in the 100 volumes of *Collected Works of Mahatma Gandhi*. He had an army of secretaries who recorded for posterity almost every word uttered by Gandhi in speeches or during personal interviews. 'No public figure has written so much over such a long period. For the greater part of his adult life, we know what he was doing and thinking at every hour of the day.'

In spite of his mistakes and failings, he rode like a colossus on the political horizon of India during the first half of the twentieth century. This period is rightly called 'the Gandhian era'. He awakened the masses and moulded them into an army of freedom fighters almost single-handedly. He had mastered the technique of winning over his enemies, which added to his greatness. At the same time, Gandhi was a very complex personality. He played the dual role of a saint and an active politician. Thus, he tried to ride two horses at the same time. 'Unfortunately, Gandhi's followers did not make this distinction and gave unto the political leader what was really due to the saint.' Even Jawaharlal Nehru, the rationalist, fell into this trap. He wrote, 'Gandhi was a unique personality and it was impossible to judge him by the usual standards or even to apply the ordinary canons of logic to him. But history must apply to him the same standards of judgment and criticism as have been applied to all other personalities, great or small, who have played any role in public affairs.'[20] The most serious mistake which the followers and admirers of Gandhi make is to attribute to him the sole credit for freeing the country from foreign rule. This does great injustice to thousands of freedom fighters and revolutionaries who sacrificed their lives to see India a free country. The most notable name among those freedom fighters is that of Subhas Chandra Bose whom the British feared most and whose exploits in Southeast Asia were the main reason of the hasty retreat of Britain from India, at

---

[20]Majumdar, R.C., *History of the Freedom Movement in India*, Firma KLM, Calcutta, 1977, p.17.

a time when Congress leaders, including Gandhi, were an exhausted and harmless lot. When the Bill on 'Granting Freedom to India' came up before the British Parliament, the leader of the opposition, Winston Churchill, took the government to task and demanded reasons for doing so. Prime Minister Attlee gave two reasons: the Indian mercenary army was no longer loyal to the British Crown (obviously referring to the raising of Indian National Army by Subhas Bose), and England was not in a position to organize and equip its army on a scale large enough to control India.

Gandhi was nowhere in the picture.

However, Mahatma Gandhi did not need any certificate from the British Government to confirm his unique services to the nation. There could be no doubt that no one in the freedom movement played as large a part as Gandhi did. At the same time, it must be conceded that he did not work on a virgin soil and did not work alone. There were thousands who sacrificed their very lives for the national cause but Gandhi certainly walked like a colossus among millions others for more than 30 years.

28

Asadullah Khan Ghalib

(1797–1869)

Ghalib's *shers* (couplets) are recited and quoted by people who do not even know the Urdu language. He is the only Urdu poet for whom a research academy has been formed by the GOI in Delhi. There seems to be no decline in his popularity with the passage of time. Even Jawaharlal Nehru used to quote Ghalib's couplets in his letters to his friends and relatives. In *Discovery of India,* Nehru wote, 'The leading poet in Urdu and one of the outstanding literary figures of the century (nineteenth) in India, was Ghalib, who was in his prime before the Mutiny.'[1] There must have been something unique about Ghalib, which the other Urdu poets lacked.

Ghalib was born on 27 December 1797 in Agra, where his father Abdullah Beg lived with his wife's parents. His father had taken service with the raja of Alwar, Bakhtawar Singh, and was killed in a battle in 1802. Thereafter, Ghalib and his siblings were taken care of by his uncle, Nasrullah Beg Khan. His uncle, who was under the service of the British, also died in 1806. The British gave his family pension, out of which Ghalib's share came to ₹750.50 annually, which he continued to receive till 1857, when the Mutiny broke out.

Ghalib wrote about his ancestry in a letter to a friend on 15 February 1866: 'I am of Seljuk, Turkish stock. My grandfather

---

[1]Nehru, Jawaharlal, *Discovery of India*, New Delhi, Jawaharlal Nehru Memorial Fund, 1946, p. 346.

came to India from beyond the river (Transoxiana), in Shah Alam's time.' The most detailed and authoritative biography of Ghalib is *Yadgar-i-Ghalib,* written by Altaf Husain Hali, who was Ghalib's contemporary and a poet of good standing himself. So, unlike many other Urdu poets, the life of Ghalib is quite well documented. His own letters to his innumerable friends in Persian as well as in Urdu are another authentic source of his life and times.

Ghalib's full name was Mirza Asadullah Khan. Ghalib was his *takhallus* (an assumed one-word name which Urdu poets use for their works). Earlier, he also wrote some poetry under the pen name 'Asad'. His childhood was spent in Agra in the home of his maternal grandparents, who were quite well-off. Ghalib's father had married into one of the most distinguished families of Agra and lived most of his life in his in-laws' house. So did his children. Early in life, Ghalib was sent to a *maktab* (school), run by Muhammad Mu'azzam, a reputed scholar of his time. Ghalib studied classical Persian prose and poetry under him. Around 1810, a Persian traveller, Abdul Samad, came to Agra and stayed with Ghalib's family for two years. Ghalib learned the intricacies of the Persian language from him. Though Ghalib had no formal *ustad* (guide), as most of the poets of his time used to have, he remained grateful to Abdul Samad throughout his life and often boasted in his letters to his friends that he had learned Persian from an Iranian.

In 1810, at the age of 13, Ghalib was married to eleven-year-old Umrao Begum, daughter of Nawab Ilahi Bakhsh Khan, brother of Ahmad Baksh Khan of Loharu. Soon after their marriage, around 1812, Ghalib came to Delhi and settled permanently there, though he frequently visited Agra. Umrao Begum gave birth to at least seven children, but unfortunately none of them survived more than a few months. Even otherwise, it could not be called a happy marriage because the couple did not have much in common. According to Hali, his biographer, 'Ghalib's wife was an exceedingly pious and sober lady, meticulous in keeping the fasts and in saying her prayers. She was as strict in her religious observations as Ghalib was lax in these matters—so much so that she even kept her own eating and drinking utensils apart from her husband's.'[2] Ghalib seems to have felt that a wife was an encumbrance and he could very well have done without one. He was a frequent visitor to courtesans and even fell in love with at least one of them. Ghalib was tall, handsome with broad shoulders and dressed like an aristocrat, even when he was in financial troubles, which he was for most of his adult life. His pecuniary troubles, to some extent, were of his own making because he lived beyond his means. At no time did Ghalib have fewer than five servants, including a maid who helped the ladies with their chores. While going out, he never walked but travelled in a palanquin carried on the shoulders of four men. The total wages of these servants came to about ₹25 per month.[3] He was also fond of rich food and expensive drinks like whisky and drank daily. He was very proud of his insignificant ancestry, which tempted him to lead a lavish lifestyle and instilled a certain unreasonable pride in him. When he was offered a job to teach Persian in the newly-founded Delhi College, he went there in a palanquin and expected the principal of the College to come out to receive him. When the principal refused to oblige him, Ghalib spurned the offer and never went back.

Due to these habits, Ghalib was always in financial trouble and spent much of his time pursuing his cases of pension from the British and appealing and accepting largesse from nawabs of Rampur and Lucknow, and later from Bahadur Shah Zafar. Much of his time and energy was wasted fighting his pension battles. His trip to Calcutta, to appeal to the governor-general, took one year and in all, he spent three years fighting his pension case. After all the trouble that he took, he lost the case. Often his friends and disciples, both Muslim and Hindu, came to his rescue.

[2]Russell, Ralph and Khurshidul Islam, *Ghalib: 1797-1869, Vol. I: Life and Letters*, George Allen & Unwin, London, 1969, p. 104.
[3]Sud, K.N., *Eternal Flame: Aspects of Ghalib's Life and Works*, Sterling Publishers, New Delhi, 1969, p. 20.

He had also started gambling, perhaps to overcome his financial difficulties. At one time, his house had become a gambling den, and was raided for this unlawful activity in 1841. He was fined ₹100 and let off by the British authorities. But he did not desist from gambling. In 1847, he was caught again. This time he was fined ₹200 and sentenced to six-month rigorous imprisonment but was released after three months. This must have been one of the most distressing experiences of his life. Most of his friends deserted him, only Nawab Mustafa Khan Shefta stood by him and used to visit him regularly in prison.

Ghalib did not believe in religious rituals. He never prayed or fasted and was accustomed to drinking daily. According to Hali, Ghalib believed:

> The long and respectable pedigree of a particular doctrine did not guarantee its correctness; that human fallibility was as evident in former days as now, and that a man must use his own judgement to decide on the correctness or otherwise of an accepted belief. His whole temperament drove him to reject any idea of the absolute finality of anything that had happened in the past.[4]

In modern parlance, he was a rationalist. Ghalib came from Sunni stock, but at some stage of his life became a Shia, or if not actually a Shia, one closely sympathetic to the Shia belief. In fact, when he died, there was a dispute between Sunnis and Shias regarding his burial ceremony. But at the end, Sunnis prevailed and he was buried as a Sunni.

He had little respect for the maulvis who preached in the mosques and made fun of them in his poetry:

Ham ko maloom hai Jannat ki haqiqat lekin, dil ke khush rakhne ko Ghalib ye khayal achha hai.

---

[4]Russell, Ralph and Khurshidul Islam, *Ghalib: 1797-1869, Vol. I: Life and Letters*, George Allen & Unwin, London, 1969, p. 34.

(We know the reality about Paradise but it is a good idea to keep oneself happy.)

And again:

Kahan maikhane ka darwaza 'Ghalib' aur kahan waiz, Par itna jante hain, kal woh jata tha ki hum nikle.

(Ghalib cannot think of the preacher entering the doors of the bar, but he knows this much that yesterday he [the preacher] was going in while he [Ghalib] was coming out.)

Muslims accepted these barbs in good humour and took this as poetic licence. Thus, Ghalib was completely devoid of religious bigotry or racial prejudices. He had as many Hindu friends as Muslims. In a letter to Munshi Gargopal Tafta, he said, 'I hold all human beings, whether Musalman, Hindu or Christian, dear to me and regard them as my brothers.' One of his servants was a Hindu, who served him throughout his life. Ghalib started composing Urdu and Persian poetry at a very young age, but he concentrated the next 25 or 30 years on writing Persian poetry. He even wrote letters to his friends in Persian during this early period. Thus, his output in Persian far exceeds that of his output in Urdu. While his *dewan* (collection) of Persian poetry has over 11,000 verses, his Urdu collection has only 2,000 verses, which were selected by Ghalib himself, after he discarded another 3,000 which he considered not up to the mark. Two compilations of Ghalib's Persian poems were published in his lifetime: *Diwan Maikhana-E-Arzoo* (1845) and *Kulliyat-e-Ghalib Farsi* (1862). His prose works in Persian are *Panjahang*, *Mehri-e-Neemroz* and *Dastanbuy*. *Panjahang* consists of five parts and contains his Persian letters which he wrote to his friends before the Mutiny. *Mehr-e-Neemroz* is the story of the Timur dynasty, which Ghalib was commissioned to write in 1850 by Bahadur Shah Zafar. Ghalib was getting an annual stipend of ₹600 for writing this. Only the first volume, which ends with Humayun's return to the throne, could be completed. *Dastanbu* was written during 1857–58, when Ghalib was holed up in his house. It describes what happened during those days in Delhi. It is mostly in praise of the British. Six out of its 80 pages are a *qasida* (ode), devoted to Queen Victoria. It must have helped Ghalib to get his pension restored by the British, which had been stopped in 1857. Ghalib also wrote a critique of a Persian dictionary *Burhan-i-Qati*, under the title *Qati-i-Burhan*, which raised a lot of controversy among the literary circles of the day.

Ghalib was proud of his Persian poetry and dismissed his Urdu poetry as of no consequence. He wrote:

Farsi bin ta babini naqsh-hai rangarang
Bigyzar az majmua-i-Urdu kibe rang-i-manast.

(Read my Persian verses if you want to see pictures of various hues. Overlook my Urdu collection for it is devoid of my true colour.)

Ironically, it is the Urdu poetry which has made him famous and popular with the masses. Very few are familiar with his Persian poetry. Later, Iqbal's Persian poetry and writings also met the same fate.

As stated above, Ghalib wrote much less in Urdu. Several versions of his *Dewan* were published in his lifetime, spanning several years. He himself selected 2,000 verses out of 5,000 and called the compilation the 'real *Dewan*' of Ghalib. But after his death, these 3,000 discarded verses have also been included in his later *Dewan*. One consolidated *Dewan* was published in 1951, by Panna Lai Bhargava, proprietor of Munshi Publishers in Lucknow. By the time Ghalib's first *Dewan* was published in the 1830s, he had already become famous and was participating in *mushairas* (poetry gatherings) held in the Red Fort by Bahadur Shah Zafar and other places like Lucknow, Rampur etc. Several nawabs and rulers of states had become his *shagird* (disciple) and used to get their verses corrected or improved by him. This correction work of various disciples and admirers, who used to send their poetry to him in a continuous stream, was done by him till his last days and he seemed to have enjoyed doing so. Ghalib's prestige was considerably enhanced in 1854, when the popular court poet Zauq died and Badshah Zafar appointed Ghalib as the court poet and his own *ustad* (master). Two of the princes also became his disciples.

Ghalib is remembered as an Urdu poet because he transformed the entire spirit of ghazal writing. According to K.N. Sud, 'He broadened its spire from a mere love prattle to encompass the whole gamut of man's life and experiences. The thought contained in Ghalib's verses is for the most part expressed in strikingly original manner.'[5] Besides the subtle style of presentation of his thoughts, he added humour into his writings, often tongue-in-cheek, which set him apart, making him a rage for a century and a half. Some of his verses are so subtle that scholars and critics have been arguing for decades about their deeper meanings. However, Hali's interpretations, given in *Yadgar-i-Ghalib,* are considered most authentic because he had discussed the interpretations of many of such verses with Ghalib himself. But Hali does not cover all of Ghalib's controversial verses.

Ghalib's prose is mainly represented in his letters, which he wrote to his friends, disciples and benefactors, during the last two decades of his life. Earlier, he used to correspond in Persian. The language of Ghalib's letters has a unique flavour. He addresses the person as if he was sitting in front of him. He had cut down the flabbiness and superfluous elements from Urdu prose. His prose sparkles with wit and drollery. Even his barbs are good-humoured, incapable of offending the person towards whom they are directed. Ghalib enjoyed repartee and people flocked to him to hear his witticisms. Ghalib had genuine love for his friends and disciples whom he tried to help in all possible ways. Of course, he had enemies and critics too, but their number was insignificant compared

---

[5]Sud, K.N., *Eternal Flame: Aspects of Ghalib's Life and Works,* Sterling Publishers, New Delhi, 1969, p. 61.

to the overwhelming number of his admirers.

Ghalib's letters throw a flood of light on his times, especially on the events that occurred during the Mutiny. He was distressed, which is evident from his letters, because many of his relatives and friends were hanged or imprisoned by the British. Two collections of his letters—*Ud-i-Hindi* (1868) and *Urdu-i-Mualla* (1869)—were compiled during his lifetime, though the latter was published a month after his death. Many other letters have been discovered and published since. Through these letters, Ghalib 'initiated a simple, natural and fascinating style of prose, which became a model for other writes and laid the foundation of chaste modern Urdu.' But Ghalib, among the multitude, is remembered for his verses only.

Ghalib never built a house and spent all his life in rented houses. He remained mostly in Gali Qasim Jan of Mohalla Ballimaran in Delhi's Chandni Chowk. The last house which he occupied was near a mosque. In the words of Ghalib:

Masjid ke zer-i-saya ik ghar bana liya
Ye banda-i-kameena hamsaya-i-khuda hai

(I have taken residence under the shadow of a mosque.
This scoundrel is now God's neighbour.)

Wit and humour did not desert him till the end.

During the last years of his life, he lost the ability to hear and his vision failed him too. After a long illness, he died on 15 February 1869 and was buried in Mazar-e-Ghalib, near Nizamuddin Dargah, besides the legendary poet Amir Khusro.

29

Aurobindo Ghose

(1872–1950)

Aurobindo was born in Calcutta on 15 August 1872. His father, Krishna Dhun Ghose, a civil surgeon, got a medical degree from Aberdeen University (Scotland), and came back fully westernized. His mother Swarnalotta was the daughter of Rajnarayan Bose, a distinguished Bengali Brahmin of the nineteenth century. Aurobindo was the third son of the five children of his parents.

Aurobindo's father was so influenced by Western culture that he wanted his children to have 'an entirely European upbringing'. The three brothers were sent to Loreto Convent in Darjeeling, an English medium school. Their father had also arranged an English nurse to train his children in English customs and manners. At home, the family spoke only English and Hindustani. Aurobindo learnt Bengali late in life.

When Aurobindo was seven, his father took the three brothers to England for their education. Aurobindo studied privately from 1879 to 1884 under Mr and Mrs Drewett. But in 1884, he was sent to St Paul's School in London, where he learnt Greek and Latin during his five-year stay. He also learnt Italian, some German and a little Spanish. It was during this time that he started writing poetry—a hobby and passion that that he carried to Cambridge and continued throughout his life. He excelled academically and won a scholarship to the King's College, Cambridge. In his final year at St Paul's, he got through the ICS open competition, getting a good position but failed in the riding test and was disqualified, much to the chagrin of his father.

Aurobindo studied at King's College from 1890 to 1892; passed the first part of the tripos but did not graduate. After staying for nearly 14 years in England, he sailed back to India and joined the Baroda State Service. From 1893 to 1906, he served in Baroda— first as a probationary officer in the revenue settlement department and later as a lecturer in French and then in English language and literature at the Baroda College. When he left the college, he was the vice-principal, getting a salary of ₹750 per month. During his stay in Baroda, he learnt Sanskrit, Marathi and Gujarati and copiously wrote prose and verse in the English language. He also contributed a series of articles in *Indu Prakash*, a periodical published in Bombay, during August 1893 and February 1894, under the title 'New Lamps for Old'. But the publication of his articles was stopped after only two articles (out of the proposed nine) as the publishers feared that they may result in a sedition charge. Thereafter, Aurobindo 'drew back in silence' and worked surreptitiously till 1905.

In 1901, Aurobindo married Mrinalini Devi, the daughter of Bhupal Chandra Bose. When Aurobindo left for Pondicherry, he did not take her with him. Mrinalini passed her days in religious pursuits and died a forlorn lady in 1918.

The partition of Bengal by Viceroy Lord Curzon resulted in the awakening of Bengal and a movement for the annulment of partition was launched, culminating in an outburst of revolt against the government. Aurobindo had been visiting Bengal during vacations in his college and had come in contact with revolutionaries like Pramathanath Mitra, president of the Anushilan Samiti, Sister Nivedita and other revolutionary leaders and had even joined a splinter group of revolutionaries for some time.

The Swadeshi Movement ushered in by the partition of Bengal brought out the sense of nationalism in the masses of India. Aurobindo could not resist the temptation to jump in and contribute his share in the national struggle. When the National Council of Education (NCE) set up the National College in Calcutta in August 1906, Aurobindo resigned from the Baroda service and became its first principal, on a nominal salary. But soon he veered round to active politics. He started writing inflammatory articles in *Jugantar*, a Bengali daily started by the revolutionaries in 1906. He joined as the editor of *Bande Mataram*, a weekly newspaper started by Bipin Chandra Pal in 1906. As *Bande Mataram* demanded his full time and attention, Aurobindo resigned from the National College. Sometime in December 1906, Bipin Chandra separated from *Bande Mataram*, leaving Aurobindo in control of the paper. In article after article in the newspaper, Aurobindo spelled out the programme and agenda of the Nationalist party and advocated complete independence through swadeshi, boycott, national education, non-cooperation and passive-resistance. In his articles, he also developed a political philosophy of revolution and wrote that many leaders 'aimed at destroying the shibboleths and superstitions of the Moderate party such as the belief in British justice and benefits bestowed by foreign government in India'. Because of this aggressive publicity (in the *Bande Mataram*), the ideas of the nationalists gained ground everywhere. The *Bande Matram* was almost unique in journalistic history in the influence it 'exercised in converting the mind of a people and preparing it for revolution.'[1] Soon Aurobindo emerged as a great nationalist along with national leaders like Bal Gangadhar Tilak and Lala Lajpat Rai. People started looking to him as the new messiah, who would deliver the nation from foreign bondage.

In 1907, the government began taking repressive measures against the press and *Bande Matram* was the first to be charged for sedition. On 16 August 1907, an arrest warrant was issued against Aurobindo for publishing a letter titled 'Politics for Indians'. However, he was acquitted on 23 September. 'The arrest and the nonchalant attitude of Aurobindo inspired Rabindranath Tagore

---

[1] *The Complete Works of Sri Aurobindo*, Sri Aurobindo Ashram, 1972, pp. 29–30.

to write a beautiful poem which begins with *"Arabinda Rabindrer laha namaskar"* (Rabindranath, Oh Aurobindo, bows to thee!).' The *Bande Matram* case added to the fame and stature of Aurobindo in national politics.

On 30 April 1908, a bomb was thrown at a carriage in Muzaffarpur (Bihar) which killed two British women, Mrs Kennedy and her daughter. The carriage had been mistaken to be that of Douglas H. Kingsford, the chief presidency magistrate who had pronounced hard sentences on the revolutionaries while posted in Calcutta. The bomb was thrown by Khudiram Bose and Prafulla Chaki who met a martyr's death. A wave of shock and consternation shook India, followed by unprecedented repression. In May 1908, 37 people were arrested for the crime, which included Aurobindo and his brother Barindra, who was active as a revolutionary. All of them were put on trial. Consequently, Aurobindo spent one year in jail. The defence council for Aurobindo was Chittaranjan Das who argued for eight days. He concluded with the statement:

> Long after this controversy is hushed in silence, long after the turmoil, this agitation ceases, long after he is dead and gone, he will be looked upon as the poet of patriotism, as the prophet of nationalism, and the lover of humanity. Long after he is dead and gone, his words will be echoed and re-echoed not only in India but across distant seas and lands. Therefore, I say that the man in his position is not only standing before the Bar of this court but before the Bar of the High Court of history.[2]

Aurobindo was released after the trial but he had already spent one year in Alipore jail. When he came out of the jail on 6 May 1909, Aurobindo was a completely changed man. Though he had been practicing yoga since 1904, in the seclusion of the prison cell, he

---

[2]Agarwal, B.R., *Trials of Independence*, National Book Trust, New Delhi, 1991, p. 69.

reached much higher in the realm of yoga and had deep spiritual experiences. But he did not quit politics immediately. After the closure of *Bande Mataram*, he had started two journals—*Karamyogin* (19 June 1909), a weekly in English, and *Dharma*, a weekly in Bengali—in collaboration with Sister Nivedita and some others. In these two journals, he wrote articles on the deeper significance of Indian nationalism. He still seemed to exert great influence on the younger generation and even the elder statesmen listened to him. His motto, 'No compromise', rankled the government and they were busy finding an excuse to nab him once again. Aurobindo got an inkling of that and wrote 'An Open Letter to My Countrymen', published in *Karamyogin* on 31 July 1909, in which he affirmed the nationalist political programme. This letter is considered as his last political will and testament. The government got even more apprehensive about his activities. In February 1910, Aurobindo received information that the office of the *Karamyogin* would be searched and he would be arrested. To avoid another arrest and jail term, he left for Chandernagore, a French enclave. After staying there for some time, he reached Pondicherry, another French settlement in India, on 4 April 1910. He spent the rest of his life there.

Soon after his arrival in Pondicherry, he was joined by a French couple Paul Richards and his wife Mirra, who later became famous as 'The Mother'. Together, they started an English monthly, *Arya: A Philosophical Review*, in August 1914, in which new truths about man's divine destiny and the path for its realization were revealed. It also elaborated on the inner meaning of the Vedas, the Upanishads and the Gita as well as on the significance of Indian culture and civilization. It contained a French section as well. *Arya* ceased publication in 1921, but its contents were later published in several books authored by Aurobindo such as *The Life Divine*, *Synthesis of Yoga*, *The Human Cycle*, *The Ideal of Human Unity*, *The Future Poetry*, *On the Veda*, *The Upanishads*, *Essays on the Gita* and *The Foundations of Indian Culture*.

Aurobindo's life in Pondicherry is a closed book, though he did react to the political situation developing in the country and the world at large. For example, in 1940, he advised the Congress to accept the Cripps proposals, which they rejected. During the Second World War, he expressed his sympathies with the British and the Allied powers, notwithstanding his antagonism to the British rule earlier. He even wrote a poem about Hitler's triumphant march through the countries of Europe, titled *The Children of Wotan* (Wotan is a Germanic god), a few lines of which read:

> Where is the end of your armoured march,
> O children of Wotan?
> Earth shudders with fear at your tread,
> The death flame laughs in your eyes.

In Pondicherry, several ex-revolutionaries and other seekers of truth and salvation joined Aurobindo. He called them *sadhaks* (seekers). Gradually, an ashram developed with strict rules of conduct. But in 1926, Aurobindo retired into seclusion, which he maintained till his death, handing over the management of the ashram to The Mother. For 40 years, he shut himself up in his ashram and refused to see people from outside. In December 1933, Gandhi expressed a desire to see Aurobindo and The Mother. When Gandhi's letter was shown to Aurobindo by a disciple he wrote on it in pencil:

> You will have to write that I am unable to see him (Gandhi) because for a long time past I have made it an absolute rule not to have any interview with anyone—that I even do not speak with my disciples and only give silent blessings to them three times a year. All requests for an interview from others I have been obliged to refuse. The rule has been imposed on me by the necessity of my *sadhana* (spiritual pursuit) and is not at all a matter of convenience or anything else. The time has not come when I can depart from it.[3]

---

[3] *Collected Works of Mahatma Gandhi,* Vol. 56, Publications Division, New Delhi, 1973, p. 499.

That gives a glimpse of Aurobindo's life in his ashram in Pondicherry.

Aurobindo died of kidney trouble on 5 December 1950, leaving behind the ashram where over 2,000 of his sadhaks live today as a well-knit community. There is also a Sri Aurobindo International Centre of Education, which runs several educational institutions on principles taught by Aurobindo. Auroville, an international community, is where nationals of various countries reside.

Aurobindo's role in the freedom movement and later as a yogi and philosopher has dwarfed his talent as a poet. Gandhi has spoken of him saying, 'Sri Aurobindo's His 'original verses as well as translations of portions of the *Mahabharat* and the *Ramayana*, devotional songs of Chandidas and Vidyapati and Bhartrihari bespeak of his poetic talents; his writings are refulgent with rich imagery, buoyancy, mysticism, originality of approach and refinedness of style. And even in his sardonic poems he could weave good poetic garlands.'[4] The culmination of Aurobindo's poetic genius is reflected 'in his supreme spiritual work' in blank verse, *Savitri,* which is perhaps the longest epic poem in the English language. An American critic called it 'a great cosmic poem'. *Savitri* was divided into three parts—the first part was published in 1950, just before Aurobindo's death, while the second and third parts were published in 1951.

Thus, with his few golden utterances and many silences, Aurobindo left an indelible mark on the hearts of his people and on the sands of history.

---

[4]Ibid. 499.

30

Gopal Krishna Gokhale

(1866–1915)

Gopal Krishna Gokhale, son of Krishna Rao Shridhar and Valubai Gokhale, was born in the Ratnagiri district of Maharashtra on 6 May 1866. They were poor but respectable Chitpavan Brahmins. Though his father died when he was only 13, Gopal had no difficulty in getting a formal education. After finishing his primary education in a village school, he studied at the Rajaram College in Kolhapur, Deccan College in Poona and Elphinstone College in Bombay, from where he graduated in 1884. He also joined a law course but left the college without completing it.

Gokhale was married at the age of 14 to Savitribai, who soon developed a chronic disease. Consequently, he was married a second time in 1887. Unfortunately, his second wife Rishibama died in 1900 while giving birth to her second daughter. Soon after, the first wife also died. Gokhale remained a widower for the rest of his life.

Soon after his graduation, Gokhale joined the Deccan Education Society founded in 1884 by Bal Gangadhar Tilak, Gopal Ganesh Agarkar and others. When Fergusson College was opened by the society in 1885, Gokhale was invited to teach English literature and mathematics. He taught in the college for 18 years, retiring in 1904. At different times, he taught history, economics, political science, besides English literature and mathematics and was nicknamed 'professor-to-order', demonstrating his wide knowledge of subjects. However, economics gradually became his favourite subject. He studied the economic conditions of the country in depth, which enabled him to use this knowledge later in his political career, especially during the Assembly debates on the budget.

In 1886, Gokhale was introduced to Mahadev Govind Ranade, an influential political leader and social reformer and Gokhale started his political apprenticeship under him. Though a high government official (he was a judge of the high court), Ranade devoted much of his time to political and social activities. Gokhale's later political life was largely shaped by his mentor's liberalism and moderate philosophy. Ranade also introduced Gokhale to journalism. To begin with, Gokhale started writing articles for *Mahratta*, an English weekly started by Vishnushastri Chiplunkar, Gangadhar Tilak, Ganesh Agarkar and other young men. When Agarkar left *Kesri* due to differences with Tilak, he had started *Sudharak*, an Anglo–Marathi weekly. Gokhale joined this venture and edited its English section for four years while Agarkar looked after the Marathi section. From 1889, Gokhale was appointed as the editor of the quarterly journal of the Poona Sarvajanik Sabha, the leading political and social organization of Maharashtra. In 1895, Gokhale started the *Rashtra Sabha Samachar* which, however, did not last long. As a journalist, Gokhale did not have the kind of impact which Tilak had with his earthy similes and bold editorials.

Gokhale joined the INC in 1889. The following year, he was made secretary of the Poona Sarvajanik Sabha. In 1893, he was elected secretary of the Bombay Provincial Conference and two years later (1895), he became joint secretary of the INC with Tilak. In 1896, he collaborated with Ranade to form the Deccan Sabha to counter the Sarvajanik Sabha which Tilak and his orthodox followers had captured earlier.

In 1897, Gokhale was among the four Indians invited to London to give evidence before the Royal Commission on the Administration of Expenditure of India, popularly known as Welby Commission (after the name of its chairman, Lord Welby). Gokhale's written and oral evidence before the Commission was universally appreciated, reflecting his deep knowledge of Indian economic problems. This first visit to England gave Gokhale a chance to meet the liberal-minded British statesmen and thinkers, including John Morley who later became the secretary of state for India and developed a lasting friendship with Gokhale. He, thereafter, became a familiar figure in London circles, visiting that country seven times between 1897 to 1914.

Gokhale was elected to the Bombay Legislative Council in 1899, from the constituency earlier represented by Tilak. Two years later, he was elected to the Imperial Legislative Council on the seat vacated by Pherozeshah Mehta. He was a member of this august body till 1911, being elected successively for three terms. In these councils, he was virtually the leader of the opposition. In the Imperial Council, he was particularly noted for his impressive participation in the annual debate on the budget. In 1904, he was awarded a CIE (Companion of the Indian Empire).

The most important year in Gokhale's life was perhaps 1905. In June 1905, he founded the Servants of India Society in Poona 'with the object of training men to devote themselves to the service of India as national missionaries and to promote by all constitutional means the national interests of the Indian people'. Gandhi, in one of his letters to his nephew in 1910, criticized the working of the society saying that 'it was simply an indifferent imitation of the West. Is it proper for the "servants" to have servants? I do feel that the aims of Phoenix (his settlement in South Africa) as well as the way of life there surpasses those of the Society'[1]. Ironically, when Gandhi returned from South Africa early in 1915, he wanted to join the Society but his application was rejected with the remarks that 'his (Gandhi's) ideals and methods of work and those of the Society were different and it would not be proper for him to join.'[2]

---

[1] *Collected Works of Mahatma Gandhi,* Vol. 10, Publications Division, pp. 138–39.
[2] Deogirikar, T.R., *Gopal Krishna Gokhale,* Publication Division, New Delhi, 1964, p. 173.

Gokhale considered the founding of the Society as his greatest achievement and the future of the society was on his mind even at the time of his death. The Society attracted important persons who devoted their lives for its work such as V.S. Srinivasa Sastri, Thakkar Bapa, N.M. Joshi, H.N. Kunzru and others.

In 1905, Gokhale went to England for a second time as a delegate of the Congress, along with Lajpat Rai, to enlighten the British public opinion about the conditions in India on the eve of the general elections there.

It was also in 1905 that Gokhale was elected president of the INC for the Banaras session and emerged as one of the leaders of the 'Moderate' group, along with Pherozeshah Mehta and Dinshaw Edulji Wacha. This was the year when militant nationalism took root in Bengal, and later in India, as a result of the partition of Bengal by Lord Curzon. The movement for the annulment of partition of Bengal was led by a section of Congressmen—Bal Gangadhar Tilak, Lala Lajpat Rai, B.C. Pal (Bal, Lal and Pal) and others—who came to be known as 'Extremists'. Thousands of youths joined the movement and resorted to terrorist activities. The government used repressive measures but the movement could not be crushed. In the Calcutta session of the Congress (1906), resolutions were passed advocating self-rule, swadeshi, boycott and national education. While Gokhale and other Moderates were opposed to the partition of Bengal and favoured swadeshi as an economic measure to ameliorate the condition of the masses, they were against self-rule, boycott and national education. Gokhale considered the British rule as an 'irrevocable necessity' which had done immense good to India. He wanted to depend on the generosity and democratic traditions of the British people to get instalments of reforms. Extremists called it the 'policy of mendicancy' and considered it to be humiliating. Gokhale also believed that Western learning was a liberating force for India and should not be replaced by national education. He was also opposed to boycott and believed that 'boycott has a sinister meaning and it implies a vindictive desire to injure another'. In short, Gokhale and other Moderates did not want to offend the British in any way. Consequently, Moderates criticized both the ultimate goal set up by the Extremists as well as their methods to achieve it.

The conflict between the two factions of the Congress came in the open in the Surat Session of the Congress in 1907. The session was controlled by the Moderates as the stronghold of Pherozeshah Mehta. They manoeuvred not to get the resolutions passed in Calcutta confirmed, going against the usual practice after each session. When Tilak went up the rostrum to move an amendment about the Calcutta resolutions, all hell was let loose. Chairs were thrown at the rival group and a shoe was hurled at Tilak who ducked and the shoe landed on the face of Pherozeshah Mehta. This was a most disgraceful incident in the history of the Congress. Tilak and other Extremists were expelled from the Congress. The Surat split not only weakened the Congress but also virtually destroyed its effectiveness till the Lucknow reunion in 1916. The Extremists were persecuted by the government; the Moderates were abandoned by their own people.

Soon followed Tilak's conviction in a sedition case in 1908 and he was sentenced to six years internment in Mandalay jail. This had grave consequences for Gokhale and his party. Gokhale was accused of being an instigator for Tilak's conviction through Secretary of State Morley while in London. He was subjected to continuous sniping in the local Marathi press. He was lampooned by cartoonists and vilified in malicious verses sung in the Ganpati festival processions in Poona.[3] To add to the dilemma of Moderates, Congress sessions had become increasingly dull and insipid. Gokhale wanted the Extremists to come back and revitalize the Congress but it could not be possible in the absence of Tilak.

Gokhale visited England thrice during 1905 to 1908. In 1905,

---

[3]Nanda, B.R., *Gokhale: The Indian Moderates and the British Raj,* Oxford University Press, 1979, p. 474.

he went in a delegation of the Congress along with Lajpat Rai
to enlighten British public opinion about the conditions in India
on the eve of general elections in that country, as stated earlier.
In 1906, he went again to plead for reforms with British liberal
leaders and parliamentarians. The visit in 1908 was essentially to
meet Lord Morley, secretary of state for India. He had several
meetings with Morley about the proposed reforms, later known
as Morley–Minto Reforms under the Act of 1909. Gokhale was
kept in the dark by Morley about the true nature of these reforms.
Gokhale evidently failed to distinguish between Morley the writer
and philosopher and Morley the bureaucrat. The reforms were much
below the expectations of the Indian people. The worst part was
the ominous clause which gave Muslims separate electorate and
other concessions. Gokhale agreeing to separate electorates for the
Muslims showed his meekness and lack of far-sightedness. Stanley
Wolpert has spoken of this, saying,

> [The reforms gave] statutory recognition at the highest
> legislative level to the communal separateness which had
> plagued Indian society with its divisive influence since the
> mass Muslim invasions of the Hindu subcontinent at the start
> of the eleventh century. Perhaps it would have been asking
> too much of him to have been able to anticipate how the
> mushrooming of this communal representational demand was
> to result within four decades in the tragic partition of the
> sub-continent. Just as the nationalist party reviled Gokhale
> for cooperating with the government so now many of his
> own Congress supporters accused him of showing excessive
> favouritism towards Muslims.[4]

Gokhale's speeches and letters are replete with criticism of the British
economic policies which had resulted in poverty and distress in the
Indian masses. He criticized heavy taxation including salt-tax and

---

[4] Wolpert, Stanley, *Tilak and Gokhale*, Oxford University Press, 1961, pp. 234–35.

unreasonably high land revenue which had ruined the farmers. He was an advocate of swadeshi along with industrialization. But his criticism of the government hardly had an effect on their policies. They just ignored what he said or wrote because they knew that it was not backed by mass agitation. His was benign criticism, they believed. Gokhale was even ready to support the government when they resorted to high-handedness. When the Indian Press Act was passed in 1910 to throttle the Indian press and was rightly condemned by public opinion throughout the country, Gokhale supported the Act in the Imperial Legislative Council saying,

> My Lord, in ordinary times I should have deemed it my duty
> to resist such proposals to the utmost of my power. The risks
> involved in them are grave and obvious. But in view of the
> situation that exists in several parts of the country today, I have
> reluctantly come, after a careful and obvious consideration,
> to the conclusion, that I should not be justified in opposing
> the principle of the Bill.[5]

It seems Gokhale was unconscious of his unpopularity.

As a social reformer, he was against the caste system, untouchability, child marriage and other ills of the society which invited the ire of the orthodoxy as was experienced by Ram Mohan Roy, Swami Dayanand and other reformers including his guru Ranade, before him.

In 1912, Gokhale was nominated as a member of the Islington Commission on Public Service. He visited England in 1912, 1913 and 1914 in connection with the interrogation work of the commission which sapped his energy. He became quite weak and tired during the later stages and lost interest in the Commission's work. By the time the Commission's work was completed and its report was submitted, Gokhale had died.

In 1912, Gokhale went to South Africa from England at the

---

[5]Ibid. 243.

invitation of Gandhi who needed his support for his satyagraha work. He was well-received there and drew appreciative crowds. Gandhi was with him all the time during his visits to various places in South Africa. He was in South Africa for 26 days, almost the whole of October.

Gokhale started having ill health even before his old age. His frequent visits to England certainly affected his health. He died when he was hardly 49 years old in Poona, in February 1915. When he saw that his end was near, he called the members of the Servants of India Society to his bedside and said, 'Do not occupy yourself with writing my biography or spend your time in putting up my statues. If you are true servants of India, dedicate your lives to the fulfilment of our aims, to the service of India.'

Tilak, who had gone to Sinhgad, a health resort for rest, rushed to Poona after hearing the news of Gokhale's death. At the cremation ground Tilak made a brief speech, 'This is time for shedding tears. This diamond of India, this jewel of Maharashtra, the prince of workers is laid to eternal rest on the funeral ground. Look at him and try to emulate him.'

31

Lala Har Dayal

(1884–1939)

Har Dayal Mathur was born on 14 October 1884 in Delhi to Bholi Rani and Gauri Dayal Mathur, who was a reader in the district court of Delhi. The couple had seven children—four sons and three daughters. Har Dayal was the sixth child. Gauri Dayal was a scholar of Persian and Urdu and Har Dayal inherited the love of these two languages from him. Later, he learnt several other languages including Sanskrit, Hindi and almost all the European languages.

Har Dayal's formal education started at the age of four when he joined the primary section of the Cambridge Mission School, Delhi. He was a very bright student with a phenomenal memory. He always stood first in class. He passed his middle school examination at the age of 12 and the matriculation examination at 14. He earned his bachelor of arts degree from St Stephen's College, Delhi and joined Government College, Lahore, from where he passed his master's in English literature in 1903 and obtained another master's degree in history the following year, standing first in both the examinations. What set him apart from other students were not only the marks that he obtained in the examinations but also his love for reading. He was a voracious reader, often finishing a book in a day and retaining everything he read. He was selected for a state scholarship by the government which provided him £200 annually for a three-year study in England. It also provided a round trip passage. He left India in 1905, at the age of 21, to join the University of Oxford. Before, he left for England, he had already been married at the age of 17 to Sundar Rani, daughter of wealthy Lala Gopal Chand. A son was born to the couple after two years of marriage but the child only lived for 10 months. A daughter Shanti was born five years later, in 1908.

At Oxford, he joined St John's College and proposed to read for the Honour School in Modern History. At the University of Punjab, Lahore, he was an Aitchison-Ram Rattan Sanskrit Scholar and continued his studies in Sanskrit at Oxford and was made a Boden Sanskrit Scholar. He also won a Casberd Exhibition in History in 1907. These honours carried with them stipends amounting to £130. There seems to be little doubt that Har Dayal made his mark in academics at Oxford. But it seems that he was feeling extremely homesick and at the end of his first term at Oxford, he left for Delhi and brought back his wife with him in spite of stiff opposition from his family as well as from his wife's family. That was in the summer of 1906. In England, Har Dayal had a wider range of friends and acquaintances than most Indian students studying there. He met George Bernard Shaw and the Poet Laureate Robert Bridges, who spoke of Har Dayal 'in the highest terms, both of his character and his intellectual attainments'. He also made the 'pilgrimage' to see Alexander Kropotkin, the Russian anarchist, who was living in England at that time. He visited London frequently and met Shyamji Krishna Verma, the Indian nationalist who had established the India House in London and was editor and publisher of *The Indian Sociologist*. In the India House, Har Dayal also met V.D. Savarkar, who was the acknowledged leader of the revolutionaries connected with the India House. Har Dayal was greatly impressed by Savarkar's nationalistic views and was initiated into the Abhinav Bharat Society, a party founded by Savarkar, and took the required oath. Har Dayal was now in the company of great nationalists and revolutionaries. This was the time when Savarkar was distributing his *Bomb Manual* to revolutionaries and trying to send arms to India. Har Dayal's association with Savarkar was noticed by the British secret agents, 'though Har Dayal was never personally identified with violence, his career was both directly or indirectly influenced by the cult of the bomb'. The arrest of Lala Lajpat Rai and Ajit Singh and their deportation to Mandalay (1907) affected Har Dayal's sensitive mind. He decided to discontinue his studies at Oxford in the fall of 1907 and decided not to accept any money in future as scholarship from the British government. He wrote to Oxford: 'I am unable to continue my studies for the Final Examination. I request the favour of your allowing me to withdraw from the College. I am sincerely sorry that I find myself unable to finish my course of studies.' He had already put in two and a half years at the College and was to finish his studies after six months. He did not give any reason for his action. Neither the university nor the government found any 'political misconduct or indiscretion' on his part.

During the interim, between the resignation of his government scholarship and his return to India, Har Dayal started wearing a kurta (a long shirt) and dhoti (a garment worn by male Hindus, consisting of a piece of material tied around the waist and extending to cover most of the legs), discarding Western clothes and he also became a strict vegetarian. Actually, Har Dayal's nationalism became an overriding commitment during his Oxford days which included his visits to the India House and meeting with revolutionaries like Shyamji Krishna Varma, Savarkar and Madam Cama. His identification with extremism was evident not only in his political views but also in his conduct. 'His almost total rejection of everything Western was more than just eccentricity.'

Har Dayal returned to India in January 1908. He wanted to be a 'political missionary' or a 'wandering friar of freedom' to the chagrin of his relatives, especially his father-in-law who saw his daughter's life being ruined. Har Dayal, however, put aside affection for his wife, their little daughter and his brothers and sisters to become 'a mendicant agitator'. During his brief stay in India, he wrote articles on different subjects in various papers, including Lajpat

Rai's *Punjabee*. In these articles, he attacked the British educational system, which he thought was the cause of many ills of the country. These articles were later published in a book titled *Our Educational Problem*. Har Dayal returned to England in September 1908. The reason for his leaving India was that 'repressive laws and spies were making further work impossible within the country'. He never set foot on Indian soil again and spent the remaining 30 years of his life in exile. On his return to England, he started living at Oxford. It is difficult to know exactly what Har Dayal was doing during his stay in Oxford (September 1908 to February 1909) beyond continuing 'to contribute his diatribes to the Lahore newspapers'. According to Madam Cama, Har Dayal lived during this period in the 'direst poverty'. 'This lifestyle', she said 'rendered him neurasthenic', and friends (which included Krishna Varma, S.R. Rana and Cama) in Paris finally persuaded him to join them. He regained his health. As Krishna Varma's *The Indian Sociologist* writings were getting 'tepid and tentative' after the assassination of Sir William Curzon Wyllie by Madan Lai Dhingra in London, Cama and Rana wanted to start a newspaper 'which would reflect a vigorous revolutionary policy'. The paper was called *Bande Mataram* and was, in a way, a continuation of the one, with the same name, started in Calcutta by B.C. Pal in 1905 and edited later by Aurobindo Ghose. Har Dayal was the obvious choice for its editor. Cama provided the financial support. The first issue of *Bande Mataram* appeared on 10 September 1909. It was almost wholly written by Har Dayal for several months and was published from Geneva. With *Bande Mataram*, Har Dayal identified himself as an advocate of open rebellion. The arrest and deportation of Savarkar, his closest political colleague if not his guru, and his impending fate, affected him very much. He left Paris and spent a few months in Algiers but found it difficult to live in a Muslim country. He returned to Paris in July 1910 and resumed the editorial work. He was living with S.R. Rana but was restless. Without consulting any of his friends, he left Paris in October 1910 for Martinique, an island in

West Indies, which was also part of the French Empire. The only account of Har Dayal's stay in Martinique has been given by Bhai Parmanand, an Arya Samaj missionary, in his autobiography *The Story of My Life*. The two friends lived together in Martinique for a month. Parmanand found that Har Dayal was living the life of an ascetic and spent his time in meditation and study. Har Dayal told Parmanand that he wanted to give a new religion to the world like Buddha did. Parmanand claims that he dissuaded him doing anything like that and suggested that he should go to the US to preach the ancient culture and philosophy of the Aryan race. After days of discussion, Har Dayal agreed.

Har Dayal arrived in the US in February 1911 and went to Harvard University to carry on his study on Buddhism. But he had hardly started when he was informed by a fellow Punjabi that there were thousands of Sikhs and Punjabi labourers working in fields or factories on the West Coast who lacked leadership in their struggle for social acceptance and economic equality. Har Dayal agreed to go to California to do something for the unfortunate Indians. He established himself in Berkeley by the end of April 1911. At Berkeley, he did not pursue any academic course but associated with campus radicals and intellectuals and introduced himself to select members of the faculty. He also met some literary personalities like the famous novelist Jack London who immortalized Har Dayal in his novel, *Little Lady of the Big House,* by introducing a character like Har Dayal in it, calling him Dayal Har. At Berkeley, Har Dayal was asked to speak on Indian philosophy at private gatherings. He was a powerful and enchanting orator and considered an intellectual giant. His fame spread and the University of Berkeley invited him to give a series of lectures on philosophy. His lectures at Berkeley attracted attention and he was offered to join the faculty of Stanford University. He refused to draw any salary. Soon after, Har Dayal started writing on subjects which the university did not approve of. He had become a Marxist and took a step still further by preaching anarchism. He advocated 'free love'. Several parents of female students objected and Har Dayal was removed from the Stanford University faculty panel.

By 1912, Har Dayal was a devout communist, nay an anarchist. To spread his gospel, he founded The Radical Club during his days in Stanford and served as its secretary. He defined its members 'as dissenters from the establishment in any social, political, or intellectual area'. It was like a clearing house for anyone and everyone to come and vent their feelings, somewhat like London's Hyde Park. It started attracting people, especially the young. The authorities of the university as well as of the government were concerned. The club could be one of the reasons for the university to have dissuaded Har Dayal to leave. By the end of 1912, Har Dayal was a figure to be reckoned with, as well-known in Washington as he had been in official circles in London, Delhi, Calcutta and Simla. His literary production (mainly articles in newspapers and journals) had made him one of the most 'avidly' read young Indians of his time. Wherever Har Dayal went, there was excitement. 'His energy and enthusiasm seemed inexhaustible, and the variety of his interests and commitments left both Indian informers and British agents bewildered and worn out.[1]

A crucial event occurred in 1912 in Delhi which brought Har Dayal back to nationalist activities. This was the assassination attempt on Viceroy Lord Hardinge. The event was celebrated in Berkeley, in which Har Dayal took a leading part. He also wrote an article titled 'Salute to the Bomb Thrower' and sent it for publication. He began lambasting the British in his writings again. To bring Indians on a common platform, he founded the Pacific Coast Hindustan Association. It was decided that the association would sponsor the publication of a revolutionary newspaper. The journal was called *Gadar* (Revolution) and Har Dayal announced the formation of Gadar Party on 1 November 1913. The first issue of

---

[1]Brown, Emily C., *Har Dayal: Hindu Revolutionary and Rationalist,* University of Arizona Press, 1975, p. 127.

Gadar was also brought out on that day in several Indian languages like Punjabi, Hindi and Urdu etc. Har Dayal was the editor and was helped by some members who knew these languages. A house at 436 Hill Street in San Francisco was purchased and was named as 'Jugantar Ashram', which was to be the headquarters of Gadar Party, and from where the journal *Gadar* was to be published. In the first formal meeting of the party, Baba Sohan Singh was elected as president and Har Dayal as secretary and editor of *Gadar*. The fame of Har Dayal rests more as the founder of Gadar Party than on anything else. A majority of the members of the party were Sikhs, working on agricultural farms and factories, who were treated shabbily by the white overlords. The recurring theme of the Gadar Party was, '*Chalo chaliye desh nun yudh karan / Eho akhari vachan farman ho gaye* (Let us go to the motherland to fight the enemy / These words [of Har Dayal] are last words and order)'.[2] But before the orders could be implemented by Gadarites, Har Dayal was arrested by the US. Immigration Department with the connivance of British Embassy on 25 March 1914 in San Francisco. He was, however, released after signing a bond of $1,000. Har Dayal left the country and after about five weeks appeared in Lausanne, Switzerland. In the Jugantar Ashram in San Francisco, the Gadar Movement and the propaganda machine had been turned over to Ram Chandra, a Punjabi, who edited the party organ.

From Switzerland, Har Dayal moved to Germany where he opened an Oriental Bureau and sought German help for armed revolution in India. He was in Germany all through the war years. During the first year of his stay in Germany, he got close to the Germans but he was completely disillusioned later on. In an article on 4 December 1918, which was published in the *San Francisco Call* he wrote, 'My residence in Germany has convinced me that German imperialism is a very great menace to the progress of

---

[2]Dharamvira, *Lala Hardayal and Revolutionary Movements of His Times,* Indian Book Co., New Delhi, 1970, p. 193.

humanity, and I rejoice to see that American arms bid fair to humble this arrogant nation.' From Germany, he crossed over to Sweden in November 1918, just before the First World War ended. That was also the end of Har Dayal, the revolutionary. He was now an adherent of the Home Rule instead of the old revolutionary party. He now advocated that India should remain a part of the great British Empire. Har Dayal lived in Sweden for almost a decade. 'He earned his rather precarious living by lecturing on Indian philosophy, art and literature.' This miserable financial condition was changed when in November 1926 Har Dayal met Agda Erikson, 'a Swedish social worker and philanthropist of significant accomplishment. She was to become his companion from then on and his acknowledged wife from the summer of 1932'.[3] She bought a cottage at Edgware when the couple moved to London later, which became their home for the rest of their lives. Agda gave him company, inspiration, financial support and much more. She was with him when he died.

Har Dayal applied to the British government for amnesty which was refused. However, the British ambassador in Stockholm issued a passport to Har Dayal for Great Britain only. Har Dayal reached London on 10 October 1927, accompanied by Agda Erikson. He was admitted to the doctoral programme at the School of Oriental and African Studies (SOAS) and submitted a dissertation, *The Bodhisattva Doctrine in Buddhist Sanskrit Literature*. He was awarded the PhD in 1930 and his dissertation was published in form of a book in 1932. It is still considered as an authoritative work in its field. Two years later, in 1934, Har Dayal's second book, and by far the most famous of his works, *Hints for Self Culture*, was published. In the brief preface he wrote, 'In this little book (it has 363 pages) I have tried to indicate and explain some aspects of the message of Rationalism for the Young men and women of all countries.' In it, the later stage of 'Hardayalism' gets manifested,

---

[3]Brown, Emily C., *Har Dayal: Hindu Revolutionary and Rationalist*, University of Arizona Press, 1975, p. 238.

'a free, united and humanly perfect India' has given way to 'a free, united, and humanly perfect world, having one state, one flag, one language, one ethic, one ideal, one love, one life'. From it, emerges Har Dayal, as the man without a country, who is finding his identification as a citizen of the world.

On 30 December 1935, Har Dayal renewed his request for amnesty because he wanted to return to his motherland. By the time the permission was dispatched to their Edgware address, Har Dayal and Agda had left for the US. They started residing in Philadelphia where Har Dayal was invited to deliver a series of lectures under the auspices of the Society for Ethical Culture. Har Dayal died on on 4 March 1939 when he was only 54. His sudden death remains a mystery. He was cremated at a simple service at which tributes were paid to him by the devotees of the 12 religions he had singled out in his book *Hints for Self Culture*. The only music at the funeral service was a rendition of *Vande Mataram*. Agda Erikson left for Sweden afterwards. She was heartbroken to discover that Har Dayal's first wife was still alive and she had married a man who was neither a divorcee nor a widower. She died on 11 January 1940 in Sweden. For the relatives of Har Dayal, Agda never existed; it was the same for many Indian biographers of Har Dayal. She had lived with him for 13 years, first as a friend and later as his wife.

When the news of Har Dayal's death reached India almost after a month, it did not go unnoticed. Most of the major newspapers devoted considerable space for recounting his career. But the most memorable tribute came from the aged and ailing Charles Freer Andrews: 'He (Har Dayal) was one of India's noblest children and in happier times would have done wonders with his gigantic intellectual powers. For his mind was one of the greatest I have ever known and his character also was true and pure.' However, as a personality, Har Dayal was elusive. As Emily C. Brown has mentioned, 'What has intrigued most of those who knew him were the seemingly abrupt changes in his actions and attitudes which occurred as he moved from a militant nationalist to a pacifist and internationalist who embraced not only the ideals but the homilies of the society he had once scorned and reviled."[4]

---

[4]Ibid. 7.

32

David Hare

(1775–1842)

The East India Company had little in common with the long line of India's traditional invaders from West Asia. Revolutionary changes were gradually introduced in administration as well as in the socio-economic structure. The important agent for these changes was the new educational system, first in Bengal and gradually in other parts of the country. The Company did not make any conscious efforts as such to spread English education and Western sciences. But the Christian missionary schools taught these subjects and gained popularity among the middle-class. The advantages of learning English and Western sciences became apparent to the Indian intelligentsia. The first decade of the nineteenth century saw a number of schools, apart from missionary schools, coming up, which taught English and Western sciences coming up. It culminated in the establishment of the famous Hindu College in Calcutta. David Hare was the founder of this great institution. He was supported by men like Ram Mohan Roy, who became his lifelong friend. Besides Hindu College, Hare was instrumental in the establishment of several other educational institutions in Calcutta. With the de-recognition of Persian as an official language in 1835 by the Company and giving the status of official languages to English and vernacular languages of each province, the spread of English and Bengali was accelerated. David Hare, along with Ram Mohan Roy, played a leading role in making these languages popular.

David Hare was born in Scotland on 17 February 1775. He did not have a college education and adopted the profession of his father, i.e., watchmaking. He came to India in 1800 and spent the remaining 42 years of his life in Calcutta. He compensated for his lack of good education by reading widely and even built his own small library. But he was no intellectual like Ram Mohan Roy.

Within a short time of his arrival in Calcutta, he built up a prosperous watchmaking business. Though he became a successful businessman, his heart was not in this profession. After making a small fortune, he voluntarily transferred his business to his assistant, Emmanuel Gray, who was perhaps his relative, early in 1820. He devoted the rest of his life doing social work, mainly in the sphere of education in Calcutta.

He soon earned the friendship of Ram Mohan Roy as both of them believed in the diffusion of English education and western sciences among Indians for India to progress. When Ram Mohan Roy visited England in 1830–33, David wrote to his relatives in England, asking them to look after him and Ram Mohan stayed with his family for some time. A niece of David attended to the needs of Ram Mohan during his last illness at Stapleton Grove where he died. All the members of the Hare family were present during Ram Mohan's last rites. David himself was, however, a lifelong bachelor.

Even before David Hare said goodbye to his watchmaking business, he was active in spreading English education. In 1814, he proposed the establishment of an English school in Calcutta to Ram Mohan. Consequently, the first English school by a native came into existence. The establishment of the Hindu College on 20 January 1817 was the result of the proposal Hare had sent to Justice Sir Edward Hyde East of the Supreme Court. The college was located on a piece of land owned by David Hare on the north side of College Square. Thus, David is considered to be the founder of Hindu College. Whether as a superintendent of the School Society's meritorious boys studying in the Hindu College or as a director of the College Managing Committee from 1925, he was a constant source of inspiration for the teachers and students. When the Calcutta School Society was formed in 1818 to look after vernacular and English schools, Hare was its European secretary. Apart from taking special interest in the activities of the students at Arpuli Vernacular School and the Pataldanga English School, he kept a close watch on the progress of the poor but meritorious students selected for study at the Hindu College by the School Society. Due to financial stringency, the two schools had to be merged and are now called Hare School and are still 'perpetuating the hallowed memory of the Scottish pioneer'.

From the beginning, Hare stressed the importance of providing Bengali education in his schools, along with English. He was also asked to lay the foundation of a Bengali Pathshala (Hindu College Pathshala) near the Hindu College on 14 June 1839.

Hare played a leading role in the establishment of Calcutta Medical College, the first medical college in India, on 1 June 1835. He was asked by the principal to be the secretary of the Calcutta Medical College—a post he held from 1837 to 1842, 'because of his influence over Hindu homes'. Hindu families were reluctant to send their children to the medical college because of the deep-rooted prejudice against dissecting dead human bodies. Hare had succeeded in convincing the friendly families of the necessity of knowing the human body for doctors and thus helping them to overcome the prejudice. According to Nirmal Sinha, 'When in January 1836, some students mustered enough courage to shake off their prejudice to dissect dead bodies, guns boomed from the Fort William, virtually welcoming the opening of a new chapter in the history of renascent Bengal.'[1]

Though a Christian himself, Hare abhorred the proselytization activities of the missionaries who were active in the educational institutions in his schools, 'who will spoil my boys', he used to say.

[1]Sinha, Nirmal, *Freedom Movement in Bengal, 1818–1904: Who's Who*, Academic Publishers, Calcutta, 1991, p. 19.

He was termed as an atheist by orthodox Christians. His inveterate hostility to the Gospel cost him the goodwill of orthodox Christians and he was denied burial in a consecrated Christian cemetery and was buried near his beloved Hindu College, in his own land.

As there was a dearth of books in English as well as Bengali, Hare founded the Calcutta School Book Society in 1818 for printing and publishing English and Bengali books. These books were distributed for free to the needy students. *The Young Bengal Address* (1831) spoke of Hare as the man who has breathed a new life in Hindu society, who has voluntarily become the friend of a friendless people, and set an example to his own countrymen and ours.[2]

Hare worked hard, along with Ram Mohan Roy, for the repeal of regulations against the press which ultimately led to the restoration of the freedom of the press by Act XI of 1835. He also took active part in securing trial by jury in civil cases in the Supreme Court. He was at the forefront of the agitation against the British practice of collecting Indian coolies for emigration to Mauritius, British Guyana (now Guyana), Trinidad and Ceylon (now Sri Lanka).

Hare's many generous benefactions, small and large, put him in financial difficulties towards the end of his life. To help him in his distress, Lord Auckland appointed him as the third commissioner in the Court of Requests in March 1840, in recognition of his services for the cause of native education, on a salary of ₹1000 per month. His appointment to this post was not liked by many. *The Friend of India* paper commented, 'He has laid the country under a debt of gratitude by his labours in the cause of education, which even the salary of a Commissioner does not repay. By the present appointment the cause of education has lost much, while the cause of justice has gained nothing.'[3]

But David Hare did not live long to serve as commissioner and

[2]Sarkar, Susobhan, *The Dictionary of National Biography*, Calcutta, Institute of Historical Studies, 1973, pp. 145–47.
[3]Sinha, Nirmal, *Freedom Movement in Bengal, 1818–1904: Who's Who*, Academic Publishers, Calcutta, 1991, pp. 22.

died on 1 June 1842 of cholera, at the age of 67. His funeral, on a soggy day, was attended by at least 2,000 grateful students and the staff of Hindu College and Calcutta Medical College along with many European dignitaries. His memory is cherished and kept alive to this day. The street on which he lived with his relative, Emmanuel Gray, was later named 'Hare Street'. The GOI has put a memorial tablet at his residence; a full-sized marble statue was erected by public subscription between Presidency College and the Hare School; and a beautiful portrait of his, which was commissioned by his students, adorns a wall of the room used by him in Hare School.

33

Keshav Baliram Hedgewar
(1889–1940)

Keshav Baliram Hedgewar was a nation builder who tried to unite Hindu society, working silently and almost imperceptibly. He created the Rashtriya Swayamsevak Sangh (RSS), an organization which is still alive and working for the national cause, without seeking any reward. In the last 15 years of his life, Hedgewar succeeded in achieving the unity and strength that Vivekananda preached and tried to implement. In one of his speeches, Vivekananda had said, 'I want a band of workers who would, as *Brahmcharins*, educate the people and revitalise the country.' Hedgewar also believed this and worked to create such a band of workers.

Keshav was born on 1 April 1889, in Nagpur in an orthodox Brahmin family. The family had migrated from Kandukur in Andhra Pradesh to Nagpur at the turn of the nineteenth century. They were by no means rich and Keshav experienced poverty right from infancy. His father Baliram Pant Hedgewar and mother Revatibai died of the plague in 1902 when Keshav was only 12 years old. Keshav was the youngest of the three brothers and had three sisters. The passing away of the parents put the family in further financial trouble but the eldest son Mahadev was able to steer the family out of difficulties.

While Baliram was still alive, he put Keshav in a modern school as he had not shown any interest in the traditional priesthood which was the profession of the family. From the beginning, Keshav was interested in history and politics, 'particularly the life and deeds of Shivaji'. He had developed a hatred of British rule while still a boy and expressed it in several ways. When the Diamond Jubilee of the Coronation of the British Empress Victoria was celebrated in his school in 1896, he threw away the sweets which were given to every child. He also took part in the 'Vande Mataram' agitation and was expelled from the school. He continued anti-British activities and was expelled from school after school. He passed the matriculation examination as a private candidate from Nagpur in 1910. By this time, Keshav came in contact with Dr Balakrishna Shivram Moonje, a militant nationalist and an admirer of Tilak. Keshav lived with Dr Moonje during much of his adolescence and he was a major influence on his life. Hedgewar went to Calcutta in 1910 to qualify as a doctor.

According to one source, 'Moonje sent Keshav to Calcutta to study medicine at the National Medical College because he wanted Hedgewar to establish contacts with the revolutionaries of Bengal.' No wonder Hedgewar joined Anushilan Samiti, the revolutionary society of Bengal, and 'rose to its highest membership category'. In the Samiti, he handled many risky jobs, under the pseudonym 'Koken'. He also identified himself with the Bengali way of life and participated in varied student movements and social service activities. He returned to Nagpur in 1916, after getting a Licentiate in Medicine and Surgery (LM&S) degree. He did not practice medicine, however, which would have enabled him to earn money and respect in society. To the dismay of his family members, he announced that he would neither marry nor practice as a doctor. And he never did. He resolved to devote his life to the revolutionary struggle. Very little is known of his revolutionary activities between 1916 and 1920. *The Nagpur District Gazetteer*, however, reported that he was the actual brain behind the revolutionary movement in Nagpur.

In 1921, Hedgewar joined the INC and participated in the Non-cooperation Movement. He was arrested on 14 August 1921 and was sentenced to a one-year rigorous imprisonment and was released on 12 July 1922. However, he was not an ardent member of the Congress. He was equally at home with revolutionaries, Congress party and the Hindu Mahasabha, and had friends and well-wishers in all these organizations. When Gandhi suddenly called off the Non-cooperation Movement in 1922, Hedgewar became increasingly disenchanted with Gandhi and his politics but did not sever ties with the Congress.

The communal riots of 1923 in Nagpur made Hedgewar think about the causes of the riots and about the timidness shown by the Hindus, though they were 150,000 against 20,000 Muslims in Nagpur. When the government banned the Dindi procession in Nagpur on the 30 October 1923, more than 20,000 Hindus marched in defiance of the order. This was done for the first time. Hedgewar had found lack of unity as the cause of the timidness of the Hindu. And the remedy was unity. Out of this incident emerged the Hindu Mahasabha, with Dr Moonje as vice president and Hedgewar as secretary. The Sabha organized more protest marches. The Hindus in Nagpur were not slow to appreciate the influence they could exert if they were organized. The intellectual basis of the birth of Rashtriya Swayamsevak Sangh (RSS) was found. Hedgewar was now convinced that our nation's malady did not lie in foreign slavery but in its disunity. Even foreign domination was a direct result of this national failing. To overcome this, a cadre of dedicated and disciplined persons was required. This was actually the task of character building.

After great thought, Hedgewar launched his new movement on Vijayadashami Day in 1925 at Nagpur. He gave it the name Rashtriya Swayamsevak Sangh. According to him, 'it is a body of those persons who have voluntarily dedicated themselves to the service of the Motherland', which results in national consciousness, brotherhood, discipline and self-sacrifice. He had come to believe that 'such a patriotic and disciplined society alone could be expected not only to throw off its foreign shackles but also offer an unfailing guarantee for the protection of the nation's freedom in future also and form the inevitable base for all future national reconstruction as well'.[1] A small group of persons gathered in an *akhara* (gymnasium) and started meeting daily. Mohite Wada grounds, near the akhara in Nagpur, was the place where the first *shakha* (group) meetings were held. Gradually, the other features which distinguish the RSS from other bodies were added—the *bhagwa dhwaj* (saffron flag) which became the guru, and a uniform of white shirt, khaki shorts and black cap as well as a stick for protection. A prayer in Sanskrit was recited every day at the shakha. The number of shakhas increased over time, first in Nagpur and then in other cities nearby. During the 1927 riots, the *swayamsevaks* (volunteers) organized defence training in the Hindu localities, demonstrating the utility of unity leading to strength. A bugle and a band were added, which was used during processions in the city. They had no newspaper or journal to publicize their activities or to do propaganda. However, a swayamsevak now stood apart from the ordinary public, the result of 'character building' process introduced by Hedgewar. The behaviour and the conduct of swayamsevaks among the public was the only source of publicity. Gradually the RSS came to be noticed. The RSS volunteers started disciplining the crowd at religious functions, getting appreciation from the public. The organizers of the December 1927 Hindu Mahasabha session, to be held at Ahmedabad, invited Hedgewar to send RSS volunteers in uniform to maintain order. The political parties saw a disciplined core for their party in the RSS. V.D. Savarkar approached Hedgewar to let his volunteers join the Hindu Mahasabha. Hedgewar politely declined. Savarkar then frequently denounced RSS for its purely 'cultural' orientation. Savarkar once publicly taunted the RSS saying that, 'The epitaph for the RSS volunteer will be that he was born, he joined the RSS and he died without accomplishing anything.' Dr Hardikar, the leader of the Hindustan Seva Dal (a wing of

---

[1] *RSS: Spearheading National Renaissance*, Prakashan Vibhag, Bangalore, 1985, p. ll.

the Congress), criticized the RSS for its refusal to get politically involved.[2] But Hedgewar was quite clear in his mind that the RSS would remain an apolitical organization devoted to the service of the Motherland. He wanted to create a nationally-conscious society through discipline and patriotism and by placing the interest of the society above the Self. This, he felt, was not possible in politics.

Despite the initial success of his venture, Hedgewar continued to be a member of the Congress party 'in his individual capacity'. He took part in the Civil Disobedience Movement and was imprisoned for nine months in 1930. But after his release from prison in 1931, Hedgewar devoted all his energies to the building up of RSS and set out to make it a national organization. He toured several states in the early 1930s, starting with Sindh, Punjab and Uttar Pradesh, founding shakhas wherever he went. He got good response in areas where Hindus were in a minority. Gopal (Babarao) Savarkar, elder brother of V.D. Savarkar, helped the RSS by merging his own Tarun Hindu Sabha as well as the Mukteshwar Dal into the RSS. He accompanied Hedgewar on trips to western Maharashtra, introducing him to Hindu nationalists. Some of them later became prominent RSS workers. The number of shakhas went on increasing; so did the membership. But RSS did not keep any written record about its branches or its members. The other unique feature of the RSS was that it was a self-supporting organization. The members contributed their share to the organization on Dussehra in the form of *gurudakshina* (an offering of money given in respect), the 'guru' being the dhwaj of saffron colour. It was unfurled daily in every shakha and every member saluted it. The other feature of the RSS was that it did not admit ladies in its cadre; it was an all-male organization. The greatest contribution of Hedgewar to Hindu society and the RSS was that it abolished caste identities

---

[2]Andersen, W.K., and Shridhar D. Damle, *The Brotherhood in Saffron: The Rashtriya Swayamasevak Sangh and Hindu Revivalism*, Vistaar Publications, New Delhi, 1987, p. 36.

and distinctions in its cadres. It is amazing how this could be achieved without consciously trying when stalwarts like Gandhi and others before him had failed. It was part of the 'discipline' and the devotion to the Motherland dinned daily in the minds of the swayamsevaks which created this miracle. Ambedkar in his address to the Sangh Camp at Pune in 1939 particularly noted the spirit of social equality and harmony in the Sangh. He said, 'This is the first time that I am visiting a camp of Sangh volunteers. I am happy to find here absolute equality between the *savarnas* (high castes) and Harijans, without anyone being even aware of such a difference existed.' So was Gandhi, when he visited the Sangh Camp at Wardha in 1934.

Till his last days, Hedgewar continued to work ceaselessly, without caring for his health. He died from high blood pressure on 21 June 1940, in the home of Babasaheb Ghatate in Nagpur. The wide roads of Nagpur saw a traffic jam for the first time as thousands of Hedgewar's admirers wanted to pay homage to the man who shunned publicity but built an organization of devoted and well-disciplined members. Even six decades after his death, whenever there is a catastrophe in the country—a cyclone in Andhra Pradesh; an earthquake in Kutch or an air-crash in Haryana—volunteers in khaki half pants and white shirts are the first to reach there to provide relief to the victims. And every time such things happen, the nation-builder, Hedgewar, is remembered with gratitude. The future historian will have to decide Hedgewar's place in modern Indian history, because so far, he has received more brickbats than bouquets at the hands of some Indian historians.

34

Allan Octavian Hume

(1829–1912)

Though the British rule is remembered more for economic exploitation, for inflicting atrocities on innocent people and for keeping thousands of Indians in the Andaman cellular jail, there were several British citizens who spent the major part of their lives in India helping people lead a better life. One such Englishman was Allan Octavian Hume. He was born in London in 1829 and is of Scottish descent. His father, Joseph Hume (1777–1855), was a qualified doctor and had served in India for 10 years in the service of the East India Company before he went back to England; became a 'radical of the deepest dye' and was recognized as the leader of the Radical Party in the British Parliament for 30 years. Allan inherited these traits of 'independent thinking and swimming against the stream' from his father. He studied medicine and surgery at the University College Hospital. He was then educated at the East India Company College in Haileybury and intended to join the navy. With that aim in mind, he joined the training college at Haileybury. However, he changed his mind and did not end up joining the Royal Navy. He had a scientific bent of mind and had cultivated a deep interest in plants and birds on his own.

In 1849, at the age of 20, he left for India to join the Bengal Civil Service and served as district officer at Etawah, a district of North West Provinces (present day Uttar Pradesh). Here, he started his social reforms along with his official duties, unlike other district officers. He started with education and opened several free schools and libraries. He instituted scholarships for deserving students for higher education. He started juvenile reformatories for disturbed children instead of throwing them in prison. He also encouraged female education. The first medical institute in Etawah was built in 1856 with his efforts. He built a commercial complex in the centre of the town, which local people called 'Humeganj'.

He also preached against alcohol and alcoholism, to the chagrin of the revenue officials who wanted to increase the *Abkaree*, which Hume openly called 'wages of sin'. While at Etawah, he studied the agricultural situation in the district including the soil composition and weather conditions and tried to help farmers in increasing the yield of their crops by adopting better methods of cultivation, based on the nature of the soil and vagaries of weather. During the 1857 uprising, he managed to ward off the rebels with the help of local population and was awarded a CB (Companion of the Bath) by the government for his services in 1860. The uprising only temporarily affected Hume's social work. For another nine years, he continued to expand and consolidate his work of reforms. This was the most productive and happiest period of his life. His wife, Mary Anne Grindall, whom he married in 1853, was there to share his work and add to his happiness.

For the next three years (1867–70), Hume worked as commissioner of customs for the North Western Provinces. In this capacity, his principal achievement was the gradual abolition of the vast customs barriers which had hitherto been kept up to protect the government salt monopoly by excluding the cheap salt produced in the Rajputana states. From 1870, Hume was the secretary of the Department of Agriculture, Revenue and Commerce at Simla. In this important position, he tried to change the policy of the department towards poor Indian farmers, the policy which was earlier concentrated 'on shearing the sheep than to feeding it'. Utilizing his knowledge of Indian agriculture gained at Etawah, he published a pamphlet, *Agricultural Reforms in India* in 1879. The pamphlet gave suggestions to the government to implement reforms that could help the poor Indian farmers lead a better life. But the Simla mandarins and the then Secretary of State in London wanted revenue to be the main concern of the department. Even Viceroy Lord Mayo could not convince the authorities in London about the need for reforms in Indian agriculture. Hume was getting too difficult for the imperialists in India and London, which resulted in them shifting him from the Simla secretariat to the Revenue Board at Allahabad. He was also removed from the ICS cadre without being given any reason. This was a severe blow to Hume. His demotion and degradation was noted by the Anglo–Indian press. *The Pioneer* termed it as 'the greatest jobbery ever perpetuated'; and *The Statesman* commented that 'undoubtedly he (Hume) had been treated shamefully and cruelly'. Almost all the leading journalists of the time believed that his offence was that he was too honest and independent.

Apart from the setback to his official career, the transfer to Allahabad dealt a disastrous blow to his scientific studies in ornithology and botany, which he was pursuing in Simla. His interest in ornithology was such that he had spent thousands of pounds in collecting bird skin and eggs and had studied them in detail. He also started an ornithological quarterly journal, *Stray Feathers*, in 1872 and published it till 1899. He also published *The Game Birds of India, Burma and Ceylon* in three volumes, in joint-authorship with C.H.T. Marshall, which is a standard work on the subject. He built an extensive ornithological museum in his beautiful home, Rothney Castle (*Sheeshe Waali Kothi*) in Simla, which was later transferred to the British Museum of Natural History as a gift. His collection of plants was transferred to South London Botanical Institute. This was the largest collection of its kind in the world.[1] It is reported that Hume was offered the lieutenant governorship of North Western Provinces by the viceroy Lord Lytton but he declined

---

[1]Wedderburn, William, *Allan Octavian Hume: Father of the Indian National Congress*, Pegasus, New Delhi, 1974, pp. 39–41.

and suggested he rather be home member which was declined by the secretary of state, Lord Salisbury. Helena Blavatsky, the co-founder of Theosophical Society, gives a different version of this episode. In a letter to her friend in Moscow dated 5 December 1881, she wrote:

> This year I was invited to Rothney Castle 10,000 feet above the level of sea by Mr Hume who had just been made Lieutenant Governor of the N.W. Provinces. He (Mr Hume) gathered some fifty people from the Society and after they had all become members of the Theosophical Society, he founded a collateral branch called "Simla Eclectic Theosophical Society"; was elected president and under the pretext that the Society needed all his time and services, sent his resignation to the viceroy declaring that he preferred Theosophy to the services of Her Majesty.[2]

What Blavatsky writes must be taken with a pinch of salt as modesty was not one of her virtues.

Hume retired from service in 1882 and embarked upon an equally important phase of his life for which he is remembered to this day. He devoted himself to the formation of an all-India organization representing various parts of the country 'that would afford a legitimate vent to the seething discontent then rife among the people, and direct it along constitutional channels'. From well-wishers in different parts of the country and from records, he received warnings of the danger to the government and to the future welfare of India. If steps were not taken to meet the challenge posed by the discontent of the people, the situation may lead to a catastrophe. The happenings of the 1857 uprising, in which he had taken an active part in thwarting the rebels in his area, were still fresh in his mind. He feared 'a terrible outbreak, destructive to India's future'. He believed that unless men like him did something to remove the general feeling of despair and avert a catastrophe,

[2]Jinarajadsa, C., *H.P.B. Speaks*, Theosophical Publishing House, Madras, 1951, pp. 33–34.

the result could be disastrous. He believed that the intelligentsia of a country, however small in number, were after all, the natural leaders of the people. He wanted such people to get together on a common platform to discuss and find solutions for the problems facing the country. He addressed an open letter to the graduates of the University of Calcutta on 1 March 1883, appealing them to take the initiative in establishing an association 'having for its object to promote the mental, moral, social and political regeneration of the people of India'. There was a good response to this appeal and the Indian National Union was formed with Hume as general secretary, the preamble of which read,

> The union is prepared, when necessary, to oppose, by all constitutional methods, all authorities, high or low here or in England, whose acts or omissions are opposed to those principles of the Government of India laid down for them by the British Parliament and endorsed by the British Sovereign, but it holds the continued affiliation of India to Great Britain, at any rate for a period far exceeding the range of any practical political forecast, to be essential to the interests of our own national development.[3]

Thus, the seed for the INC was sown by Hume. The next meeting of the Union was held in Bombay on 27 December 1885. The name of the Union was changed to the Indian National Congress, which has survived to this day with various ups and downs and with noble and ignoble deeds. 72 delegates coming from different parts of the country attended the meeting. Hume continued to be the general secretary till 1893, painstakingly noting down the proceedings of each session.

There was strong opposition to the Congress by Sir Syed Ahmad Khan who was quite vehement in condemning the formation of the Congress, calling it a Bengali Hindu conspiracy to grab power and

---

[3]Pradhan, R.G., *India's Struggle for Swaraj*, Low Price Publications, Delhi, 1993, p. 20.

advised Muslims not to join it and was quite successful in doing so. Very few Muslims sought membership of the Congress. Hume considered this opposition unimportant, and held that, 'excluding an inappreciable fraction, the whole culture and intelligence of the country was favourable to Congress'. The number of delegates went on increasing every year, attracting almost all the stalwarts of the country like Dadabhai Naoroji, Justice Ranade, Pherozeshah Mehta, W.C. Bonnerjee, Krishna Swami Iyer, Tilak, Gokhale and others, increasing Hume's work as general secretary, which he continued to do diligently. The activities of the Congress were confined to meeting once a year and passing resolutions for the consideration of the government. But Hume's work did help the government in understanding the sentiments and aspirations of the intelligentsia, and through them, of the nation. After putting the Congress on a firm footing, Hume left for England in 1894, but even in England, he was elected secretary year after year until he relinquished the post in 1906, at the age of 77. He continued his propaganda and started a journal called *India* in 1892, to put before the British public and Parliament, information about India and grievances of Indians. During the last 18 years of his life, he carried on the work of the Congress from England, though he had retired to a quiet little home, a few miles from London, where he spent most of his time with his first love—plants. In 1910, he established the South London Botanical Institute (SLBI).

On 31 July 1912, Allan Octavian Hume died peacefully at the age of 84. There were more mourners in India than in England. Even after 45 years, the people of Etawah remembered him and shops in the town were closed in his memory. At the Bankipore session in December 1912, the Congress party placed on record that Allan Octavian Hume was the father and founder of the INC. 'He taught us how to fight bloodless battles of constitutional reform. Well may we, our children and our children's children remember the name of Mr Allan Hume through succeeding generations with gratitude and reverence.'

35

Muhammad Iqbal

(1877–1938)

Muhammad Iqbal was an important member of the fraternity of Muslim leaders who preached Muslim separatism after the collapse of the Muslim rule in India. The earlier proponents were Shah Waliullah (1704–1762), Syed Ahmad Barelvi (1786–1831), Jamal al-Din al-Afghani (1838–1897) and Sir Syed Ahmad Khan (1817–1898). In Pakistan, all these leaders are considered as freedom fighters who laid the foundations of Pakistan. Mohammad Ali Jinnah only completed the work which these leaders had started. It must be added that Iqbal, besides creating a schism between Muslims and non-Muslims, contributed greatly in some other fields also. He was one of the greatest Urdu and Persian poets after Ghalib. He was an intellectual and also wrote treatises attempting to construct a philosophy out of Islamic scriptures.

Muhammad Iqbal was born on 9 November 1877 in Sialkot, West Punjab. His ancestors were Kashmiri Brahmins who had been converted to Islam some generations earlier due to unknown reasons. Iqbal's grandfather, Sheikh Muhammad Rafiq, migrated to Sialkot from Srinagar in early nineteenth century. Iqbal's parents, Sheikh Noor Muhammad and Imam Bibi, were almost illiterate but had a religious bent of mind. Iqbal had one brother called Ata Muhammad. His was from a middle-class family, devoid of any intellectual pursuits.

Iqbal's initial education was in a traditional *maktab* (school).

One of his teachers was Sayyid Mir Hasan, the famous Oriental scholar. Iqbal learnt Urdu, Persian and Arabic there. He started composing Urdu poems while still studying at the maktab. After completing his education there, he joined the Sialkot Mission School from where he passed the matriculation examination. For higher studies, he joined the Government College, Lahore, from where he attained his bachelor's degree in 1897 and then his master's in philosophy in 1899, topping the list of successful candidates, thus demonstrating his intellectual acumen. He was appointed as a lecturer in Arabic at the local Oriental College. But soon he shifted to Government College, his alma mater, as assistant professor of philosophy and was greatly influenced by Thomas Arnold, who was working as professor of philosophy in the College. All these years till 1905, he had been writing beautiful Urdu poetry without any trace of the fanaticism or Pan-Islamism that is reflected in his later poetry. *Tarana-e-Hindi (Sare Jahan Se Achha, Hindustan Hamara)*, *Naya Shiwala* and *Aftab* (translation of Gayatri) were all composed by him, before 1905. He also wrote beautiful Urdu poems for children, which remain unrivalled to this day.[1]

Professor Arnold, impressed by the talents of Iqbal, advised him to go to England for higher studies. He joined the Trinity College, Cambridge and did research under Mac Taggart and James Ward and was greatly influenced by these two thinkers. He also studied law and was called to the Bar in 1908. He must have worked very hard those three years in Europe because besides getting a degree from Cambridge and qualifying as a barrister, he also got a PhD from Munich University, Germany in 1907. The topic of his dissertation was *The Development of Metaphysics in Persia*.

He came back to Lahore in 1908 and was appointed as a part-time lecturer of philosophy and English literature at the Government College. He was allowed to practice as a barrister as well. However, Iqbal's heart was not in the legal practice and

---

[1]Iqbal, Muhammad, *Bang-e-Dara*, Shaikh Mubark Ali, Lahore, 1924.

thus he could not be a successful lawyer. After his return from Europe, there was a complete transformation in his thinking. He was deeply concerned with the fate of Islam in the world and almost all his writings during this period are devoted to that sentiment. He now stopped singing praises of 'Hindustan' and instead wrote on Pan-Islamism. He also condemned nationalism. His *Tarana-e-Milli*, starts with the lines: '*Chino-Arab hamara, Hindustan hamara; Muslim hain, hum watan hai, sara jahan hamara* (China and Arabia are ours and India is ours; for we Muslims, the whole world is our country).' Was he the same Iqbal who wrote *Tarana-e-Hindi* only four years earlier? He expressed his views about nationalism in a short poem, *Wataniyat*: 'Among the newly discovered gods, the greatest is the country; But the apparel of this god is the shroud of religion.' Was he referring to *Vande Mataram* here? His two poems, *Shikwa* and *Jawab-e-Shikwa*, depict the sorry state of Muslims who had drawn swords in the name of God. The second poem *Jawab-e-Shikwa* is the reply of God who tells the Muslims that they had forgotten the message of Muhammad the Prophet. In this poem, Iqbal exhorts Muslims to go back to early Islam and shed their timidness. In his famous *Asrar-e-Khudi (The Secrets of Self)*, he tells Muslims to have confidence in themselves and know their intrinsic powers. It was translated by Prof. R.A. Nicholson, the famous Orientalist of Cambridge, and as a result, Iqbal came to be discussed in the Western academic circles. He was conferred knighthood in 1922 for his literary eminence. By 1928, he had earned a reputation as a great Muslim philosopher and was invited to deliver lectures in Hyderabad, Aligarh and Madras. These lectures were later published as *The Reconstruction of Religious Thought in Islam* (1930), which is his major prose work. In it, he makes an attempt, as he himself says, 'to construct Muslim religious philosophy with due regard to the philosophical traditions of Islam and the more recent developments in the various domains of human knowledge'.

As his legal practice, which had never been lucrative any way, dwindled, Iqbal decided to try his luck in politics. In the 1926 elections, he stood as a candidate and was elected to the Punjab Legislative Council. After that he became an active member of the Muslim League and in a way its policymaker. He joined Aga Khan and Jinnah to denounce the Nehru Report (1928), putting forward 'demands' for the safeguards of Muslim interests. In that year he was elected as secretary of the All-India Muslim League. He presided at the 1930 session of the Muslim League in Allahabad. His presidential address marks the formal beginning of the demand for a separate home for the Muslims and deserves to be quoted:

> Communalism, in its higher aspects, is indispensable to the formation of a harmonious whole in a country like India. The units of Indian society are not territorial as in European countries. India is a continent of human groups belonging to different races, speaking different languages, and professing different religions. The principle of European democracy cannot be applied to India without recognizing the presence of communal groups. The Muslim demand for the creation of a Muslim India within India is, therefore, perfectly justified. I would like to see Punjab, the NWFP, Sindh and Baluchistan amalgamated into a single state, self-governing within the British Empire, or without the British Empire. The formation of a consolidated North-West Indian Muslim state appears to me to be the final destiny of the Muslims, at least in Northwest India.[2]

Iqbal's selection of the north-west as the most appropriate region for the establishment of a Muslim state had an interesting history behind it. Apart from its being a compact Muslim majority area, it was the geographical link between India and the Muslim world of Central and Western Asia. The memory of the Wahhabi state founded in this region by the advocates of *Dar-ul-Islam,* like

---

[2]Zaidi, A.M., *Evolution of Muslim Political Thought in India,* S. Chand, New Delhi, 1978, pp. 60–70.

Syed Ahmed Barelvi, was still fresh in the minds of the fanatical Muslims.[3]

Iqbal also attended the Second and Third Round Table Conferences (London) in 1931 and 1932, 'where his only contribution was to oppose every suggestion for the introduction of joint-electorates and the formation of federation in India'.

Iqbal's last years were not happy. He was keeping ill and two deaths in the family shattered his equanimity. Still, his mind was active. He was worried about the future of Islam and of Muslims in India. His admirers gathered at his residence daily and he discussed with them what was foremost in his mind. During these sittings, Iqbal censured territorial nationalism and the doctrine of separation of Church and State. He categorically asserted that narrow nationalism was the antithesis of Islam, which believed in an international brotherhood of Muslims (Pan-Islamism). He criticized the concept of a common Indian nationality.[4] Iqbal believed that Islam was perfect and eternal as a guide for social and political life. Thus the 'philosophy' of Iqbal comes down almost to the level of a fundamentalist clergy.

He remained the president of the Provincial Muslim League of Punjab, though he could not take active part in its activities. He regularly corresponded with M.A. Jinnah, expressing his views about the political developments in India vis-a-vis Muslims. In a letter to Jinnah in 1937, Iqbal wrote, 'The construction of a polity on Indian national lines, if it means the displacement of the Islamic principle of solidarity, is simply unthinkable to a Muslim.'

He died in Lahore on 21 April 1938, at the age of 61 and was buried in the backyard of the Badshahi Mosque, built by Aurangzeb.

It is difficult to assess Iqbal. 'He was too contradictory and unsystematic to permit a systematic assessment.' The fact that he

---

[3]Banerjee, A.C., *Two Nations: The Philosophy of Muslim Nationalism*, Concept Publishing Comapny, New Delhi, 1981, p. 203.
[4]Khairi, Saad R., *Jinnah Reinterpreted: The Journey from Indian Nationalism to Muslim Statehood*, Oxford University Press, Karachi, 1966, p. 341.

put forth his philosophy in poetic form, adds to the confusion. According to Jawaharlal Nehru,

> He was very far from being a mass leader; he was a poet, an intellectual and a philosopher with affiliations to the old feudal order. He supplied in fine poetry, which was written both in Persian and Urdu, a philosophic background to the Moslem intelligentsia and thus diverted its mind in a separatist direction. His popularity was, no doubt, due to the quality of his poetry, but even more so, it was due to his having fulfilled a need when the Moslem mind was searching for some anchor to hold on to.[5]

[5]Nehru, Jawaharlal, *The Discovery of India*, John Day Company, 1946, pp. 350–51.

36

Kasturi Ranga Iyengar

(1859–1923)

During the freedom struggle, some newspapers and their editors with nationalistic leanings played an important role in the formation of public opinion. One such editor was Kasturi Ranga Iyengar of *The Hindu*.

Kasturi Ranga was born on 15 December 1859 in an orthodox Brahmin family. His father Sesha Iyengar was a revenue official under the district collector of Tanjore. Kasturi Ranga started his education in village schools in Innambur and Kabisthalam, where his father got posted. But at the age of 12, he was sent to Provincial School and College at Kumbakonam, where his elder brother was studying. After completing his matriculation at Kumbakonam, Kasturi Ranga joined Presidency College, Madras, from where he took his Arts Degree in 1879. While he was still in school at Kumbakonam, Kasturi Ranga was married to ten-year-old Kanakammal. When he was 17, his father, Sesha Iyengar, died. Kasturi Ranga continued his studies and joined the law course in Presidency College but failed in the first attempt. He joined the post of a sub-registrar in the Registration Department in 1881, which did not carry any salary but he earned commission on the stamp value of registered documents which came to about ₹40 per month. After serving as sub-registrar for three years, he applied for a law degree again and got through (1884). He started his apprenticeship under V. Bashyam Ayyangar, a leading lawyer of Madras. After his apprenticeship,

Kasturi Ranga was enrolled as a *vakil* (lawyer) in March 1885. Instead of setting up his legal practice at Madras he opted for Coimbatore, a smaller place. In a short time, he had a lucrative practice. He was also motivated to play an active role in the public life of the town. He was elected to the Municipal Council, appointed honorary magistrate as well as a jail visitor. Later, he was nominated to the Coimbatore District Board. After nine years of practice at Coimbatore, Kasturi Ranga moved to Madras (1894), hoping to augment his practice and to play a greater role in public affairs. His calculation about increasing his legal practice did not fructify but he started taking greater interest in politics as well as in journalism. His public activities naturally brought him in close touch with *The Hindu*, an upcoming newspaper in Madras, and its manager and editor. He also took great interest in the activities of Madras Mahajan Sabha, a leading social and political society of Madras, whose office was located in the premises of *The Hindu*. In 1895, Kasturi Ranga became legal adviser to *The Hindu*, which was then edited and managed by two of its founders, G. Subramania Iyer and M. Veeraraghavachariar respectively. As the two did not devote much time to the monetary aspect, *The Hindu* had run into financial difficulties. In addition to being the legal adviser, Kasturi Ranga was a regular contributor to the columns of *The Hindu* on legal, political and social issues.

In 1905, Kasturi Ranga took the most important decision of his life. He purchased *The Hindu*. His first concern after the takeover was to reorganize the business set-up of the paper. And within a month, he had to take up the entire burden of editorial responsibilities. Simultaneously, he started strengthening its news services. He subscribed to a fuller service from Reuters, which was the sole news agency covering Indian and foreign affairs. He also appointed correspondents in a number of places. He expanded the 'Letters to the Editor' columns to know the reaction of the readers and introduced several other features to make *The Hindu* a popular newspaper.

Even when Kasturi Ranga was preoccupied with the affairs of *The Hindu*, he took an active part in politics. He was in agreement with the policies of Bal Gangadhar Tilak and was critical of the Moderates. When after the Surat Congress in 1907, the Moderate faction took over the Congress, Kasturi Ranga practically retired from active politics for nearly 10 years. He returned to politics when there was rapprochement between the two adversaries in the Congress in 1916 after Tilak's release from prison. He played an important role in formulating the Congress–Muslim League Pact of 1916 (Lucknow Pact), along with other important leaders of the Congress such as Tilak. He also supported the Home Rule Movement of Annie Besant and Tilak (1916). During the First World War, Kasturi Ranga gave cautious support to the Allies headed by Britain. In August 1918, the British government invited a small team of five journalists from India to visit Britain to witness the goings-on in the battlefield on the Western Front. Kasturi Ranga was one of those five journalists. Writing about the invitation to Britain, Annie Besant wrote in her paper, *New India*: 'Mr Kasturi Ranga Iyengar holds easily a very high place among the Indian journalists who have contributed not a little to the public life and the formation of influential public opinion in the country.'[1] The visit lasted for five months and he learnt a great deal from the visit which was reflected in the despatches he sent from the War Front for *The Hindu*. When Mahatma Gandhi started the Non-cooperation Movement in 1920, he gave selective support to the movement but was an ardent supporter of the freedom movement as such. During the critical years of 1920–22, the support of *The Hindu* was a great asset for the freedom struggle. Kasturi Ranga used his position as the editor to influence the views and decisions of men in power as well as in the INC. When the Non-cooperation Movement was suspended in February 1922 after the Chauri Chaura

---

[1]Narasimhan, V.K., *Kasturi Ranga Iyengar*, Publication Division, New Delhi, 1963, p. 138.

incident and Gandhi was arrested the following month, a committee was constituted by the AICC (headed by Hakim Ajmal Khan) to review the situation. The other members of the committee were Motilal Nehru, C. Rajagopalachari, V.J. Patel and Kasturi Ranga Iyengar. The committee members were divided among those who wanted to change the nature of the movement and enter legislatures and those who wanted no-change and opposed the Council entry proposal and recommended doing 'constructive work' as advised by Gandhi. Kasturi Ranga was among those who opposed the Council entry proposal. Though he supported the Congress party and its policies through the editorials and write-ups in *The Hindu*, he never courted arrest.

From the very beginning of his takeover of *The Hindu*, Kasturi Ranga did not hesitate to risk the displeasure of the authorities. For instance, highlighting the failure of the banking firm of Arbuthnot & Co. and the misdeeds of its proprietor, Sir George Arbuthnot, who was found guilty of misappropriation of public funds in the paper, resulted in his getting 18 months rigorous imprisonment. By taking up such public causes, *The Hindu's* circulation increased and it became self-supporting and stopped accepting donations within a few years. In a span of only 18 years (1905–1923), Kasturi Ranga made *The Hindu* one of the best produced and most influential newspapers in India.

Late in his life, Kasturi Ranga emerged as a labour leader. In March 1920, he helped to organize the South Indian Railway Employees Association at Tiruchirappalli. The inaugural meeting was held under his presidentship and he was elected the association's first president. In 1921, when 10,000 labourers were locked out of the Buckingham and Carnatic Mills, it was *The Hindu*, under the editorship of Kasturi Ranga, that came forward and defended their cause. During the strike, Kasturi Ranga, in spite of poor health, attended a public meeting of the citizens at the Triplicane beach to express sympathy for the workers. He donated ₹500 for the Strikers Relief Fund and was elected as a member of the committee that was formed to help the strikers. Thus, he helped the striking workers both with his pen and his money.[2]

At the end of 1922, Kasturi Ranga fell ill. He was suffering from liver trouble and also had to be operated upon for hernia. He was in bed for a whole year and died on 12 December 1923 in Madras.

Kasturi Ranga Iyengar was a leading journalist and nationalist of the twentieth century. K. Santhanam has spoken of him, saying, 'His single-minded patriotism and strict adherence to truth in the publication of news and features and freedom from malice or personal prejudices in dealing with those with whom he did not agree, entitle him to respect and gratitude and a high place among the builders of modern India.'[3] *The London Times,* in an obituary, described him as 'one of the most influential of extremist journalists in India'. A more detailed tribute was paid by Mahatma Gandhi when he was invited to unveil a portrait of Kasturi Ranga at *The Hindu* office, Madras (22 March 1925). Gandhi said,

> I believe that Kasturi Ranga Iyengar represented some of the best that is to be found in Indian journalism. He had a style of his own. He commanded a sarcasm which was also, so peculiarly, his own. Whenever he wrote as an opponent or as a friend, you could not fail to admire his style in which he wrote. I think it can be fairly claimed for him that he never wavered in his faith in his own country. And although he was always a courteous critic, he was also one of the most fearless critics of the Government. I had on many an occasion to differ from him. But I always valued his decision because I understood thereby wherein lay the weakness of my argument or my position. Very often it appeared to me that he occupied, if I may take such a parallel, about the same

---

[2]Ibid. 197–98.
[3]Santhanam, K., *Dictionary of National Biography,* Institute of Historical Studies, Calcutta, 1973.

position in this Presidency that the editor of *The London Times* occupies in England.[4]

Kasturi Ranga Iyengar had three daughters and two sons. When he died in 1923, his two sons Kasturi Srinivasan and K. Gopalan, inherited the paper. Kasturi Srinivasan (1887–1959) was more talented and was a worthy son of a worthy father. *The Hindu* became highly respected and internationally known under his direction. The paper, even after a century and a quarter, maintains the same position successfully.

---

[4]*Collected Works of Mahatma Gandhi*, Vol. 26, Publications Division, Government of India, pp. 368–69.

37

Mukund Ramrao Jayakar

(1873–1959)

Mukund Ramrao Jayakar was born on 13 November 1873 in Bombay, in a middle-class family. His father, Ramrao, was a junior official in the Bombay secretariat. His mother, Sonabai, was able to create a religious atmosphere in the family. Mukund was brought up by his grandfather, Vasudeo Jagannath Kirtikar, after the early and untimely death of his father. Vasudeo was a reputed scholar, philosopher and lawyer and greatly influenced Mukund. Thus, Mukund was brought up in an ambience of scholastic studies, religiosity and sobriety, resulting in him becoming a multifaceted personality. He was educated in the Elphinstone High School and at St Xavier's College, Bombay. He graduated in 1895 and passed his master's in 1897 and bachelor of laws (LLB) in 1902. In 1903, he left for England, joined law and was called to the Bar in 1905. After returning to India in the same year, he started practising at the Bombay High Court. In 1907, he joined the Bombay Law School as a professor but resigned in 1912, when an Englishman who was at a junior position, was appointed principal instead of him. He started practising at the Bombay High Court again and became one of the leading barristers of Bombay. M.C. Chagla, who at the time was working as Jinnah's assistant, wrote: 'Jayakar was an erudite lawyer and argued his cases with words which were carefully chosen, and which bore the impress of a scholar. He rose to great eminence and eventually became a member of the Privy

Council.'[1] Before becoming a member of the Privy Council of London, he had accepted an appointment as judge of the Federal Court of India in 1937.

At the age of 26, Jayakar married Sushilabai in 1899. They had one son and three daughters. Jayakar became interested in politics but he did not join any political party formally, though his inclinations were towards Hindu Mahasabha, like those of Madan Mohan Malaviya, as he was deeply imbued in Hinduism. However, he played an important role, along with Tej Bahadur Sapru, as a Liberal and moderate leader, political negotiator and peacemaker. In 1918, the Poona District Conference at Lonavala was held under the chairmanship of Jayakar. 'This Conference', he said, 'was an assertion of the political tenets of Maharashtra, professed since the days of Ranade, Tilak and Gokhale.' At this time, Jayakar was a follower of Annie Besant. He was a member of the Home Rule League deputation, led by Besant, which waited upon Viceroy Lord Chelmsford and Secretary of State Montagu in November 1918. Later, Jayakar was drawn towards Gandhi but he never became a Gandhian. The deportation of B.G. Horniman (1919), editor of *Bombay Chronicle,* brought them nearer as Gandhi had taken up the Horniman's illegal deportation case and closure of his paper. Jayakar revived *Bombay Chronicle,* spending considerable time and money on it. He became the chairman of the board of directors of the paper.

The Congress Punjab Enquiry Committee (formed after the Jallianwala Bagh tragedy) brought Gandhi and Jayakar closer as Jayakar replaced Motilal Nehru as a member of the Committee. The Congress had assigned Jayakar the work of writing the report and seeing it through the press. Gandhi collaborated with him in scrutinizing the final proofs. When the report was ready, it was decided to send someone to London to inform the British public

---

[1]Chagla, M.C., *Roses in December: An Autobiography,* Bharatiya Vidya Bhavan, Bombay, 1973, p. 92.

about what really had happened in Jallianwala Bagh and about the atrocities committed on the innocent public under Martial Law. In a letter to Jayakar dated 28 March 1920, Gandhi wrote: 'I consider that I am the fittest to go, but my going is a virtual impossibility. You come next in my view, because you are student like me and we want a man of application and studious habits and possessing a level head.'[2] However, the idea of sending someone to England with the report was dropped because of Jayakar's illness. In July 1921, Gandhi came to Poona in connection with the Tilak anniversary and visited Jayakar, who was still ill and in bed. Jayakar gave ₹25,000 to Gandhi for the Tilak Swaraj Fund.

Jayakar was a powerful speaker, both in the assemblies and outside. He was leader of the Swaraj Party in the Bombay Legislative Council (1923–25). His speeches were informative, thought-provoking and backed by statistical data. In 1926, he was elected to the Central Legislature, where he acted as deputy leader of the Nationalist Party (1926–30).

Along with Tej Bahadur Sapru, his role as a mediator and peacemaker gave a turn to history. The Gandhi–Irwin Pact (March 1931) was the outcome of the ceaseless efforts of the Jayakar–Sapru duo. He was mainly instrumental in effecting the Poona or the Yerwada Pact between Gandhi and Ambedkar (1932). He did his work, along with Sapru, in a silent and unobtrusive manner. 'Their non-alignment with the Congress and Gandhi gave them a stature and they often struck a line of rapprochement when dark clouds were ominous.' Jayakar participated in the three Round Table Conferences in London (1930–32) and took active part in the negotiations between the Indian leaders and the representatives of the British government. He was a keen observer of the political developments in the country and unhesitatingly warned the leaders when he thought that a wrong step was being taken. He wrote a strong letter on 21 January 1942, to Rajagopalachari, who was going

---

to meet Jinnah, for a settlement of the Hindu–Muslim question conceding to the Muslims 50 per cent share in central and state legislatures as well as in government services. He wrote,

> You have publicly spoken of the fifty-fifty basis being acceptable to you with Jinnah as Prime Minister. I am not worried about the Prime Ministership, which may go to Jinnah or anyone else. But it is my duty to warn you that the fifty-fifty basis at the Centre or in the provinces or in the Services or administration will not be acceptable to the Hindus.[3]

He had written a similar letter to Gandhi before he went to meet Jinnah, in his Malabar Hill residence in Bombay (September 1944), to offer him the Rajaji Formula, which was the virtual acceptance of Pakistan. Jayakar was a very upright man and a nationalist to the core.

Apart from his interest in politics, Jayakar was an eminent educationist. He set-up the Aryan Education Society and was its chairman for several years. He was a member of the Bombay University Reforms Committee (1924–25). In 1941, he was appointed chairman of the committee set up to consider the establishment of Maharashtra University, which materialized in the establishment of University of Poona, with Jayakar becoming its first vice-chancellor. He ably performed his duties for two terms (1948–56). He was instrumental in securing funds and generously donated to the Bhandarkar Oriental Research Institute (BORI), enabling the publication of a critical edition of the Mahabharata. He was an extremely erudite Sanskrit scholar. In 1924, he edited *Studies in Vedanta*, written by his grandfather, V.J. Kritikar. His contributions on Hindu law were also widely acclaimed. As an educationist, he was invited by several universities to deliver convocation addresses.

---

[3]Pandey, B.N., *The Indian National Movement, 1885–1947: Select Documents*, Macmillan, London, 1979, pp. 167–69.

Jayakar was a great lover of art and music and spent several years studying classical music and fine arts. His presidential address at the Akhil Bhartiya Gandharva Mahavidyalaya Mandal in Bombay is considered an outstanding and original contribution to modern music.

Jayakar was also greatly interested in social activities. He was the president of the Indian National Social Conference (founded by Ranade) held at Nasik in 1917. He also worked for the eradication of untouchability. In 1924, Jayakar, as a member of the Depressed Classes Mission Society of India, sought Gandhi's help in assisting the Harijans build their own temples, schools and hostels in Bombay. A number of letters were exchanged between Gandhi and Jayakar on this issue.

Jayakar lived a very fruitful and varied life. His patriotism and liberality were reflected in whatever he did. In spite of being a devout Hindu and being close to several Hindu Mahasabha leaders, he was considered a liberal even by his enemies.

After a prolonged illness, he died on 10 March 1959 in Bombay, at the age of 86. His autobiography, *The Story of My Life* (published in two volumes), describes the important events and personalities of his time in an objective and unobtrusive manner.

38

Mohammad Ali Jinnah

(1876–1948)

Mohammad Ali Jinnah was born in Karachi to Jinnahbhai Poonja and Mithibai. The family had moved to Karachi from Rajkot in Gujarat a generation earlier. Jinnah's grandfather was a Hindu (of Bhatia caste) who got converted to Islam for unknown reasons. They were now Khoja Muslims, a business community among Muslims who are followers of Aga Khan. Mohammad Ali Jinnah was the first of six children of his parents. Surprisingly, his date of birth is still under dispute. But according to his own assertion, he was born on Christmas day (25 December) in 1876 and that is the day that is officially celebrated as his birthday in Pakistan. His father was a hide merchant and had prospered since the arrival of the family in Karachi. When Mohammad was about six, his father arranged a tutor for him but the boy was not interested in studies. His aunt (father's sister), Manbai, tempted him to visit her in Bombay and put him in a school there. In Bombay, he studied for an uncertain but brief period at the Gokul Das Tej Primary School. Returning to Karachi in 1887, he was enrolled in Sindh Madressatul Islam (SMI) University in December 1887; however, he studied there only for a few years. Later, he studied in Church Mission High School. He was fond of horse riding and his father owned several horses. Reading bored him. He was not easy to control even as a child. It is doubtful if he learnt enough Gujarati (his mother

tongue), Hindi or Urdu. We find Gandhi writing to him on 28
June 1919: 'I have your promise that you would take up Gujarati
and Hindi as quickly as possible.'[1]

Jinnah's father's firm was closely associated with a British
firm called Douglas Graham & Company. The company's general
manager, Leigh Croft, developed a liking for the young, energetic
lad and suggested to his father that his son should be sent for an
apprenticeship in the company's head office in London. Jinnah's
father agreed but his mother insisted that her son should marry
before he left for England. So, in 1892, the sixteen-year-old Jinnah
was married to a Khoja girl, Emibai, two years his junior. In January
1893, Jinnah left for England. Not long after arriving in London,
he abandoned business for law. He shortened his name to 'M.A.
Jinnah', for the convenience of his British friends and acquaintances.
He was called to the Bar from the Lincoln's Inn in 1896. While
in London, he used to visit the House of Commons and listened
to the debates there. He also fell in love with theatre. After three
and a half years in England, Jinnah sailed back to his country,
reaching Karachi in 1896. 'His home-coming was grim. His mother
and wife had died and his father's business was on the verge of
collapse.' Instead of settling in Karachi, he decided to seek his
fortune in Bombay. He had to struggle hard for some years but
his law practice soon picked up. In time, he had earned a name
as a brilliant barrister; his income soared and he started living in
luxury and was always immaculately dressed. He lived more like a
British than an Indian and was something of a dandy.

Jinnah had two brothers and three sisters but the only sibling
with whom he established a close and continuing relationship till the
end was his sister Fatima, 17 years younger than him. Jinnah defied
Muslim conventions by sending Fatima to a Catholic boarding
school and later encouraged her to study dentistry. But Jinnah

---

[1]*Collected Works of Mahatma* Gandhi, Vol. 15, Publications Division, Government
of India, p. 399.

never tried to usher in any reform movement among the Muslim community as such.

Besides his legal practice, Jinnah developed an interest in politics. He was influenced by Dadabhai Naoroji, Gopal Krishna Gokhale and Pherozeshah Mehta (in whose chambers, he worked for some time when he was trying to establish himself). It was at the Calcutta session of the Congress in 1906 that Jinnah made his debut in politics. Dadabhai presided over the session and Jinnah served as his secretary. Jinnah formally joined the Congress party that year. Gradually his flirtations with the Muslim League (which was founded in 1906 at Dhaka) started. Though not a member of the Muslim League, he addressed their sessions in 1910 and 1911. In 1910, he was elected to the Imperial Legislative Council (ILC) from the Muslim constituency of Bombay. The separate constituencies for Muslims had been created under the 1909 Act. Except for 1913, when he was nominated, he was elected often unopposed, from Muslim constituencies in 1915, 1923, 1926 and 1934. During his election in 1910 and again in 1915, he was still a member of the Congress. He had a long and brilliant career as a legislator and vied for prominence with stalwarts like Motilal Nehru, Lajpat Rai, Madan Mohan Malaviya and M.R. Jayakar. He started enjoying his political outings, and along with law, politics became his second passion. In fact, apart from law and politics, he had no other interests. 'He seldom, if ever, read a serious book in all his life. His staple food was newspapers, briefs and law books.'

In 1913, he formally joined the Muslim League and the interest of the Muslim community became the prime concern of his life. It is true that he did not believe in Islamic taboos like eating pork and in rituals like going to the mosque for prayers and to Mecca for salvation. For him, these were non-essential things. What he did during the rest of his life was to get the maximum benefits for the Muslim community so that they could become a power to reckon with. His brilliant legal brain produced the document called 'Lucknow Pact' in 1916, when he presided over the Lucknow session of the Muslim League at Kaisarbagh in Lucknow. Nobody else but Jinnah could get as many provisions for the Muslims as he got under the Lucknow Pact. Separate electorates for Muslims were retained; Muslims got heavy weightage in legislatures—one-third at the centre and in Bombay, one-half in the Punjab, 40 per cent in Bengal, 30 per cent in the United Provinces, 25 per cent in Bihar and Orissa and 15 per cent in Central Provinces and Madras. Muslims also got virtual veto during the enactment of new legislation in the assemblies. In return, the Muslim League promised to work with the Congress in their fight for swaraj. In spite of these concessions to the Muslims in the Lucknow Pact, the loss of majority rankled Jinnah for years and he wanted to annul that clause which went against the interest of the Muslims. In 1924, he said, 'As a party to the Lucknow Pact, I can say that it was never intended to be permanent. I suggest that in Bengal and Punjab, Muslims should be restored to their majority.'[2]

Jinnah had been a widower for more than two decades when he thought of marrying again. His choice was a beautiful, young and vivacious Parsi girl, Rattanbai or Ruttie, daughter of one of the wealthiest Parsis in Bombay, Sir Dinshaw Maneckji Petit. Jinnah was 42 and she was 19 when they got married on 19 April 1918, against the wishes of her father. Three days earlier, Jinnah got her converted to Islam. 'Sir Dinshaw never forgave his daughter, never saw her again and even when she died, he refused to attend the funeral or even to see her body.' The couple had only one daughter, Dina, born in 1919. The marriage proved to be a disaster. Apart from the age factor, the natures of husband and wife were distinctly different from each other. 'Ruttie had married Jinnah because of the glamour of his personality, and there was nothing in common between them. Jinnah used to pore over his briefs every day, and what little time he had to spare was given to politics. Ruttie was a young woman, fond of life and frivolities of the young. They

---

[2]Nagarkar, V.V., Genesis of Pakistan, Allied Publishers, California, 1975, p. 172.

gradually drifted apart.'[3] While Jinnah found solace in his briefs and politics,

> Ruttie had nothing to fall back on. She became a mental wreck and tried to find solace in drugs, Theosophy, seances and her pets. But nothing seemed to work for her and she died in the prime of her youth, in February 1929. Before she died, she had confided to her dear Parsi friend, Kanji Dwarkadas, that she would like to be cremated. But Jinnah ignored her last wish and got her buried under Muslim rites. Ruttie was a true nationalist and kept Jinnah on the right track so long as she was alive. After her death, Jinnah's sole companion at home was his sister Fatima, who was even more communal minded and partly responsible for the transformation brought about in Jinnah subsequently. There is reason to believe that Jinnah rehearsed his speeches before her. She enjoyed Jinnah's diatribes against the Hindus, and if anything, injected an extra dose of venom into them.[4]

The year 1920 proved to be a turning point in the life of Jinnah, and for India. It was the year when Gandhi promised swaraj in one year and got his non-cooperation resolution passed by the Congress. When Jinnah stood up to oppose 'Mr Gandhi's resolution' at the Nagpur session of the Congress he was howled down with cries of shame. 'Not "Mr" but say *"Mahatma"*,' the unwieldy crowd yelled. Jinnah, taken aback, tried to argue but was shouted down. He left the stage in disgust and the Congress for good, 'the searing memory of his defeat at Nagpur permanently emblazoned on his mind.' He waited for revenge. The importance of Jinnah remained outside the Congress. In 1923 and 1926, he was elected to the Central Legislature from Muslim constituencies. His community still believed in him and he decided to serve them with renewed

---

[3]Chagla, M.C., *Roses in December*, Bharatiya Vidya Bhavan, Bombay, 1973, p. 120.
[4]Ibid. 119.

vigour, as president of the Muslim League.

In 1924, he was appointed a member of the Muddiman Committee, which was to examine the working of the India Act of 1919. He was also nominated a member of the Skeen Committee, along with Motilal Nehru, which was to examine the problem of Indianization of army officers. It was evident that the government considered him as one of the most important members of the Central Assembly. When the all-white Simon Commission visited India in 1928, the Jinnah faction of the Muslim League joined the Congress in boycotting the commission which was appointed to assess the working of the 1919 Act and to propose further legislation leading towards self-government. Simultaneously, the All Parties Conference appointed a committee, headed by Motilal Nehru, in February 1928 'to report on the principle of a constitution for independent India'. The committee submitted its report (later called the Nehru Report) at the Lucknow meeting in August 1928. The main recommendations were—dominion status; joint electorates and weightage to minorities etc. The parties agreed to the proposals. But the agreement did not last long and when the conference met on 22 December 1928, Muslims, under the leadership of Jinnah, made four new demands in the form of amendments. These were 33 and a half percent representation for the Muslims in the Central Legislature; reservation of seats on population basis in Punjab and Bengal; residuary powers with the provincial governments and separation of Sindh from Bombay. The amendments were turned down and Jinnah left the Conference disappointed calling it 'parting of ways'. After wrecking the All Parties Convention in Calcutta, he reached Delhi to attend the All Parties Muslim Conference. Aga Khan, who presided over the meeting, welcomed the prodigal son to the Islamic fold. Jinnah's four points in Calcutta swelled to 14 by the time he reached Delhi. The elaborate demands put forward in Jinnah's famous 14 points were not yet Pakistan, 'but almost its early embryo, within a weak federal womb'. He threw away his nationalist and secular mask which he was wearing since the

Lucknow Pact days. 'I have no future in any Hindu dominated body,' he declared. The Muslim League elected him as its lifelong president.

Jinnah sailed for England on 4 October 1930, along with his sister Fatima and daughter Dina, to attend the Round Table Conference as a Muslim nominee. There he put forward a wide range of demands of special Muslim interests contained in his 14 points, adding a few more to it. The vision of Pakistan was getting clearer in his mind. It will remain a mystery why Jinnah was not invited to attend the Second and Third Round Table Conferences. But according to his own admission, 'I was not invited to the later sittings of the Conference because I was the strongest opponent of the Federal Scheme.' Disappointed, Jinnah decided to stay on in England to practice before the Privy Council but without much success. However, when The Communal Award was announced in 1932, all his 14 points had been conceded by the British government and more concessions were given to the Muslims than what they had asked for.

At the request of several Muslim friends and well-wishers like Muhammad Iqbal and Liaquat Ali, Jinnah returned to India in 1934 to lead the Muslim community. Muslims were in need of a dynamic and cunning leader as many Muslim leaders of national stature had died between 1928 and 1936—Ajmal Khan, Mohammad Ali, M.A. Ansari, Muhammad Shafi and Fazl-i-Hussain. Leaders like Sikandar Hayat Khan in Punjab and A.K. Fazlul Huq in Bengal were busy in provincial politics. The burden of rejuvenating the moribund Muslim League fell on Jinnah's shoulders and he seemed to like the role assigned to him. The Communal Award had given a new orientation to the communal politics in the country and Jinnah emerged as the saviour of the Muslim community. In the Bombay session of the Muslim League (April 1936), a resolution was adopted rejecting the Federal Scheme of the 1935 Act, while recommending the Provincial Scheme to be tried out for what it was worth. Elections to the provincial legislatures were held in 1937, under the 1935 Act. The results of the elections were extremely disappointing from Jinnah's point of view. Of the 485 Muslim seats, the League could win only 108 seats in all the 11 provinces; the remaining Muslim seats went to other Muslim groups. Congress won almost all the general seats and formed ministries in seven out of 11 provinces. The defeated Jinnah started vicious propaganda against the Congress ministries, charging that all the inequities and injustices were being inflicted on the Muslims in the 'Hindu Raj'. To add weight to the accusations, a committee headed by Raja of Pirpur was formed to 'look into the grievances of Muslims under Congress rule'. Another committee was formed in Bihar to go into the details of Muslim suffering under Congress rule which was even more intemperate.

> At this distance of time their truth or untruth matters little. What was important is the technique adopted by Jinnah to incite the Muslim masses by making them believe that Islam was in danger. The Muslim masses flocked to the League, the membership jumping from a few thousand to over a hundred thousand in the United Provinces alone. Jinnah had become a mass leader, tens of thousands of people greeting him with cries of *"Allah-hu-Akbar"* and *"Quaid-e-Azam Zindabad"*.

To Jinnah's delight, the Congress ministries decided to resign in November 1939, after the Second World War broke out. This, not a very wise act of Congress, left the political field entirely to be exploited by the Muslim League. Under Jinnah's orders, the Muslims observed 22 December 1939 as the 'Day of Deliverance'. Only a few months later, Jinnah was bold enough to demand a separate area of the country for the 'Muslim nation' in the Lahore session of the Muslim League (March 1940). Pakistan had arrived. Henceforth, Pakistan became a passion and a mania with Jinnah. He evolved a strategy to deal with the Congress, which puzzled and bewildered the Congress leaders and to a lesser degree the British government. Every Congress error was irreversibly exploited by Jinnah and the

Congress, led by Gandhi, managed to commit many such errors during 1940–47. In the words of H.V. Hodson, 'Never was the Gandhian leadership less relevant to practical politics; never did the Congress need more to recognize its own shortcoming.'[5] Gandhi's launch of the Quit India campaign (1942) without proper planning and the government, put almost all the Congress leaders behind bars, leaving the political arena open for Jinnah to exploit to achieve his end. The repeated contradictory announcements by Gandhi that Muslims have a right to ask for the division helped Jinnah to be adamant in demanding division of the country. The worst thing Gandhi did was to go to Jinnah's house in Bombay daily for 18 days in September 1944, with the offer of Pakistan contained in the Rajaji Formula. Jinnah, the superb tactician, humbled Gandhi on the last day of their meeting by pointing out that Gandhi did not represent any political organization. Jinnah emerged as the most important leader to decide the destiny of the country. Even before Gandhi's disastrous journey to Jinnah's residence in 1944, several Congress leaders including Jawaharlal Nehru, Rajendra Prasad and Subhas Chandra Bose had tried to convince Jinnah about his unreasonable attitude, through correspondence and personal meetings. But Jinnah was adamant and wanted that the Congress recognize Muslim League as the sole representative of the Muslims. Congress could not accept that because it claimed to represent all Indians irrespective of caste and creed. Jinnah's technique of getting the other man to make an offer so that he could turn it down and ask for more was difficult to counter and paid him rich dividends. His intransigence became a rewarding strategy and his obstinacy his great asset. Through these tactics, he almost got the Hindu majority reduced to a minority in legislature and services during the Simla Conference (1945) and Cabinet Mission (1946) discussions. His greatest triumph came during the December 1945 elections for the Central Assembly, in which Muslim League won

---

[5]Hodson, H.V., *The Great Divide*, Oxford University Press, Karachi, 1985, p. 526.

all the Muslim seats in the Central Assembly securing 87 per cent of Muslim votes. There was a chance for India to remain united when the Congress and the Muslim League agreed to the proposals of the Cabinet Mission (March–June 1946). There was some dispute about the 'grouping' of provinces but that was almost resolved. However, Nehru issued a statement on 10 July 1946, immediately after taking over as president of the Congress, stating that the Constituent Assembly was a sovereign body and was capable of changing the accepted plan. This gave Jinnah an excuse to reject the Cabinet Mission proposals. Sensing that the vast majority of Muslims were with him, he changed his strategy. In the last week of July, the Muslim League Council met at Bombay and passed a resolution, the significant sentence of which was: 'The time has come for the Muslim nation to resort to Direct Action to achieve Pakistan.' When a correspondent asked Jinnah if the Direct Action would be violent or non-violent, Jinnah retorted, 'I am not going to discuss ethics.' Direct Action was launched in Calcutta on 16 August 1946, as planned. A lot of violence, killings, stabbing, looting, arson and rape continued for three days, leaving 5,000 dead. Gandhi's reaction to the Calcutta carnage was quite typical of him. 'If through deliberate courage, the Hindus had died to a man that would have been deliverance of Hinduism and India and purification of Islam in this land.' The riots spread to East Bengal and then to several parts of India. When Hindus retaliated in Bihar, Jinnah was unnerved and he pleaded for a complete exchange of population on 20 November 1946. But the Congress leadership ignored his proposal.

Though the Cabinet Mission proposals were rejected, the formation of an Interim government and the Constituent Assembly was implemented by the Government. After initial reluctance, the Muslim League joined the Interim Government, headed by Nehru, with more Muslim members than the Hindus. The League never participated in the Constituent Assembly of united India. While the Bihar riots were ruthlessly suppressed under Nehru's guidance, riots in other parts of the country continued and Jinnah looked the other way. The worst affected area was Punjab. By March 1947, the riots became more serious and Hindus and Sikhs started leaving many parts of Punjab. Gandhi and his creed of non-violence had made the Muslim League's task easier. According to B.R. Ambedkar, 'The riots were a sufficient indication that gangsterism had become a settled part of their strategy in politics. They seem to be consciously and deliberately imitating the Sudeten Germans in the means employed by them against the Czechs.'[6] Congress leaders were utterly shaken and on 8 March 1947, they passed a resolution asking for the partition of Punjab and Bengal. This was virtually accepting partition of the country. At the same time, the British were in a hurry to leave the country as they were in no position to hold on to India after the Second World War. Things moved fast after that. British Prime Minister Attlee, announced in Parliament, that the British will be leaving India by June 1948. They sent Lord Mountbatten as viceroy in March 1947 to wind. He advanced the date to 14–15 August 1947. The country was divided on that day and two dominions, Bharat and Pakistan, emerged, with Jinnah accepting Pakistan. The last meeting of the Muslim League was held in Delhi on 9–10 June 1947 in which Jinnah had a difficult time for the first time. He was accused of 'betrayal' for accepting partition of Punjab and Bengal. *Khaksars* (a name taken from Persian; roughly translating to humble people) ried to lynch him but the Muslim League National Guards came to his rescue. But the most intriguing aspect about the creation of Pakistan is the way in which Jinnah managed to delude his co-religionists in the Hindu majority provinces into believing that Pakistan was good for them. Jinnah flew to Karachi, with his sister, Fatima, on 7 August 1947. His daughter, Dina, refused to accompany him as she had married a Parsi converted to Christianity, Neville Wadia (owner of commercial and textile empire Bombay

---

[6]Ambedkar, B.R., *Pakistan or the Partition of India*, Thacker & Co., Bombay, 1946, p. 269.

Dyeing). According to M.C. Chagla, when Jinnah learnt about his daughter's intention to marry a non-Muslim, he was furious and said: 'There are thousands of Muslim boys to choose from. Why you want to marry a non-Muslim?' The girl retorted, 'Father, there were thousands of Muslim girls who would have liked to marry you, why did you marry a Parsi girl?' Jinnah had no answer to her question but he disowned his daughter and left most of his property to his sister. In poetic exuberance, Sarojini Naidu described Jinnah as an ambassador of Hindu–Muslim unity during the earlier decades of the last century. This label, however, deserves scrutiny. Jinnah's actions and his concern for Muslim interests from the very beginning of his political career cast a doubt over his ever being a nationalist or a secularist.

Jinnah had appointed himself as governor-general of Pakistan but he was a dying man and he knew that too. Some years earlier, doctors had told him that tuberculosis had devoured his lungs and he did not have many years to live. During his 13 months as Pakistan's governor-general, he was fighting ill-health most of the time. He died on 11 September 1948 in Karachi.

What kind of a man was Jinnah? People, who came to know him, assessed him in different ways. In July 1946, when Gandhi's biographer Louis Fischer asked Gandhi, 'What did you learn from your eighteen days with Jinnah?' (September 1944), Gandhi replied, 'I learned that he was a maniac. I could not make any headway with Jinnah because he is a maniac.'[7] Mountbatten, after a series of meetings with Jinnah, reported to his staff that he considered, 'Mr Jinnah was a psychopathic case'. He later added that, 'Until he had met Mr Jinnah, he had not thought it possible that a man with such a complete lack of sense of responsibility could hold the power which he did'. The reaction of Lord Ismay, Mountbatten's chief of staff, was, 'The dominating feature in Mr Jinnah's mental structure

---

[7] Collected Works of Mahatma Gandhi, Vol. 85, Publications Division, Government of India, p. 514.

was his loathing and contempt for the Hindus. He apparently thought that all Hindus were sub-human creatures, with whom it was impossible for the Muslims to live.' Paying a backhanded compliment to Jinnah, V.D. Savarkar said in one of his speeches, 'Jinnah is a true representative and custodian of Muslim rights. Hindus needed a leader like Jinnah.'[8] B.R. Ambedkar gave a detailed assessment of Jinnah,

> He (Jinnah) may be too self-opinionated, an egotist without the mask and has perhaps a degree of arrogance which is not compensated by any extraordinary intellect or equipment. It may be on that account he is unable to reconcile himself to a second place and work with others in that capacity for a public cause. He may not be overflowing with ideas but he was also not, as his some of his critics make him out to be, an empty-headed dandy living upon the ideas of others. It may be that his fame was built up more upon art and less on substance. At the same time, it is doubtful if there is a politician in India to whom the adjective 'incorruptible' can be more fittingly applied. No one can buy him.[9]

---

[8]Wolpert, Stanley, *Jinnah of Pakistan*, Oxford University Press, New York, 1984, p. 319.
[9]Ambedkar, B.R., *Pakistan or the Partition of India*, Thacker & Co., Bombay, 1946, p. 328.

39

Kumaraswami Kamaraj

(1903–1975)

Kumaraswami Kamaraj was born on 15 July 1903 in Virudhunagar (in the district of Ramnad in Tamil Nadu) to Kumaraswami Nadar and Sivakami Ammal. He had a sister called Nagammal. The family belonged to Nadar caste. His father had a small coconut shop but died when Kamaraj was only six years old. An uncle came to the rescue of the family and supported them for some time. Kamaraj had very rudimentary education and he often played truant during his school days. Throughout his life, he could learn no other language other than his mother tongue, Tamil. At the age of 12, he started assisting his uncle at his cloth shop. While sitting in the shop, he used to read newspapers and started taking an interest in political developments around the world and in India. The First World War was in progress at the time and exciting things were happening. Then came the Jallianwala Bagh tragedy (1919), which proved to be a turning point in his life. Freedom from foreign rule became the passion of his life. Gandhi had emerged as the national leader by 1919 and Congress as the national party. Kamaraj joined the Congress and became a devoted follower of Gandhi. But for years, he was content to remain a rank and file Congress worker. He had a brief stint in the insurance business but gave it up after a few months. From then onwards, political activity became his sole occupation. Another important decision which he made during this time was to remain a bachelor throughout his life.

The Nadar community, to which he belonged, was relatively affluent among the lower-castes. They were upwardly mobile and considered themselves to be Kshatriyas. They were largely pro-British, so it was hard to work as a Congress volunteer among them. During the Non-cooperation Movement, he worked for the propagation of khadi and prohibition of British goods but somehow was not arrested. After the withdrawal of the Non-cooperation Movement in 1922, the Congress party was divided between no-changers (who still believed in non-cooperation), led by Rajagopalachari in Madras, and those who wanted to enter the legislative bodies 'to wreck their working from within'. The latter group, was led by S. Satyamurthi and S. Srinivasa Iyengar, in the South. Kamraj joined this group of pro-changers. Satyamurthi became his political guru and Kamaraj started working closely with him though he was a Brahmin. It required some courage because the anti-Brahmin Justice Party had emerged as a powerful political force in Madras and had even formed the first ministry in Madras under the 1919 Act. Kamaraj remained in the Congress party and worked for the emancipation of the poor masses of Madras, irrespective of caste or language. He had few domestic responsibilities and led a semi-bohemian life, roaming about villages of the taluka selling khadi and preaching freedom from foreign rule. He was still a silent worker, partly because he was not a good speaker and rabble-rouser.

However, he was gradually being drawn more and more into the political arena. In 1925, he was elected to the Tamil Nadu Congress Committee (TNCC) from Cuddalore. In 1930, he took part in the Salt Satyagraha in his taluka; was arrested and sentenced to two years imprisonment, which he spent in Bellary jail. However, he was released in March 1931, under the Gandhi–Irwin Pact. He came back to his native place, Virudhunagar and received a hero's welcome. During the Civil Disobedience Movement, he was arrested again in 1932 and lodged in Vellore jail.

In the 1936 assembly elections, the Justice Party was routed and the Congress Party formed ministry, under Rajagopalachari, in 1937.

Kamaraj was elected to the Madras Assembly from Sathur. However, he kept himself almost completely in the background and hardly took part in the debates. He was not cut out for parliamentary work. Another reason was that the Assembly was completely dominated by Rajaji and his men and Kamaraj, as everyone knew, was a Satyamurthi man, who was a bête noire for Rajagopalachari.

In 1940, Kamaraj fought the election for the presidentship of Tamil Nadu Congress against Rajaji's candidate, C.P. Subbiah Mudaliar, and won by a narrow margin. This election marked, in a very real sense, a turning point in the political career of Kamaraj. But he was arrested during individual satyagraha in December 1940; was kept in Vellore jail and released in November 1941. He was arrested again during the Quit India Movement on 16 August 1942, and sent to Vellore jail again and later to the Amravati jail. He was released in June 1945. After his release, he continued as president of the TNCC, as fresh elections could not be held during the Second World War years. During this time, several things happened. Kamaraj's mentor Satyamurthi died in 1943. Rajagopalachari re-joined the Congress with the blessings of Gandhi and without the knowledge of TNCC President Kamaraj, which irked him. Further friction was caused when during a tour of the South, Gandhi pleaded for Rajaji's resumption of leadership of the Congress in Tamil Nadu. In an article in the *Harijan* (10 February 1946), Gandhi paid tribute to Rajaji and wrote that he was 'pained to find a "clique" against him. It is a clique that evidently counts in the official Congress in Madras, but the masses are devoted to Rajaji'.[1] Kamaraj felt that Gandhi's accusation was a reflection on him and his colleagues and resigned from the TNCC Parliamentary Board. However, there was no doubt that there was a strong feeling among Congressmen in Tamil Nadu against Rajaji for his Pakistan resolution and for leaving the Congress party in 1942. However, in the election of 1946, the Congress party swept the polls and

---

[1] Narasimhan, *V.K., Kamaraj: A Study*, Bombay, Manaktalas, 1967, p. 34.

Kamaraj was elected from the Sattur–Aruppukottai Constituency. He was also elected to the Constituent Assembly in 1946 and served as a member of the AICC from 1947 to 1969. In the 1952 election, Kamaraj was elected as a member of the Lok Sabha from Srivilliputhur Constituency. C. Rajagopalachari was sworn in as the chief minister of Tamil Nadu in April 1952. However, opposition to his education policy grew and he had to resign in April 1954. Kamaraj was then elected as the leader of Congress Legislative Party and was sworn in as chief minister a week later and consequently resigned from the Lok Sabha. He remained the chief minister of Tamil Nadu for nine years (1954–63) and was elected to the Assembly for three terms, in 1954, 1957 and 1962 consecutively. His long tenure as chief minister is 'generally regarded as an outstanding success for laying the infrastructure of economic development, for accessible, firm, and impartial administration, and for striking at caste hierarchy without undue confrontation or rhetoric'.[2] By the time he resigned as chief minister in 1963, Madras state had made notable progress on all fronts—food, agriculture, industry, education, power, irrigation and roads.

Then a political event happened which catapulted Kamaraj to the national scene. It was what later came to be known as the 'Kamaraj Plan', for which he is remembered the most. In June 1963, Kamaraj met Jawaharlal Nehru at Hyderabad and expressed his anxiety for the decline in the prestige of the Congress and suggested that all the senior leaders should resign their executive posts as cabinet ministers and chief ministers and devote their time in rejuvenating the party. The prime minister should decide whom to retain as cabinet ministers and chief ministers. Kamaraj himself offered to resign. Nehru quickly realized what a powerful weapon Kamaraj had put into his hands. On 21 August 1963, Kamaraj was urgently called to Delhi to decide with the Prime Minister who should be axed. An understanding was soon reached.

---

[2]Ibid.

While all the Union ministers and all the chief ministers submitted their resignations, only those of six cabinet ministers and six chief ministers were accepted. The cabinet ministers who had to go were—Morarji Desai, S.K. Patil, Jagjivan Ram, Lal Bahadur Shastri, K.L. Shrimali and Gopala Reddi. Among the chief ministers, Kamaraj, C.B. Gupta, Biju Patnaik, Ghulam Mohammed, B. Jha of Bihar and B.A. Mandloi were let off. The 'purge' at the highest level neatly dispensed with some of the 'less desirable' candidates in the run-up to Nehru's succession. The most prominent among them was, of course, Morarji Desai. Soon after, Lal Bahadur was brought in as minister-without-portfolio to lessen the burden of the Prime Minister. Kamaraj, on the other hand, got elected as president of the Congress party, an office which he held till 1969. As Congress president, Kamaraj became a crucial figure during the months before Nehru's death and even after his death.

He was an astute politician who came to the fore when he succeeded in the selection of prime minister twice in a matter of a few years. After the death of Nehru, he manoeuvred to get Lal Bahadur Shastri unanimously elected as the leader of the Parliamentary Party. After Shastri's death in 1966, Kamaraj saw to it, with the help of his coterie (which had come to be known as the Syndicate), that Morarji Desai was defeated in the quest for prime ministership by Indira Gandhi. Earlier, when his well- wishers had suggested that he should put his claim for prime ministership, Kamaraj's reaction was: 'No English, no Hindi, How, how?' using the few words of English which he had learnt.[3] Later on, his relations with Indira Gandhi became strained, especially after Indira Gandhi devalued the rupee by 57.5 per cent under US pressure, without consulting Kamaraj, who was party president. She did not consult Kamaraj because she knew that he was vehemently against devaluation. Kamaraj who had ensured that Indira, rather than Desai, became prime minister,

---

[3]Frank, Katherine, *Indira: The Life of Indira Nehru Gandhi*, Harper Collins, London, 2001, p. 299.

reportedly moaned saying 'a big man's daughter, a small man's mistake'. Kamaraj, along with the Syndicate and Desai wanted Indira to be out. But she outmanoeuvred them all by splitting the Congress party into two, with the old guard naming their party as Congress (O). Indira Gandhi's faction was called Congress (R) and later became Congress (I).

The glorious days of Kamaraj were now behind him. He lost the Parliamentary election in 1967 to a twenty-six-year-old student leader of the Dravida Munnetra Kazhagam (DMK). His popularity and his power slid downwards. There was some respite when he won the by-election in 1968. But he never regained the position which he enjoyed during the early 1960s. The 1967 election brought DMK to power in Tamil Nadu and pushed the Congress into opposition. Kamaraj went to the villages to meet the rural folk—his first love and his strength. But he was a spent force now and died in 1975. He was posthumously awarded the Bharat Ratna in 1976.

The rise of Kamaraj as a shrewd Congress leader, who was able to guide the destiny of the country during a crucial decade, is nothing short of a phenomenon. Coming from a poor family, belonging to a low caste, without much schooling, not knowing Hindi or English--he overcame all hurdles through his humility, hard work, subtle manoeuvring and sheer grit. He is remembered for his work as the chief minister of Madras, for his Kamraj Plan and as 'kingmaker' to this day.

40

Dhondo Keshav Karve (Maharishi)

(1858–1962)

Dhondo Keshav Karve was the foremost social reformer and educationist from Maharashtra who devoted his life for the emancipation of widows and for female education.

Karve was born in Murud, a small village in the Konkan region of Maharashtra, in a middle-class family. His father, Keshav Bappunna Karve, was the manager of a small estate in Ratnagiri district and got a meagre salary.

Dhondo (later known as Annasaheb) had his primary education in his village, Murud. Later, he went to Bombay and joined Robert Money School and passed the matriculation examination rather late in 1881, at the age of 23, due to certain family circumstances. He, however, obtained good marks and was able to join the prestigious Elphinston College, Bombay, from where he got his bachelor's degree in 1884. Mathematics was his favourite subject.

While still a student, Dhondo was married at the age of 15 to a nine-year-old, Radhabai. Ten years after their marriage, their first son, Ighunath, was born. Two more sons were born later.

After his graduation, Dhondo settled in Bombay and started his career as a teacher. From 1888 to 1891, he taught mathematics in the Cathedral Girl's High School, the Alexandra High School and the Maratha High School, Bombay. In September 1891, Karve joined Fergusson College in Poona, as a professor of mathematics. There, he came in close contact with Gokhale who had a very high opinion of him. Unfortunately, his wife died in the same year. Karve was heartbroken but busied himself in his teaching work. In April 1892, he was elected a Life Member of the Deccan Education Society. He taught in Fergusson College for 21 years and retired in 1914.

While still teaching at the Fergusson College, Karve devoted his time to social work. He was influenced by the work done by Ram Mohan Roy and Ishwar Chandra Vidyasagar for the emancipation of Hindu widows in Bengal. In Maharashtra, Pandita Ramabai had opened Sharda Sadan in 1889, for giving education to widows in Poona. Ramabai had converted to Christianity and got money from foreign missions. Karve wanted to help widows while remaining in the fold of Hinduism. To set an example, Karve married Godubai, a widow, in March 1893. The couple was ex-communicated by the orthodox Brahmin community, to which Karve belonged. But both of them showed exemplary courage and weathered the storm. Karve was determined to change social opinion about widow marriage. He founded a society, Vidhava Vivahottejak Mandali (Society for the Promotion of Widow Marriages), in 1893. In 1895, the name of the society was changed to Pratibandh Nivarak Mandali (Society for the Removal of Obstacles to Widow Marriages). Karve toured all over Maharashtra to popularize widow marriage. He also collected donations for the Mandali and his efforts for the emancipation of widows bore fruit. Gradually, people began to appreciate the need to help the unfortunate women rejected by society for no fault of theirs. In 1898, Karve started the Mahilashram (Women's Home) in Poona, a home for destitute women to live safely and with dignity. In 1900, the ashram was shifted to Hingane, a village 10 km from Pune, where it still functions.

Karve soon realized that unless women, including widows, were educated, their condition and status could not be improved and they would not be able to fend for themselves. With great foresight, he reasoned that if girls were sent to school, their marriages could be postponed thus reducing the possibility of child marriage and early widowhood. Karve was convinced that education was the key to the emancipation of women.

With this object in mind, he started Mahila Vidyalaya, a residential school for girls in 1907. The school not only taught the reading, writing, and arithmetic but also imparted training in different skills to make women self-reliant and self-confident. The ashram and the school became the centre of social reform. Here widows did not lead a life of misery and helplessness. They looked forward to a meaningful and exciting future. Educated widows were trained to take up teaching and administrative jobs in the school and the ashram. Some students even took up jobs outside the ashram. The success of the ashram and the unique school earned the admiration of several important personalities. The renowned Indologist, R.G. Bhandarkar became the honorary president of the ashram.[1] The news about the work being done for women, especially the widows, reached the far shores of South Africa. Gandhi, who was in South Africa at that time, wrote in the *Indian Opinion,*

Thousands of widows, mostly among Hindus, spend their whole life to no purpose. To that extent the wealth of India is being wasted. To prevent this waste, the benevolent Prof. Karve of Poona has dedicated his life to the country. He has been running, for several years, an institution in Poona for the education of widows. There, women are given training in midwifery and nursing. The work of the institution has been expanding. Because he is rendering honorary service himself, he is able to get similar assistance from others too. Moreover, he goes about from place to place collecting funds. There are so many things which can be done through sheer self-help and without Government aid.[2]

---

[1]Panandiker, Surekha, *Remembering Our Leaders*, Children's Book Trust, New Delhi, 1989, pp. 38–39.
[2]*Collected Works of Mahatma Gandhi*, Vol. 7, Publications Division, Government of India, p. 29.

In 1908, Karve started the Nishkam Karma Math, a self-sacrificing institution to train workers for the Ashram and Mahila Vidyalaya. In 1914, Karve, who was now endearingly being addressed as 'Annasaheb' by his admirers, retired from Fergusson College. Now, he was free to devote all his time to the working and developing the institutions which he had established almost single-handedly. Inspired by the Women's University of Tokyo, Annasaheb founded the Women's University in Poona (later shifted to Bombay) in 1916. The following year, a training college for primary school teachers was added, and Karve became its first principal. Running a university required more money than what Annasaheb had imagined. But a huge donation came from an unexpected source which gave the University a stable base. The donation was from Seth Vithaldas Thackersey. While giving the donation, he had requested that the university should be known as 'Shrimati Nathibai Damodar Thackersey (SNDT)' Women's University and should be located in Bombay. Thus, SNDT Women's University came about and it is one of the leading universities in the country financed by the University Grants Commission (UGC) now. Recently, it moved to its new campus in Bombay.

Annasaheb's name as a social worker and as an educationist was now known outside India. He was invited by several social and educational organizations in England and Europe to address select gatherings. He left for England in March 1929. He attended the Primary Teacher's Conference and later spoke on 'Education for Women in India' at a meeting of the East India Association at Caxton Hall, London. From July to August, he was in Europe and spoke on 'The Indian Experiment in Higher Education for Women' in Geneva and Elsinor, Denmark. He went to the US from Europe and delivered lectures and exchanged views at several places on women's education and social reform in general, with particular reference to India. He returned to India via Japan, where he visited the Women's University in Tokyo which had inspired him to start a similar university in India resulting in the establishment of SNDT. He continued to collect money for it wherever he went. He returned to India in April 1930. In December of the same year, Karve left for Africa. He visited Kenya, Uganda, Tanganyika, Zanzibar and South Africa, collecting money for his institutions as usual. He was back in India in March 1932.

He was in his 70s now, an age at which most people ideally retire. But Annasaheb was still very active, planning to do more for widows, women and society at large. With the funds collected during his foreign tours, he started the Maharashtra Gram Prathmic Shikshan Mandal in 1936. The Mandal took up the task of opening schools in villages, a field which Karve felt he had neglected because he had been busy with widows' problems and women's education. Another important organization was established by him in 1944 the Samata Sangh. The aim of the Samata Sangh was to preach equality among people and inculcate the feeling of oneness in society. This was essentially a fight against caste distinctions and untouchability, which were prevalent in Maharashtra in extreme form. Soon, 300 like-minded people joined the Samata Sangh to spread its message of equality and fellow feeling.

Many honours were bestowed upon Annasaheb during his long life. BHU awarded him the Doctor of Letters degree, so did SNDT and Bombay University. When he turned 91, President Rajendra Prasad presented him with a purse of ₹1 lakh, which Annasaheb distributed among the institutions founded by him. He was awarded the Padma Vibhushan in 1955 and the Bharat Ratna in 1958. Jawaharlal Nehru attended the main function in Bombay, and in a brief speech, observed, 'Who am I in front of his personality? I have come to seek his blessings. We will be lucky if we can inculcate even a small bit of his great qualities—dedication and simplicity.' Doordarshan also made a film on his life and achievements. He was called a *Maharishi* (the great sage) by his admirers and fellow workers.

Karve did not write much, being more of a doer. However, he started a monthly bulletin called *Manavisamata* in 1947 to popularize the message of the Samata Sangh. He wrote only two small books—his autobiography, *Atmavrutta* (1928) and *Looking Back* (1936).

He died on 9 November 1962, at the age of 104, leaving behind a chain of memorabilia, in the form of ashrams, schools and a university. Not many people in India have as much for widows and female education as Karve did in his life.

41

Abdul Ghaffar Khan

(1890–1988)

Abdul Ghaffar was born in 1890 (the exact date remains unknown) in Utmanzai village, in the Peshawar district of NWFP, in an aristocratic family. He belonged to the Pathan tribe of Mohamadzai. His father, Khan Sahib Bahram Khan, was the headman of the village and commanded respect among his tribe and in the surrounding villages.

At the age of five, Ghaffar Khan was sent by his parents to a *maktab* (school) attached to a mosque. There the sole teacher was a *mullah* (priest) who made the students learn the Holy Quran by heart. Ghaffar Khan continued his education at the Municipal Board High School in Peshawar and later went to the Edward Memorial Mission High School. It is difficult to explain why he changed so many schools—from Peshawar to Campbellpur (now Attock) to Qadian and finally to Aligarh. However, he could not pass the matriculation examination and returned home. That was the end of his formal education. Quite obviously, Ghaffar Khan was not a good student and he could not communicate in the English language even later in life, which was somewhat of a handicap during his political career. Some British officials like Lord Wavell passed snide remarks about him because of this reason. It is believed that Ghaffar Khan had been selected as a commissioned officer in the army while he was still in school but did not join after he saw an Indian officer being insulted by a British officer who was his junior.

During his school days, Ghaffar Khan was influenced by Haji Sahib of Turangzai, who was a pioneer educationist in NWFP. On his return from Aligarh in 1911, he associated with the Haji of Turangzai in opening several schools, for both boys and girls in NWFP. He believed that the emancipation of the Pathans lay in getting educated. During this period, he began to subscribe to Urdu papers like *Al Hilal* (1912–14), edited by Maulana Azad, and *Zamindar,* edited by Zaffar Ali Khan. That was his initiation into political thinking.

In 1912, at the age of 22, he was married to a Pathan girl. The following year, his son, Abdul Ghani Khan, was born.

Ghaffar Khan was soon drawn into active politics. When the Khilafat Movement, in support of the Khalifa of Turkey, was started in 1919–20, he attended a big political meeting at his village Utmanzai and was arrested along with his father but both were soon released. He met Gandhi for the first time at the Khilafat Conference in Delhi in early 1920 and was drawn to him and his philosophy of non-violence. He also attended the Nagpur session of the Congress, in which the resolution of non-cooperation was passed. From then onwards, he took an active part in the activities of the Congress. To begin with, he organized the Khilafat Movement in the NWFP, which was spearheaded by the Congress. He was arrested and sentenced to three years rigorous imprisonment and was transferred to various prisons in Punjab where he came into contact with Hindu and Sikh prisoners and found that there was so much common in Hinduism, Islam and Sikhism. He studied the *Gita* and the *Guru Granth Sahib* with them and taught them the essence of the *Quran.* He was released in 1924 and started doing social and constructive work among his people as advised by Gandhi, after the failure of the Khilafat Movement. Later, he took part in the Bardoli Satyagraha (1928) and gave impressive speeches. But his main area of work remained in NWFP. To organize the work he was doing, he started a movement called *Khudai Khidmatgars* (God's Servants). It was not just a political movement. It taught the *pathans* love and brotherhood that inspired them with a sense of unity. It also inculcated in them the virtues of non-violence, thus harnessing he martial spirit of the Frontiersmen in constructive channels. The *Khudai Khidmatgars* (also known as Red Shirts, because of the colour of their uniform) became shock brigade of every Non-cooperation Movement and were proving a bogy to successive Governments.[1]

The British had a tough time during the nineteenth century in the NWFP and were very much concerned about the potential danger of Pathans getting organized. The government, therefore, unleashed a reign of terror of the worse kind, imprisoning and torturing thousands of Khudai Khidmatgars, including Abdul Ghaffar, under the Frontier Crimes Regulation Act. But he and his followers remained disciplined and bore all the punishments and atrocities stoically, something rare for the Pathans. In spite of the government's reprisal, the number of Red Shirts went on increasing and the number crossed 100,000 at one point of time. Ghaffar Khan's followers started calling him 'Badshah Khan'. He attended the Karachi session of the Congress in 1931 and brought thousands of Khudai Khidmatgars in their red uniforms with him. Badshah Khan's presence at the Karachi session gave the entire Congress leadership a greater dimension, proving that it was not a party of the Hindus only. After this, Badshah Khan emerged as a national leader. He was a member of the CWC between 1930 and 1946. He was arrested in 1930 and was in prison for one year. Once again, he was arrested in 1934 for taking part in the Congress Satyagraha. In fact, he was in and out of British jails for about 14 years between 1920 to 1947. At one time, his entry into NWFP and Punjab was banned and he spent months with Gandhi in his Sabarmati Ashram or in Wardha Ashram when Sabarmati Ashram was abandoned in 1933. During Gandhi's prayer meetings, he used to recite verses from the *Quran*.

---

[1]Hodson, H.V., *The Great Divide: Britain-India-Pakistan*, Oxford University Press, Karachi, 1985, pp. 227–78.

To spread his message to a larger number of Pathans, Badshah Khan started a Pashto monthly *Pakhtun* whose first issue appeared in May 1930. Unfortunately, it had to be closed down after Badshah Khan's arrest. It was revived the following year but had to be closed down again. After a few years, it was brought out as *Das Roza* in April 1938 and ran till 1941. It was revived in 1945 as a weekly and was closed after the Partition in 1947.

Elections to the provincial assemblies were held in 1937, under the 1935 Act. The Congress party, led by Badshah Khan and his elder brother Dr Khan Sahib, won a majority of seats in the NWFP Assembly and formed the ministry, with Dr Khan Sahib as chief minister. The Muslim League did not win a single seat. Badshah Khan never held any office throughout his life. Even when he was offered presidentship of the Congress in 1934, he declined saying that he would rather be an ordinary worker. His brother Khan Sahib, was certainly better-suited for the highly important job of chief minister. He was a qualified doctor and had studied in India as well as in England and was an able administrator.[2]

In October–November 1938, Gandhi went on a tour of the NWFP, accompanied by Badshah Khan, starting from Utmanzai and ending at Taxila. They ran into an embarrassing situation when Hindus of Bannu complained that their life and property were not safe in the NWFP because tribes like the Waziris raided their houses regularly, looting and burning their homes and property. After hearing them, Gandhi remarked, 'After studying all the facts I have gained the impression that the situation in respect of border raids has grown worse since the inauguration of the Congress Government. I therefore feel that unless Dr Khan Sahib can cope with the question of the raids it might be better for him to tender his resignation.'[3] It was a great embarrassment for the host Badshah

---

[2]Nagarkar, V.V., *Genesis of Pakistan*, Allied Publishers, 1975, p. 277.
[3]*Collected Works of Mahatma Gandhi*, Vol. 68, Publications Division, Government of India, pp. 55–56.

Khan, but he kept quiet. It was evident that the Khan brothers did not hold influence on all the Pathan tribes. However, Dr Khan Sahib did not resign, ignoring Gandhi's advice.

Badshah Khan took part in the Quit India Movement of 1942 and was imprisoned along with other Congress leaders. He was released in 1945. By that time, the British had made up their mind to leave India. Partition was in the air and the Congress leadership was yielding to the unreasonable demands of the Muslim League. In this atmosphere, elections were held in December 1945. While the Muslim League won all the Muslim seats in the Central Assembly, it could not win majority in any of the Muslim-majority provinces. In the NWFP, the Khudai Khidmatgar Ministry was formed, headed by Dr Khan Sahib. Badshah Khan and Abdul Kalam Azad were elected members of the Constituent Assembly in 1946 from NWFP, which also served as the Indian Parliament.

A bolt from the blue came for Badshah Khan when the Congress party accepted the partition of the country in the Working Committee meeting on 3 June 1947, without consulting NWFP leaders. Badshah Khan was present in the meeting and 'he was completely stunned and for several minutes could not utter a word'. His fate and that of the NWFP was sealed. As per agreement, a plebiscite was to be held, giving the electorate the option of joining India or Pakistan. The Khudai Khidmatgars wanted another option—an independent Pashtunistan. The demand was rejected even by India. Khidmatgars boycotted the plebiscite. Consequently, the Muslim League won by an overwhelming majority. NWFP became part of Pakistan. 'They (the Congress) have thrown us to the wolves,' Badshah Khan lamented. Undaunted, he started an agitation for the creation of Pashtunistan. He was pitted against a powerful and remorseless enemy. He was put in jail by the Pakistan authorities while Dr Khan Sahib had reconciled to his fate and accepted Pakistan. He was made a minister for some time. But his younger brother, Badshah Khan, rotted in Pakistan's prisons for 16 long years. In 1969, Badshah Khan came to India at the invitation of the then Prime Minister Indira Gandhi, to attend the Gandhi centenary celebrations. To the correspondents who wanted him to say something, he repeated what he had said in 1947 '*Aap ne to humein bhedion ke samne phenk diya.* (You have thrown us to the wolves).' He went back to Jalalabad in Afghanistan, where he settled to live a peaceful life, taking his shattered dreams with him. He could come back to his village only in 1972. He was awarded the Bharat Ratna by the Indian government in 1987. He died on 20 January 1988, at the age of 98. Thus ended the long journey of a man who was honest, fearless, a devout Muslim and a great nationalist. He has left behind his memoir, *My Life and Struggle: Autobiography of Badshah Khan*, published in 1969.

42

Syed Ahmad Khan

(1817–1898)

Syed Ahmad Khan was born to Mir Muhammad Muttaqi and Aziz-un-Nisa on 17 October 1817. His ancestors had come to India from Persia during the reign of Shahjahan and enjoyed the patronage of the Mughal emperors. Ancestors from his mother's side of the family had held important posts under the Mughal kings. Aziz's grandfather, Khwaja Fariduddin Ahmed, was the prime minister of Emperor Akbar II for some time. He also enjoyed the patronage of the East India Company and was sent on a diplomatic mission to Persia (Iran) and later to Burma. Among his ancestors, Syed Ahmad was most influenced more by his maternal grandfather as he had spent his childhood in his house.

Syed Ahmad had no formal education but learnt Arabic, Persian, Urdu and some mathematics from private tutors, besides the study of Quran. But it must go to the credit of Syed Ahmad that despite his rather unsystematic education, he developed a taste not only for reading, but also for writing and was able to author some significant books and tracts. However, he picked up only a smattering of the English language and could not gain mastery over it even later in life. Almost all of his written works are in Urdu.

His father died when Syed was 21 years old and the family was hard pressed for money. Through the good offices of his uncle, Maulvi Khalilullah, he succeeded in securing a job in the employment of the East India Company—that of a petty judicial officer or a *sheristadar*. In 1839, he was promoted to the post of *Naib Mir Munshi* or assistant to the commissioner of the Agra division. Privately, he studied law and qualified in 1841 for the post of a *munsif* (judge). In this capacity, he worked for many years in Delhi (1846–54) and in different towns in Uttar Pradesh— Bijnor (1855–60); Moradabad (1860); Ghazipur (1862); Aligarh (1864); Banaras (1867); and Aligarh again (1877). He retired as a subordinate judge in 1878.

During these long years of service under the British government, he had come to believe that it would not be possible to dislodge the British from India. The atrocities committed by the British on the Indians after the 1857 Mutiny also convinced Syed Ahmad that it would be better for the Muslim community not to antagonize the British in the future. While he was posted at Bijnor, Syed Ahmad saved the lives of about 20 Europeans from the wrath of the mutineers. The role played by Syed Ahmad in Bijnor earned him a distinguished position in the official circles and he fully utilized it for the upliftment of the Muslim community. Even in service, he set before himself the twofold task of bringing about a rapprochement between the British government and the Muslims and to introduce modern education among the Muslims so they could compete with the Hindus. Through his writings, he tried to convince the British that Muslims were not against the British rule. He started with a pamphlet *Tarikh-e-Sarkashi-i-Bijnor,* followed by *Risalah Khair Khwahan-e-Musalmanan-i-Hind* (*The Loyal Muslims of India*) in two parts in 1860 and *Asbab-e-Baghawat-e-Hind*, which he got translated into English as *The Causes of Indian Revolt*. In it, Syed Ahmad tried to prove that the main cause of the revolt was the lack of communication between the rulers and the ruled. Copies of it were sent to members of the British Parliament in London.

He also wanted the Muslims to shed their antagonism to Christianity. While at Ghazipur (1862), Syed Ahmad started writing *Tabyin-ul-kalam*, a commentary in Urdu on the Old and New Testament. In this book, he emphasized the points of similarity between Islam and Christianity and the fundamental unity that ran through the two faiths and among the 'People of the Book'.

To achieve his second objective, of educating the Muslims about Western science and literature, he founded the Translation Society for the translation of important English books into Urdu in 1864 while he was posted in Ghazipur. Soon after, he was transferred to Aligarh and he took the office of the Society with him, changing its name to The Scientific Society of Aligarh. There, he got several important English works translated into Urdu. In 1866, the society started a journal, *The Aligarh Institute Gazette,* to put the views of Muslims before the government on various issues. In 1869, his son, Syed Mahmud was awarded a scholarship to study in the Cambridge University. Syed Ahmad accompanied his son to England, taking his second son, Syed Hamid, with him. He stayed in England for 17 months. There he met several British officials and literary men including Thomas Carlyle. While in London, he wrote *Khutbat-e-Ahmadiya (Essays on the Life of Mohammed),* in which he refuted the charges against Islam in William Muir's *The Life of Mahomet.* His visit to England inspired him to propagate the English system of education for the Muslim community in India with even greater zeal. In fact, 'he had been much impressed by what he had seen of European civilization, and indeed some of his letters from Europe indicate that he was so dazed that he had rather lost his balance'.[1] After his return from England in late 1870, Syed Ahmad settled in Aligarh and started to implement his plans of educating the Muslim community, on the lines of British schools and colleges. He could foresee the antagonism of the Muslim orthodoxy. To explain his ideas about modern education and culture, he started another Urdu weekly, *Tahzibul Akhlaq* (December 1870). Through the columns of this weekly, he started vigorous propaganda against the fanatical *ulama (Muslim scholars)* and in favour of social reform.

---

[1]Nehru, Jawaharlal, *The Discovery of India,* Jawaharlal Nehru Memorial Fund, New Delhi, 1946, p. 345.

He immediately became a controversial figure. The ulama reacted sharply to his unorthodox ideas and issued fatwas, condemning him as a *kafir* (infidel). To meet the challenge of the orthodoxy, he wrote a commentary on the *Quran* called *Tafsir-ul-Quran* (which he could not complete in his lifetime), giving a liberal interpretation and a rapprochement between religion and science which further infuriated the ulama who were accusing him of making sacred religious beliefs subordinate to science. All this opposition by the orthodoxy could not shake his conviction that the emancipation and progress of the Muslims was impossible without higher education along the Western pattern.

Undaunted, he succeeded in establishing the Muhammadan Anglo–Oriental (MAO) College in 1875 at Aligarh. The college was raised to the status of a university—Aligarh Muslim University (AMU), in 1920. The foundation of the college was laid by the Viceroy Lord Lytton in January 1877. In the address presented to the Viceroy, Syed Ahmad explained that the aim of the College was:

> To educate the students so that they might be able to appreciate the blessings of the British rule; to reconcile Oriental learning with Western literature and sciences; to make the Muslims worthy and useful subjects of the Crown and to inspire in them that loyalty which springs not from servile submission to foreign rule, but from genuine appreciation of the blessings of the good government.[2]

By making such faithful exhortations, he could easily win the favour of the government. It is surprising that even Syed Ahmad could not completely rid himself of Muslim orthodox beliefs and practices. In the MAO College, the history of India commenced from the medieval period and students were given instruction in the traditional Shia and Sunni theology and religious laws. Even the religious instruction was based on the traditional interpretation of

---

[2]Nagarkar, V.V., *Genesis of Pakistan*, Allied Publishers, New Delhi, 1975, p. 37.

Quran and the Sunnah. The students were thoroughly indoctrinated through the columns of the *Aligarh Institute Gazette*. Namaz was compulsory for both Shia and Sunni students. There was a prescribed uniform for students—a black *achkan* (gown) and red *fez*. There was no sign of liberalism in the college.

Morris Dembo, an American scholar of Indie Islam and Urdu literature, opines that, 'The puritan rational (or shall we say, Wahhabi) steak is, quite clearly evident in Syed Ahmed's character. It was not in jest that Sir Syed once answered a question about his religion from an English official by saying "I am a Wahhabi".[3] Sir Syed's sympathy for the militant anti-British movements of his day is most strikingly seen in his great work on the monuments of Delhi—*Athar-al-Sanadid*. This book was translated into French in 1861 by French Orientalist, Garcin de Tassy. The pro-British preaching of Syed Ahmad got a big jolt when Wahhabi jihad against the British government continued even after the 1857 revolt. In September 1871, John Norman, judge of the Calcutta Supreme Court, was assassinated during a Wahhabi trial in the court itself. This was followed by the murder of Viceroy Lord Mayo in February 1872 by a Wahhabi prisoner in the Andamans. W.W. Hunter, in his book *The Indian Musalmans* (1871), devotes three of the four chapters on the Wahhabi Movement and the jihad against the British government. The Wahhabi streak in Syed Ahmad impelled him to come forward in the defence of the Wahhabis. In a letter to *The Pioneer* dated 14 April 1871, Syed Ahmad argued that the Wahhabi jihadis were not true Wahhabis, therefore innocent men had been falsely charged. The forceful and persistent pro-British stance of Syed Ahmad prevailed upon the British to accept his pleadings in good faith. The Wahhabi Movement was completely crushed by the early 1870s, anyway. It is surprising how the British Government gradually changed their attitude from anti-Muslim to pro-Muslim

---

[3]Dembo, Morris, *Political Profile of Sir Sayyid Ahmad Khan*, Adam Publishers, Delhi, 1993, p. vi–vii.

within two decades after the Mutiny. The whole credit for this change must go to Sir Syed Ahmad and the resultant benefits he got from the government for his community.

Syed Ahmad had to face anew, the wrath of the Muslim orthodoxy, because of his decision to include English and Western sciences and philosophy in MAO College curriculum. They had started a virulent attack on Syed Ahmad once again. Many fatwas were circulated, declaring Syed a kafir again. Maulvi Ali Baksh Khan even went to Mecca to go against Syed Ahmad and his university. A part of the fatwa read: 'No assistance is allowable to the institution. May God destroy it and its founder. No Mohammedan is allowed to give assistance to or countenance the establishment of such an institution.'[4] Consequently, Syed Ahmad was obliged to seek financial assistance from the non-Muslims, especially in Punjab and NWFP. His oft-quoted speech, in which he has metaphorically compared Hindus and Muslims as the two beautiful eyes of a bride, belongs to this period. However, soon the gentry of Uttar Pradesh, Punjab and other Muslim dominated areas started sending their wards to the college and started giving it financial support. Syed Ahmad did not need the monetary help of non-Muslims. Gradually a sea change came in his thinking, especially after the formation of the INC in 1885. In this, he was supported and even guided by Theodore Beck, who had joined the MAO College in 1883 as principal at only 24 years of age. Inexperienced and amateur as he was, Syed Ahmad started depending on Beck and he became an important member of the team which guided the destiny of the college and the political movement started by it, which came to be called as the Aligarh Movement.

From the very birth of the INC, Syed Ahmad started a campaign against it and he advised the Muslims not to join it in his speeches. It is not difficult to understand the antagonism of

---

[4]Muhammad, Shan, *Sir Syed Ahmad Khan: A Political Biography*, Meenakshi Parkashan, Meerut, 1969, pp. 71–72.

312 • 50 Captivating Lives

Syed Ahmad towards the Congress. The Congress, from its very inception, demanded a representative government on British lines. This meant rule of the majority community. As the Muslim formed only one-fourth of the total population of the country, they would always be dominated and ruled by the Hindus in a democratic set-up, Syed Ahmad argued. He felt this was not in the interest of the Muslim community. Hence, his virulent attack on the Congress. Thus, Syed Ahmad gave a distinctly new turn to Muslim politics which became anti-Congress and also anti-Hindu, because he looked upon the INC as a Hindu organization. In a speech at Meerut on 16 March 1888, Syed Ahmad said,

> Suppose that the English community and the army were to leave India, taking with them all their cannons and their splendid weapons and all else, who then would be the rulers of India? Is it possible that under these circumstances, two nations— the Mohammedans and the Hindus—could sit on the same throne and remain equal in power? Most certainly not. It is necessary that one of them should conquer the other. To hope that both could remain equal is to desire the impossible and the inconceivable. At the same time, you must remember that although the number of Mohammedans is less than that of the Hindus, and although they contain far fewer people who have received a higher English education, yet they must not be considered insignificant or weak.—This thing—who after the departure of the English would be conquerors would rest on God's will. But until one nation has conquered the other and made it obedient, peace cannot reign in the land.[5]

So explicitly, Syed Ahmad had sown the seeds of the two-nation theory. He gave similar speeches at Lucknow and other places, with only minor variations.

[5]Zaidi, A.M., *Evolution of Muslim Political Thought in India*, New Delhi, Michika and Panjathan, New Delhi, 1975, p. 48.

When Badruddin Tyabji presided over the Congress session in 1887 at Madras, he was reprimanded by Syed Ahmad through letters to the press and also through personal letters addressed to Tyabji. He was so unnerved that he wrote to Hume, secretary of the Congress, that 'the main object of the Congress to unite different communities and provinces have miserably failed; that the Mohammedans were divided from the Hindus in manner they were never before, that the gulf was becoming wider day by day'. He suggested that the Congress should be prorogued for five years. Of course, his suggestion was not accepted.

The last 10 years of Syed Ahmad's life were devoted mainly to politically awakening the Muslims against the INC and the Hindus. In August 1888, Syed Ahmad formed the Indian Patriotic Association. The nomenclature was changed to United Indian Patriotic Association, with himself as secretary and Principal Beck as treasurer. He said that the association was formed as a rival to the Congress. Initially, both Muslim and Hindu landed gentry, who were opposed to the Congress, had joined the association. But after the Council Bill of 1892 was passed, the association was wound up in December 1893 and a purely Muslim organization called Mohammedan Anglo–Oriental Defence Association was established. In 1896, this association prepared a memorandum, highlighting the Muslim demands for separate communal electorate, weightages in local bodies etc. Syed Ahmad in a speech broadly hinted that if the demands were not conceded the Muslim minority might be forced to take up sword to prevent the tyranny of the majority. This is actually what the Muslim League did in 1946 through 'Direct Action'. The memorandum formed the basis of the Simla Deputation to Lord Minto in 1906. In 1886, Syed Ahmad founded the All India Muhammadan Educational Congress (the world 'Congress' was changed to 'Conference' in 1890) to propagate the idea of the Aligarh Movement throughout the country, by holding annual conferences at various places.

The role of Principal Beck in directing the activities of Syed

Ahmad, during the last 15 years of the latter's life, cannot be over-emphasized. Soon after he joined as principal of MAO College, Beck had become Syed Ahmad's right-hand man—indeed, his friend, philosopher and guide. Syed Ahmad's lack of mastery over English made him depend on Beck for many crucial decisions. Beck made a systematic effort to alienate the Muslims from the Hindus and thus contributed considerably towards anti-Hindu bias in the Aligarh Movement. The personal influence exerted by Beck upon Syed Ahmad was believed to be so great that one Muslim writer humorously remarked that 'the College is of Syed Ahmed, but the order is of Beck'. Mr Morrison, who succeeded Beck after the latter's death in 1899, followed the same policy as that of Beck. According to V.V. Nagarkar, 'Thanks to the efforts of the founder and the first two Principals of Aligarh College, an open manifestation of uncompromising hostility against the Indian National Congress formed the basic creed of the Aligarh Movement.'[6] It is interesting that one Britisher (Hume) was guiding the destiny of the Congress, while another Britisher (Beck) was attacking it through the Aligarh Movement.

To be fair to Syed Ahmad, one must try to understand the reasons for his pro-British and anti-Congress policy. As explained by R.C. Majumdar,

> The Aligarh Movement was to the Muslims what the Renaissance and National Movement of the nineteenth century was to the Hindus. It raised the Muslim community from the slough of despondency in which it had sunk after the Mutiny and transformed it from the Medieval into the modern age. Syed Ahmed, who ushered in this movement, deserves the highest praise for his love of Muslim community and the far-sighted vision which he displayed regarding the problems of the Muslims.[7]

---

[6]Nagarkar, V.V., *Genesis of Pakistan*, Allied Publishers, New Delhi, 1975, p. 52.
[7]Majumdar, R.C., *History of the Freedom Movement in India*, Firma KLM, Calcutta, 1988, p. 434.

At the same time, it must be admitted that in the process he created a schism between the Hindus and Muslims which ultimately resulted in the division of the country. Aga Khan in his *Memoirs* wrote that the independent sovereign nation of Pakistan was born in the Muslim University of Aligarh. The famous Pakistani historian, Ghulam Ali Allana, wrote, 'Pakistan owes as much to Aligarh, as Aligarh owes to Sir Syed Ahmad Khan for its conception, establishment and development. In other words, Sir Syed Ahmed's contribution in the cause of the Pakistan Movement has been a spectacular one and deserves honourable mention in the annals of our freedom movement.'[8]

Syed Ahmad received many well-deserved honours and positions in life. In 1878, he was nominated a member of the Viceroy's Council. In 1887, he was made a member of the Public Service Commission. In 1888, he was decorated with KCSI (Knight Commander of the Order of the Star of India) and an honorary doctorate was conferred on him by the University of Edinburgh in 1899. But his greatest reward was when in 1920 his MAO College became AMU.

In February 1938, Jinnah visited Aligarh. 'I have from you today the greatest message of hope', he told the students of Syed Ahmad Khan's university. 'Henceforth Aligarh was to be the "arsenal of Muslim India".'[9] Even after four decades, the message of Syed Ahmad was reverberating in the corridors of his college. No educational institution ever played such a decisive role in the fortunes of any nation as Aligarh did in the case of Indian Muslims.

Syed Ahmad died in Aligarh at the age of 81 on 27 May 1898, after leading an eventful life. He is revered in both India and Pakistan.

---

[8]Allana, G., *Eminent Muslim Freedom Fighters, 1562–1947*, Low Price Publications, Delhi, 1993, p. iii.

[9]Khairi, Saad R., *Jinnah Reinterpreted: The Journey from Indian Nationalism to Muslim Statehood*, Oxford University Press, Karachi, 1996.

43

Khuda Bakhsh

(1842–1908)

Rarely does a person devote his life and spend his fortune on building a library for public use; that too, a man of modest means. Khuda Bakhsh (which means 'gift of God') was one of the greatest bibliophiles this country has produced, and an authority on Islamic bibliography, covering Arabic and Persian manuscripts and books.

Khuda Bakhsh was born in Chapra in Bihar, on 2 August 1842. His father, Muhammad Bakhsh, was a pleader and a devoted bibliophile. Khuda Bakhsh's education started at the Patna High School and he studied there till 1859. The school was, however, closed after the uprising of 1857–58 and the boy was sent to Calcutta for further studies. He passed the University of Calcutta's entrance examination in 1861. Soon after, his father fell ill and the responsibility of supporting the family fell on Khuda Bakhsh. He came back to Patna and worked as a *peshkar* or presenter (a peshkar keeps a record of the actual courtroom proceedings in Hindi) of the district judge. After sometime, he resigned and got the post of a deputy inspector of schools. In 1869, Khuda Bakhsh passed the pleadership examination and started practicing at the Patna Bar. He soon had a lucrative practice and earned a name in the local courts as a pleader.

Khuda Bakhsh was married early in life, but his wife died childless. He married twice thereafter. From the two wives, he had five sons and two daughters. At least two of his sons, the eldest,

Salahuddin, and the second, Shihabuddin, have made their mark as Orientalists. One of his wives, Razia Khatun, was an Urdu poetess of some merit.

Khuda Bakhsh's reputation as a pleader and as a forensic expert came to the notice of the government and he was made a Government Pleader of Patna in 1880. Besides his professional activities, he ungrudgingly gave time to public causes, for which he was rewarded. For his work on the School Committee, he got a Certificate of Honour at the Delhi Durbar of 1877. He was the first vice-chairman of the Patna Municipality and the Patna District Board, when these self-governing bodies were created by Lord Ripon. A *Khan Bahadurship* (an honorific title conferred in British India on Muslim senior civil servants) was conferred on him in 1881 and a Companion of the Indian Empire (CIE) in 1903. He was also a Fellow of the Calcutta University, thanks to his academic interests. He was appointed chief justice of the Nizam's High Court, Hyderabad in 1895 for a term of three years. He returned to Patna in 1898 and started his practice at the Bar again. But unfortunately, he had a paralytic stroke (the disease which also killed his father) in the same year and did not fully recover from its ill effects. He was, however, appointed secretary of the library on a monthly salary of ₹200. He had stopped earning at the Bar and was in deep financial trouble. The government made him a grant of ₹8,000 for the liquidation of his debts so that he could die in peace.

All the honours which were conferred on him pale into insignificance before the magnificent library he built in Patna and which is now called the Khuda Bakhsh Oriental Public Library. His father, Muhammad Bakhsh, must share part of the credit for its inception as he was the one who handed over 1,400 manuscripts to his son and asked him to enlarge the collection and build a library for public use when he was on his deathbed in 1876. Khuda Bakhsh endeavoured throughout his life to give a concrete shape to the wish of his father and started collecting rare manuscripts from various parts of India and various Islamic countries. In this, he found a powerful rival in the Nawab of Rampur, who was also collecting manuscripts for his library. However, Khuda Bakhsh was able to entice a collector in Rampur's service, an Arab, Mohammad Maqi, and employed him at a regular salary of ₹50 a month, besides commission. For 18 years, Maqi worked for Khuda Bakhsh, hunting and procuring rare manuscripts (mostly Arabic) from Syria, Arabia, Egypt and Persia. It was also Khuda Bakhsh's practice to pay double railway fare to every manuscript seller who visited him with manuscripts. Thus, he became famous as a collector and was given the first choice by every manuscript seller.

Not all the manuscripts were collected by honest means. In the words of V.C. Scott O'Connor,

> The founder's sons relate with a dash of pride not unmixed with humour, that many of the manuscripts were stolen. The love of letters, it is said, carried both the founder and the library and his emissaries with an impetus that was stayed with no scruples, over the fine—and shall we say the trivial—line that divides one man's property from that of another.[1]

Khuda Bakhsh and his collectors did not allow the Penal Code to come in the way of their adventure of acquiring manuscripts, legally or otherwise. Khuda Bakhsh used to tell his friends, with a mischievous twinkle in his eyes, 'There are three classes of blind men: those who were bereft of sight; those who lent valuable books even to a friend; and those who returned such volumes, once they had passed into their hands.'

As the years rolled by, the number of manuscripts increased and his house proved to be insufficient to keep them in some order. He started thinking of a separate building to house his valuable collection. He also remembered the promise he gave to his father

---

[1]Scott O'Connor, V.C., *An Eastern Library: An Introduction to the Khuda Bakhsh Oriental Public Library*, Khuda Bakhsh Library, Patna, 1977, pp. 6–7.

on his deathbed. Khuda Bakhsh started getting the building for the library constructed in 1886, which was completed in 1888. By the time the building was completed, Khuda Bakhsh had spent ₹80,000 on it—several millions at the current price level. The library soon came to the notice of the Government of Bengal and they became its patron and sponsor. It was formally opened to the public after the opening ceremony performed by the then Lieutenant Governor, Sir Charles Elliot, in 1891. The importance of the library and its building can be gauged from the fact that when the chief architect Sir Edwin Lutyens planned New Delhi in the thirties of the last century, he did not include a public library in his extensive plans for the new Imperial city. The main branch of the Delhi Public Library is still housed in a canteen built during the Second World War for American soldiers. After more than five decades of Independence, it is still functioning from that canteen building. Even the Indian National Library at Calcutta is functioning in a building which was once the residence of the governor-general and viceroy. And here was a man, Khuda Bakhsh, who, with his own efforts, not only acquired a valuable collection, but also built a magnificent building to keep the books and manuscripts properly along with providing reading halls for the users. He also had a taste for binding and hundreds of volumes in the collection have excellent binding, many in leather.

Khuda Bakhsh loved his library and its valuable collection more than anything else in the world. The British Museum made him a magnificent offer for his collection, but he declined it. He said, 'I am a poor man and the sum they offered me was a princely fortune, but could I part for money with that to which my father and I have dedicated our lives.' As he said this, his clean-cut features betrayed a singular emotion; his large luminous eyes welled up with tears. 'No,' he said, 'the collection is for Patna, and the gift shall be laid at the feet of the Patna public.'[2]

---

[2]Ibid. 8.

Khuda Bakhsh was not just a collector of books; he was also a scholar. He knew his books well—not only their titles, authors and their rarity, but also their content. The famous historian Jadunath Sarkar visited the Khuda Bakhsh library several times while he was doing research on medieval India and had a chance to meet and discuss his projects with him. Prof. Jadunath Sarkar wrote,

> I remember how one day he (Khuda Bakhsh) poured out the copious store of his memory, full list of Arabic biographers and critics from the first century of the Hijra to the eighth, with running comments on the value of each. Most of these manuscripts he had himself collected. Next to the acquisition of a rare manuscript, what gave him most delight was to see anybody using his library in carrying on research.[3]

Khuda Baksh's scholarship is quite evident in a detailed article which he wrote in the *Nineteenth Century*. He also translated Bacon's essays to Persian which shows his mastery over Persian prose.

Not only scholars, but some British bureaucrats also visited the library to see the rare and beautiful collection. Sir Antony MacDonnell, acting lieutenant governor, visited the library in 1903 and wrote that, 'I had not expected to see anything so fine.' In the same year, Lord Curzon, the viceroy, also visited the library. 'The sanction for the construction of the reading-hall and the preparation of the descriptive catalogue, under the supervision of Dr Denison Ross, were the direct outcomes of the Viceroy's visit.'

In the rare collection, one can find manuscripts which were once the property of Mughal emperors like Akbar, Shahjahan, Jahangir and Adil Shahi and Qutb Shahi Sultans. There are charming and matchless specimens of Eastern painting and Persian calligraphy. There are numerous rare manuscripts on Islamic law, history, philosophy, theology, science and medicine. The importance of the Khuda Bakhsh Public Library was recognized by the GOI and the

---

[3]Sarkar, Jadunath, *Khuda Bakhsh: The Indian Bodley*, Modern Review, 1908.

library was declared as an Institution of National Importance in December 1969 and the management of the library was completely passed on to the GOI.

Khuda Bakhsh was a man of striking personality, of average height and was rather slim. He was a devout Muslim, saying his prayers five times daily. The Muslim community and its welfare were always taxing his mind, but he was not a bigot. The last two years of his life were spent in misery. The paralytic attack had immobilized him and he was penniless. He died on 3 August 1908 and is buried in the precincts of the library which he built almost single-handedly.

Since 1969, when the Indian government took the library under its wings, the library has progressed and is better managed than most of the manuscript libraries in the country. The number of manuscripts has gone up to over 20,000 and the number of printed books to 25,000. A staff of 60 people, both trained and untrained, look after the upkeep of the library. 36 printed volumes of the *Descriptive Catalogue* of manuscripts have been published which, however, cover only one-third of the collection. The compilation, editing and publishing of the remaining volumes of the *Descriptive Catalogue* will take several decades, it seems. In the absence of such a catalogue, the full use of the rare manuscripts is not possible. However, the dream of its founder has come to fruition beyond his expectations and the future of the library is secure under government patronage.

44

J.B. Kripalani

(1888–1982)

Jivatram Bhagwandas (J.B.) Kripalani was born in Sindh (now in Pakistan) in 1888, in an upper middle-class family. His father, Bhagwandas Kripalani, was a *tehsildar* (revenue and judicial officer) in the British government. Jivatram had six brothers and one sister and was the sixth child of his parents.

Kripalani went to school in Hyderabad, Sindh and passed the matriculation examination in 1906. He was an intelligent, spirited and mischievous boy and was not very fond of studies, having a healthy contempt for book learning. In 1906, he joined Wilson College in Bombay. Those were the days of the Bengal partition and consequent agitation. The turmoil had spread to other parts of the country, including Bombay. Wilson College students agitated against the partition of Bengal, with Kripalani taking a leading part. He was expelled from Wilson College and joined D.J. Sindh College in Karachi. Here, too, he got himself involved in a strike by college students against the principal of the college who had denigrated Indians in one of his speeches and, here too, he was rusticated. He went to Poona and joined Fergusson College, run by Indian nationalists. He graduated in 1908 and went on to get a master's degree in history and economics in 1911.

Surprisingly, he chose teaching as his profession in spite of his dislike for books. From 1912 to 1917, he taught English and history at Langat Singh College in Muzaffarnagar, Bihar. There, he met Gandhi for the first time and joined him in his fight against the indigo planters who were exploiting the poor farmers of Champaran. He accompanied Gandhi during his travels around the villages of Champaran. There were some things about Kripalani that appealed to Gandhi—his sincerity, simple way of living, and passionate concern for the poor peasants and downtrodden villagers. It did not take much time for Gandhi to realize that he had found a new and powerful disciple. On his part, Kripalani felt that he had found a great guru and was ready to follow in his footsteps. It must be pointed out that though Kripalani never became a devotee of Gandhi's religious beliefs and he could say sharp and bitter things about Gandhi's fads and eccentricities, he never wavered in his faith in Gandhi as such.[1] He became a firm believer in non-violence and swadeshi as preached by Gandhi. Thinking about the Champaran days, Gandhi wrote,

> Professor Kripalani could not but cast his lot with us. He was my gatekeeper-in-chief. For the time being he made it the end and aim of his life to save me from seekers. He warded off people, calling to his aid his unfailing humour, now his non-violent threats. At nightfall he would take up his occupation of a teacher and regale his companions with his historical studies and observation, and quicken any timid visitor into bravery.[2]

In 1918, Kripalani joined BHU; first, as the secretary of Madan Mohan Malaviya, and later, as a professor of political science. When Gandhi started the Non-cooperation Movement in 1920 and asked students and teachers to leave the universities and colleges which were being aided by the government (which included BHU), Kripalani was the only lecturer serving in the university who quit

---

[1]Payne, Robert, *Life and Death of Mahatma Gandhi*, Rupa Publications, New Delhi, 1997, p. 307.
[2]Gandhi, M.K., *An Autobiography*, Navajivan Publishing House, Ahmedabad, 1927, p. 349.

his job. He founded an ashram in 1920 in Banaras and named it
'Shri Gandhi Ashram'. Some students who had quit the University,
along with Kripalani, started living in the ashram. The main purpose
of the ashram was to produce khadi and to propagate its use among
city folks and villagers alike. Among all the ashrams started with
the same purpose, Kripalani's ashram was one of the best and
professionally managed. It had several departments—production,
dyeing, printing, washing, calendaring and sales. The ashram became
a profit-making body, and when it was shifted to Meerut later,
they had saved enough money to purchase a building of their own.

In 1922, Gandhi asked Kripalani to join Gujarat Vidyapith.
He served as its principal for five years (1922–27). About his stay
at the Vidyapith, Gandhi wrote, 'Acharya Kripalani was borrowed
from the Kashi Ashram, which is his own creation. I relieved
him as I had promised to do so. Under his leadership, too, the
Vidyapith has not taken a retrograde step. At the time of the
student's strike, we saw that he had stolen the heart of the students.
Acharya Kripalani was a second gift that Sindh gave to Gujarat.'[3]
Gandhi used to address Kripalani as 'professor' or 'acharya'. After
leaving the Vidyapith, Kripalani came back to his ashram and started
propagating khadi work once again. But from the early 1930s,
Kripalani started devoting himself completely to Congress party
work. He served as the general secretary of the Congress from 1934
to 1942 when he was arrested, along with other Congress leaders,
during the Quit India Movement and was kept in Ahmednagar
jail. During the rift between Subhas Chandra Bose and Gandhi
on the issue of the election of Congress president, Kripalani sided
wholly with Gandhi.

An event of great significance happened in 1936. Kripalani
decided to marry at the age of 48. He had met Sucheta Majumdar,
who was teaching at the Women's College of BHU. Though there

---

[3] *Collected Works of Mahatma Gandhi,* Vol. 42, Publications Division, Government
of India, p. 328.

was a difference of 20 years in their ages, they were attracted to each other and got married with the blessings of Gandhi. Sucheta also played a significant role in the Freedom Movement and served as the chief minister of Uttar Pradesh after Independence. They were married for almost 40 years but had no children.

In 1946, Kripalani was elected president of the INC and steered the organization through the critical days of the transfer of power. During the AICC meeting held on 14–15 June 1947, in which the 3 June Plan for the division of the country was to be discussed and approved (which had already been accepted by the CWC two days earlier), Kripalani, as the president, made a most memorable speech at the conclusion of the discussion. He graphically described what was happening in some parts of the country, especially in Punjab. Concluding his speech, he observed,

> The Hindus and Moslem communities have vied with each other in the worst orgies of violence. I have seen a well where women with their children, 107 in all, threw themselves to save their honour. In another place, a place of worship, fifty young women were killed by their menfolk for the same reason. I have seen heaps of bones in a house where 307 persons, mainly women and children, were driven, locked up and then burnt alive by the invading mob. These ghastly experiences have no doubt affected my approach to the question. Some members have accused us that we have taken this decision out of fear. I must admit the truth of this charge but not in the sense in which it is made.[4]

He argued that it had become imperative to accept the partition of the country, as laid down in the 3 June Viceroy's statement, to avoid such bloodshed in the future. Nehru, Patel and Gandhi had already spoken for the partition of the country but Kripalani's speech was

---

[4]Majumdar, R.C., *Struggle for Freedom*, Bharatiya Vidya Bhavan, Bombay, 1988, p. 781.

more graphic. The resolution, when put to vote, was carried by 157 votes for and 29 against, with 32 members remaining neutral. After Independence, Kripalani found that the Congress president was not part of the decision-making process of the government. On the other hand, Nehru and Patel felt that the government cannot, and need not consult the party president while taking important decisions. In protest, Kripalani resigned from the party presidentship in 1947. After his resignation, he was offered the governorship of Bihar but he declined. He wanted to be free of official duties in order to publicly express his disagreement with the government's policies. In 1950, he started a political weekly, *Vigil,* to express his own views as well as those of like-minded people. In 1951, he resigned from the Congress party. He formed The Kisan Mazdoor Praja Party (KMPP) in 1952 but soon merged it with the Socialist Party, giving it the new name, The Praja Socialist Party (PSP), of which he was elected chairman. During the 1952 general elections, PSP polled the largest number of votes, after the INC. Soon differences cropped up in the party—not only on ideological issues, but also about the relationship to be maintained with the Congress and the Communist party. The discord resulted in the resignation of Kripalani from the PSP in 1954. He became an 'independent' candidate for the rest of his parliamentary career. He was elected to Parliament for four consecutive terms. His parliamentary life came to an end in 1971. During his parliamentary career, Kripalani was very popular for his forceful and fearless speeches. In 1977, Kripalani, along with Jayaprakash Narayan, helped in the formation of the Janata Party, and in getting Morarji Desai elected as the prime minister. He was, however, disillusioned when the Janata Party split and when it had to quit office before completing its term.

Kripalani wrote a number of books mainly on Gandhi and Gandhism. Some of them are: *Non-violent Revolution, The Gandhian Way, The Indian National Congress, The Fateful Years, The Politics of Charkha, The Future of the Congress, The Gandhian Critique, Where Are We Going?* and *Freedom in Peril.* He also regularly contributed to leading Indian newspapers and journals. Some of these articles were published, under the title *Some Stray Thoughts* (1979), by Navajivan Publication House in Ahmedabad. Kripalani had a distinct style of his own—simple, crisp but forceful. It is said that 'Kripalani was a tall, elegant, somewhat saturnine man with a gift for sharp humour and a passionate concern for the peasants and the poor.' He was loving and kind at heart, but at times, showed quick temper which eclipsed many of his virtues. Although he did not wield power, his contribution to the national upliftment will be long remembered.

When Kripalani's wife, Sucheta, died in 1974, he said, 'Mysterious are the ways of God. I was to go first, but instead she, much younger than myself, preceded me.' He died on the 19 March 1982 at the Harijan Ashram in Ahmedabad. He willed his assets, worth about ₹4 lakh, to various public institutions. He was cremated on the banks of the Sabarmati River.

45

Rani Lakshmibai

(1835–1858)

Rani Lakshmibai of Jhansi is perhaps the best remembered freedom fighter in India. Her heroic tale has inspired generations and she is still a role model for millions of girls. She has become a legend. It is now difficult to distinguish between the myths and facts that surround her.

Lakshmibai's maiden name was Manikarnika, abbreviated as 'Manu'. She was also affectionately called 'Chhabili' in her in-laws' household. She was born in Banaras to Moropant Tambe and Bhagirathi Bai, who were Karhade Brahmins from the Satara district. Her date of birth remains uncertain. Some Indian historians put the date of her birth as 19 November 1835 while some believe she was born in 1928. Some British sources believe that the Rani was 29 or 30 years of age during the mutiny Manu's mother died when she was still a small child. Her father, Moropant, was a member of the retinue of Chimnaji Appa, brother of Peshwa Baji Rao II, at Banaras. After the death of Chimnaji Appa, Moropant took employment with the last Peshwa Baji Rao II at Bithur, near Kanpur, where the Peshwa had settled. Manu was three years old at the time.

At Bithur, Manu grew up with the Peshwa's sons, Nana Saheb and Bala Rao (better known as Rao Saheb), and with Tatya Tope, whose father was a retainer of Baji Rao. She hardly had any female playmates and became skilled in horse riding, shooting and swordplay while playing with older boys in the palace. She also became a good judge of horses. There, she also learned to read and write.

In 1842, at the age of seven (or 14, whichever date of birth we accept), she was married to Gangadhar Rao, the ruler of Jhansi, a man in his 40s. She was given the name 'Lakshmibai' by her in-laws. Her father accompanied her to her new home in Jhansi against the established Hindu custom. In 1851, she gave birth to a son who unfortunately died after three months.

Gangadhar, never a healthy man, died on 21 November 1853, leaving the teenage Rani a widow. By that time, she had developed a magnetic personality, high-spirited resolve and an enchanting demeanour. The dying Raja, just two days before his death, adopted Damodar Rao (alias Anand Rao), a five-year-old relative, as his heir, in the presence of two English officers, Major Ellis and Captain Martin, whom he had invited to officially witness the adoption. They were both given copies of the Raja's will.

After the death of Gangadhar Rao, Rani Lakshmibai sent her petition (3 December 1853) to the governor-general seeking confirmation of the adoption, followed by a number of petitions. Governor-General Lord Dalhousie turned down the Rani's pleas and did not recognize the adoption and decided to annex Jhansi under his Doctrine of Lapse. After Dalhousie's proclamation of the annexation, the Rani continued to send appeals, at times through her counsel, John Lang, who was a British barrister practising in Calcutta. But the Governor-General was adamant and did not recognize the adoption.

Lord Dalhousie, a church going Presbyterian, the most unscrupulous and wily of all governors-generals who were sent to India, was obsessive about extending the territories of the British Empire and filling the coffers of the East India Company. He applied the Doctrine of Lapse to at least eight Indian states during his eight year-stay in India. He was a sick man when he left India at the age of 35 in 1856, on a stretcher. It is believed that his illness was the cause of his behaviour and obsessions. It is also believed that his dealings with Indian rulers were the main cause of the uprising of 1857. *The Hindu Patriot* wrote on 18 May 1854, 'Lord Dalhousie is determined to shame the devil and beat even Nicholas hollow in the matter of forcible appropriation of neighbouring states, without the shadow of a pretext to colour his grasping policy.'[1] But nothing moved Dalhousie to change his mind.

Consequently, in May 1854, Jhansi came under British administration, with Alexander Skene as superintendent of police, Captain Gordon as deputy commissioner and Captain Dunlop in the command of the troops in Jhansi. Under the new arrangement, the Rani was to leave the fort and the palace within while keeping her smaller palace in the town. A paltry amount of ₹5,000 per month (or £6,000 a year) was settled as pension for the support of the Rani and her retinue, which she refused to accept and decided to live on her deceased husband's private estate. She believed that the acceptance of pension would mean acknowledging the 'lapse' of Jhansi, something she could never do.

Several official measures taken after the lapse offended the religious feelings of the Rani and her people. The refusal to allow her to draw on the maharaja's trust for her adopted son Damodar Rao's sacred-thread ceremony was one of them. Other insulting measures followed—lifting the ban on cow slaughter; resumption of two villages whose revenue used to support the temple of Mahalakshmi (a temple on the east of the town wall, which was associated with the Newalkar Dynasty [Gangadhar's] family and regularly visited by the Rani); and the Maharaja's debt being deducted from the Rani's pension. As if that was not enough, the Jhansi grasslands, which used to be the private property of the Maharaja, as well as the state buildings, were taken from the Rani's control. The government's deliberate acts to humiliate the Rani must have hurt

---

[1]*Freedom Struggle in Uttar Pradesh, Vol. 1,* Publication Bureau, Uttar Pradesh, 1957, p. 33.

her sentiments but she was helpless. The only recourse was to send appeals and petitions to Fort William in Calcutta, the seat of British government in India at the time.

In May 1857, the sepoys at Meerut rose in rebellion and occupied Delhi. The news rapidly spread to Jhansi where tension among the sepoys was already brewing. On 5 June, the sepoys in Jhansi rose in rebellion and occupied the Star Fort in the cantonment area where the treasury and the munitions were stored by the British officials. The next day, the entire garrison at Jhansi rebelled and killed Captain Dunlop and a few other British officers. Captain Skene and Gordon took all the Europeans from the city to the main fort, which was also soon attacked by the rebels. On 7 June, three English officers—Andrews, Scott and Purcell—left the fort to seek the Rani's help but were intercepted on the way and killed. In the meantime, Captain Gordon was also killed by the mutineers' bullets. On the fourth day of the siege, i.e., on the afternoon of 8 June, Captain Skene, baffled as he was at the death of Captain Gordon and other officers, hung out a flag of truce. The rebel leaders promised safe conduct of the besieged English if they would vacate the fort and lay down arms. Accepting the terms, Captain Skene led the besieged and came out of the fort, when they were 'seized, bound and taken to Jokhan Bagh outside the city wall where all men, women and children were massacred'.

There is nothing to indicate that the Rani was involved in the mutiny or the massacre that followed. It is certain that the insurgents, prior to the mutiny, did not consult the Rani. On the contrary, they all went to the palace of the Rani with loaded guns and demanded assistance and supplies. She was obliged to yield and to furnish guns, ammunition and supplies to save her life and honour. The same treatment was administered to Bahadur Shah Zafar at Delhi by the mutineers who had arrived from Meerut.

After the departure of the rebels for Delhi on 11 June 1857, the Rani wrote to Major Walter Erskine, the commissioner for Jhansi, narrating the events that took place and deplored the massacre. Erskine, while forwarding the Rani's letters to Fort William, Calcutta, remarked that the Rani had had no complicity with the mutineers.

Erskine, in response to the Rani's letters to him, authorized her to manage the state of Jhansi till a new arrangement was made and issued a proclamation to this effect. When the Rani assumed charge of Jhansi (June 1857), she devoted herself to manage the state with the help of her chief minister, Lakshman Rao Bande, efficiently and with all sincerity. However, the British officials, including Dalhousie, still suspected her of connivance with the mutineers.

Ever since June 1857, when she was authorized by Erskine to manage Jhansi, the Rani kept on writing and appealing to the British officers at Jubbulpore (now Jabalpur), Agra, Jalaun and Gwalior till January–February of 1858, seeking help as she was facing trouble from neighbouring *satraps (governing officials)*. But there was no response from the English. According to R.C. Majumdar, 'Rani gradually became disillusioned and disappointed with British failure to respond. She felt a growing apprehension that the British might capture and try her, even hang her. She was faced with two alternatives, namely death by hangman's rope or a heroic death in the battlefield. She chose the more honourable course.'[2]

As soon as the Rani decided to fight the British, she began recruiting troops and sought help from Tatya Tope, her childhood friend and a general of Nana Sahib. Help also came from other sources. The Rajas of Banpur and Narwar arrived with their troops by 15 March 1858, to help her. The Rani moved from the city palace into the fort with all her troops. She personally supervised the defence. Soon, she came face to face with the British forces. The British forces, under the Central India Field Forces Commander Hugh Rose, arrived at Jhansi on 21 March 1858 and invaded the

---

[2]Majumdar, R.C., *History of Freedom Movement*, Firma KLM, Calcutta, 1988, p. 147.

city the following day. The Rani and her troops took shelter in the fort. They put up stiff resistance under her spirited leadership and faced the British for 10 days. Then, Tatya Tope arrived with 20,000 men and a fierce battle took place near Jhansi. But the powerful British army defeated Tatya Tope, who retreated with his army to Kalpi. The Rani, to the anguish of the British, slipped from the fort on 4 April, taking her adopted son and a few loyal soldiers with her and galloped to Kalpi to join Tatya Tope. Rose's army pursued them. Battles were fought at Konch and Kalpi and the British proved superior. Rao Sahib, the adopted son of the last Peshwa, joined them. They proceeded to Gopalpur, 46 miles from Gwalior, where they conceived a daring plan to invade Gwalior. When their combined forces reached Gwalior, almost the entire army of Maharaja Scindia joined the rebels and he fled to Agra. The rebel forces entered Gwalior in triumph and Rao Sahib was proclaimed Peshwa. However, their triumph was short-lived and Rose's forces soon encircled Gwalior. Rani faced the British forces at Kota-ki-Serai, about four miles from Gwalior, attired in battle dress and mounted on horseback. A squadron of eight *hussars* (European cavalry members) charged through the rebel lines. While fighting on horseback, the Rani was struck by a hussar; she fell from the horse and the wounds proved fatal. So died Rani Lakshmibai on 18 June 1858, heroically fighting the British. Commander Rose, when he learnt about her death, described her as 'the best and bravest of the rebel leaders'.

This is the commonly held narrative of her exploits and death, mostly written by British historians. But there are other versions as well. The myth gets mingled with facts now and it is difficult to distinguish between the two. While the British blame her for killing 66 British officers, women and children, calling her 'the Jezebel of India'[3], her story has become a legend in India.

---

[3]In the Bible, Jezebel was the wife of Ahab, the king of Israel, who killed the Prophets. Now, her name is alluded to connote wickedness.

According to Joyce Chapman Lebra,

Her courage against her adversaries and her martyrdom in battle stimulated the growth of an epic and transformed her from a woman who lived and died into a legend that is immortal. There is no doubt that her heroism has left an indelible imprint on the Indian imagination. But the Rani of Jhansi has taken a significant part in the historiography of the rebellion as well. While questions remain about aspects of her historical role, the actions she took in battle make her place in history secure.[4]

---

[4]Chapman Lebra, Joyce, *Rani of Jhansi: A Study in Female Heroism in India*, Jaico Publishing House, Bombay, 1988, p. 165.

46

Madan Mohan Malaviya

(1861–1946)

A great nationalist and educationist, Madan Mohan Malaviya was born in an orthodox and devout Brahmin family belonging to Allahabad, on 25 December 1861. He was the fifth son and eighth child of Pandit Brijnath Prasad. His ancestors hailed from Malwa in Madhya Pradesh and thus the family was called 'Mallais', which gradually changed to 'Malaviyas'. Madan Mohan's grandfather, Pandit Premdhar, as well as his father Brijnath, were learned Sanskrit scholars. Madan Mohan inherited their scholarship. He had his early education in Sanskrit at home under the guidance of his grandfather and father. Later, he was sent to Haradeva's Dharma Gyanopadesh Pathshala and then to the Vidyadharma Vardhini Sabha Pathshala. At the age of eight, he joined the local government Zilla School and passed the entrance examination in 1879, after which he took admission in the Muir Central College in Allahabad which was affiliated to the University of Calcutta. He graduated in 1884. In college, Malaviya was a favourite student of Pandit Aditya Ram Bhattacharya, who had a great hand in moulding his life and character. When the BHU started functioning in 1921, Malaviya requested Bhattacharya to be its pro-vice-chancellor, a post from which he resigned after two years due to ill-health.

While still a student, Malaviya was married to Kundan Devi in 1878. They had five sons and three daughters. After graduation, Malaviya joined classes for his Master's degree but was compelled to leave studies due to financial difficulties. He accepted an appointment as an assistant teacher in the Government High School at Allahabad. There were no restrictions imposed by the government on its employees joining political parties at the time. Malaviya attended the second session of the INC at Calcutta in December 1886, and made his maiden political speech there, which was highly appreciated by everyone including A.O. Hume. In fact, Malaviya had started public speaking while he was still a child and used to give discourses at religious gatherings. He also took part in dramatics as a student. In later life, he became a forceful speaker, in both Hindi and English. In his school days, Malaviya also composed poems and wrote stories and essays on various topics which were published in magazines. Raja Ram Pal Singh of Kalakankar (Rampur) heard about Malaviya's work and offered him the editorship of the Hindi weekly paper *Hindustan*, of which he was the proprietor. Malaviya accepted the offer and worked there from July 1887 to the end of 1889, converting it to a daily paper. The success of Malaviya as an editor brought him fame in journalistic circles and emboldened him to launch a number of papers of his own later.

At the persuasion of friends, Malaviya took up the law course at the newly established Allahabad University, passed the LLB examination in 1892 and entered the Bar as a junior to Beni Ram Kanyakubja. Soon, he set up a lucrative practice of his own and came to the rank immediately after Sir Sunder Lai and Motilal Nehru. However, Malaviya was not interested in amassing wealth in the legal profession because his heart was in social work and upliftment of the Hindus, for which he devoted all his energies during his lifetime. He was actively associated with 'Hindu Samaj', a social service organization set up in 1880, largely through the efforts of Aditya Ram Bhattacharya, Malaviya's Sanskrit teacher in Muir Central College. When the Kendriya Hindu Samaj (Central Hindu Samaj) was formed in 1884, Malaviya took an active part in it. The Samaj held its annual functions from 1884 to 1891 at different places. Malaviya continued serving Hindu interests and tried organizing the community during this period. He founded the Hindu Dharma Pravardhini Sabha at Prayag in 1906. On the occasion of the Kumbh Mela at Prayag in January 1906, Malaviya called a grand assembly of the Sanatan Dharma Mahasabha, where he encouraged Hindus to follow the ideals of Sanatan Dharma and revealed his scheme for founding a Hindu University at Banaras for the first time. The Sanatan Dharma Sabha became the All India Sanatan Dharma Mahasabha in 1928 and under its auspices, two weekly journals were brought out in 1933—*Sanatan Dharma* edited by Malaviya from Banaras and *Vishwabandhu* from Lahore (the office and the library of which was shifted to Hoshiarpur in Punjab after Partition).

By 1909, Malaviya had almost given up his practice at the Bar and was devoting all his energies for social welfare of the community. However, he made an exception when he accepted the brief in the lawsuit of 225 accused in the Chauri Chaura incident of 1922, and saved 170 accused from the gallows or transportation for life through his brilliant defence. He did not charge them any fee. In 1912, Malaviya founded the Seva Dal to look after the comfort of pilgrims who came to have a dip in the Sangam in Prayag. The Dal, under the presidentship of Malaviya, did commendable work during the Ardh Kumbh Mela in 1912 and Kumbh Mela in 1918. Malaviya, along with Lajpat Rai, was a very popular leader in Punjab and did much to promote the welfare of the Hindus and for safeguarding their religious beliefs. After the Jallianwala Bagh tragedy in April 1919, he toured Punjab with Swami Shraddhanand, located the affected Hindu and Sikh families and provided monetary and other help to the families of the deceased. Both of them collected funds for the purpose and people responded enthusiastically. Malaviya had no inhibition in joining the Arya Samaj leaders in making the Shuddhi Movement a success, their differences notwithstanding. He was against untouchability and took active part in opening the doors of temples for all Hindus. He treated B.R. Ambedkar as his son and Ambedkar had great respect for Malaviya. As one of the founders of the Akhil

Bhartiya Hindu Mahasabha, Malaviya figured prominently in it, presiding consecutively over its annual functions from 1922–24 as well as in 1935.

Malaviya, from his early years, took active part in promoting the cause of Hindi in the Devnagari script. Along with some other Hindu leaders, Malaviya played an important role in securing the order of the government in April 1900 for the use of Devanagari script, along with the Persian script, in the courts. When in 1910, the first Hindi Sahitya Sammelan was convened in Banaras, Malaviya presided over it. He continued to take active part in the promotion of Hindi.

After his early journalistic stint in *Hindustan* as an editor, Malaviya launched his own papers. He started *Abhudaya*, a Hindi weekly in 1907, which was converted to a daily in 1915. He started *Maryada*, a Hindi monthly in 1910. He also started another Hindi monthly, *Kisaan* in 1921, to fight for the cause of the poor peasants of Oudh. His greatest journalistic venture, however, was *Leader*, an English daily, started on 24 October 1909. Both *Abhudaya* and *Leader* played an important role in the cause of national movement, as envisaged by Malaviya and his associates.

Malaviya had joined the Congress party way back in 1886 and attended almost every session during his lifetime. He was elected president for the 1909, 1918, 1932 and 1933 sessions, though he could not be present during the 1932 and 1933 sessions as he was in jail. However, Malaviya did not always approve of the Congress policies, especially after it came to be controlled by Gandhi. Because of his independent views, he was never elected a member of the CWC. In politics, Malaviya was essentially a Moderate or a 'Responsivist' or a 'Responsive Co-operator' (responding positively for those actions of the government which he thought were good for the country). When Gandhi started the Non-cooperation Movement, Malaviya opposed it strongly. He openly preached against Gandhi's move of closing down educational institutions, boycott of legislative assemblies and burning of foreign clothes. He defied Gandhi on the question of closing of schools, colleges and universities because Malaviya believed that the existing educational system could be made to serve the aim of national regeneration and questioned the wisdom of Gandhi's policies.

When Gandhi visited Banaras in 1920 to preach Non-cooperation, Malaviya invited Gandhi to address the students and staff of BHU on 27 November 1920. Malaviya himself presided over the meeting and let Gandhi have his say. Gandhi told the students, 'Advantages are dangled before us. There are a number of facilities in this University. There is instruction in engineering and various other facilities. For the good of India, these things must be sacrificed.'[1] Malaviya did not contradict Gandhi in the meeting because he was confident about the sanity of his students and teachers. Hardly any student or teacher left the university. Not only did Malaviya not close the university, he invited the Prince of Wales (later, King Edward VIII) to declare the newly constructed buildings of the university open on 13 December 1921. BHU also conferred the honorary degree of Doctor of Letters on the Prince of Wales, to the chagrin of Gandhi and his followers, who had boycotted his visit to India.[2]

The BHU remains the greatest achievement of Madan Mohan Malaviya. With the joint efforts of Malaviya and Annie Besant, the Banaras Hindu University Act was passed by the government in 1915. Viceroy Lord Hardinge laid BHU's foundation stone in 1916. Malaviya had collected over a crore to build the campus. The Maharaja of Banaras donated hundreds of acres of land for the purpose. The University had started functioning in the buildings of the Central Hindu College, which Annie Besant had founded in 1898 at Banaras. It moved to the new campus in 1921 and many subjects of science, technology, arts and commerce were soon

---

[1] *Collected Works of Mahatma Gandhi*, Vol. 19, Publications Division, Government of India, pp. 35–36.
[2] Dar, S.L., and S. Somaskandan, *History of the Banaras Hindu University*, BHU Press, Varanasi, 1966, p. 530.

introduced, along with the study of Hindu religion and culture. Malaviya served as the vice-chancellor of the University from 1919 to 1938, after which he resigned because of ill-health but remained as Rector till his death. BHU soon became pre-eminent among Indian universities and still retains that status. It is interesting to note that Gandhi, who wanted the university to be closed in 1921, was the chief guest on its silver jubilee in January 1942.

Malaviya was a member of the Allahabad Municipality for many years and was elected as its vice-chairman twice. In consequence of the active work which he did for the Allahabad Municipality, he was elected to the Provincial Legislative Assembly in 1902 and to the ILC in 1909. He remained a member till 1920, and again from 1923 to 1930. He was one of the most important members of the Council. When the Swaraj Party was formed by Chittaranjan Das and Motilal Nehru in 1923, Malaviya joined the party because he was vehemently against the boycott of legislatures as advocated by Gandhi. However, when he realized that the Swaraj Party could not protect the interests of the Hindus who were suffering during communal riots in the country, he, along with Lajpat Rai, resigned from the Congress as well as from the Swaraj Party. They founded the Indian Nationalist Party and fought the 1926 general elections under its banner. The Swaraj Party was completely routed in Uttar Pradesh and Punjab and its number of seats depleted in other provinces. After the announcement of the Communal Award in 1932, Malaviya was greatly upset. He had attended the Second Round Table Conference as a Hindu nominee of the government. Though the Round Table Conference ended in failure, he did not expect such an award from the British government. The award had recommended separate electorate and heavy weightage, and much more for the Muslims at the expense of the Hindus. The Congress, while condemning the Commual Award as 'intrinsically bad' and 'anti-national', decided neither to support nor oppose it. Malaviya, along with M.S. Aney, M.R. Jayakar, Ramanand Chatterjee and others, once again resigned from the Congress and founded the

Congress Nationalist Party in 1934. During the 1935 elections to the Legislative Assemblies, their party won all the general seats in Bengal and all but one in Punjab. Again, Malaviya was upset with the Congress's Muslim appeasement policies and opposed them with remarkable success. In spite of his great regard for Gandhi, who was eight years his junior, he never succumbed to Gandhi's gimmicks like spinning the charkha. He felt that he had more important things to do in life. Along with Theology and Oriental learning, Malaviya advocated the use of Western science and technology to build large-scale industries in the country. The BHU was one of the first universities to start departments like mining, metallurgy, geology and various branches of engineering. Graduates from these departments played a significant role towards the industrialization of the country. Because of his interest in industrialization, Malaviya was appointed a member of the Indian Industrial Commission (or the Holland Commission) in 1916. In his minute of dissent, he made some important suggestions.

During the last years of his life, Malaviya stopped taking an active part in politics. He spent his days in BHU's extensive campus and was mighty pleased to see his dream come true. He died on 12 November 1946 in Banaras, at the age of 85 and was mourned by millions throughout the country. Nehru, in his autobiography, wrote,

> His (Malaviya's) long record of public service in various fields from early youth upwards, his success in establishing a great institution like the Banaras Hindu University, his manifest sincerity and earnestness, his impressive oratory, and his gentle nature and winning personality, have endeared him to the Indian public, particularly the Hindu public, and though many may not agree with him or follow him in politics, they yield him respect and affection. Both by his age and his long public record he is the Nestor of Indian politics.[3]

---

[3]Nehru, Jawaharlal, *An Autobiography*, Jawaharlal Nehru Memorial Fund, New Delhi, 1980.

47

Pherozeshah Mehta

(1845–1915)

Pherozeshah Mehta, son of Merwanji Mehta, was born on 4 August 1845, in Bombay, where he spent most of his life. He belonged to a middle-class Parsi merchant family. His father was a partner at Madam Cama and Company. Beginning his education in Ayrton's School, he passed the matriculation examination in 1861 and graduated from Elphinstone College in 1864. He was married the same year, at the age of 19. A good student of history and English literature, he was awarded a scholarship at the recommendation of his college principal, Sir Alexander Grant, which enabled him to go to England for further studies. He left for England in December 1864, entered Lincoln's Inn, took three years to qualify and was called to the Bar in 1868 and left for home.

While in England, he used to meet Dadabhai Naoroji and was influenced by his liberal thinking, which resulted in him joining the liberal school of Indian politics, the important members of which were M.G. Ranade, W.C. Bonnerjee, Gopal Krishna Gokhale and Dinshaw Wacha. After the death of Ranade and Bonnerjee, Pherozeshah Mehta and Gopal Krishna Gokhale led this group of Congressmen. They came to be known as the Moderates, as opposed to the Extremists, another group led by Gangadhar Tilak, Lajpat Rai, B.C. Pal and Aurobindo Ghose.

After his return from England, Pherozeshah started his legal practice in Bombay and soon became successful as a criminal lawyer.

His services were requisitioned in almost all parts of the Bombay Presidency, including Gujarat and Kathiawar. He also acted as a legal consultant for some Indian rulers, like those of Kathiawar and Junagarh.

While in England, Pherozeshah had joined the East India Association, for which Dadabhai and Bonnerjee were working. On his return to India, he was selected as one of the secretaries of the Bombay branch of the East India Association and used to deliver lectures under its auspices.

Pherozeshah's public life began with his involvement with Bombay Municipal Corporation, which he joined in 1872 and remained connected with for four decades. It was his speech in 1872 that paved the way for the introduction of the principle of election in the municipality. The Municipal Laws of 1872 and the Municipal Act of 1888 were, to a large extent, the result of Pherozeshah's untiring efforts. He was president of the Bombay Municipal Corporation in 1884, 1885, 1905 and 1911. His involvement in the municipal affairs of Bombay had reduced him to a provincial leader and so he hardly had any following in large parts of India.

Along with K.T. Telang and Badruddin Tyabji, Pherozeshah formed the Bombay Presidency Association in 1885, of which he became honorary secretary. Under his stewardship, it served as the organizational wing of the INC in the metropolis for nearly 30 years (1885–1915). He continued to take part in the working of the Bombay branch of the East India Association. In 1886, Pherozeshah became a member of the Bombay Legislative Council, and he was elected to it when the Council was reconstituted in 1892. He represented Bombay in the ILC during 1894–95, but he resigned in January 1896 because of poor health and left for England for treatment. He came back from England in February 1898, stood for election and got re-elected to the ILC in 1898 itself and continued as member till 1901, when he finally resigned on health grounds once again. In the legislative bodies, he distinguished himself by his eloquent speeches which criticized the government's economic policies, as did most of the Moderates, starting with Dadabhai Naoroji. But because they sang praises of the British rule and swore by constitutional methods, the government never took them seriously. In a way, they were a contradiction in themselves. They were called 'mendicants' by the Extremists.

Pherozeshah had some role in founding the INC, and presided over its 1890 session at Calcutta and twice served as the chairman of the reception committee at the Bombay sessions of 1889 and 1904. Gradually, he became a dominant figure in the Congress in the first decade of the twentieth century. His main endeavour in those days was to keep the Extremists, led by Tilak, from dominating the Congress and he was largely successful in this, though the Congress suffered grievously under his autocratic control. His most unprincipled act was during the Surat session of the Congress in 1907. The session was scheduled to be held in Lahore; he got the venue changed to Nagpur and from Nagpur to Surat where he had influence. He realized that he could not get his way in Lahore (where Lajpat Rai was a dominant force) nor in Nagpur (where Tilakites had the sway). He, along with Gokhale, did not want to get the resolution about swadeshi, boycott, national education and swaraj, which was passed in 1906 at Calcutta, confirmed in 1907. The intention of the Moderates became clear when during the Provincial Conference in April 1907 at Surat, the resolution about boycott was omitted and also when they refused to accept Lajpat Rai as president of the Surat Congress to be held in December. Lajpat Rai later withdrew to avoid controversy and the Moderates elected Rash Behari Ghosh as president. Aurobindo wrote an article in the *Bande Mataram* under the caption 'Pherozeshahi at Surat' castigating the autocratic nature of Pherozeshah.[1] Not heeding the criticism, Pherozeshah resorted to unethical and unparliamentary

---

[1]*Aurobindo, Collected Works*, Pondicherry, Sri Aurobindo Ashram, Vol. 1, 1972, p. 246.

methods to teach the Extremists a lesson at the Surat session of the Congress. He is said to have kept ready some hired men, armed with sticks, to forcibly expel the Extremists, if such a need arose. The Surat session ended in pandemonium when Tilak went up the rostrum to move an amendment about the Calcutta resolution. The Extremists were expelled from the Congress and remained expelled as long as Pherozeshah was alive.

Pherozeshah behaved in the same autocratic manner when he was elected president of the Congress to be held at Lahore in 1910. He changed his mind about presiding at the eleventh hour as he feared that the session would not be a peaceful one and he would not be able to have a repeat of Surat at Lahore. He refused to go to Lahore, leaving the Reception Committee in a dilemma. Pherozeshah's biographer, Homi Mody, wrote about the incident, 'The country was bewildered. Not even the closest friends of Pherozeshah suspected his intentions or could guess at the reasons that prompted this extraordinary step which threw the Congress into utter confusion. The President elect was as silent and mysterious as the Sphinx.'[2]

Whatever be the reasons, the whole episode was in bad taste. Madan Mohan Malaviya presided over the Lahore session then. Being so autocratic by nature, Pherozeshah could not have a mass following and merely remained a provincial leader.

However, Pherozeshah's apolitical contribution to the nation was not insignificant. As a supporter of indigenous industries, he was one of the first to invest in cotton textile mills. He also raised an indigenous bank, which later came to be known as the Central Bank of India, a leading Indian bank even today. Mehta had a deep interest in education, both primary and higher. Like so many other leaders of his time, he believed that Western education was one of the most precious gifts of the British rule. He had been connected

[2]Modi, Homy, *Sir Pherozeshah Mehta: A Political Biography*, Asia Publishing House, New York, 1963.

with the University of Bombay since 1868, when he was nominated as a Fellow of the Senate. He took active interest in the university affairs, and helped to promote the Graduate Association, along with Ranade, doing useful work in the educational field in Bombay in 1886. He was elected dean of the faculty of arts at the Bombay University. In March 1915, he was appointed vice-chancellor but he died soon after. He was awarded the Doctor of Letters degree by the University of Bombay in the same year.

The British government was always quick to honour the Moderates. Pherozeshah was honoured with a CIE in 1894 and a knighthood in 1904.

Pherozeshah did not dabble in journalism nor did he write any book or tract. However, he was mainly responsible for the founding of an English newspaper, *The Bombay Chronicle,* in 1910, which became an important source for expressing Indian opinion, under the editorship of B.G. Horniman.

Pherozeshah was a born leader of men, and those who came in contact with him, seemed to succumb under the charms of his personality. Wacha, Setalvad, Jinnah, Baptista and Jayakar had their early lessons in public life in Pherozeshah's chambers.

In Western India, Pherozeshah is remembered mainly as the maker of the modern Bombay Municipal Corporation and as the father of civic life in that city. His magnificent statue in front of the Bombay Municipal Corporation building is a symbol of that contribution.

He died in Bombay in 1915, at the age of 70.

48

V.K. Krishna Menon

(1896–1974)

Vengalil Krishnan Krishna Menon was born on 3 May 1896, in Panniyankara, a suburb of Calicut (Kozhikode). His father, Komathu Krishna Kurup, was a successful lawyer at the Calicut courts. His mother, Vengalil Lakshmikutty Amma, was a gifted lady, with high erudition in Sanskrit and was an accomplished musician. It was a respectable, wealthy and talented Nair family in which Krishna Menon was born.

He started his education at the Municipal Lower Secondary School and at Brennen High School, where he studied only for a year. In 1910, the family moved to Calicut and Menon was enrolled at the Native High School (now known as Ganapati High School) and passed the matriculation examination in 1913. He passed the Intermediate examination from Zamorin's Guruvayurappan College in Calicut in 1915 and his bachelor's from Presidency College in Madras in 1918. Then, he joined the Law College in Madras but did not complete law studies and started taking an interest in politics. He was a voracious reader and tried to imbibe the writings of Western thinkers like John Locke, John Stuart Mill and others. Later, he was influenced by the writings of Karl Marx and Engels. He hardly had any interest in Indian literature, religion, epics or philosophy.

While in Madras, Menon came under the influence of Annie Besant and joined the Theosophical Society. He moved into Adyar and into a new life. He was also a lecturer at the National University, founded by Annie Besant, for some time. He devoted his energies to social and political work, under the aegis of the Theosophical Society. Additionally, he joined and worked for the Indian Boy Scout Association, which was also founded by Annie Besant (she was its chief scout commissioner). Krishna Menon worked for the Scouts Movement in Madras, and later, in his home district in Malabar in 1918. Impressed by the talent and devotion of the young Menon, Dr George Arundale and Besant decided to send him to England for a short course on education so that he could come back and serve the National University better after getting exposure to a more enlightened atmosphere. Menon left for England in June 1924. His father agreed to his son's going to England in the hope that he would pursue law there and become a barrister and practice law on his return.

Menon got a teacher's job on his arrival in London, at St Christopher School in Hertfordshire, run by the Theosophical Society. In July 1925, he joined the London School of Economics (LSE) to study political science. He was a student of Professor Harold Laski, who was greatly impressed by Menon's intellectual acumen. Menon passed BSc from LSE in 1928 with first class honours. He continued his studies and got a master's degree from University College in London and an MSc degree from LSE in 1934. In the same year, he was called to the Bar from the Middle Temple. Menon was 38 by the time he completed his formal education. However, he had also been taking part in political activities since his arrival in England. Annie Besant had founded Commonwealth of India League in 1923, which was an auxiliary of her Home Rule League started in 1916. Krishna Menon started working for the League, as desired by Besant, and became its joint secretary. With his efforts, several branches of the League were opened in places like Manchester, Bristol and Liverpool. The end of the Commonwealth of India League came with extreme suddenness. At the end of an unfinished annual meeting in 1928, the majority of members in support of outright independence (in place of dominion status) adjourned elsewhere. The same day, they decided to form a new body, calling it 'India League', with Menon as its honorary secretary. Annie Besant resigned from the Commonwealth of India League, leaving the field for Krishna Menon to run the new India League, which he did, almost single-handedly for the next 17 years. He managed to get ideal premises for the office of the India League on Strand Street. The League was formally inaugurated on 11 November 1931. Its aim was 'educating the British people on India, appealing to their conscience, lobbying among the Members of Parliament, making the India League platform available for all visiting national leaders, publishing pamphlets on India'.[1] Menon also kept the Indian public informed about the activities of the India League and the political developments in England vis-à-vis India through his write-ups in Indian newspapers. He, at one stage, represented a dozen Indian newspapers in London. He also regularly wrote letters to British newspapers whenever he found misrepresentation of facts about India. The INC tried to utilize his services. Though not formally affiliated with the Congress, the India League became an outpost of the Congress in England and Krishna Menon its unofficial representative.

Through his teacher, the socialist Harold Laski, Menon was able to befriend several socialists and Labour party leaders like Sidney and Beatrice Webb, Stafford Cripps, Bertrand Russell, Clement Attlee and others. In 1932, Menon succeeded in convincing some British Parliament members to visit India to see what was happening there. The India League Parliamentary Delegation, consisting of three Labour Members of Parliament, with Menon as secretary, reached India in August 1932. They travelled to different parts of India, including the villages. During their 83-day sojourn, the delegates were shocked by the atrocities committed by the government

---

[1]Kutty, Madhavan, *V.K. Krishna Menon*, Publications Division, New Delhi, 1988, p. 43.

on innocent people who participated in the Civil Disobedience campaign. The 536-page report, when submitted to the government, sent shock waves among people interested in Indian affairs in Britain and the Congress, led by Gandhi, got powerful support for their campaign. The report became a landmark in the history of the India League and was considered as a personal triumph of Krishna Menon. This also resulted in closer association with the Labour Party, his socialist leanings helping him greatly. Menon joined the South West Pancras Labour Party in 1934. He was elected councillor repeatedly for 13 years until he became the Indian high commissioner in the UK in 1947. Another achievement of Menon in England was in the publishing industry. He is credited with launching the 'paperback revolution'. Along with Allen Lane of Bodley Head, he started the publishing company, Penguin. Later the Pelican series, with Krishna Menon as its general editor, was started.

In 1939, Menon was selected by the Labour Party as a candidate for the Dundee Constituency Parliamentary seat. But his participation in the *Daily Bazaar*, a people's war platform, revealed his leanings towards communism. He was declared a communist among labour circles and his candidature was cancelled. The repercussion of this in was even stronger in the US. He came to be regarded as a mouthpiece of the Soviet Union. He was shunned by the Labour Party and the socialists henceforth. His communist leanings came to the surface even when he was the Indian high commissioner in London. In a letter to Jawaharlal Nehru, Sardar Patel (6 January 1949) wrote about the accusations made by Krishan Menon (in an interview with T.G. Sanjeevi Pillai, director of the Intelligence Bureau [DIB], against the GOI. Menon was perturbed by the action taken by the GOI against the communists who had committed atrocities in Hyderabad, Madras, Bengal and other parts of the country, and indulged in murders, pillage, arson, loot and armed insurrection. He was not convinced and shouted at Sanjeevi and blamed the Intelligence Bureau for murdering the communists. In reply, Nehru wrote to Patel (6 January 1949): 'I can only explain and excuse it to some extent by imagining that he (Menon) was under some deep mental strain and consequently completely upset. He is often rather ill and sometimes his nerves give way when he is unwell.'[2] The views held by Menon about communism and communists are of consequence because Nehru, as prime minister, was guided by Menon on foreign and economic affairs for years, resulting in Nehru making some grievous mistakes.

Menon and Nehru maintained their intellectual and emotional links ever since they met in London in 1935. Of course, socialism was the common link. But Nehru was obliged to Menon for projecting him as one of the greatest men of their time. Perhaps Menon sincerely believed that only Nehru could lead free India. After Independence, Menon was appointed as the Indian high commissioner in London, in which capacity he worked for five years and retired on 13 June 1952. During his tenure, there was the famous Jeep Scandal, which coincided with the 'Police Action' in Hyderabad (1948). Menon was charged 'with having entered into a business deal with persons of no substance for the purchase of defence equipment in order to oblige friends'. Prime Minister Nehru had a hard time defending his friend in the Parliament. Nothing could be definitely found against Krishna Menon and the matter was eventually dropped.

Soon after, Nehru sent him to the UN as a member of the Indian delegation, with Vijayalakshmi Pandit as the leader. Following her election as president of the UN General Assembly (UNGA), Menon became the leader of the Indian delegation. When the Kashmir question came up for discussion, Menon is believed to have made the longest speech in UN history. He was successful in converting a lost case to one of complexity, to the chagrin of Britain and the US who wanted to see Kashmir independent as well as disarmed. Menon also suggested solutions for many controversial international

---

[2]Shankar, V., *Select Correspondence of Sardar Patel, 1945-50*, Navajivan Publishing, 1977, pp. 371–75.

issues, including those concerning Korea and Vietnam, which the great powers did not relish.

Menon returned to India in 1956 and was taken in the Union Cabinet as minister without portfolio. He was elected a member of the Lok Sabha in 1957, and again in 1962. In 1957, he was appointed as the defence minister. Two major events attracted global attention during Krishna Menon's term of office as Defence Minister. One was the integration of Goa in December 1961 and the other was the conflict with China in 1962. The Goa affair was a smooth operation but invited strong reaction from the Western block which was eyeing Goa as a naval base. Even Mountbatten, a friend and admirer of Krishna Menon, lamented,

> Krishna Menon—got this invasion of Goa linked up without Nehru understanding or knowing about it. In doing so, he destroyed Nehru. Nehru was the great idealist, who had always said that force must never be used. In forcing Nehru to bless the invasion of Goa he destroyed him, not only his credibility, his prestige, his reputation, but he destroyed his faith in himself, for he felt that he had been betrayed. And he later killed him with the disastrous Chinese war.[3]

The debacle during the war with China in 1962 will go down in history as the blackest spot in the political career of Krishna Menon as well as that of Nehru. Before his death in 1950, Sardar Patel, in a detailed letter to Jawaharlal Nehru, had warned him about the intentions of China. Nehru had ignored the warning and Menon perhaps never cared to read that letter. Worse, when the army chief, General Subayya Thimayya, informed Nehru and Defence Minister Krishna Menon about Chinese forces' incursions into Indian territory, Menon blew up and accused Thimayya of 'lapping up CIA agent provocateur propaganda'. It is believed that General Thimayya

---

[3]Collins, Larry, and Dominique Lapierre, *Mountbatten and the Partition of India, Vol. I: March 22–August 15, 1947*, Vikas Publishing House, New Delhi, 1983, p. 46.

submitted his resignation after the incident. According to Michael Edwards, 'Fearing that it might be used further to criticize the Government and in particular the Defence Minister, who were already under heavy attack for neglecting border defence, Nehru persuaded Thimayya to withdraw his resignation, but news of it leaked out.'[4] Krishna Menon's perception of Chinese policy was coloured by his communist leanings and he believed that China would never attack India. He and Nehru had convinced themselves that China, under Communist regime, was a friend of India and was morally bound to be friendly towards India as a co-sponsor of Panchsheel (the Five Principles of Peaceful Co-existence). They seemed to have never learnt the basic precept of statesmanship—there are no permanent friends, only permanent national interests in politics. The arrogant Menon would not listen to the plea of the army generals for upgradation of the army to face the Chinese. The Chinese knew that the Indian army was not well armed and was much smaller in number. The voices against Krishna Menon started getting louder in the media, among the general public and in Congress circles. Nehru continued to shield his friend but after the India–China War debacle in 1962, when the Chinese force almost reached the Indian plains without much resistance by the Indian army, Nehru found it difficult to protect Menon. He had to resign from the post of defence minister and the prestige of Nehru as a world leader also came under a cloud. Menon's political career almost came to an end. He had no following in the Congress party and was denied a Congress ticket in the 1967 Parliamentary elections. So, he resigned from the Congress party. After Nehru's death, he was almost pushed into oblivion. He started to practice at the Supreme Court as a 'progressive' lawyer, taking up cases of the leftist leaders like E.M.S. Namboodiripad. His health deteriorated and he was in and out of hospitals most of the time. He died on 6 October 1974 in Delhi.

---

[4]Edwards, Michael, *Nehru: A Political Biography*, Vikas Publishing House, 1971, p. 290.

An agnostic and a bachelor throughout his life, Krishna Menon made few friends. With his haughty, arrogant and superstitious nature, it was easy for him to make enemies. No Indian politician faced more bitter criticism, both at home and abroad, than he did. People have forgotten his service to the nation through India League and him fighting for Indian independence in a foreign land for more than two decades. They only remember the humiliation which the country suffered at the hands of the Chinese when he was defence minister.

He did not write much about himself. Whatever we know about him is through his friends and his enemies. He did not write any book of substance, only some pamphlets, though he was certainly a distinguished intellectual. Lord Greenwood, who knew Krishna Menon from his court days in London, paying a tribute to Krishna Menon after learning about his death, said, 'Vitriolic, intolerant, impatient, exigent—Yes! But generous, sensitive, considerate, a great teacher, too. I doubt if I shall ever meet a great man, or one who will leave behind him so many so deeply in debt to him, for all the lessons he taught to those of us who will cherish his memory.'[5]

---

[5]Kutty, Madhavan, *V.K. Krishna Menon*, Publications Division, New Delhi, 1988, p. 43.

49

Syama Prasad Mukherjee

(1901–1953)

Syama Prasad was born in one of the most illustrious families of Bengal on 6 July 1901. His father, Ashutosh Mukherjee, had become a legend in his own time and had occupied a unique position as the vice-chancellor of University of Calcutta and as judge of the Calcutta High Court. Syama Prasad's mother, Jogamaya Devi Mukherjee (who outlived him), possessed a strong character and played a character-forming role while bringing up her three sons —the eldest Rama Prasad, the middle child Syama Prasad and the youngest, Bama Prasad. His father's scholarship, which was reflected in the huge collection of books he had amassed on various subjects, attracted the intelligentsia of Calcutta to their *bari* (house) in Bhawanipur. Ashutosh's personal library now forms an important section of the National Library of India in Calcutta. The Mukherjees were devout Hindus and puja celebrations in their house were well-attended. Such was the atmosphere—a blend of religious and scholastic—in which Syama Prasad grew up.

He started his education at the Mitra Institution in Bhawanipur, from where he passed the matriculation examination at the age of 16 and won a scholarship. For college education, he joined Presidency College in Calcutta, getting a bachelor's degree in 1921 and securing a first class. For his master's, he opted for Bengali rather than English or any other subject. While studying for his master's, Syama Prasad got married to Sudha Devi in 1922. They had four children—two sons and two daughters. However, they could lead a happy married life only for 12 years as Sudha Devi died in 1934. Syama Prasad was only 33 at the time of her passing, but he never remarried.

Ashutosh Mukherjee died in 1924, creating a void in the educational circles of Calcutta, which was later filled by his son, Syama Prasad. He was elected to the Senate and Syndicate of the University in 1924 itself. He enrolled as an advocate in the Calcutta High Court and did legal practice for some time. In 1926, he left for England to study for the Bar, joined the Lincoln's Inn and was called to the Bar in 1927. On his return, he did not practice at the Calcutta High Court as he was drawn to University work as a member of the Senate and Syndicate. In 1934, he was appointed vice-chancellor of the University of Calcutta for two successive terms, 1934–38. He was the youngest vice-chancellor at the time. As vice-chancellor, he brought innovative changes in the university. Even after 1938, he remained the most important member in the Syndicate and continued to guide the university affairs. His involvement in education was not restricted to the University of Calcutta. He actively participated in the affairs of the Asiatic Society of Calcutta and was a member of the Court and Council of the Indian Institute of Science (IISc) in Bangalore, where C.V. Raman and Homi Bhabha were working at the time. He was also chairman of the Inter-University Board. Thus, education was his main activity for 13 years.

Thereafter, he entered into the sphere of politics. He was elected to the Bengal Legislative Council as a Congress candidate in 1929, representing the University of Calcutta. But the following year, he resigned when the Congress party decided to boycott the legislatures and he was elected as an independent candidate from the same constituency. Thereafter, he was actively involved in politics.

In August 1939, Veer Savarkar visited Bengal, bringing with him his new ideology of the Hindu Mahasabha. Syama Prasad met him and was impressed by his concern for the Hindus. He has written about this saying,

> Being then greatly perturbed at the helpless position of Hindus—whom the Congress failed to rouse and protect— some of us were drawn to Savarkar's influence and it gradually took root. My tour in eastern Bengal in September 1939, further made me realise how desperate the position of Hindus had become, and I saw how the spirit of resistance against an outrageously communal aggression was dying out—slowly but surely.[1]

He joined the Hindu Mahasabha and became its acting president. As a member of the Bengal Legislative Council, he quickly learnt a few lessons. He found that no political party cared to look after the interests of the Hindus. The Communal Award had crushed the Hindus politically. The number of Hindu seats had been drastically reduced. Initially, he was attracted towards the Congress because he considered it to be the most organized and representative political body, which depended mainly on Hindu support. However, he soon found that the high command of the Congress did not properly assess the ground realities in Bengal. In the 1939 elections, Krishak Praja Party, headed by A.K. Fazlul Huq, emerged as the largest party in the Council, while the Congress won almost all the Hindu seats. Fazlul Huq wanted to form a coalition ministry with the Congress. However, the Congress refused to cooperate with him, compelling Fazlul Haq to form coalition ministry with the Muslim League. Thus, Bengal Hindus had a taste of a Muslim League ministry (1939–41) in the form of communal riots in Dacca (now Dhaka) and other places. Syama Prasad worked hard to topple the ministry before further damage was done. He rallied non-Congress and non-League members and succeeded in forming a Progressive Coalition ministry, which was headed by Fazlul Huq. Syama Prasad joined

---

[1]Mukherjee, Syama Prasad, *Leaves From a Diary*, Oxford University Press, 1993, p. 29

the Ministry as finance minister. New and dangerous developments were taking place in the country during this time. Japan had joined the Second World War on the side of the Axis powers and had run through most of East Asia and was knocking at the India's door. Britain had adopted the 'scorched earth' policy—destroying crops, stocks and means of communication in East Bengal, without taking the Bengal ministry into confidence. 'The Governor, John Herbert, was interfering in the day-to-day working of the ministry, thus rendering so-called provincial autonomy into a meaningless farce.' Exasperated by the attitude of the governor, Mukherjee resigned on 16 November 1942. While he was still in the Ministry, the Gandhi-led Congress had started the Quit India Movement, resulting in the imprisonment of all the Congress leaders. Syama Prasad's nationalism came to the fore and he addressed a letter to Viceroy Lord Linlithgow, on 12 August 1942, three days after the arrest of Gandhi and other Congress leaders. Though he was acting president of the Hindu Mahasabha at the time, he defended the Congress in his letter, saying that 'the demand of the Congress, as embodied in its last resolution, virtually constitutes the national demand of India as a whole'. He further wrote: 'What is regarded as the most unfortunate decision on the part of the British government was its refusal to negotiate with Mahatma Gandhi.'[2] That shows that Syama Prasad was not anti-Congress per se, but a true nationalist.

The 'scorched earth' and 'denial' policy of the British government resulted in a terrible famine in Bengal in 1943, in which more than a million lost their lives. Syama Prasad organized relief measures in Calcutta, saving thousands of lives, heading the Bengal Relief Committee and Hindu Mahasabha Relief Committee. After the famine was over, he worked to strengthen the Hindu Mahasabha, of which he was elected president in 1943 (after Veer Savarkar relinquished office in 1942). He presided over the Silver Jubilee Session of the Hindu Mahasabha at Amritsar in December 1943.

[2]Ibid. 191–93.

In his speech, he revealed that the Mahasabha volunteers had urged Hindu and Sikh youth to join the army, navy and air force in large numbers. As a result of their efforts, the proportion of Hindus and Sikhs in the armed forces had increased from one-third to three-forth. 'Free India will need their services', he asserted. Prophetic words! Under his leadership, the Hindu Mahasabha tried to avoid the vivisection of the country. However, the Congress, as the largest party in the country had already conceded Pakistan under what has come to be known as the Rajaji Formula. When Pakistan became a reality, Syama Prasad concentrated his efforts to get Bengal and Punjab divided on the same basis on which India was divided. On 11 May 1947, Syama Prasad wrote to Sardar Patel: 'We demand the creation of two provinces out of the present boundaries of Bengal—Pakistan or no Pakistan.' Congress also passed a resolution demanding the partition of Bengal and Punjab. In the meanwhile, a new situation arose when Sarat Chandra Bose and Huseyn Shaheed Suhrawardy of the Muslim League jointly pleaded for a sovereign Bengal. Syama Prasad, in speech after speech delivered in various places in Bengal, denounced Sarat Bose's efforts and demanded the partition of Bengal and Punjab. He succeeded in his efforts. It used to be said that Jinnah partitioned India and Syama Prasad partitioned Pakistan.

In 1946, Syama Prasad was elected to the Constituent Assembly, which was also serving as the Parliament of India. In August 1947, he was invited by Jawaharlal Nehru to join his Cabinet. He became the minister of industry and supply. India was passing through a period of acute scarcity of goods of every kind at that time and Syama Prasad did a commendable job as a minister, establishing industries and looking after the proper distribution of the scarce goods. However, in 1950, differences cropped up between Nehru and Syama Prasad, when the former signed the Nehru–Liaquat Pact, under which Pakistan could interfere with the internal affairs of India regarding minorities (Muslims). Syama Prasad gave seven reasons for his resignation in a comprehensive statement before the Parliament, besides tracing the pitiable condition of Hindu minority in Pakistan. Sardar Patel, in a letter to Syama Prasad, dated 15 April 1950, appealed to him to retrace his steps 'in obedience to the call of both of us, the demand of the Party and the interest of your province and country'.[3] But Syama Prasad had already made up his mind and did not withdraw his resignation. Along with him, K.C. Neogy, Union minister of Relief and Rehabilitation, also resigned.

Syama Prasad resigned from the moribund Hindu Mahasabha and founded a new party, the Bharatiya Jana Sangh, whose membership, unlike Hindu Mahasabha's, was open to all. He returned to the Lok Sabha from North Calcutta in the 1952 elections. Only two other Bharatiya Jan Sangh candidates could win. Even then, Syama Prasad became the virtual leader of the opposition in Parliament by bringing together a few smaller parties under the banner of the National Democratic Party. As a parliamentarian, he earned respect even from the then Prime Minister.

Soon after Syama Prasad entered Parliament, the situation in Kashmir drew his attention. He found it strange that though Kashmir was an integral part of India, it had its own prime minister, separate flag, separate constitution—virtually a sovereign state within the Republic of India. The Jammu Praja Parishad was agitating at the time, demanding that Jammu and Kashmir be integrated with India like other states. Indians had to seek a permit from the Kashmir government to even enter the state. He had a lengthy correspondence with Sheikh Abdullah and Jawaharlal Nehru on the Kashmir question, pointing out the dangerous implications of the situation but to no avail. Nehru had full confidence in Sheikh Abdullah at that time, which he regretted later on. To know the ground realities first-hand, Syama Prasad entered Jammu and Kashmir on 11 May 1953. He was immediately arrested and taken to Srinagar. He died in detention on 23 June 1953. Several

---

[3]Patel, Vallabhbhai, *Sardar's Letters, Mostly Unknown: The Year 1950*, Sardar Vallabhbhai Patel Samarak Bhavan, Ahmedabad, 1983, p. 35.

leaders, crossing party lines, including M.R. Jayakar, Jayaprakash Narayan, M.V. Kamath, Purushottam Das Tandon, suspected foul play. Syama Prasad's mother wrote to Nehru, requesting him to hold an enquiry into the circumstances of her son's death in detention. Nehru did not agree to that and tended to believe what Sheikh Abdullah told him. Many feel that Syama Prasad Mukherjee died a martyr's death. He was cremated in Calcutta on 24 June.

Even while being involved in politics, Syama Prasad was interested in cultural and religious activities. From 1947, he was president of the Maha Bodhi Society of Calcutta. He also presided over the Nikhil Bharat Banga Sahitya Sammelan at Cuttack in 1952. He was also actively associated with the Asiatic Society of Calcutta for many years.

50

Lord Louis Mountbatten

(1900–1979)

Lord Louis Mountbatten was the last viceroy and the first governor-general of free India. He was born on 25 June 1900, and was the youngest child of Prince Louis of Battenberg and Princess Victoria of Hesse (Germany). He was christened Louis Francis Albert Victor Nicholas of Battenberg, but the exceedingly complicated name remained only in official records. Among his family and friends, he came to be known as 'Dickie'. He had one brother, George, and two sisters, Princess Louis (married to King Gustav VI of Sweden) and Princess Alice (married to Prince Andrew of Greece, whose son Philip, the duke of Windsor, was married to Queen Elizabeth II of Britain). Dickie was related to at least six royal houses of Europe and the Czars of Russia. And on top of that, he was the great-grandson of Queen Victoria, whose daughter Alice was married to Louis IV, grand duke of Hesse. Dickie was proud of his ancestry and tracing his lineage was his most absorbing hobby.

His father, Prince Louis, had come to Britain from Germany and had joined the British navy. In due course, he became a naturalized citizen. Due to the anti-German mania of the British public during the First World War, he changed his name from Battenberg to Mountbatten in 1917, renounced his German titles and became the first marquess of Milford Haven. Henceforth, the family came to be known as the Mountbattens. Following the example of his father, Dickie joined the British navy at an early age. He loved the navy more than anything else in the world. He came to India in 1921, as ADC to Prince of Wales, his cousin, who was on a tour of South Asia. They were guests of Lord Reading, the viceroy. Here Dickie proposed to Edwina Ashley, with whom he had fallen in love and brought with him to Delhi. The room where Dickie proposed to Edwina is now room Number 13 of the Registrar's Office in Delhi University. Both of them developed a sentimental attachment to India, which played some part in their coming to India later as viceroy and vicereine. They were married in 1922, when he was 22 and she was 21. Edwina inherited fabulous wealth in 1921, after the death of her maternal grandfather, Ernest Cassel, a German Jew, who was the richest man in the world at the time. On the other hand, Dickie had very a limited source of income, besides his salary in the navy. This disparity in income played a significant role in their discordant married life. Soon after their marriage, the couple found that there was a serious lack of compatibility in their characters. Dickie was not the reflective type and had not studied much beyond technical manuals and P.G. Wodehouse. Thus, his intellectual resources were limited. The gadgets which he used to design and invent for the navy and the hours he spent on his genealogy did not interest Edwina. There was nothing which could excite or interest her. Most of his friends agreed that Dickie was dull. There were strains in the marriage and the couple indulged in infidelities, started by Edwina as early as 1924, to overcome the ennui. Both of them opted for lovers; Edwina more than Dickie. Their physical intimacy had ended by 1929 and they had arrived at a pact that their marriage would not come in the way of them having lovers. They both adhered to it till Edwina's death in 1960. Thus, their marriage was more of an alliance than a union. Even then, two daughters were born to Edwina—Patricia (1924) and Pamela (1928), who came to India with their parents in March 1947. The relationship which the couple developed with Jawaharlal Nehru, during their viceroyalty and after, must be seen in the light of these early developments in their married life.

Mountbatten was a very handsome man—tall, athletic, full of energy and verve. He lived in style, made possible by his wife's millions. It was but natural that women fell for him. Even years later, when he kissed the famous writer of romantic novels, Barbara Cartland, on the cheek, she wrote, 'A streak of fire ran through me as if I had been struck by lightning. From a woman's point of view, the power was devastating.'[1] Others less privileged than Cartland still found the impact of his personality almost overwhelming. He radiated ineffable self-confidence. The impact of his personality was not confined to women, as Indian leaders in 1947 found to their chagrin. It is rather strange that the personality which overwhelmed and fascinated most people did not enamour his wife. The treatment meted out to Dickie at the hands of his wife and the resultant sense of inferiority was, perhaps, partly responsible for his ambition to reach at the top of his career. He worked furiously to achieve that end. He wanted to show that though he might have been unsuccessful as a husband, he was an exceptional and talented naval officer, respected and feared by men. This attitude helped Mountbatten to achieve great success as a distinguished leader of men, for which he is remembered. Love for his career sustained Mountbatten through the rough patches of his married life. He meticulously planned to climb the professional ladder, step by step, and put all his energies and talents towards that end. The Second World War came as a blessing in disguise for Mountbatten. The harassed British were in search of a commander who could take risks. Churchill surprised everyone when he appointed Mountbatten as chief of the Combined Operations in Europe. When the tide was turning in favour of the Allied and Japan was proving a greater menace, Mountbatten was sent as a supreme allied commander in South East Asia (1943) to tackle the Japanese. Japan was defeated

---

[1]Ziegler, Philip, *Mountbatten: The Official Biography*, Collins, London, 1985, p. 483.

with the help of the Americans and Mountbatten emerged as a hero for the demoralized British public and establishment.

The British had won the war but were in no position to retain the Empire. Their economy was shattered; the best of their manpower had been killed. Their cities were in ruin. There was shortage of almost everything—food, petrol, clothes and coal. All of a sudden, Britain became a poor country. After two centuries, the British were worried about themselves. They had been ruling India with the help of the Indian army. The formation of INA and the navy mutiny in February 1946 had cast doubts about the Indian army's reliability. The British were convinced that they could no longer hold on to India. They feared an uprising similar to the one in 1857, or worse. They wanted to get out of India before it was too late. To their chagrin, they found that their man on the spot, Viceroy Lord Wavell, was incapable of doing what was needed. Therefore, Prime Minister Attlee selected Mountbatten for the job. To the British Parliament, he explained the reasons for his choice, saying: 'Mountbatten is an extremely lively, exciting personality. He has an extraordinary faculty for getting on with all kinds of people.' The Parliament agreed. According to Mountbatten, when Attlee told him about his plan to send him to India as viceroy, 'he was staggered'. He was not telling the truth. His close friends and those who knew him in official circles believe that his eyes were set on the viceroyalty while he was still in SouthEast Asia. As Richard Hough said, 'All this business about being surprised when he was offered the job of going away to India as viceroy— and then first refusing it—is all my eye.'[2] It was part of the great plan. By feigning reluctance and by being difficult, Mountbatten managed to extract several concessions from the Prime Minister. He managed to take with him some of his own trusted men, a private four-engine plane and a specific date for the withdrawal. He

[2]Hough, Richard, *Edwina: Countess Mountbatten of Burma,* Weidenfeld and Nicolson, London, 1983, p. 179.

was given greater liberty in making his arrangements and writing his own instructions 'than had traditionally been allowed to even the most magnificent of viceroys'. It is, however, doubtful if he enjoyed plenipotentiary powers, as he later claimed.

When everything was decided, he went around and met several people. First was his mother. She was 84 but still active. She warned her son that he was going to fail just like Linlithgow and Wavell had failed. She asked him what made him think that he would succeed? Dickie replied, 'You have so little faith in your own son as to think I am not slyer than them. I'm going to tie them up in such knots that I shall succeed at their expense.' When he met Churchill, the latter told him: 'I am not going to tell you how to do it, but I will tell you one thing—whatever arrangements you may make, you must see that you don't harm a hair on the head of a single Muslim.' Dickie promised Churchill that no Muslims would be harmed and some of his actions must be seen in this light as a viceroy and governor-general must be seen in this light.

Mountbatten arrived in India on 22 March 1947, along with his wife Edwina and daughter Pamela. They were received at the Delhi airport by Nehru, Liaquat Ali Khan and Commander-in-Chief, Claude Auchinleck. He was officially sworn in on 24 March. His brief was precise: 'Hand over India to the Indians by June 1948'. Mountbatten's arrival had irked many civil servants who regarded Mountbatten as a jumped-up ex-playboy and Edwina as a spoilt Jewish playgirl of doubtful morals, in spite of what they had done during the War.[3] Mountbatten started interviewing Indian leaders one by one—Nehru, Patel, Jinnah, Liaquat Ali, Gandhi and lesser mortals, giving one hour to each. The Indian leaders were at a disadvantage during these meetings. While Mountbatten had been briefed by his predecessors Linlithgow and Wavell as well as by the ICS clique about the Indian leaders and their standing in their party; the leaders were completely in the dark

---

[3]Ibid. 188–89.

about the seamy side of Mountbatten's character. Most of the Indian leaders, including Gandhi, were dazzled by his personality, his royal connections, his informal affability. But those who had worked with Mountbatten knew that he delighted in intrigue. He would never give a straight answer to a straight question. 'Dickie was a born intriguer. If there was a choice between open dealing and a corkscrew approach, he always chose the latter,' a friend of his remarked. Field Marshal Richard Temple once exploded across a dinner table, 'Dickie, you are so crooked that if you swallowed a nail, you would shit a corkscrew.'[4] During his 15 months of stay in India, he indulged in intrigues of the worst kind, including double talk. According to Chaudhry Muhammad Ali, former prime minister of Pakistan (1955–56), 'Mountbatten won the confidence of both, the leaders of Congress and the Muslim League, by denouncing one to the other. At the very time when he was wooing Congress leaders day and night, he was portraying them to Jinnah as unreasonable men.'[5]

Despite Dickie's friendship with Nehru, he had a fondness and admiration for the Muslims and hardly any sympathy for the Hindus and much less for the Sikhs. According to his own admission,

Muslims were mostly the people from the officer's class of the Indian Army—much more than the Hindus. I wasn't pro-anybody, but I really did like the Muslims. I had so many friends. I think you'll find this one of the things that's not completely understood. The British out there were naturally more easily friends with Muslims because they played polo, they went out shooting, they mixed freely and they didn't have any sort of inhibitions.

The Hindus didn't get along so well with the British. Frankly, no Muslim ever took part in any plotting against

[4]Ziegler, Philip, *Mountbatten: The Official Biography*, Collins, London, 1985, p. 528.
[5]Rajmohan Gandhi, *Eight Lives: A Study of the Hindu-Muslim Encounter*, Roli Books, New Delhi, 1986, p. 174.

the British. They wanted the British to remain; it secured their position. The last thing that Jinnah wanted was that we should go. But the Hindus wanted us to go.[6]

This affinity of Mountbatten towards Muslims was not only shared by Churchill but by almost all the British officials of any consequence in India. It did not come as a surprise to anyone when three Governors and scores of ICS officials decided to serve Pakistan after Partition and hardly any chose India. Many of the actions of Mountbatten also must be seen in this background—his advice to Maharaja Hari Singh of Kashmir to opt for Pakistan; his exaggerated description of the sufferings of Muslim refugees in Delhi while ignoring those of Hindu and Sikh refugees who were in much greater number and in much worse condition; his exploitation of the naivety of Gandhi to go on a fast to coerce the government to release ₹55 crore rupees to Pakistan, a country at war with India.

After consultations with Indian leaders, Mountbatten set to work 'to hand over India to the Indians'. By this time, he was convinced that the partition of the country could not be avoided. It was not difficult to convince the Congress leaders about the inevitability of Partition, harassed as they were by the tactics of the Muslim League members in the Interim Government. In the meeting of the CWC of 8 March 1947, a resolution for the partition of Punjab was passed (later Bengal was added to it), thus accepting the partition of the country by implication. That made things easier for Mountbatten. He had started with the Cabinet Mission Plan but soon abandoned it. Next, he, with the help of his aides, prepared what has come to be known as 'Plan Balkan'. His 'hunch' deceived him when he showed this plan to Nehru, who was with him in Simla. Nehru rejected the plan, as it presented 'a picture of fragmentation, conflict and disorder'. A new plan was hurriedly drafted, with the help of V.P. Menon, the poltical

---

[6]Collins, Larry, and Dominique Lapierre, *Mountbatten and the Partition of India*, Vikas Publishing House, New Delhi, 1983, pp. 59–60.

reforms commissioner. Mountbatten flew to London on 18 May, with the new plan; he was able to convince the authorities about its viability. He, along with Lord Ismay, returned to Delhi on 31 May. Any apprehension about the rejection of the revised plan by Indian leaders was taken care of. 'I will drive them forward at a pace which would make it impossible for anyone to have second thoughts or fuss much over the details,' he told his staff on his return. On 3 June, he announced that the power would be handed over to Indians on 15 August 1947 instead of June 1948, as had been announced by Attlee earlier in the British Parliament. The reason given by Mountbatten was that 15 August was the second anniversary of the Japanese surrender. Within 73 days of his arrival in India, the partition plan had been announced. After 72 more days, two independent countries would emerge on the corpse of the Empire.

Mountbatten was a hustler. He often took decisions without caring for the consequences. This was one such decision. 72 days was a short time to bifurcate a country of India's size, especially when communal riots were becoming uncontrollable. The whole of North India was in the grip of communal frenzy, from Peshawar to Noakhali. The deadline of 15 August 1947 did not allow time for proper precautions and arrangements to be made. It took three years to separate Burma from India and two years to separate Sindh from Bombay, but only 72 days to divide the whole of India. Maurice Zinkin, formerly of the ICS, said, 'Wavell represented the Indian point of view in England. Mountbatten was not basically interested in India but represented British interests. He did the job with dash and deftness but without compassion.'[7] The British were in such a haste to leave the country that the Indian Independence Bill was hurried through the British Parliament in unprecedented haste and they got the Royal assent on 18 July 1947, clearing the deck for the transfer of power.

---

[7]Hatch, Alden, *The Mountbattens*, W.H. Allen, London, 1966, p. 359.

It did not take much time through voting in the legislatures or through referendum as to which states would form a part of Pakistan. The whole of NWFP, Baluchistan, Sindh and the district of Sylhet in Assam were to go to Pakistan. The most serious problem was the bifurcation of Punjab and Bengal on the basis of Muslim and non-Muslim majority areas. Such areas were not distinctly clear. To decide the issue, a Boundary Commission was formed under the chairmanship of Sir Cyril Radcliffe. Radcliffe arrived in India on 8 July and submitted his report, in a sealed envelope, on 13 August to the Viceroy. In less than five weeks, two lines were drawn, dividing the two provinces of Punjab and Bengal on the basis of contiguous majority areas. To control the communal riots in Punjab—where thousands of innocent people were being massacred, their houses burnt, their property looted, their women molested and children killed before the eyes of their parents—a Boundary Force was raised on 1 August 1947, with 55,000 army personnel under Major-General T.W. Rees. A major segment of the force was stationed in East Punjab, while the worst carnage was being enacted in West Punjab. The riots and killings continued unabated. The Boundary Force came under fire and was disbanded on 29 August.

Most of the Indian states in the Indian territory were integrated with the Indian Dominion by 15 August due to the deft handling of the princes by Sardar Patel, as head of the States Department. It must go to the credit of Mountbatten that not only did he reiterate on 25 July (while addressing the Chamber of Princes) what Patel had told them on 5 July, but as the Crown Representative, advised them to join either of the proposed two Dominions because Paramountcy would lapse on 15 August. After hearing Mountbatten, all the princes who were still reluctant, signed the Instrument of Accession, except Kashmir, Hyderabad and Junagarh.

As the time of the transfer of power approached, the intensity of the communal riots increased. Uncertainty about the Boundary Commission's Award made things worse. Though Radcliffe had sent the details of the Award on 13 August, Mountbatten did not make it public. On 14 August, Mountbatten and Edwina flew to Karachi to participate in the celebrations of the birth of Pakistan, leaving the envelope sent by Radcliffe unopened on the table. To dramatize the event, a canard went around that there was a plan to assassinate Mountbatten and Jinnah by the Sikhs and the RSS men. That was just like Mountbatten. There was hardly any presence of Sikhs in Karachi or of the RSS men. There was no way for them to execute such a plan. But it did add to the drama. At times, it was difficult for Mountbatten to distinguish between truth and untruth. According to Philip Ziegler, 'The truth in his hands was swiftly converted from what it was to what it should have been. He sought to rewrite history with cavalier indifference to the facts to magnify his own achievements.'[8]

Back in India, Mountbatten participated in the Independence celebrations in Delhi. The fate of millions of Indians still lay sealed in the envelope sent by Radcliffe; millions still not knowing to which Dominion they would belong. 'Let the Indians have the joy of their Independence Day,' he said nonchalantly. 'They can face the misery of the situation after.' When the details of the Boundary Commission's report were made public on 17 August, all hell was let loose! Almost the whole of West Pakistan was cleansed of Hindu and Sikhs by September. Similarly, East Punjab was cleansed of Muslims. In the eastern part of Pakistan, there were riots to, but of lesser intensity. Nobody is sure how many people were killed in this carnage, the worst in the history of the world. Nobody really knows. Estimates vary from two million to a quarter of a million. When Mountbatten relinquished the office of governor-general, returned to England and met Churchill, the first thing Churchill said was, 'So, you got two million Indians killed.'

Mountbatten emerged as the saviour of the British residents in India and as a 'true friend' of India. Indians were so obliged to

---

[8]Ziegler, Philip, *Mountbatten: The Official Biography*, Collins, London, 1985, p. 701.

372 ▪ 50 *Captivating Lives*

him for handing over India to them that he was asked to be the first governor-general of free India. Jinnah had refused him this honour and appointed himself as governor-general of Pakistan, to the great disappointment of Mountbatten, who wanted to be governor-general of both the Dominions. Mountbatten remained governor-general of India till 21 June 1948, after which C. Rajagopalachari took over. Indians trusted Mountbatten, but true to his character, he deceived India by creating the 'Kashmir problem'. While accepting the accession of Kashmir to India, as proposed by Maharaja Hari Singh, Mountbatten, as head of the Dominion, added this sentence to the document: 'It is my government's wish that as soon as law and order have been restored in Kashmir and her soil cleared of the raiders, the question of State's accession should be settled by reference to the People.' Mountbatten also advised Nehru to stop fighting and refer the matter to the UN in November 1947. The Kashmir problem, created by Mountbatten, remains unsolved to this day and has cost India dearly in terms of men, money and material. Another act of treachery on the part of Mountbatten was talking Gandhi into a fast to give ₹55 crore to Pakistan. On 12 January 1948, Sardar Patel, in a press statement, had categorically said: 'We would not agree to any payment until the Kashmir affair was settled.' Gandhi started his fast the next day, on 13 January 1948. Mountbatten later boasted that it was he who convinced Gandhi. Later he admitted, 'I acted as a kind of forwarding agent for Pakistan because I felt, to some extent, they'd been pushed and I therefore had to remain to see it.' Mountbatten must share the blame for the assassination of Gandhi.

'Nehru's motives in the Kashmir affair remain opaque. Why did he promise a plebiscite? Why was the issue taken to the United Nations and the offer repeated? It seems clear that the initiative both for the holding of a plebiscite and referring Kashmir to the United Nations came from Mountbatten.'[9] Edwina had played an

---

[9]Ziegler, Philip, *Mountbatten: The Official Biography*, Collins, London, 1985,

important role in politics, which none of the earlier vicereines had done. Her relationship with Nehru added a new dimension to the policymaking process in India. When Edwina died in February 1960 and was buried at sea, as she had willed, Nehru ordered the Indian frigate, *INS Trishul,* to escort the British frigate, *HMS Wakeful,* which carried her body to the south coast of England.

Mountbatten returned to the navy in October 1948 to command a cruiser squadron in Malta. His career in the navy was on expected lines. He became the First Sea Lord in 1955 and the chief of the Defence Staff in 1958. He retired from active service in 1965. He was a lonely man, and after Edwina's death, his share of her wealth came to a shilling for every pound and he was worried about his financial position. On 27 August 1979, he died when his boat was blown to pieces by Irish revolutionaries. Two of his companions and a child also died with him in the blast. His assassination became world news. Though he did not serve India well during his 15-month stay as viceroy and governor-general, he served his own country well.